Praise for
American Television during a Television Presidency

"Since the broadcast of the first of the Nixon/Kennedy debates in September 1960, U.S. politics have been inextricably entwined with television. None more so than reality TV star turned president—Donald Trump. McNally's exhaustive edited collection covers every aspect of the Trump presidency through the prism of television. From the presidency itself, textual analyses of dramas screened through the four years of his term, how his disruptive politics impacted television genres and gender politics, *American Television during a Television Presidency* deserves its place in the canon of titles dealing with American politics, presidencies, and how they impact television. This is a timely publication and one that deserves to be read, and then read again, in order to understand how Trump's politics impacted and influenced the medium of television."

—Kim Akass, professor of radio, television,
and film, Rowan University

"*American Television during a Television Presidency* offers a wide-ranging look at how the Trump era fundamentally changed the way America makes and consumes popular culture. Full of fascinating case studies, the book forcefully illustrates just how deeply politics has become ingrained in the world of entertainment. Anyone interested in understanding today's television landscape is sure to learn and enjoy."

—Matt Sienkiewicz, associate professor of
communication, Boston College

American Television
during a
Television Presidency

Contemporary Approaches to Film and Media Series

A complete listing of the books in this series can
be found online at wsupress.wayne.edu.

GENERAL EDITOR

Barry Keith Grant
Brock University

American Television

DURING A

Television Presidency

Edited by

Karen McNally

WAYNE STATE UNIVERSITY PRESS
DETROIT

ISBN (paperback): 978-0-8143-4935-9
ISBN (hardcover): 978-0-8143-4936-6
ISBN (ebook): 978-0-8143-4937-3

Library of Congress Control Number: 2021951002

Cover art © Sagittarius Pro / Shutterstock and Wuttichok Panichiwarapun / Shutterstock. Cover design by Brad Norr Design.

Wayne State University Press rests on Waawiyaataanong, also referred to as Detroit, the ancestral and contemporary homeland of the Three Fires Confederacy. These sovereign lands were granted by the Ojibwe, Odawa, Potawatomi, and Wyandot nations, in 1807, through the Treaty of Detroit. Wayne State University Press affirms Indigenous sovereignty and honors all tribes with a connection to Detroit. With our Native neighbors, the press works to advance educational equity and promote a better future for the earth and all people.

Wayne State University Press
Leonard N. Simons Building
4809 Woodward Avenue
Detroit, Michigan 48201-1309

Visit us online at wsupress.wayne.edu

In memory of Lena and Eddie McNally

CONTENTS

I.
Donald Trump and a Media Presidency

II.
Fact, Fiction, and Critique

III.
Genre, Style, and Reception

IV.
Power and Gender

V.
Renegotiating the Past

Acknowledgments

My thanks go firstly to each of the contributors to this volume, with whom it has been a joy and an honor to work on this book. Their absorbing and groundbreaking chapters have made editing a pleasure, and I am immensely grateful for all the work that has gone into producing such exceptional essays. The immediate enthusiasm for the project shown by Marie Sweetman, acquisitions editor at Wayne State University Press, and Barry Keith Grant, series editor for Contemporary Approaches to Film and Media, has been hugely encouraging, and their feedback and advice in guiding this book to publication have been invaluable. My gratitude goes as well to the readers who gave of their time to provide such supportive and useful comments on the manuscript. The energy and thoughtfulness this takes is fully acknowledged here, and I am extremely grateful.

INTRODUCTION

A PRESIDENCY MADE FOR TELEVISION

Karen McNally

Following the result of the US election on November 9, 2016, David Remnick in the *New Yorker* described Donald Trump's victory over Hillary Clinton as "nothing less than a tragedy for the American public, a tragedy for the Constitution, and a triumph for the forces, at home and abroad, of nativism, authoritarianism, misogyny, and racism."[1] The *New York Times* predicted, "Mr. Trump will thoroughly reimagine the tone, standards and expectations of the presidency, molding it in his own self-aggrandizing image."[2] While the first statement is politically charged, there can be no doubt that Donald Trump presided over a norms-smashing presidency that emerged out of and was fixed around the inflated egotism that Trump had for decades constructed as a persona and a brand of politics intended to substantially alter the contemporary culture of the United States.

Three areas that have caused consternation at home and abroad largely defined Trump's presidency. His combative attitude and aggressive posturing, physically signaled by his elbowing past NATO leaders at the Brussels summit in May 2017, characterized his relationship with European allies. Moving in 2019 to pull the United States out of the 2015 Paris Agreement on climate change and repeatedly threatening to withdraw the United States from NATO left European nations with a sense of deep unease as they constructed strategies to accommodate or loosen ties with the United States during the years of the Trump administration. Trump's parallel cozying up to the United States' opponents such as Russia and North Korea and his praise for their authoritarian leaders prompted criticism on the world stage, as well as suspicion at home as to the president's motives. The much-vaunted deal with North Korea's Kim Jong Un stalled indefinitely, but not without Trump having described the "beautiful letters" he exchanged with the Supreme Leader and praising the dictator whom he once referred to as "little rocket man." Trump's cultivation of a seemingly close relationship with Vladimir Putin disturbed international allies, particularly when stretched to the US president's attempt to reintroduce Russia into the G7 group of nations.[3] At home, moreover, Trump's siding with Putin against US intelligence reports of Russian intervention in the 2016 election during the 2018 summit in Helsinki and his silence on intelligence in June 2020 that Russia paid bounties for the killing of US troops in Afghanistan suggested, as the *Washington Post* put it, an American president repeatedly "advancing Russian interests and . . . consistently shying away from rebuking Putin."[4]

Trump's infamous July 2019 telephone call to the president of Ukraine, Volodymyr Zelensky, in which he suggested, "I would like you to do us a favor though," to investigate former vice president and future 2020 election opponent Joe Biden, seemed to reinforce the accusation of a combined lack of unequivocal support for democracies and indifference to the basic ethics that govern presidential conduct. Such concerns resulted in Trump becoming the third US president in history to be impeached. Combined with the administration's multiple attempts under Attorney General Bill Barr to intervene in legal cases concerning the president's allies—including those of convicted felons Roger Stone and Paul Manafort—that personalized the justice system and the role of the attorney general, fears for the long-term impact of the Trump presidency on the United States' democratic system of government have been widespread. Citing Trump's denial of climate change, suggestions of a new arms race, and his determination to control the Supreme Court for the Republicans, Princeton professor of sociology and public affairs Paul Starr wrote in the *Atlantic* in May 2019, "In short, the biggest difference between electing Trump in 2016 and reelecting Trump in 2020 would be irreversibility. . . . If we cannot focus on what matters, we may sleepwalk into a truly perilous future."[5] Trump's initial denial of the severity of the COVID-19 pandemic in early 2020, followed by a serious mishandling of the response, which pushed the United States to the top of the World Health Organization's table of recorded deaths worldwide, underscored his leadership failings and simultaneously the fundamentals at issue in the 2020 election.[6] The unprecedented events of January 6, 2021, when Trump supporters launched a violent assault on the Capitol following the president's "Save America" rally, further fueled by court cases denying the legitimacy of the election result, became an astounding illustration of the apparent danger to American democratic institutions. The legacy for

Trump's presidency was a second impeachment trial, making him the most impeached president in US history.

The other central element of Trump politics with a substantial and persistent impact has been the culture war waged against liberal values. Trump announced his run for the presidency in 2016 with an assault on Mexican immigrants in which he claimed, "They're bringing drugs. They're bringing crime. They're rapists. And some, I assume, are good people." Trump's "Make America Great Again" nationalist agenda has been a central tenet of his strategic appeal to the white, middle-America base of his support and was repeatedly demonstrated by a "Build that wall" rally cry, the description of neo-Nazis marching in Charlottesville in August 2017 as "very fine people," an attempt to institute a ban on Muslims from entering the country, and repeated attacks on NFL players including Colin Kaepernick "taking the knee" at football games. Similarly, Trump has displayed an identifiably misogynistic attitude toward women and female equality, evident in his infamous "grab 'em by the pussy" comments on the *Access Hollywood* tape released during the 2016 presidential campaign, his comment after the Fox News Republican debate that Megyn Kelly had "blood coming out of her wherever," the multiple accusations of sexual harassment and assault made against him, the "nasty woman" remark made about Democratic opponent Hillary Clinton during the 2016 campaign, and his particularly vitriolic relationship with Speaker of the House of Representatives Nancy Pelosi. A viral photo taken at a White House meeting in 2017 showing Speaker Pelosi standing with her finger pointing toward a seated Trump at a table surrounded by men was released by Trump and intended to illustrate the Speaker's "unhinged meltdown!" but was adopted by Pelosi as her Twitter profile photo and heralded by liberals as an image of a strong woman disturbing a patriarchal power dynamic. As Molly Roberts put it in the *Washington Post*, "It's a Rorschach test for an America cleaved into two."[7] Attempts to reverse legislated workplace equality and female reproductive rights through attacks on *Roe v. Wade* and on efforts to ratify the Equal Rights Amendment, with the attendant urging of Trump's evangelical supporters, have made the future position of women in the 2020s a similarly fraught battleground in the United States.

Resistance against the cultural direction of travel suggested by Trump's election in 2016 was immediate and continuous, emphasizing the clearly delineated divisions that dominated his term in office. The Women's March that was held in Washington, DC, on January 21, 2017, and was replicated across the country and worldwide, the Time's Up campaign, and the #MeToo movement have all highlighted gender inequalities still prevalent in American society and created an intended barrier to regressive political action. The Black Lives Matter movement, which began in 2013 after the killing of Trayvon Martin and has become increasingly focused around police brutality, has received heightened attention and urgency during the Trump presidency. Following the police killing of George Floyd in Minneapolis in May 2020, the national and international marches that followed as a call for urgent changes in racially defined strategies of policing were met with antagonism from the president, who compared peaceful protestors to "terrorists" and sent in unidentified federal forces to quell disturbances in Portland, Oregon.[8] The late civil rights leader and representative John Lewis remarked of Donald Trump that his words and actions were those of a man "who knows something about being a racist. It must be in his DNA, in his makeup."[9] Trump pointedly refused to attend the lying-in-state of the congressman in the Capitol Rotunda, and in a widely ridiculed television interview with the journalist Jonathan Swan, he declined to acknowledge Lewis's life as "impressive," citing Lewis's nonattendance at the 2017 presidential inauguration.[10]

While the result of the 2016 election was a surprise to many people worldwide, the manner of Trump's presidency should not have been to anyone with even a passing acquaintance with Donald Trump over several decades. Appropriately spurred on by belittling comments made by then–*Saturday Night Live* (NBC, 1975–) regular Seth Meyers at the 2011 White House Correspondents Dinner, Trump's ascendance from a real-estate mogul and reality-television celebrity wholly inexperienced in political office has defined a presidency born and conducted through American television. Trump's election campaign was initiated by a combination of three key elements that would go on to define his term as president, those of unfiltered right-wing extremism, reality TV celebrity, and the kind of media event created for television. His celebrity had been built on extensive self-publicizing during his real-estate years in New York and his accompanying multiple marriages, appearances on television news and chat shows (even infamously phoning in live in the guise of his imaginary publicist "John Miller" or "John Baron"),[11] and most effectively his self-branding as billionaire creator of a business empire and television celebrity on *The*

Apprentice and *The Celebrity Apprentice* (NBC, 2004–15). Descending the escalator at the gold-emblazoned Trump Tower in June 2015 (he would later boast about the event, "It looked like the Academy Awards"),[12] Trump used the location as a television event that traded on his existing celebrity persona as he attempted a reframing as a future celebrity president. Trump's rambling speech, which included attacks on President Obama and references to himself as the ultimate deal-maker, simultaneously established the racially divisive, news-grabbing political approach that would dominate his campaign and presidency with his infamous comments on Mexican immigrants.

Even if Trump was unable to assume complete control over his depiction on television during the campaign—the release of the *Access Hollywood* tape being an obvious example—the television event would dominate his campaign. Trump's experience on *The Apprentice* illustrated the power of television to amplify celebrity, transforming his infamy in New York real-estate circles into national and international fame. The "Make America Great Again" rallies that traversed the country veered from the traditional strategy to capture votes in key Electoral College states adopted by Hillary Clinton and were instead aimed at a national television audience eager to watch the "You're fired" guy swear, encourage violence, and put on a show. Trump's stalking of Hillary Clinton around the stage of the televised presidential debate in October 2016 and his response to an onslaught of sexual harassment allegations—staging a press conference with accusers of President Bill Clinton in advance of the same debate—were similar strategies to command the attention of the television camera and its audience. As the *New York Times* critic and author of *Audience of One: Donald Trump, Television, and the Fracturing of America* James Poniewozik puts it, "Donald Trump had one friend who stuck by him his entire campaign, one partner who never left his service. When he spoke, he spoke to one audience: not the moderators at the debates, not the throngs at his rallies, not the 'forgotten man and woman' that his speechwriters kept referring to. He spoke to the red light."[13] Trump's limited ability to exploit a similar television strategy in 2020 in the midst of the restrictions of the COVID-19 health crisis—despite several "super spreader" events—impacted substantially on a campaign style so defined by televisual performance.

Donald Trump's event-television approach to politics was identifiable in his 2016 campaign and continued into his presidency as part of the simultaneous extension of his celebrity persona. In a 2016 article published during the election cycle, the cultural historian Neal Gabler drew on Daniel Boorstin's notion of "pseudo-events" and their connection to celebrity to describe the alternative political strategies playing out. Boorstin argued in *The Image* (1962) that the press conferences, presidential debates, and photo opportunities that are without content, function, or meaning other than that of being reported and televised are framed in America's cultural history of fabricated public spectacle going back to the days of P. T. Barnum. Alongside the modern phenomenon of the celebrity famous for their fame, these strategies become markers of a contemporary politics fundamentally driven by television and the media.[14] Megan Garber, writing in the *Atlantic*, pointed to Boorstin's acknowledgment of the audience as enabler and the factor assuring the persistence of the pseudo-event in the modern age: "We are living, still, he suggests, within the sparkle and the spectacle and the fog of P. T. Barnum—whose core insight, after all, was not just that people could be fooled, but that, in fact, they wanted to be fooled. . . . Today, living as we do in the shadow of a man who is most readily associated with gaudy circuses, Americans tend to take performance for granted as a feature of political and cultural life. We often assume that, since we ask politicians to entertain us as celebrities do, they will probably pretend like them, as well."[15] For Gabler, Trump's "pseudo-campaign," indeed, represented the perfect confluence of these modern vacuums, enabled by a media eager to consume both. As his scathing critique of the reality TV candidate and his favored medium suggested, "While celebrity may not be much of a recommendation for the presidency, it is a hell of a recommendation for a presidential aspirant performing before a media that is far more interested in creating a reality show than presenting a process for selecting a leader. Trump is the Kardashian of politics."[16]

In *Audience of One*, Poniewozik more specifically traces the development of US television alongside the emergence of Donald Trump as celebrity president. Exploring the increasing significance of reality television in the 2000s, Poniewozik asserts that, contrary to accepted narratives of quality television, it was less dramas such as *The Sopranos* (HBO, 1999–2007) or *Mad Men* (AMC, 2007–15)—or even the trend of dark superhero films—that established the antihero as a central figure in contemporary television than it was the proliferation of the reality show. The latter, after all, centered on a competitive format and therefore encouraged individuals to create a persona that would command attention on the screen, use personal narratives (however fictional), and ruthlessly battle to a victorious conclusion. The shows asked their protagonists to "get out there and do what you've got to do. Sometimes you have to work the dark side."[17] Trump emerged from television, therefore, as one of the architects of a format that suggested that being unpopular was what winning was all about. It became a central element of his strategy in his move into the political arena and a key factor in the popularity achieved among his base. As *The Apprentice* was discarded in favor of *The Celebrity Apprentice* as a response to a sharp decline in ratings, Poniewozik argues, even the concept of business rapidly disappeared as contestants exploited their celebrity to acquire money for charity. Trump had, in any case, throughout the show represented "the *idea* of a businessman. That was Donald Trump. It was the entire point of him."[18] With the addition of a side dish of politics with a weekly slot on *Fox and Friends* (Fox News Channel, 1998–) in 2011, it was this antihero character, fictionalized businessman, reality-television celebrity persona that Trump brought to the presidency.

Trump's use of the media during his term as president certainly has historical precedent going back to Franklin Delano Roosevelt's famous "Fireside Chats" during the Great Depression and World War II and televised presidential addresses to the nation at times of political crisis. While these largely represented a source of information and acted as calming succor for US citizens, however, Donald Trump's exploitation of his television and social media presence has been both unrelenting and aimed at directly communicating with the American public and increasingly with his base support. When the president's threatening tweet during the former US ambassador to Ukraine Marie Yovanovitch's testimony at the November 2019 impeachment hearings was read out on live television by committee chair Adam Schiff, its breaking of the fourth wall represented not only Trump's self-imaging as a dominant televisual force but also one further example of his attempts to bypass traditional media and his own White House administration with messaging directed at his core audience.[19] News organizations at the same time were strongly criticized for their calls for more "pizzazz" that would define the hearings as television events, seeming to assume the mantle of Trump's culture of televised political theater.[20]

Trump's news-grabbing, impromptu press conferences on the White House lawn throughout his presidency, usurping the role of his various press secretaries, featured as a central aspect of his pseudo-events television strategy. Similarly, his rambling press conferences at the height of the COVID-19 health crisis, aimed at challenging the data on the United States' spiraling case numbers, were temporarily abandoned only when broadcasters ceased carrying them on live television.[21] The diminishing effectiveness of Trump's attempt to control his political messaging through television pseudo-events is exemplified by the photo opportunity—more accurately describable as a TV opportunity—constructed during the Black Lives Matter protests against police brutality in June 2020. The clash of images created by a scene of peaceful protestors being beaten and tear-gassed out of Lafayette Square outside the White House before the president, Ivanka Trump, Bill Barr, and a crew of White House staff walked to St. John's Church, where Trump posed uncomfortably with a Bible held aloft, signaled both a transparent incongruity in his attempt to clothe himself in religion and an unashamed disregard for the political moment that called for basic American equality.[22] The clashing imagery that occurred on January 6, 2021, as the president and members of his family celebrated the "Save America" rally rolling out on television screens shortly before the attack on the Capitol suggested a final reckoning for the symbiotic relationship between television and the Trump presidency. Indeed, the media conversation about a more appropriate response to Trump's damaging invention of an alternative reality was immediate, if self-evidently late.[23]

With the overwhelming focus of the Trump campaigns and presidency on dominating political messaging and screen time through television, the extent to which the small screen has consistently engaged with the daily news, dramas, and controversies of the Trump era is unsurprising. At the same time, the recognizable shifts in both the style and content of the presidency as conducted by Donald Trump, Republican cheerleaders in Congress like Lindsey Graham and Jim Jordan, and various White House advisers such as Trump's son-in-law Jared Kushner and daughter Ivanka have pitched television alongside its audience into a jarring experience that simultaneously fascinates and repels. The destabilizing effect of a presidency consumed by television and to which television has been similarly, if necessarily, addicted is nevertheless a cultural and political phenomenon that defines the Trump era and its aftermath and has driven the direction of television since 2016. Whether the documenting of a political period during which the workings of Washington politics play out repeatedly on television or the explicit or implied critiques of a divisive political culture through a variety of genres, the medium has been transfixed by a presidency consistently conducted with television in mind.

American Television during a Television Presidency positions itself within a field of books that have argued for the recognition of presidential politics and culture as a potentially dominant factor in screen representation. Jane Feuer's *Seeing through the Eighties: Television and Reaganism*, for example, illustrates how television programming and industry developments display the political and economic conservatism of the 1980s, and in *Cinema Wars: Hollywood Film and Politics in the Bush-Cheney Era*, Douglas Kellner considers the political agendas surrounding 9/11, the Iraq War, and other events revealed and critiqued in the period's fiction and documentary film. Issues of cultural identity that might define a presidency are the focus of books including Susan Jeffords's *Hard Bodies: Hollywood Masculinity in the Reagan Era* and David Garrett Izzo's *Movies in the Age of Obama: The Era of Post-Racial and Neo-Racist Cinema*. The connections made by Jeffords between the Hollywood blockbuster and Reagan's branding of national identity around his constructed male image and the increased visibility of the Black experience in Obama-era Hollywood explored in Izzo's volume, alongside the cinematic retracing and reinforcement of otherness, point to screen engagement with the cultural temper created by and around presidential politics.[24]

This book emerges simultaneously within a context of works that consider Donald Trump as a text represented in film, television, and the wider media. Jack Holland's *Fictional Television and American Politics: From 9/11 to Donald Trump* connects the various eras of contemporary US politics, developing a historical narrative that demonstrates the central space for political engagement in fictional television. Stephen Hock's volume *Trump Fiction: Essays on Donald Trump in Literature, Film, and Television* explores the cultural depiction and referencing of Trump across fiction both prior to and since his ascent to the presidency. Most specifically, Victoria McCollum's volume *Make America Hate Again: Trump-Era Horror and the Politics of Fear* addresses TV horror as a genre whose characteristics and concerns arguably make it ideally placed to respond to the contemporary political climate.[25] *American Television during a Television Presidency* draws on a variety of these approaches to television's engagement with presidential politics. Collapsing the borders between political agendas and their cultural framing and moving between factual and fictional programming, the book seeks to open up new territory in which to critically analyze television's complex relationship with Donald Trump, his presidency, and the politics and culture that pervade this era.

Part 1 of the volume, "Donald Trump and a Media Presidency," focuses on Donald Trump as president and the extent to which his term in the White House has been defined by his association and interplay with television. In chapter 1, Martin Murray takes a psychological approach to Trump and his persistent desire for media celebrity. Considering the narcissistic tendency the president displays and his conduct as a businessman, television celebrity, and president, "The Imaginary President: Donald Trump's Narcissism and American TV" explores how the identity Trump constructed to attract media attention and its mediation through television became effective strategies for a reality-television presidency. In "*Our Cartoon President*: Donald J. Trump's White House as an Animated Comedy," Rafał Kuś examines Showtime's animated sitcom *Our Cartoon President* (2018–), which uses comedy, satire, and the animated form in a televisual representation of a sitting president. Framing the show within a history of television comedy, the animated sitcom, and the mockumentary as political forms, the chapter explores *Our Cartoon President*'s representation of Trump, his family, and his presidency, as well as the show's critical reception, arguing that the show becomes both a political critique and a humanization of its subject. In "The Mob, the Reds, and the TV President: The Changing Role of Televised Hearings in a Post-Decency Era," the congressional hearings that have been a feature of Trump's tenure in the White House are the subject, as Kathryn Castle positions the Kavanaugh, Russia, and impeachment hearings in US political history. Tracing the thread that binds Trump to McCarthyism and the organized-crime hearings of the 1950s, Castle draws parallels with the camera-grabbing performances that have dominated the televised hearings during the Trump administration and investigates television's ability nevertheless to expose and reveal.

Part 2, "Fact, Fiction, and Critique," explores some of the contemporary American television shows that play out as commentaries on the Trump presidency as they dramatize and satirize the political era. In "The Political Is Personal: Disturbing Form, Revisiting Liberalism, and Resisting Trump's America in *The Good Fight*," Karen McNally explores how the show continuously disturbs the style and form of the television legal drama to explicitly critique the politics of the Trump era. As the characters of *The Good Fight* (CBS All Access, 2017–)[26] become consumed personally and professionally by current events and liberalism becomes radical, the chapter contends, the narrative reflects on both the increasing personalization of politics and the lawlessness and chaos of the Trump administration. Simon Stow's chapter, "On the Value of Uncertainty in Uncertain Times (Or, "Pay Attention, You Assholes!"): Donald Trump, David Simon, and *The Plot Against America*," explores HBO's 2020 television adaptation of Philip Roth's novel imagining a Charles Lindbergh presidency during World War II. As Stow examines critical reception of the miniseries that views its portrayal of rife anti-Semitism, capitulation to fascism, and the aviator's celebrity presidency as a polemic against Trump, the chapter considers whether David Simon's promotion of critical perspective through narrative and thematic ambiguity in the depiction of an alternative past to inform our understanding of the present ultimately becomes instead a call for engagement in the democratic process as part of the creation of the United States' future. Dolores Resano, in "From Political Depression to 'Satiractivism': Late-Night in the Tribal Era of Trump," explores the comedic and politically charged arena of late-night satire on US television. Examining the Trump-dominated satire of shows such as *Saturday Night Live* (NBC, 1975–) and *Last Week Tonight* (HBO, 2014–), Resano considers how they might reflect the tribalism of the nation's contemporary politics, promote political activism, or push their viewers further into an abyss of Trump fatigue.

Part 3, "Genre, Style, and Reception," explores how the generic frameworks and styles of comedy, science fiction, and horror impact on both the representation and reception of contemporary politics in fictional television. Teresa Forde delves into a controversial series in the *Star Trek* franchise in "*Star Trek: Discovery* and Controversy: 'The War Without, the War Within.'" Addressing the social media backlash from sections of *Star Trek* fandom against the message of diversity in *Discovery* (CBS All Access, 2017–), Forde argues that the racial divisions of the Trump era sparked a culture war around a key example of television's sci-fi genre and moved the utopian vision of the franchise toward critique and activism. K. Scott Culpepper examines the immersion of the anthology series *American Horror Story* (FX, 2011–) in Trump-era politics in his chapter, "Paranoia, the Hive Mind, and Empowered Sisterhood: *American Horror Story*'s Trump-Haunted World." As symbolism and generic tropes are used to address themes including the powerful influence of new technology and social media and a political culture of division and extremism, Culpepper argues that the drama simultaneously makes space for hope alongside the horror through its depictions of female resistance and the ultimate possibility of healing. In "Teaching

Demons and Eating Nazis: Morality in Trump-Era Fantasy Comedy," Hannah Andrews and Gregory Frame explore the ways in which television comedy confronts the United States' neoliberal politics. Examining NBC's *The Good Place* (2016–20) and *Santa Clarita Diet* (2017–19) on Netflix, the authors contend that the shows' framing of characters and narratives around questions of ethics that seek to challenge moral and philosophical assumptions become implicit critiques of the contemporary political arena. Michael Mario Albrecht's chapter, "First as Farce, Then as Tragedy: The Hilarious Nihilism of the Trump-influenced Final Season of *Veep*," continues looking at comedy, taking up the theme of fictional political satire. Examining the persistently hyperbolic take of *Veep* (HBO, 2012–19) on the venality of US politics in the midst of the chaos and corruption of the Trump administration, Albrecht argues that the show's final season faces the problem of how to provide an exaggerated portrayal of an unethical political landscape when an unscrupulous presidency becomes real.

Part 4, "Power and Gender," commences with Steven Cohan's essay "*Fosse/Verdon* and the #MeToo Moment," which explores the FX limited series and its portrayal of the creative partnership and personal relationship between Bob Fosse and Gwen Verdon. While much of the promotion and reception of the show in 2019 circulated around #MeToo and the attempt to both reclaim Verdon's legacy and acknowledge Fosse's abuses of power, the narrative's focus on the better-known achievements of Fosse, Cohan argues, means that the show ultimately fails to fittingly capture the moment and redress this balance. In "'Grab Them by the Pussy': The Sexual Politics of Touch in *The Handmaid's Tale*," Donna Peberdy considers the show's representation of touch as both a means of control and a signal of defiance. The sexual politics that define *The Handmaid's Tale* (Hulu, 2017–), Peberdy contends, reflect not only a political climate hostile to women's sexual autonomy and reproductive rights but also a presidency dominated by masculine aggression and, moreover, an activist female response. In "The Sound of Money and Power: Musical Scoring in Trump-Era Television Drama," Aimee Mollaghan takes a close look at the musical scoring of the quality television dramas *Succession* (HBO, 2018–) and *The Good Fight*. Exploring how these scores draw on the extravagance of seventeenth- and eighteenth-century orchestral music as accompaniments to narratives framed by themes of power and excess, the chapter considers the ways in which musical scoring becomes integral to the shows' representation of the chaos and absurdity of the Trump era.

The essays in Part 5, "Renegotiating the Past," address various approaches to memory, beginning with Kwakiutl L. Dreher's chapter, "Remember the Time When: Annotations on Black Histories in Kenya Barris's *Black-ish*." In an examination of the show's disruption to the American sitcom's racially exclusive utopian ideal, Dreher demonstrates the essential imperative in *Black-ish* (ABC, 2014–) to memorialize Black history, asserting the significance of re-presenting the Black experience in an amnesic post-Obama, Trump-administration climate. Jessica Ford and Martin Zeller-Jacques examine contemporary reboots of situation comedies in "You Can't Go Home Again: The Recuperative Reboot and the Trump-Era Sitcom." Focusing in particular on *One Day at a Time* (Netflix, 2017–19; Pop, 2020) and *Roseanne* (ABC, 2018), the authors highlight the limitations evident in the reboot's aim to both exploit audience nostalgia and reframe shows for a new era in the light of contemporary cultural attitudes, as issues of genre, stardom, the American family, and an alternative social and political arena are raised. Oliver Gruner's chapter, "'The Cost of Lies': *Chernobyl*, Politics, and Collective Memory," closes the volume with an examination of the HBO show and its revisiting of a catastrophic event whose reverberations have been wide-ranging, global, and persistent. Exploring the show's visual use of realism and horror tropes in the shaping of its narrative, alongside the depiction of contaminated and disintegrating physical and national identity, Gruner explores themes from collective memory to surveillance, the environment, and the corruption of truth, illustrating how the show's concerns are informed by a political past, present, and future.

These chapters address the wide-ranging ways in which the politics and culture of the Trump era are drawn across contemporary American television. Exploring how TV documents, dramatizes, satirizes, and critiques an astonishing period in US politics, the authors consider the diverse ways that television engages with themes and issues that are raised, confronted, and challenged across an era defined by a presidency. Taking approaches that position contemporary television both historically and in the specificity of the contemporary moment, these chapters illustrate the indelible links that exist between television, US politics, and the nation's broader culture. Interrogating a presidency played out through the lens of the TV camera and delving into a television climate immersed in its compelling and inescapable subject, this book sets out to explore what defines the television of the Trump era as a distinctive time in the medium's history and to discover the textured layers of the relationship between television and US politics and culture that this unsettled and simultaneously groundbreaking period reveals.

Notes

1 David Remnick, "An American Tragedy," *New Yorker*, November 9, 2016, https://www.newyorker.com/news/news-desk/an-american-tragedy-2.
2 Matt Flegenheimer and Michael Barbaro, "Donald Trump Is Elected President in Stunning Repudiation of the Establishment," *New York Times*, November 9, 2016, https://www.nytimes.com/2016/11/09/us/politics/hillary-clinton-donald-trump-president.html.
3 Maggie Haberman, "Trump Postpones G7 Summit and Calls for Russia to Attend," *New York Times*, May 30, 2020, https://www.nytimes.com/2020/05/30/us/politics/trump-g7-russia.html.
4 Paul Sonne, "Trump Remains Silent on Putin Despite Uproar over Alleged Russian Bounty Payments," *Washington Post*, July 4, 2020, https://www.washingtonpost.com/national-security/trump-remains-silent-on-putin-despite-uproar-over-alleged-russian-bounty-payments/2020/07/03/00a692a6-bc81-11ea-86d5-3b9b3863273b_story.html.
5 Paul Starr, "Trump's Second Term. It's More Likely than Most People Think—and Compared with His First Term, Its Effects Would Be Far More Durable," *Atlantic*, May 2019, https://www.theatlantic.com/magazine/archive/2019/05/trump-2020-second-term/585994/.
6 World Health Organization, WHO Coronavirus Disease (COVID-19) Dashboard, accessed September 10, 2020, https://covid19.who.int/table.
7 Molly Roberts, "The Nancy Pelosi Photo Is a Rorschach Test for an America Cleaved into Two," *Washington Post*, October 17, 2019, https://www.washingtonpost.com/opinions/2019/10/17/nancy-pelosi-photo-is-rorschach-test-an-america-cleaved-into-two/.
8 Paul LeBlanc, "Trump Shares Letter That Calls Peaceful Protestors 'Terrorists,'" CNN.com, June 5, 2020, https://edition.cnn.com/2020/06/04/politics/trump-letter-protesters/index.html; Emily Badger, "How Trump's Use of Federal Forces in Cities Differs from Past Presidents," *New York Times*, July 23, 2020, https://www.nytimes.com/2020/07/23/upshot/trump-portland.html.
9 Amanda Terkel, "John Lewis Went against Donald Trump When Few Democrats Would," *Huffington Post*, July 18, 2020, https://www.huffingtonpost

.co.uk/entry/john-lewis-trump_n_5e0e3fa0e4b0843d360f8964?ri18n=
true.

10 Tim Elfrink, "'I Don't Know John Lewis': Trump Bashes Deceased Civil
    Rights Leader for Skipping His Inauguration," *Washington Post*, August 4,
    2020, https://www.washingtonpost.com/nation/2020/08/04/trump-john
    -lewis-axios-swan/.

11 Marc Fisher and Will Hobson, "Donald Trump Masqueraded as Publi-
    cist to Brag about Himself," *Washington Post*, May 13, 2016, https://www
    .washingtonpost.com/politics/donald-trump-alter-ego-barron/2016/05/
    12/02ac99ec-16fe-11e6-aa55-670cabef46e0_story.html.

12 Michael Kruse, "The Escalator Ride That Changed America," *Politico*,
    June 14, 2019, https://www.politico.com/magazine/story/2019/06/14/
    donald-trump-campaign-announcement-tower-escalator-oral-history
    -227148.

13 James Poniewozik, *Audience of One: Donald Trump, Television, and the
    Fracturing of America* (New York: Norton, 2019), 195.

14 Neal Gabler, "We All Enabled Donald Trump: Our Deeply Unserious
    Media and Reality-TV Culture Made This Horror Inevitable," *Salon*,
    March 14, 2016, https://www.salon.com/2016/03/14/we_all_enabled
    _donald_trump_our_deeply_unserious_media_and_reality_tv_culture
    _made_this_horror_inevitable/.

15 Megan Garber, "*The Image* in the Age of Pseudo-Reality," *Atlantic*, Decem-
    ber 1, 2016, https://www.theatlantic.com/entertainment/archive/2016/12/
    the-image-in-the-age-of-pseudo-reality/509135/.

16 Gabler, "We All Enabled Donald Trump."

17 Poniewozik, *Audience of One*, 107.

18 Poniewozik, 139–41, 119.

19 James Poniewozik, "The President Bursts through the Virtual Courtroom
    Doors," *New York Times*, November 15, 2019, https://www.nytimes.com/
    2019/11/15/arts/television/trump-tweet-hearing.html.

20 Aaron Rupar, "Coverage of the First Impeachment Hearing Illustrates How
    the Media Is Falling Short," *Vox*, November 14, 2019, https://www.vox
    .com/2019/11/14/20964668/impeachment-hearing-pizzazz-nbc-reuters.

21 Tyler Hersko, "The Decision Not to Air Trump's Coronavirus Briefing
    Is Commendable—and Overdue," *IndieWire*, April 3, 2020, https://www
    .indiewire.com/2020/04/cnn-msnbc-not-airing-trump-coronavirus
    -briefing-1202222521/.

22   Katie Rogers, "Protestors Dispersed with Tear Gas So Trump Could Pose at Church," *New York Times*, June 1, 2020, https://www.nytimes.com/2020/06/01/us/politics/trump-st-johns-church-bible.html.

23   Ben Travers, "TV Is Starting to Cut Ties with Trump, as His Legacy Wreaks Havoc on Reality," *IndieWire*, January 7, 2021, https://www.indiewire.com/2021/01/capitol-attack-tv-trump-coverage-reality-1234608059/.

24   Jane Feuer, *Seeing through the Eighties: Television and Reaganism* (London: BFI, 1996); Douglas Kellner, *Cinema Wars: Hollywood Film and Politics in the Bush-Cheney Era* (New York: Wiley-Blackwell, 2009); Susan Jeffords, *Hard Bodies: Hollywood Masculinity in the Reagan Era* (New Brunswick, NJ: Rutgers University Press, 1994); David Garrett Izzo, *Movies in the Age of Obama: The Era of Post-Racial and Neo-Racist Cinema* (Lanham, MD: Rowman and Littlefield, 2014).

25   Jack Holland, *Fictional Television and American Politics: From 9/11 to Donald Trump* (Manchester, UK: Manchester University Press, 2019); Stephen Hock, *Trump Fiction: Essays on Donald Trump in Literature, Film, and Television* (Lanham, MD: Lexington Books, 2019); Victoria McCollum, *Make America Hate Again: Trump-Era Horror and the Politics of Fear* (Abingdon, UK: Routledge, 2019).

26   CBS All Access was rebranded as Paramount + in March 2021.

PART I

Donald Trump and a Media Presidency

THE IMAGINARY PRESIDENT

DONALD TRUMP'S NARCISSISM AND AMERICAN TV

Martin Murray

There is a synergetic relationship between the American public, the media, and Donald Trump, one that involves dynamic and significant exchanges in which all parties are affected. Despite what most Democrats think, the various events, interactions, and consequences involved in these exchanges have not all been bad ones. For example, Trump's term in office has made media bigger and richer, as its revenue has expanded through increased coverage and ratings, partly generated by Trump himself.[1] The US economy has grown overall too, although nowhere near as much as Trump has claimed.[2] Yet Trump's presidency has failed to make him or US voters happier, at least not in any demonstrable or enduring way. Their relationship plays out largely as a drama of love and hate. Those who are against Trump do not just dislike him but despise him. They are appalled by his tweets and his policy announcements (which are sometimes, in any case, indistinguishable). They abhor his support for armed protesters and his suggestion that Americans ingest disinfectant to guard against the coronavirus.[3] This "theatrical trauma" of anti-Trumpism is fully covered in the media and acted out in news stories, on news shows, or even on entire channels such as MSNBC or CNN by celebrity anchors like Rachel Maddow or Don Lemon.[4] It is provoked, reflected, and sustained in comedy and chat shows like *The Late Show with Stephen Colbert* (CBS, 2015–), *The Tonight Show Starring Jimmy Fallon* (NBC, 2014–), and *The Daily Show* (Comedy Central, 1996–) or in print media such as the *New York Times* or the *Washington Post*. The drama is enacted in (and is a reaction to) the dysfunctional and melodramatic powerplay in which the president engages through his tweets, press briefings, executive orders, interviews, and rallies. Yet it is also the case that Trump's supporters—and sometimes Trump himself—are delighted by the show. His advocates flock to his televised rallies and hang on his words; they laugh at his jokes and cheer his insults, accusations, and promises of revenge. Trumpists could not care less if what Trump says is untrue; he entertains them.[5] If he offends liberals, they love him even more. As Trump put it himself, "I could stand in the middle of Fifth Avenue and shoot somebody and I wouldn't lose any voters."[6] Trump is as reactive as his opponents are horrified and is as outrageous as his supporters want him to be. The Trump-media-public relationship is a mutually dependent one. Everyone watches it and thus participates in it, even if they are not starring in it. A great deal of it takes place on television.

The Script

Trump is a TV baby (the moniker fits him perfectly). He watches TV as avidly as he craves being on it.[7] He is as addicted to consuming it as he is to conducting televised rallies, and he had a bank of televisions in his bedroom at the White House, where he reportedly spent most evenings. Trump prefers televisual representations of the American people, people overseas, and his family to the flesh-and-blood personification of them he sometimes has to encounter outside his bedroom door.[8] The American people are Trump's audience. He communicates with them through television, which simultaneously mediates and forms them. Trump seeks out his audience through his television appearances, attempting to reach it by presenting himself in a relatable (even if unlikable) way. Trump and Americans come together via TV, and all three are key elements of the analysis that follows.

Many mental health professionals have described Trump as narcissistic, adopting a psychological approach to their analysis of him, one that references psychiatry, clinical psychology, and psychoanalysis. This is a perspective that I will also broadly adopt in this chapter.[9] Television has always been an appropriate vehicle for Trump's pathology, allowing him to create various personae as ideal versions of himself that appeal to him and that he thinks will appeal to others. This feeds his overwhelming need to be liked, admired, or loved or at least to be the center of everyone's attention (which being hated can achieve just as well as being loved). Trump's narcissistic personae both connect with audiences and have a significant effect on them, one that it would not be hyperbolic to call world-changing and that has been facilitated, shaped, and even encouraged by the media in general and television in particular. In what follows, I show that television's technology, economy, location in culture, and audience have each altered substantially during Trump's lifetime and career. Trump has understood this, and his TV personae have changed and adapted accordingly. The success of this adaption has contributed significantly to his success as a celebrity and, by extension, to his election to the presidency. In what follows, I make some references to Trump's presidential appearances, but for reasons of space (and because those appearances deserve an essay to themselves), my analyses focus mainly on his preelection broadcasts and recordings on television.

Narcissism

Narcissism is something that is commonly, and not inaccurately, thought of as self-love. The term is taken from the Greek myth of Narcissus, who, having fallen in love with his reflection in a pool, was unable to bear the fact that the object of his love was only an image and consequently killed himself.[10] Psychologically speaking, narcissism is not necessarily pathological, however tragically it affected Narcissus. As Craig Malkin notes, a normal, stable, creative, and productive personality will include some measure of narcissism, enough to provide it with an adequate level of confidence to facilitate successful human activity, to accomplish satisfying life goals, to form relationships, and to survive. One needs an adequate level of narcissism to feel good enough about oneself to be able to live successfully. Thus, healthy narcissism amounts to the effective (if occasionally unrealistic) portion of self-regard that permits achievement of a productive and happy enough personal and interpersonal life.[11]

Trump's representation of himself is as someone whose personality might meet these criteria of healthy narcissism. He has famously represented himself as "stable" and "smart" and as having "tremendous" relationships with everyone with whom he works. Unfortunately for Trump and for Americans, his self-assurance is neither as measured nor as constructive as he would have everyone believe. His claims about his stability and smartness were accompanied by a declaration of his own "genius." Trump's comments were made in the context of a questioning of his mental health, and he inadvertently responded with an excessive display of narcissism, putting the very health he was declaring in question.[12] His descriptions of his relationships as "tremendous" have been misleading, to say the least. He clashed with almost every senior member of his own cabinet. Most had fallen out with him by the time they left their posts, and many have gone public with reports of his egotism and incompetence. One in a long line is former national security adviser John Bolton.[13] Trump clearly exhibited a dysfunctional pattern of relationships with senior officials. He praised them when he hired them, clashed with them when they disagreed with him, and then, unlike his television persona on *The Apprentice* (NBC, 2004–17), had them fired. FBI director James Comey, for example, learned of his sacking when he saw it reported on TV.[14]

It is worth noting that although Trump's narcissism is destructive, it contains *traces* of its healthy incarnation (as most narcissism does). When manifest in attractiveness or charisma, healthy narcissism can have a beneficial effect beyond its subject and on its objects. Actors and comedians, who often score above average on indexes of narcissism, are good examples.[15] They want to be liked and admired by others and achieve their ends via a type of generosity and charm. The personalities they adopt—at least onstage or onscreen—are intended to entertain others or to make others feel good, at least for a while. They hope, by the investment of good feeling that acting involves, to get that good feeling back. This type of narcissism-via-the-other is clearly recognized in psychoanalytic theory. Freud describes it as a direction of self-love toward an object, one that is presented as love for that object but that intends and hopes that the love expended will be returned. He calls this psychical strategy "anaclitic narcissism."[16]

Trump's behavior shows some traces of healthy narcissism, or at least its strategies, even though it is not beneficial for anyone overall. His behavior also involves anaclitic narcissism. Trump's performance of self-regard can be charming, and this charm is clearly intended to flatter its objects and to get something in return. He hosted *Saturday Night Live* (NBC, 1975–) in 2004 and delivered a monologue on the same show a year later. On both occasions, he parodied himself (and allowed himself to be parodied by impersonators) as egotistical, boastful, and vulgar. The audience loved it and liked Trump as a consequence. Historically, the show has mocked him, encouraging the audience to laugh at Trump rather than with him. Yet Trump deployed his narcissistic charm to turn that effect around. He knows how to make people like him. His critics often fail to see this due to their antipathy toward him, yet Trump garners admiration from his supporters all the same.

Trump's narcissistic displays have practical and financial aims and effects as well as psychological ones. His cultivation of his image as a hugely successful real-estate billionaire was part of his financial success. Being known as a rich and successful developer helped him to finance his deals, giving investors confidence in him. Being a big spender, a playboy, and someone who always had an attractive woman on his arm made him attractive to others, including his financiers and the consumers of his products. His was an achievement of the American Dream that many people craved, particularly in the 1980s, when that dream was mostly built around material success and/or fame. Trump projected success; he *performed* it. "The show is Trump," he said, "and it is sold out performances everywhere."[17] He most obviously performed it on *The Apprentice*, although it was apparent before the show that made him a television celebrity. The performance involved sex, power, and the indulgence of his own wishes. These were obviously all narcissistic pleasures for him in the sense that they made him feel good about himself, but they also involved narcissistic investment and return insofar as they made others love and/or admire him too. These others (business partners, television audiences, voters) probably felt good about Trump at the time, even though many of them have felt abused, lied to, and exploited by him since. Like many destructive narcissists, Trump has a character that bears traces of, and can at least impersonate, good narcissism too.

It is worth briefly thinking about *how* this sort of exploitation can happen, how people can be tricked into thinking they are being loved and gratified when, ultimately, they are not. It depends on a sort of *identification*, one that involves a narcissistic exchange. Identification is the psychological process of bonding with someone on the basis of a perceived similarity or affinity. It usually (but not exclusively) involves "liking" someone and/or thinking that one is "like" them. One of Trump's main political achievements is to have persuaded others to identify with him enough to facilitate his election to the presidency. Remarkably, he achieved this even though most people who voted for him are *unlike* him in important ways. Many of his admirers are ordinary and/or working-class people, and there is a huge disparity between their wealth and his. Trump nevertheless persuades people to aspire to be like him. They would like to live in the Trump Tower apartment he showed off in season 1 of *The Apprentice* or the luxurious homes he paraded on television in *Lifestyles of the Rich and Famous* (Paramount, 1984–95). Trump knows this. In 1987, he explained, "I play to people's fantasies. People may not always think big themselves. But they can still get very excited by those who do."[18] He provokes a wish in his audience to be like him by both displaying his wealth and turning on his charm. He even suggests they *are* like him *already*. How so? Because (he says) he is *like them*. Despite being a "billionaire," he is realistic, brash, iconoclastic. He rails against the elite (even though he is one of them) as ordinary working people do. As Michael Kranish and Marc Fisher suggest in their biography of Trump, "Despite living in a golden palace high above Fifth Avenue and jetting to rallies in a private jet, Trump pitched himself as the voice of the beaten-down working class."[19]

In order for this identification between Trump and the downtrodden to take hold, he has done more than to be charming and funny. He has channeled a sort of rage. Irrespective of the origins of that rage, he has turned it against objects that ordinary or deprived people dislike or hate. Added to Trump's antipathy toward the elite is a list of common hate objects for him and his supporters that include liberals, Mexican immigrants, the Chinese, and transnational institutions (World Health Organization, NATO). During the past twenty years, this more negative and caustic aspect to Trump's narcissism, and its function as a point of political identification, has come to the fore. It has become very apparent in his televised rallies, which, while replete with charm and jokes, are also bitter and accusatory. As the *New Yorker* television critic Emily Nussbaum has pointed out, Trump has increasingly become "a hot comic, a classic Howard Stern guest . . . the insult comic, the stadium act, the ratings-obsessed headliner who shouted down hecklers. His televised rallies boil with rage and laughter, which are hard to tell apart."[20] At this point, Trump's narcissism, wit, and charm, which were never entirely benign in any case, tip over into something much nastier. This brings me to the matter of the negativity of Trump's narcissism, its pathology and malignancy.

Malignancy

Ultimately, there is very little true or honest about the narcissistic self-image that Trump projects into the world via the media. His narcissism *is not* beneficial, in toto. Narcissism becomes pathological when an individual's capacity and/or need for self-love is greater than an amount that is consistent with normal, decent, functional human behavior. In such cases, narcissists will lie and cheat to maintain their image of themselves as lovable or admirable and will exploit those around them to do so.[21] Trump's biography is replete with examples of precisely these traits. He has made untruthful statements throughout his presidency. The earliest of these were his claims to have won the popular vote in the presidential election and his insistence that the crowd size at his inauguration was the largest ever. Typically, he claimed that it was the news media, including television news, that misrepresented the numbers.[22] A similar major untruth was his claim in an interview with the Fox anchor Chris Wallace that Joe Biden has sanctioned and supported initiatives to defund the police.[23] More recently and infamously, Trump claimed to have won the 2020 US presidential election, both before and after the result was confirmed. He patently did not.

Trump's intentionally false statements have usually been intended to smear and defame his opponents. In June 2017, the *New York Times* established an inventory of "Trump's lies," comprising Trump's statements while in office that can be demonstrably proven false. It shows that in the first three months of his term, he lied about not only his election but also immigration figures, insurance rates, government savings, the *New York Times*, opposition protestors, terrorism, the US murder rate, Iraq, Democratic senators, the judiciary, Hillary Clinton, job creation, corporations, "Obamacare," lobbyists, prisoner releases, Sweden, NATO, government investment, Steve Bannon, Congress, and more. The *New York Times* continued to publish the inventory until near the end of Trump's first year in office, until his lies became so constant and numerous that it was no longer worth recording them individually.[24] In case it were doubtful that these lies derived from anything other than Trump's narcissism, the *Washington Post* has a complementary index, one that records his false boasts, in other words, the untrue things he has stated with the clear purpose of inflating his own ego and his image in the eyes of others.[25]

Lying is not the only major feature of pathological narcissism or the only one more than manifest in Trump's behavior. Malkin lists three characteristics of pathological narcissism: entitlement, exploitation, and empathy-impairment. All three are identifiable in Trump's personality and history, and it is easy to provide examples of activities that suggest his character contains them. While he was expanding his real-estate empire in Manhattan in the late 1970s, he felt entitled to huge grants and tax breaks to help finance developments. When an unsympathetic mayor and administration resisted this, Trump sued them.[26] He has a reputation, while developing, of not paying, or of underpaying, his suppliers. There are numerous examples of this sort of exploitation of business partners during the 1980s that include nonpayment of funds for the decoration and renovation of Trump's larger investments like his casinos.[27]

Trump's empathy deficit is apparent in his tendency to drop or reject people when they are no longer of use to him, even when they are struggling. A notable example is the lawyer Roy Cohn, who is, ironically, often credited with teaching Trump his provocative, aggressive, and disruptive business style. Trump was close to Cohn for over a decade. When Cohn, a closeted gay man, was dying of AIDS in the mid-1980s, Trump avoided him.[28] Trump's narcissism is as evident in his television persona and work as it is in his business identity. It was while engaged in television work, on the way to record an episode of *Access Hollywood* (NBC, 1996–), that Trump displayed his predatoriness with women, famously boasting to the show host Billy Bush that his strategy for sexual conquest involved kissing them without warning them and trying to "grab 'em by the pussy."[29] Unambiguous accusations of rape, sexual assault, or sexual harassment have been made against Trump by more than twenty-five women since the 1970s. Forty-three further accusations have been added in a recent book.[30]

The News

It seems obvious that what Trump cares about most, given his narcissism, is himself. This is what he wants others to care about too. There is nothing Trump loves doing more than putting himself in the public eye, and in the early part of his career, this meant being in the news. As a young property developer during the 1970s and 1980s, he flattered and bullied the media, especially television news media, into covering him and doing so as favorably as possible. Unlike most developers, Trump actively engaged with journalists, inviting them into his offices and homes for interviews and regaling them with stories of his wealth and ambition. He attended elite nightspots like Studio 54, where he consorted with the richest, most famous, most fashionable people on the planet, and as a consequence, he frequently appeared in gossip columns and on celebrity and entertainment shows. He flaunted his wealth, his lavish lifestyle, his influence, and his power and did so while accompanied by beautiful women, only one of whom was his wife, Ivana.[31] It goes without saying that as much of Trump's celebrity life as he could arrange took place on TV.

Yet by the 1990s, Trump's narcissistic self-image was becoming more difficult to sustain as his massively overleveraged and indebted construction empire began to collapse. Trump's property holdings, which included three casinos, numerous high-value Manhattan residential properties, and overseas ownerships and investments, were not making sufficient money to be financially sustainable, and his business accrued estimated debts of over $1 billion. He was effectively and massively bankrupted, and it took a consortium of international banks and financiers to bail him out. Crucially, Trump never admitted to having failed and has been disingenuous and misleading about his real wealth ever since. His billionaire friends sometimes say that Trump is nowhere near as wealthy as he says he is. Yet he has continued to present himself as rich, in fact as super-rich, maintaining a celebrity lifestyle to match with yachts, planes, limousines, helicopters, mansions, multimillion-dollar weddings, Miss World contestant companions, celebrity friends, and so on. All of this is manifestly for show and as much for business reasons as for personal ones.

By the early 1990s, Trump had realized that the future of his business was branding and in fact that his brand was himself. Even before the change in his fortunes, he used his celebrity to convince investors that his projects would yield a return. The idea was to show that he was successful and that investments in him would be successful too because consumers would buy or rent his developments or spend money in his casinos to try to be like him. After his financial collapse, Trump was unable to stimulate investors' confidence by showing them his real financial successes as a developer because so many of his developments had failed. His new strategy was to sell, or rather rent, his image of *himself* rather than of his buildings, suggesting to investors that his celebrity is what consumers (for example, hotel and casino customers) respond to, even though the idea that he was truly wealthy was false. Both investors and consumers bought what Trump was selling. Banks and wealth funds took over his properties but left Trump's name on them (for example, the Trump Taj Mahal). They let him keep his plane and his helicopter. Trump made money from his name, branding products as diverse as games, books, drinks, dolls, and (most lucratively of all) golf courses and hotels. What does this all show? Trump's business has been and still is himself. He has consistently used the media to create, sustain, and inflate that self and to make money using it.[32] The key medium he has exploited to do this is television.

The Mirror

From his interviews in the 1970s and 1980s to his cameos and guest appearances in the decades that followed, Trump has always sought to cultivate and, as far as possible, stage-manage his television appearances. For Trump, they have all been about selling himself and about getting others to give him their business and/or their attention. Television has always been both a vehicle for his narcissism and a mirror in which his desirability, success, power, and influence can be reflected back to both him and others. When the structure and the process of narcissistic mirroring are considered in the context of Trump's television appearances, it becomes possible to see how they are both addressed to an audience and intended for the gratification of his ego.

Lacan's account of the assumption of identity, the "mirror phase," represents the best-known psychoanalytic theory using the figure of reflection in the mirror as a model for narcissism. The "mirror phase" is equivalent to the narcissistic phase and is at least as central to its author's theory as narcissism is to Freud's. The infant is captivated by their image in the mirror, plays with it, gains some control over it, and begins to recognize it as theirs. This self-ownership is their first experience of a sense of identity. Yet this identity is fragile and fraught with tension. Despite wanting to be and appear unified, that is "themselves," the child feels divided and fragmented. They are prone to "motor incapacity and nursling dependence," which is evident in "turbulent movements" that are symptoms of both their lack of coordination and their primal distress. In response, they "fix" their self-image in their mind's eye, seeking a "symmetry" in it. This turns it into a sort of "statue," one that is ostensibly secure but actually immobile and alienated.[33] Lacan's account places great emphasis on the role of *the image* as the mediator of narcissistic identity. Identity is both found in and facilitated by the mirror image. The most important point about this image is that it is *other*. Put both more accurately and more subjectively, it is other than me as well as being me. This is partly because it is *in* something other than me: the mirror.

There are a number of important consequences of this alterity of the self-image: *my* self-image. Because it is both an image and other than me, there is a sense in which it fails to coincide with me. One implication of this is that the image does not entirely belong to me, however much I would like it to. It can be seen by others, and they can identify with it or not. More crudely, they can accept or reject it, love it or hate it, as they wish. Another important implication of the alterity of my self-image is that it is *imaginary*. It is not objectively real but exists in the mirror and in my head. It is not something that anyone can touch, so much as something subjective and phantasmatic and hence imagined. It is not reality, even if it sometimes appears as if it is.

The Screen

The television screen, like the mirror image, is a kind of interface. The image that program makers like to see reflected back to them onscreen corresponds with what they want their program to be: entertaining, funny, intelligent, truthful, objective, provocative, and so on. Similarly, those who appear on television want to see themselves as they wished or imagined themselves to be while conceiving or recording their performance: attractive, charismatic, informed, insightful, witty, or iconoclastic. In both cases, an ideal image is wished for, one that can both form and confirm the program makers' or actors' self-image. The image is both looked for on and projected onto the screen, where it might be reflected back and owned as a sort of self-validation. Of course, the television image, at least as much as the self-image, is seen by others. The makers of television self-images would obviously like others to see those images as they do too.

Trump's projection of his own image on television has always been intended both to gratify his narcissistic need to see himself in a certain way and to seduce others into seeing him in the same way. This is quite obvious in his earliest television appearances. He first appeared on NBC's *Today Show* (1952–) in 1980. He had already developed a few large Manhattan sites into upmarket apartment buildings and had just broken ground on what was to become Trump Tower. Trump's demeanor on the show was smooth as he answered questions assertively but politely from the journalist Tom Brokaw, who noted that an apartment in Trump's new building might cost up to $11 million. Trump nodded gently. He seemed happy to acknowledge the sum and also to confirm that for someone like him or his buyers, the amount was no big deal, as such amounts were simply the ones in which the rich and famous traded. Trump manifestly avoided bragging or becoming defensive during the interview, and when asked if he wanted to be a billionaire, he indicated that this was not particularly his aim. Rather, he was happy to "keep busy and keep active."[34]

There is a kind of ease and apparent modesty about Trump's performance here that says something not only about how he wishes to be seen but also about how he wants others to see him. The aim of much of network television during the 1970s and 1980s was to retain its audience on a single channel through the course of an evening with a stream of connected and somewhat-conservative programming. Trump's understanding of this agenda meant that he sought to create an enviable television persona that exuded wealth yet remained unobjectionable. That persona was also on display in 1981, when he appeared on *Rona Barrett Looks at Today's Super Rich*. Trump was filmed in his apartment overlooking Central Park. Again, he was quietly spoken and unassuming but confident. When asked if he had political ambitions, Trump said he did not. He said he had political opinions but also indicated that they were controversial. Being a tough businessman, he surmised, might make him "unpopular," and the electorate might prefer someone inoffensive "with a big smile." He concluded that the necessity of an agreeable image was "because of television," revealing in this comment that he was purposely containing his own aggressive and disruptive tendencies in the celebrity businessman persona he was adopting as he spoke, which had to be cultivated for television purposes just as much as the image of a politician.[35]

Moderated though his persona was for television, Trump was unable and unwilling to present himself as anything other than rich and powerful. After all, wealth and power were not only aims and objects of his narcissism but also tools of it. He needed to display them for business reasons as well as to gratify his ego. This means that he has always indulged in vulgar displays of wealth and brash performances of power, especially in the 1980s, when such behavior was more than socially acceptable in the United States. Since that time, Trump's television appearances have repeatedly highlighted the views from his apartment (the top three floors of Trump Tower) as the most expensive in New York—they are worth over $100 million. Attention is drawn in them to the twenty-four-carat-gold plating, the marbling, the faux-classical paintings on the ceilings, and the furnishings modeled on a French eighteenth-century royal palace. The apartment is a hugely and inadvertently camp display of wealth similar to Trump's limousines, airplanes, and an unsailable yacht. All of these have appeared across documentaries and a variety of chat-show, lifestyle, and reality TV features about Trump through the decades.

Beyond the 1980s, however, Trump increasingly began to understand that in order to retain a level of popularity, his image would need to transcend brashness. The "greed is good" philosophy of *Wall Street* (Oliver Stone, 1987) shifted in the 1990s to the "kinder, gentler nation" politics of President George H. W. Bush, and Trump had to find a way to appeal to rather than alienate television's changed audience. He achieved this less by changing his persona than by standing outside it and creating an ironic distance between himself and his image, from which it could be gently and warmly mocked. Trump performed cameos in several comedy shows during the 1990s, offering himself as an object of fun as he paraded his wealth and power while attempting to remain relatable. On *The Fresh Prince of Bel-Air* (NBC, 1990–96), he turned up to buy the Banks family's house with a suitcase full of cash; on *Suddenly Susan* (NBC, 1996–2000), he beat the guys at poker; on *Sex and the City* (HBO, 1998–2004), Trump was the object of the attentions of Samantha Jones (played by Kim Cattrall), just as Elizabeth Hurley would flirt with him on *The Job* (ABC, 2001–2002). He gave out-of-towners assistance and baseball tickets on the *Drew Carey Show* (ABC, 1995–2004) and provided advice to the mayor on *Spin City* (ABC, 1996–2002). In each of these cases, Trump was both playing and sending up his persona as a rich, handsome, successful, available businessman, attempting to replace selfishness and crassness with self-deprecation. His persona, which amounted to both his self-image and the image of himself that he wanted the audience to see, was crafted with the intent of appearing confident, even arrogant, but not unselfconscious to the extent that he looked either foolish or ruthless. His self-consciousness was also intended to reassure his audience that he was not the kind of billionaire that would fall into the trap of hubris and failure, even though he already had done so. The performance was instead aimed at obscuring or detracting from his failure by giving the impression that there was a new Donald Trump who had bounced back or, indeed, had never failed at all. Trump's thirty-plus mock-egotistical, audience-pleasing appearances on

Late Show with David Letterman (CBS, 1993–2015) were there to back up his story, if need be.

In 2004, Trump embarked on his biggest, most successful television vehicle, *The Apprentice*, which he hosted for fourteen seasons. Huge ratings guaranteed Trump undisclosed increases in his fees as host, alongside the substantial remuneration he received as executive producer. It was a very successful business model for him. *The Apprentice* is a knockout reality game show in which aspiring young executives are pitted against each other to win the prize of a job in one of Trump's businesses. Trump was essentially the judge in the show, the authority who decided which competitor was "fired" each week because of their performance. His clear intention was to appear powerful, successful, and therefore admirable. Trump appeared like Caesar with his consuls, descending the escalator in Trump Tower with his executive lieutenants or overseeing his holdings from its summit or supervising massive building projects as he ordered his minions not to "screw it up." He sat at the head of the boardroom table, deciding who would survive each week and who would not. He dispensed wisdom, justice, and favors, executing the loser and granting the winners access to his world of enormous success and wealth. Weekly prizes, for example, included a glimpse of his Trump Tower apartment, a picnic in the grounds of his Connecticut mansion, and dinner at Mar-a-Lago in Florida. The aim of Trump's image in *The Apprentice* was not so much to make him likable but to show that he "came back" (as the show's prologue has it) to reclaim the wealth and power that was rightly his. Like many reality shows, *The Apprentice* represents a work of fiction, but it is one in which the contestants and audience colluded in a suspension of disbelief over the course of its run. As a culmination of developments in his television persona, Trump's *Apprentice* identity was not designed specifically to elect him. Nevertheless, it did anticipate his persona as president, whether consciously or otherwise. Perhaps the question posed by the election of Donald Trump is whether the presidency, like reality television, was partly imaginary all along.

Notes

1 "Entertainment and Media: What's Going On?," *Chief Executive Officer North America* (blog), January 12, 2019, https://www.ceo-na.com/business/innovation-business/entertainment-and-media-whats-going-on/.

2 "US Economy under Trump: The Greatest Ever?," *BBC News*, February 17, 2020, https://www.bbc.com/news/world-45827430.

3 Ben Collins and Brandy Zadrozny, "In Trump's 'LIBERATE' Tweets, Extremists See a Call to Arms," NBCNews.com, April 17, 2020, https://www.nbcnews.com/tech/security/trump-s-liberate-tweets-extremists-see-call-arms-n1186561.

4 Bret Easton Ellis, *White* (London: Macmillan, 2019), 247.

5 Dave Eggers, "'Could He Actually Win?': Dave Eggers at a Donald Trump Rally," *Guardian*, June 17, 2016, https://www.theguardian.com/books/2016/jun/17/could-he-actually-win-dave-eggers-donald-trump-rally-presidential-campaign.

6 Collins and Zadrozny, "In Trump's 'LIBERATE' Tweets."

7 James Poniewozik, *Audience of One: Donald Trump, Television, and the Fracturing of America* (New York: Norton, 2019), 3–14.

8 Michael Wolff, *Fire and Fury* (London: Hachette, 2018), 123.

9 Craig Malkin, "Pathological Narcissism and Politics: A Lethal Mix," in *The Dangerous Case of Donald Trump: 37 Psychiatrists and Mental Health Experts Assess a President*, ed. Bandy X. Lee (New York: St. Martin's, 2019), 51–68.

10 Robert Graves, *The Greek Myths: The Complete and Definitive Edition* (London: Penguin, 2017), 286–88.

11 Malkin, "Pathological Narcissism and Politics," 54–55.

12 William Cummings, "Trump Again Calls Himself a 'Stable Genius,' Adds 'Great Looking,'" *USA Today*, July 11, 2019, https://www.usatoday.com/story/news/politics/elections/2019/07/11/trump-again-calls-himself-stable-genius/1703154001/.

13 John Bolton, *The Room Where It Happened: A White House Memoir* (New York: Simon and Schuster, 2020).

14 Bob Woodward, *Fear: Trump in the White House* (New York: Simon and Schuster, 2019), 162–66.

15 Malkin, "Pathological Narcissism and Politics," 56.

16 Sigmund Freud, "On the Universal Tendency to Debasement in the Sphere of Love," in *On Sexuality*, trans. Translated by James Strachey (Harmondsworth, UK: Penguin, 1984), 249.

17 Michael Kranish and Marc Fisher, *Trump Revealed: The Definitive Biography of the 45th President* (New York: Simon and Schuster, 2017), 70–140.

18 Kranish and Fisher, 105.

19 Kranish and Fisher, 316.

20 Emily Nussbaum, "How JokesWon the 2016 Election," *New Yorker*, January 16, 2017, https://www.newyorker.com/magazine/2017/01/23/how-jokes-won-the-election.

21 Kranish and Fisher, *Trump Revealed*, 57.

22 Wolff, *Fire and Fury*, 34–46.

23 "Transcript: 'Fox News Sunday' Interview with President Trump," Fox News, July 19, 2020, https://www.foxnews.com/politics/transcript-fox-news-sunday-interview-with-president-trump.

24 David Leonhardt and Stuart A. Thompson, "President Trump's Lies, the Definitive List," *New York Times*, June 23, 2017, https://www.nytimes.com/interactive/2017/06/23/opinion/trumps-lies.html.

25 "Tracking All of President Trump's False or Misleading Claims," *Washington Post*, accessed January 20, 2021, https://www.washingtonpost.com/graphics/politics/trump-claims-database/.

26 Kranish and Fisher, *Trump Revealed*, 77–78, 97–99.

27 Kranish and Fisher, 123–39.

28 Kranish and Fisher, 59, 90, 11–12.

29 Wolff, *Fire and Fury*, 18–20.

30 Barry Levine and Monique El-Faizy, *All the President's Women: Donald Trump and the Making of a Predator* (London: Hachette, 2019).

31 Kranish and Fisher, *Trump Revealed*, 70–101.

32 Kranish and Fisher, 210–40.

33 Jacques Lacan, *Ecrits: The First Complete Edition in English* (New York: Norton, 2006), 75–81.

34 Poniewozik, *Audience of One*, 20–23.

35 Kranish and Fisher, *Trump Revealed*, 272–73.

Our Cartoon President

Donald J. Trump's White House
as an Animated Comedy

Rafał Kuś

Cartoon sitcoms have come a long way since the emergence of early shows such as *The Flintstones* (ABC, 1960–66) and *The Jetsons* (ABC, 1962–63). Exploring real-life dilemmas in ways that live-action shows were unable (or unwilling) to, they have grown into a staple genre of modern television thanks to the trailblazing *The Simpsons* (Fox, 1989–) and several 1990s series inspired by the onscreen success of Springfield's most famous citizens. These included both shock-value teen fare, such as *Beavis and Butt-Head* (MTV, 1993–97, 2011), and more sophisticated shows offering unconventional insight into contemporary social and cultural problems (*Futurama*, Fox, 1999–2003; Comedy Central, 2008–13) or eventually evolving into some of the sharpest commentaries on American life in audiovisual media (*South Park*, Comedy Central, 1997–).

Our Cartoon President (Showtime, 2018–) draws not only from this tradition. Its broadcasting history (first as a segment in a comedy program, then as an independent feature) is reminiscent of classic 1950s sitcoms such as *The Honeymooners* (CBS 1955–56), and its drawing style resembles web animations of the early 2000s, while its content represents another item in the long procession of television's presidential-themed satire, including, among many others, *Saturday Night Live* sketches (NBC, 1975–), *That's My Bush!* (Comedy Central, 2001), and the present-day "fake news" shows starring such comedians as Stephen Colbert, John Oliver, and Trevor Noah. Colbert, a veteran of US comedy journalism and the host of a popular late-night show, is actually one of the creators and executive producers of the sitcom.

Released to a largely mediocre critical response, *Our Cartoon President* has nevertheless been twice renewed since.

This chapter explores several aspects of the series, including the way it portrays the president himself, its comedy style, the range of topics presented in the sitcom, its perceived political sympathies and positions, its intended audience, its critical reception, and viewers' reactions. The Showtime broadcast is presented here against a comprehensive historical background of political situational comedy, from the earliest adaptations of radio entertainment shows to recent developments in the genre. Comparing *Our Cartoon President* to other productions, the chapter attempts to define the role the show is trying to play in today's pop-cultural (as well as ideological) landscape and to assess its impact on the TV audience. Crucial for this consideration is the dichotomy between "relevant" (based on contemporary social and political issues) and "escapist" (deliberately avoiding such topics) TV shows. The argument of this chapter is that *Our Cartoon President* combines both these traits in an idiosyncratic manner.

The Sitcom as a Political Television Format

There is no denying that the situational comedy can be ranked among the most popular audiovisual genres. From its not-so-humble beginnings back in the Golden Age of Radio, when millions of American families tuned in every night to listen to their favorite radio comedy shows, to its postmodern incarnations with clever, multilayered writing and fancy visuals attracting new and wide cohorts of viewers, it has always been the staple food of broadcasting in the United States. It might also be argued that the sitcom is actually the most conservative of all major television formats, with its individual specimens seldom diverting from the tried-and-true list of common features. These include a short running time of about twenty-five minutes, a permanent cast of lovable characters placed in a family or workplace environment, formulaic plots revolving around the little joys and worries of everyday life, and—frequently—the laugh track, either coming from a live audience or prerecorded and then artificially inserted into the show. On the other hand, however, the amazing ability of the genre to be redefined and adapted to new television eras has been proven many times, with numerous innovations such as the single-camera setup, the mockumentary format, and self-referential humor giving fresh blood to the format in recent years.

The political history of situational comedies, balancing in their scripts between realistic depictions of social issues and escapist fantasies, mirrors to a large extent the evolution of television trends from the very beginning of the medium. The pioneering TV shows of this genre, such as *The Goldbergs* (CBS, 1949–51, continuing on other networks) and *Amos 'n' Andy* (CBS, 1951–53), were adaptations of successful radio shows. Those early broadcasts usually concentrated on family life and, in vivid contrast to sitcoms of the late 1950s and 1960s, were not shy of including ethnic minorities among the characters. Yet their stereotypical portrayals of certain social groups could sometimes be accurately described as downright offensive (and became increasingly controversial).

CBS's *I Love Lucy* (1951–57) was an original sitcom that went on to define the genre for decades to come. Its recipe for success was the charisma of Lucille Ball and Desi Arnaz, high production values (unlike many New York City–based shows of that time, the series was made in Hollywood), and the fact that it was recorded on tape, allowing for the redistribution of previous episodes in syndication, which has been emulated countless times in subsequent decades. As the premiere of *I Love Lucy* roughly coincided with the introduction of the Code of Practices for Television Broadcasters (which stifled the medium's potential for tackling controversial issues), the sitcom became a standard bearer for a new wave of family-friendly comedy series, devoid of any social or political undertones and frequently venturing into imaginative scenarios, for example, *Gilligan's Island* (CBS, 1964–67) and *The Addams Family* (ABC, 1964–66). This was especially true for the many rural-based shows of the 1960s, such as *The Andy Griffith Show* (CBS, 1960–68) and *Green Acres* (CBS, 1965–71), presenting an idyllic vision of life in the American countryside. Even if the political scene was used as a setting for the comedy, as happened occasionally, for example in the short-lived *Mr. Smith Goes to Washington* (ABC, 1962–63), it represented more often a play on the universal motif of a clash between an honest man and a corrupt environment (i.e., the "fish out of water" trope), rather than acting as a meaningful examination of contemporary issues. The escapist character of television humor in the 1960s was perhaps best embodied by *Gomer Pyle, U.S.M.C.* (CBS, 1964–69), a popular military-themed sitcom that scrupulously avoided any mention of the ongoing Vietnam War.

Not until the early 1970s did social and political issues begin to permeate television programming. Groundbreaking situational comedies such as *All in the Family* (CBS, 1971–79) and *The Mary Tyler Moore Show* (CBS, 1970–77) offered viewers sharp, well-written satire based on the controversies of the day. Writing about the former series, Harry Castleman and Walter J. Podrazik suggest that "by carefully mixing the humor and politics, *All in the Family* avoided heavy-handed preaching and became an almost subliminal national self-examination."[1] Individual episodes of the show, famously featuring Carroll O'Connor as the ultraconservative, clueless, yet charming patriarch Archie Bunker, covered much of the social unrest of the period, including such issues as the sexual revolution, women's rights, ethnic minorities, and the Vietnam War.[2] Moore's show, on the other hand, presented the audience with a new role model, a thirty-something woman not afraid to chase her own romantic and career-oriented dreams, in striking contrast to television's other leading ladies, seen mainly as beautiful accessories to their onscreen partners (this included also Mary Tyler Moore's previous big success as the perfect housewife in *The Dick Van Dyke Show*, CBS, 1961–66).

The popularity of such "relevant" TV sitcoms began to wane in the middle of the decade, due to viewers' changing tastes and the general disappointment in politics and public life after Vietnam and the Watergate scandal, bringing about a new wave of family shows.[3] These included the nostalgic *Happy Days* (ABC, 1974–84), transferring the audience back to the 1950s in a sort of "return of innocence" fantasy for many of its fans, and numerous other high-concept shows that were deprived of any connection with real-life issues. It was only in the early 1980s, with the popular Reagan administration bringing back the feel-good factor to US politics, that such themes reappeared in situational comedies. A prime example of this development is NBC's *Family Ties* (1982–89), featuring Michael J. Fox as Alex P. Keaton, a teenage Republican sympathizer growing up in a liberal, idealistic baby-boomer household. While in this case, unlike that of *All in the Family*, the political bickering generally constituted only an added flavor in an otherwise warmhearted family series, this setting allowed for an intriguing reversal of the typical depiction of a generational conflict, with hip parents and square kids, perfectly catching the ideological dynamics of a large part of US society in Ronald Reagan's era.

The advent of the premium cable industry in the 1980s not only unleashed the creative potential of the medium (bringing about the so-called Second Golden Age of Television with a plethora of new quality shows) but also served as a game-changer for the whole broadcasting sector. Suddenly it became apparent that the TV market is much more capacious than it was thought to be in the past, as new cable channels and terrestrial broadcasters snatched a large part of the audience pie from the traditional Big Three networks. There was more of everything, and the increased competition resulted in numerous new paths explored by creators of situational comedies. One of them was the mockumentary format, pioneered in the medium of television by Robert Altman's dramatic series *Tanner '88* (HBO, 1988), and another that of the animated sitcom.

Although *The Flintstones* (ABC, 1960–66) was the first cartoon series to hold a prime-time slot, it is safe to argue that it was not a major hit among its intended adult audience, as the lackluster show "reached [its] most effective penetration of the market when the show ended its primetime run and moved to its natural home, the Saturday morning kiddie circuit."[4] The first true champion of the animated sitcom was *The Simpsons*, a successful series created by Matt Groening that was highly praised for the quality of its writing.[5] Offering witty, hard-hitting satire, *The Simpsons* has been able to lampoon virtually every facet of American life during its long run, becoming a precursor of and inspiration for many similar shows, including such modern hits as *Rick and Morty* (Adult Swim, 2013–) and *BoJack Horseman* (Netflix, 2014–).

Perhaps the most interesting of those animated series is Trey Parker and Matt Stone's *South Park* (Comedy Central, 1997–). Originally known for both juvenile humor and shock value (the sitcom's most famous character, Eric Cartman, could be described as an exaggerated version of the incorrigible Archie Bunker of *All in the Family* and was, in fact, based on him), the show quickly evolved into an intelligent social commentary, never avoiding controversial topics and not afraid to express the opinions of its creators. The growing political involvement of *South Park* resulted in in-depth media scrutiny of the series's ideological positions, which included the commentator Andrew Sullivan's assertion that the sitcom is conservative at heart and a lighthearted démenti from Parker and Stone themselves in one of its episodes, "The Tale of Scrotie McBoogerballs" (14.2). The quality that distinguished *South Park* from virtually all of its contemporaries was the fact that the deliberately primitive visual style of the show allowed for an extremely short production time (less than a week) for an individual episode.[6] Its creators were able to use this opportunity to deliver up-to-date commentary on politically charged events, including the cases of Elian Gonzalez (a child refugee sent back to Cuba; "Quintuplets 2000" 4.4) and Terri Schiavo (a comatose woman allowed to pass away in 2005; "Best Friends Forever" 9.4). Both episodes were broadcast merely days after the incident in question took place.

The office of the US president has been used as the setting for a situational comedy several times over the decades. Such shows included vehicles for the veteran stars Patty Duke (*Hail to the Chief*, ABC, 1985) and George C. Scott (*Mr. President*, Fox, 1987–88). The latter series was part of Fox's inaugural season comedy lineup (together with *Married . . . with Children* and *The Tracey Ullman Show*), which exemplified the will to innovate, characteristic of new broadcasters in that period, while the sitcom ultimately failed to stay on air for long. *That's My Bush!* (Comedy Central, 2001), featuring George W.'s look-alike Timothy Bottoms as the forty-third president and created by Trey Parker and Matt Stone, was an exercise in form rather than substance, mercilessly lampooning sitcom clichés but leaving political controversies aside: "Even the bits touching on issues that remain hotly debated don't come down on any particular side. In the abortion episode, the moral Bush learns is that the pro-life and pro-choice camps came by their views sincerely, and therefore each side needs to respect the other."[7] Another Comedy Central series, *Lil' Bush* (2007–8), may well be seen as *Our Cartoon President*'s predecessor, employing animated visuals to portray the forty-third president and his entourage. The show was, however, short-lived, critically panned, and arguably aired too late in Bush's presidency to attract any major interest from the audience.

Recent years have brought about a new wave of presidential-themed sitcoms, including *The First Family* (syndicated, 2012–15) and *1600 Penn* (NBC, 2012–13). Perhaps the most successful of these shows has been *Veep* (HBO, 2012–19), starring Julia Louis-Dreyfus as the eponymous vice president (and later president) of the United States. Adapted from the BBC series *The Thick of It* (2005–12), filmed in cinéma vérité style, and showered with industry awards during its seven-year run, the sitcom offered a sharp satirical view of the political proceedings in Washington. While the main characters of *Parks and Recreation* (NBC, 2009–15) did not reside on 1600 Pennsylvania Avenue and did not operate in the highest echelons of federal politics (at least not until the very last episode), this workplace series focused on a determined and lovable female public servant and politician.

The mockumentary format employed by its creators allowed them to lampoon the inner machinery of a local political institution in a fresh, modern manner.

For some shows, Donald J. Trump's unexpected victory in the 2016 presidential election meant an abrupt revision of already-devised plotlines; even *South Park*'s Trey Parker and Matt Stone were taken by surprise and struggled to meaningfully utilize the new US president in their scripts during the subsequent months. "You know, it was like what was actually happening was way funnier than anything we could come up with," suggested Parker. "So . . . we decided to just kind of back off."[8] Nonetheless, a surge of comedy content featuring Trump emerged in US television schedules during the presidential campaign and shortly afterward. This included countless late-night shows, as well as a few serialized broadcasts: the crude web program *You Got Trumped: The First 100 Days* (Blackpills/Vice TV, 2016–17), as well as Comedy Central's equally controversial sketch series *The President Show* (2017). Then, on February 11, 2018, *Our Cartoon President* premiered on Showtime.

Our Cartoon President as Animated Sitcom

Just like many successful sitcoms of earlier decades (including *The Honeymooners* and *The Simpsons*), *Our Cartoon President* began as a recurring segment of another show, the popular *The Late Show with Stephen Colbert* (CBS, 2015–). Its host, Stephen Colbert, best known as the star of the parody news show *The Colbert Report* (Comedy Central, 2004–15), often lampooned Trump in his comedy and is regarded as one of the harshest critics of the Republican in network media, despite inviting him to *The Late Show* early during the 2016 presidential campaign, holding a relatively friendly, relaxed conversation when Trump was "still seen as a long shot GOP candidate."[9] Trump himself does not publicly conceal his enmity toward Colbert, having lambasted the comedian on several occasions.

While satirical news programs, and late-night shows in some of their segments, rely on up-to-date reporting to "mock the formulas that real TV news programs have long used" and "present an informative and insightful look at current events," fictional genres such as situational comedy obviously do not need to offer a commentary on current events.[10] Their task, as suggested already by Aristotle in *Poetics*, is to capture the imagination of viewers, allowing them to experience the good and the bad of what is happening to the characters. The narratives of fanciful occurrences, thrills, and agonies told in works of fiction do have to be intense or (in some sense) exaggerated to attract the audience, but they do not require the quality of being based on specific events in order to deliver a message. In the case of political sitcoms, the very restrictions of the format prevent them from being up-to-date, with few exceptions, such as *South Park*; the production of a single, twenty-something-minute episode takes much longer than shooting a sketch or an animated short for a late-night show segment.

The creators of *Our Cartoon President* aimed for a middle approach, combining preprepared scripts with short audio inserts dubbed into the episodes in postproduction.[11] Yet it might be argued that even this task was far from easy due to the hectic pace at which the Republican administration generated controversy: "In this age of the warp-speed news cycle, an animated series will have a hard time staying on top of the latest Trump scandal."[12] Thus, even though the show has occasionally been able to align itself in the same time frame with a political occurrence (of the planned-in-advance sort, of course), such as the 2018 State of the Union address, which coincided with the premiere of the first season, *Our Cartoon President* feels much more like a traditional sitcom than a political satire program. "The show is just timely enough to be outdated. References to Stormy Daniels . . . seem ages old," argues *New York Times* critic James Poniewozik, with another critic pointing out that "with late-dubbed references . . . the show feels simply stale instead of fossilized."[13]

Instead of striving for detail and currentness, the series uses the simple, reductionist approach of distilling the thunderous, grandiose, and absurd traits of Trump's administration into the individual quirks and idiosyncrasies of its representatives. The focal point of the ensemble is, of course, Donald J. Trump himself. His portrayal is based on two major traditions of sitcom leading men: the naïve, infantile, yet ultimately sympathetic patriarch (in the mold of *Family Guy's* Peter Griffin; Fox, 1999–), and the incompetent, buffoonish boss (not unlike Michael Scott from *The Office*; NBC, 2005–13), rendering the series an amalgam of family and workplace formulas of television comedy. The rest of the cast is built on similar but predictably less developed notes, also drawing heavily from the menagerie of sitcom clichés. Trump's politically active sons, Donald Jr. and Eric, are *Our Cartoon President's* variation on Beavis and Butt-Head of the notorious

MTV show of the same name. Their depictions are also among the least flattering and most memorable in the whole show, with Jr. portrayed as a spoiled, impudent brat alongside an intellectually handicapped, childlike Eric. Daughter Ivanka's character is that of a self-obsessed businesswoman speaking in marketing lingo: "My values are American values and the duty, love of family, smart, good scarves, fragrance, children, inspiration, and genuine human emotions with Ivanka Trump, soft-shell outerwear with a belt for all" ("Disaster Response" 1.2). Wife Melania, on the other hand, gets surprisingly soft treatment from the show's creators, who portray her as a generally likable person (in stark contrast to the more vitriolic portrayals of the First Couple in several other comedy shows), oftentimes serving as a "straight man" for her husband's antics. Worth noticing is the fact that the other Trump children—Tiffany and Barron—are absent from the *Our Cartoon President* lineup, as the series focuses "only on family members who have influence in the administration."[14] Other characters include the dull and boring Pence couple, annoying Ted Cruz, and many other recurring or one-time dramatis personae. In the very beginning of the show's run, the *Our Cartoon President* writers followed the old sitcom principle of switching the show's focus from character to character between individual episodes in order to better acquaint the audience with the cast. During the second season, the show's roster was enlivened by more prominent roles given to Democratic politicians competing for their party's nomination in the 2020 presidential election.

The decision of a series's creators to use animated visuals has wide-reaching ramifications for the artistic direction of the whole broadcast. On the one hand, animation may emphasize the symbolic, theatrical character of a show's presentation, while lending it a distinctive style. On the other, it allows for easy ventures into the whimsical and unusual, as even the most spectacular sceneries and fanciful characters might be created with no additional budget for special effects. *Our Cartoon President*'s animation design, overseen by Tim Luecke, might be placed somewhere between the primitive visuals of *South Park* and the realistic drawing conventions of *King of the Hill* (Fox, 1997–2010).[15] With its intense, bright shades, clear lines, and picturesque watercolor backgrounds, the series is certainly on the cheerful side of the animated-sitcom spectrum, in contrast to the many deliberately grotesque or gloomy cartoons, such as *Beavis and Butt-Head* and *Aaahh!!! Real Monsters* (Nickelodeon, 1994–97). The realism of individual depictions may vary, from the more mundane designs of Jared Kushner, Melania Trump, and Justin Trudeau to the Master Yoda–inspired, long-eared Jeff Sessions, big-foreheaded Stephen Miller (bearing an uncanny resemblance to Roger in *American Dad*; Fox, 2005–14, TBS, 2014–), and the show-stealing, perpetually open-mouthed Eric Trump. Yet all the characters are perfectly recognizable. The series's "two-dimensional avatars," as Showtime's official website for *Our Cartoon President* calls them, may be seen as reminiscent of Flash-based internet animations due to their flat, clean-cut design and uniform textures.

Our Cartoon President largely follows the standard sitcom formula of self-contained episodes, as opposed to multiepisode story arcs. As noted earlier, plotlines of individual episodes are only loosely inspired by real-life events and issues. The range of problems covered by the show is wide and extends from the 2018 midterm elections, Robert Mueller's investigation, and the impeachment proceedings to the establishment of the US Space Force and climate change. An important recurring motif satirizes Donald J. Trump's affinity for the conservative *Fox and Friends* show (the forty-fifth president is known to have regularly watched the morning series).[16] Still, many of those issues are seen by the writers merely as opportunities to utilize one of sitcom's stock scenarios (not unlike Parker and Stone's *That's My Bush!*). A case in point would be the fifth episode of the first season, "State Dinner," in which an official visit of the Canadian prime minister Justin Trudeau leads Trump to try to best his guest in every possible way, only to see his attempts effortlessly fended off by the charming Trudeau. This is, of course, reminiscent of the myriad situation-comedy scripts in which an overambitious character gets entangled in a silly competition he cannot win. Such things happened on many occasions, for example, to *The Big Bang Theory*'s Sheldon Cooper in "The Wheaton Recurrence" or "The Good Guy Fluctuation" and to *South Park*'s Eric Cartman—until ultimately notoriously reversed—in "Scott Tenorman Must Die" and so on.

The Critical Reception of *Our Cartoon President*

It is perhaps safe to say that *Our Cartoon President* has not been a major television hit, either with the audience or with the critics. In the United States (obviously the show's main market), it attracted 198,000 viewers on average in its first season, with only the first two episodes—both aired in February

2018—surpassing the threshold of 400,000 viewers. Things got even worse during the second season, as the sitcom's ratings fell by 27 percent on average to 144,000 viewers for an individual episode in 2019 (see figure 2.1). These numbers relegate Stephen Colbert's show to the lower strata of television programming, with its niche status clearly seen in comparison not only with industry blockbusters, such as *The Big Bang Theory* (13,222,000 viewers on average watched during the final season of the sitcom), but also with more established animated comedy series such as *South Park*, which got 817,000 viewers per episode in 2019.[17]

The critical response to the sitcom has been mediocre as well. *Our Cartoon President* holds a 42 percent score on the Metacritic aggregate review website, with predominantly "mixed" opinions from professional critics. The show's ratings have been even lower (32 percent for the first season) on the Rotten Tomatoes website's "Tomatometer," measuring the professional critical response to TV shows and movies. Among the most commonly criticized aspects of the show include the very idea of creating a sitcom that is bound to reprocess jokes already made elsewhere, given the lightning speed of news cycles involving Donald J. Trump and the extreme levels of media interest in his presidency, as well as the show's tendency to avoid creative risks and the overall quality of writing. "You have to bring

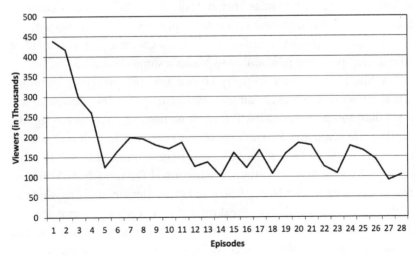

Rating numbers for the broadcasts of the first twenty-eight episodes of *Our Cartoon President*.

something especially smart and inventive to the table to excel in the over-crowded, increasingly stale world of Trump humor," argues Jen Chaney, "and *Our Cartoon President* isn't either one of those things."[18] On the other hand, critics generally liked the sitcom's gleeful visuals and the excellent, "eerily accurate" voice performances from the cast, including Jeff Bergman as the forty-fifth president.[19]

The Politics of *Our Cartoon President*

Questions about potential bias often arise in the case of shows such as *Our Cartoon President*, with commentators attempting to interpret and cate-gorize them along ideological lines. In fact, much of the media discourse around the Showtime sitcom is focused on the alleged political sympathies of the show. Surprisingly enough, taking into consideration the strong and distinctive opinions of producer Stephen Colbert, most of it suggests that the show does not go after the forty-fifth president hard enough, with its writing arguably too tepid for the cut-throat political polarization of the Trump era. "It's a sympathetic portrayal of a family whose actual behavior errs on the side of fascistic," asserts *Slant*'s Julia Selinger. "The series ulti-mately hinges on the premise that these people are innocuous doofuses and not insidious politicos."[20] Her sentiment is seconded by Melanie McFarland of *Salon*, who argues that since Trump "is dividing families and threatening their lives, health and homes via draconian policies he implements without fully comprehending the ramifications, merely coloring him in as an idiot who doesn't pay enough attention to Melania simply doesn't cut it."[21]

While it might be effectively argued that the preceding opinions reveal far more about their authors' expectations for *Our Cartoon Pres-ident* than about the series itself, there is no denying that there is signifi-cantly more sympathy for the Republican here than in Colbert's acerbic late-night show. In fact, some observers have contended that "the show attempts to be non- or bipartisan, poking fun at Senator Chuck Schumer, House Minority Leader Nancy Pelosi and other Democrats."[22] In what can be described as a fourth-wall-breaking moment, cartoon Trump actually discusses this issue at the very beginning of the premiere episode of the animated sitcom ("State of the Union"), saying, "Now, some are worried that this show might humanize me. Well, too late, folks. After my recent physical, Dr. Ronny assured me that I am a human being, and there's no cure for that. I'm also our cartoon president, and our show—but really mine—begins now." Stephen Colbert himself emphasized the difference between his two programs, arguing that, unlike *The Late Show*, which feeds on news related to Trump and his administration, the Showtime sitcom "does not exist to serve that. The show is the interpersonal relationships of the people you don't get to see."[23]

So, is *Our Cartoon President* an essentially apolitical, commercial television show that uses the image of a controversial celebrity (who also now happens to be a statesman) and an intriguing setting of the Washington circles of power in order to attract the audience? Maybe, as it is indeed difficult to find a clear target for the sitcom among American political aficionados: "The . . . real problem with 'Our Cartoon President' is that half the country doesn't need it and the other half doesn't want it," argues David Wiegand.[24] Still, many of the show's topical jokes would be incomprehensible for viewers without the knowledge of their context, so it is also hard to imagine the show's allure for someone with no interest in politics at all. While these problems might limit the universal appeal of the broadcast for the US audience (and at the same time explain the middling ratings of the Showtime series), one might wonder if perhaps the show's true (and par excellence political) intended purpose was not to serve as a sort of national psychotherapy, allowing those Americans who are concerned about recent developments in politics to peek at the world through *Our Cartoon President*'s intense, brightly colored prism. For the divided nation, this really could be the best medicine.

Conclusion

While *Our Cartoon President* will most certainly not make US television history the way shows such as *I Love Lucy*, *All in the Family*, and *The Simpsons* did, it arguably has its place in contemporary television schedules. For one, its relative longevity (as mentioned earlier, the program has already been renewed twice) and flexibility (the show's third season evolved enough to focus on the Democratic side of the presidential race, with the catchphrase "Who will be the next Our Cartoon President?" heavily featuring in its promotion) put it in contrast with other series inspired by real-life political events, of which the vast majority is merely novelty television, based on one-time joke portrayals of public figures. The other circumstance is that because the show lampoons both Republicans and Democrats, its appeal might actually be wider than TV's predictably partisan political comedies, with viewers of all ideological persuasions able to enjoy *Our Cartoon President*.

Perhaps the key to understanding the apparent paradox of Colbert's sitcom and controversies surrounding it is related to the escapism-versus-relevance dichotomy in US television, as discussed earlier.[25] While undoubtedly belonging to the relevance category, the Showtime program feels oftentimes more like an escapist show, using political issues as bricks to build a familiar, happier environment for viewers. And since there is absolutely no shortage of hard-hitting, up-to-date satire in today's television, this—for a change—might not be a bad idea after all.

Notes

1 Harry Castleman and Walter J. Podrazik, *Watching TV: Eight Decades of American Television* (Syracuse, NY: Syracuse University Press, 2016), 220.

2 Les Brown, "The American Networks," in *Television: An International History*, ed. Anthony Smith (New York: Oxford University Press, 1998), 155.

3 Robert J. Thompson and Steve Allen, "Television in the United States: The Late 1960s and Early '70s: The Relevance Movement," *Encyclopodia Britannica*, accessed April 10, 2021, https://www.britannica.com/art/television -in-the-United-States/The-late-1960s-and-early-70s-the-relevance -movement.

4 Castleman and Podrazik, *Watching TV*, 141.

5 Paul Austerlitz, *Sitcom: A History in 24 Episodes from "I Love Lucy" to "Community"* (Chicago: Chicago Review Press, 2014), 208.

6 Rafał Kuś, "Republikanie z kreskówki? Jak South Park komentuje rzeczywistość polityczną USA," in *Post-soap. Nowa generacja seriali telewizyjnych a polska widownia*, ed. Mirosław Filiciak and Barbara Giza (Warsaw: Scholar, 2011), 123–24.

7 Ryan Vlastelica, "Politics Was Not the Satirical Target of *That's My Bush!*," *AV Club*, June 15, 2017, https://tv.avclub.com/politics-was-not-the-satirical -target-of-that-s-my-bush-1798248469.

8 Laura Bradley, "Why *South Park* Might Never Be Able to Really Tackle Trump," *Vanity Fair*, December 7, 2017, https://www.vanityfair.com/ hollywood/2017/12/south-park-recap-season-21-finale-recap-trump.

9 Allyson Chiu, "Stephen Colbert Had Trump on His Show Once Before: The Host Says He Won't Do It Again," *Washington Post*, August 15, 2019, https://www.washingtonpost.com/nation/2019/08/15/stephen-colbert -donald-trump-anderson-cooper/.

10 Richard Campbell, Christopher R. Martin, and Bettina Fabos, *Media & Culture: Mass Communication in a Digital Age* (Boston: Bedford Books / St. Martin's, 2017), 474.

11 Kelly Lawler, "Review: Stephen Colbert's Trump Satire 'Our Cartoon President' Lacks Bite," *USA Today*, December 15, 2019, https://eu.usatoday .com/story/life/tv/2018/01/26/review-stephen-colberts-trump-satire-our -cartoon-president-lacks-bite/1066963001/.

12 Julia Selinger, "Review: *Our Cartoon President: Season One*," *Slant*, February 8, 2018, https://www.slantmagazine.com/tv/our-cartoon-president -season-one/.

13 James Poniewozik, "Review: 'Our Cartoon President' Misses a Huuuge Target," *New York Times*, February 9, 2008, https://www.nytimes.com/2018/ 02/09/arts/television/our-cartoon-president-review-trump-showtime .html; Daniel Fienberg, "'Our Cartoon President': TV Review," *Hollywood Reporter*, February 9, 2018, https://www.hollywoodreporter.com/review/ cartoon-president-review-1083328.

14 Daniel Holloway, "Stephen Colbert on How 'Our Cartoon President' Differs from 'Late Show,'" *Variety*, January 6, 2018, https://variety.com/2018/ tv/news/colbert-late-show-cartoon-president-1202655661/.

15 Jen Chaney, "*Our Cartoon President* Should Probably Be Impeached," *Vulture*, February 8, 2018, https://www.vulture.com/2018/02/our-cartoon -president-showtime-review.html.

16 Matthew Gertz, "I've Studied the Trump-Fox Feedback Loop for Months. It's Crazier than You Think," *Politico*, January 5, 2018, https://www.politico .com/magazine/story/2018/01/05/trump-media-feedback-loop-216248.

17 TV Series Finale, "Cancelled and Renewed TV Shows," accessed March 15, 2021, https://tvseriesfinale.com.

18 Chaney, "*Our Cartoon President* Should Probably Be Impeached."

19 Sonia Saraiya, "TV Review: 'Our Cartoon President' from Executive Producer Stephen Colbert," *Variety*, February 9, 2018, https://variety.com/ 2018/tv/reviews/our-cartoon-president-stephen-colbert-showtime-tv -review-1202692370/.

20 Selinger, "Review."

21 Melanie McFarland, "'Our Cartoon President': That Joke Isn't Funny Any-more," *Salon*, February 10, 2018, https://www.salon.com/2018/02/10/our-cartoon-president-that-joke-isnt-funny-anymore/.

22 David Wiegand, "'Cartoon President' Timely and Too Much," *San Francisco Chronicle*, February 7, 2018, https://www.sfchronicle.com/tv/article/Cartoon-President-timely-and-too-much-12557068.php.

23 Holloway, "Stephen Colbert."

24 Wiegand, "'Cartoon President' Timely and Too Much."

25 Thompson and Allen, "Television in the United States."

THE MOB, THE REDS, AND THE TV PRESIDENT

THE CHANGING ROLE OF TELEVISED
HEARINGS IN A POST-DECENCY ERA

Kathryn Castle

There have been warnings since the early days of television that this new medium possessed the ability to create a demagogue and to challenge the rule of democracy. The argument against this happening in the United States has been raised by those who point to the checks and balances in the US government, which were designed to prevent just this possibility. They point to Joseph McCarthy and his eventual unmasking in the glare of the TV lights. But what happens when a president comes to office on a tide of right-wing populism, takes near total control of a political party, and has a major TV network working for him? Can Trump and television undermine the safeguards in the Constitution and co-opt not just the executive but also the legislative branch into a congressional reality TV show? The nonimpeachment victory speech of the president sounded remarkably like that of an Emmy winner thanking all those (mainly Republican members of Congress) who helped produce the award-winning production on Capitol Hill.

The highly polarized and escalating conflicts of the president's first term played out in the important nexus between the legislative and executive branches of government: contested appointments, claims of corrupted elections, clashes between the FBI and the executive, Ukraine and impeachment, and criticism of Trump's handling of the crises of COVID-19 and Black Lives Matter protests against police brutality. President Trump is said to have consumed up to eight hours a day of cable television, and these networks,

alongside mainstream providers, carry the important congressional proceedings. In the hearings since Trump's election in 2016, Republican legislators defended his actions and vied for his attention, while the president
seemed captivated by the aggressive and at times outrageous behavior of his
loyalists. These surrogates, many of whom eagerly pursued Hillary Clinton
in the Benghazi hearings, performed for the man in the Oval Office. In
return, the president's tweets reflected high presidential ratings for those
who fought his corner. The emperor and his gladiators, refracted through
the Trumpian prism of World Wrestling Entertainment (WWE), became an
indispensable element on the congressional channel of Trump TV.[1]

This is not the first time that congressional committees have offered
riveting viewing to the American public. There is a temptation to see President Trump as a one-off, novel, unique, boundary-shattering, and truth-
challenging individual. He may be most of these, but he is not without
precedent. There are earlier political actors who help us understand the
dynamics of the present and provide perspective on the nature of Trump's
TV government. To many people, what Trump represents is the resurfac-
ing of a dark thread in US political and media history.[2] There are two congressional committees from nearly seventy years ago that work to connect
Trump to a history of media in government. Watching the earliest televised
congressional hearings of the 1950s (Kefauver and Army-McCarthy) alongside those of the Trump era, the resonance, even on the superficial level of
sound and fury, invites comparison. The very small screen in the infancy
of television produced extraordinary images of mobsters and the ultimate
Red Scare demagogue. Even now, the public memory understands when
politicians reach for iconic references to McCarthyism and mob hearings,
like Representative Kevin McCarthy accusing Adam Schiff and Jerry Nadler
of being the modern versions of McCarthyism, or Adam Schiff accusing
Trump of being a Mafia shakedown guy in his *Godfather* moment before
the House Intelligence Committee. This is despite the revolutionary changes
in the scale, mode, and channels of viewing in the contemporary United
States.[3]

The Eyes and Ears of the People

Congressional committee hearings were conceived from the earliest republic as essential to the legislative branch's constitutional oversight of the

executive. In their role of investigating, interrogating, and approving the activities and appointments of the president, they were understood to be acting as the eyes and ears of the people. Bipartisanship was viewed as central to the credibility of the proceedings, then and now. Prior to the twentieth century, these congressional powers were often rolled out in troubled times, as in the Civil War's Joint Committee on the War and Reconstruction. This early committee was set up specifically to curb presidential power, in both the case of Abraham Lincoln as wartime leader and the later impeachment case against Andrew Johnson in 1868.

In the midst of hearings on the Trump administration, there were references to the Teapot Dome Scandal of 1922. This was the biggest scandal to hit the executive before Watergate, and it was a Senate committee that found corruption in the executive. This affair jeopardized the presidency of Warren Harding and led to the first imprisonment of a cabinet member for bribery by oil interests and contempt of the Senate. One interesting result of these hearings, the Revenue Act of 1924, established the precedent that the secretary of the Treasury furnish tax records to a relevant committee. Teapot Dome shocked the public and enhanced the Congress's investigative powers.[4]

The creation of the House Un-American Activities Committee (HUAC) in 1938 with an anticommunist and antifascist remit showed the potential for politically motivated investigations. The first chair, Martin Dies (R-Texas, 1938–45), was clearly hostile to Franklin Roosevelt's New Deal and included the Roosevelts in his investigation of left-wing activities. The committee would come into its own in the Cold War partisanship of 1947. Newsreels show the intimidation and bullying of accused communists and fellow travelers in the federal government, schools, and Hollywood. Both HUAC and the McCarthy hearings have echoes in the Trump playbook. Trump's promise to drain the swamp can be seen as a contemporary version of attacking the enemy within. The country was, like now, divided and in turmoil.[5]

In the mid-twentieth century, concerns surfaced over committee members playing to the audience and injecting populist politics into the proceedings. Before TV coverage, print journalism, radio reports, and newsreels brought political highlights to a receptive audience. Political careers could be built on this exposure: Richard Nixon's strident anticommunism in HUAC made him a household name, and Harry Truman assumed a reputation for honesty and public service from his chairmanship of a War Spending Review in 1941. The political combat and personal ambition found in this arena are not the invention of Trump TV.

Television came of age in America in the 1950s. The first congressional hearings to take advantage of the new medium were those chaired by Senator Estes Kefauver, Democrat of Tennessee, in 1950–51. Thirty million viewers tuned in to watch on nearly ten million television sets.[6] This Senate investigation into organized crime across the United States offered the nation a range of witnesses straight from Hollywood's central casting. It quickly became a TV spectacle, broadcasting from local stations on a road tour around the country and ending with a live telecast from New York City in the spring of 1951. According to *Life* magazine, "The week of March 12, 1951 will occupy a special place in history. . . . People had suddenly gone indoors into living rooms, taverns, and clubrooms, auditoriums and back-offices. There, in eerie half-light, looking at millions of small frosty screens, people sat as if charmed. Never before had the attention of the nation been riveted so completely on a single matter."[7] *Time* magazine wrote, "From Manhattan as far west as the coaxial cable ran, the U.S. adjusted itself to Kefauver's schedule. Dishes stood in sinks, babies went unfed, business sagged and department stores emptied while the hearings were on."[8]

The daytime live coverage (and evening highlights) provided a riveting diet of nonincriminating mobsters and their molls. The audience was transfixed by Frank Costello, by both his willingness to talk and the stipulation that only his hands could be televised. Virginia Hill Hauser, "Queen of the Mob" (played by Annette Bening to Warren Beatty's Bugsy Siegel in Barry Levinson's 1991 film *Bugsy*), was a great success with the viewing public. After testifying to her ignorance of drugs and illegal activity, delivered in her silver-gray mink, she exited the room hitting and kicking the reporters who got in her way. It was a classic parting shot: "I hope the f*****g atom bomb falls on every one of you." The ratings for the hearings in New York were phenomenal, estimated at nearly twenty times the normal viewing figures. Even recent stunts played out by Republican Trumpists pale against this drama.[9]

Senator Kefauver was regarded as media savvy, and it is clear that he recognized the opportunities for positive exposure as chair of the proceedings. Kefauver never quite made it to the presidency, however, although he

was the vice presidential nominee on Adlai Stevenson's losing challenge to
Eisenhower in 1956. His reputation, though, was firmly tied to his chairmanship of the first live TV hearings. "Estes Kefauver came off as a sort
of Southern Jimmy Stewart, the lone citizen-politician who gets tired of
the abuse of government and goes off on his own to do something about
it," writes David Halberstam in *The Fifties*.[10] An Emmy in 1952 for the live
coverage of the crime hearings brought acclaim to the senator and the TV
stations for "bringing the workings of our government into the homes of the
American people."[11] Kefauver went on to hold hearings on comic books and
the threat of juvenile delinquency.

While the Kefauver hearings were instrumental in creating an audience for live congressional drama, it was the Army-McCarthy hearings
three years later that "changed the political landscape into a TV event."[12]
McCarthy's focus was on a very different enemy within than criminals
and their corrupted political allies. Unlike the Kefauver hearings, where
the forces of good and evil seemed relatively clear, the Army-McCarthy
hearings attacked traditional elites and revered institutions for being soft
on communism. Viewers were not surprised to see Frank Costello on the
stand but were much more uncomfortable witnessing the browbeating of
State Department and Army officers. Tactics that have become normalized
in our time were employed in this select committee, as they had been in
McCarthy's own Senate committee hearings. It was in this setting that the
term "executive privilege" as a defense against fact finding was first used.[13]
The repeated interruptions by Joseph McCarthy and Roy Cohn with shouts
of "point of order" have become commonplace Republican strategies in
disrupting the proceedings of the current House Judiciary and Intelligence
Committees. Repeated "big lies" and doctored exhibits were McCarthy and
Cohn's stock-in-trade, tactics that have been revived and replayed in our
time. Then, as now, the Republican Party was accused of condoning these
actions.

Bullying and intimidation of witnesses, characteristic of the Red Scare,
were eventually seen as distasteful by the public and demeaning of the process. By 1954, with the senator's accusations against the churches and the
Army, public opinion was beginning to turn. Television exposure and an
audience of forty-five million who were still capable of outrage and righteous anger began to turn the tide. When McCarthy was "outed" on TV by
Edward R. Murrow on *See It Now* (CBS, 1951–58) and then pinned onscreen

by Joseph Welch's interrogation of decency, television was giving the American people a long close-up of the face of McCarthyism. Joseph Welch noted afterward to Eisenhower, "If the hearings had accomplished nothing else," they had kept McCarthy on television sets so the public could "see how disgracefully he acted."[14] Afterward, reflecting on the impact of public exposure, all parties were worried about their reputations and revenue in the continuing Cold War climate. Congressional hearings only returned to prime time in the Watergate hearings of 1974, when the public interest was such that television was deemed crucial to the deliberations. The power of television in politics had been proved, but how to control it had not. McCarthy's experience remained as a cautionary tale.

Where's My Roy Cohn?

In the age of Trump, when a sense of history seems to have evaporated, one might wonder why a phenomenon of the 1950s has become such a touchstone. One reason is clear: "McCarthyism" is a term that many Americans understand or have at least encountered in a high school civics class. They may have seen movies that dramatize the era, like *Good Night, and Good Luck.* (George Clooney, 2005) or *The Front* (Martin Ritt, 1976).

McCarthy, a PBS American Experience series, aired in January 2020, while the documentary *Where's My Roy Cohn?* (Matt Tyrnauer, 2019) takes its name from Trump's lament. Americans know the meaning of a blacklist and a witch hunt when they hear it. Many have viewed the meltdown of Joseph McCarthy under questioning by Joseph Welch. They know why the McCarthy hearings are generally considered the low point of congressional broadcasting and a shameful episode in the history of the United States. Whenever McCarthyism has been evoked by former president Trump, his loyalists, Democrats, journalists, or commentators, it resonates with a significant section of the public.

With Trump, however, it is always personal, and that places Roy Cohn as the conduit between Joe McCarthy and Donald Trump. From being McCarthy's young sidekick and trusted counsel in the anticommunist hearings, he would emerge disgraced from the senator's downfall and censure in 1955, only to reinvent himself as a powerful New York attorney. It was Cohn who represented Fred Trump and mentored the young Donald in the 1970s and 1980s. When Trump was besieged by hostile political opponents and insufficiently loyal appointments of his own choosing, he was heard to ask, "Where is my Roy Cohn?" Commentators concluded that he was finally found in the figure of Attorney General William Barr.[15]

Roy Cohn's advice to the young Donald, "Always attack, always deny, never apologize," was honed in his partnership with McCarthy and publicly aired in the televised hearings.[16] McCarthy and Trump share a love of the red light of TV cameras. The legendary journalist James Reston reflected after the first day of the Army hearings, "When the red lights of the TV cameras go on, the Senator automatically produces sound."[17] In James Poniewozik's excellent book *Audience of One*, he devotes an entire chapter to Trump and the red light, arguing that the president is only really alive in the light of the cameras.[18] As for what you can get away with in a political style without boundaries, there is a striking comparison between the two figures and the loyalty of their bases. The pollster George Gallup's comment on McCarthy after his fall from grace in 1954 was telling: "Even if he killed five innocent children, they would probably still go along with him." This sounds remarkably like candidate Trump's now-infamous assertion, "I could stand in the middle of Fifth Avenue and shoot somebody and I wouldn't lose any voters."[19] These examples lend weight to the assertion that the former president is the McCarthy of our time.

The Apprentice: Congressional Version

Fast-forward to the Trump-era congressional committee room, and Republican legislators mainly followed Roy Cohn's advice. Trump reportedly told his staff to see every day as an episode in a reality show in which he defeats his enemies.[20] His friends in Congress certainly took that on board. Trump's constant monitoring of his presidency on news outlets extended into his compulsive watching of hearings when he was part of the business at hand. His acolytes—Matt Gaetz, Kevin McCarthy, Jim Jordan, Devin Nunes, Mark Meadows, and others, some veterans of the Benghazi hearings—spoke for him. These loyalists were the stand-in McCarthys of the hearings, bullying, berating, yelling endless points of order, interrupting, and constantly grandstanding. Jim Jordan, with jacket off, ready to wrestle, threatened to impeach Adam Schiff for treason. As in the McCarthy era, the elitists of the State Department were suspected of Deep State allegiances and undermined when testifying. The disdain for anyone associated with the Obama administration mirrors McCarthy's hatred of the New Deal and its East Coast elites. Disruption is the end game.[21]

Participants and observers have regularly described the proceedings as a site where the remit of serious governmental operations has been hijacked into an unseemly circus. The language used to describe the actions of congressional interrogators and the testimony of witnesses is full of performative references. Trump loyalists on the House committees are described as "taking the role of a cocksure reality TV contestant."[22] *InfoWars* staff attended and disrupted proceedings on camera; Republican loyalists stormed the secure meeting room. Trump loved it. There is an awareness that this was what the audience that matters wanted. Trump and his base care little about institutions or traditions favored by elites.

The Kavanaugh Hearing, Senate Judiciary Committee, September 27, 2018

The issues raised in Brett Kavanaugh's Supreme Court confirmation hearing could not have been more central to the Trump presidency. Adding another very conservative judge to the court was a crucial part of right-wing support for this president. Senate confirmation of Kavanaugh would tip the balance of power on the increasingly politicized court and increase the potential to roll back progressive legislation in the area of reproductive rights and abortion. The emergence of sexual assault charges against Kavanaugh, stalwart of the judicial Right and staunch Catholic family man, occasioned an extraordinary day in Washington.

The Senate Judiciary Committee confirmation hearing was held just five weeks before the midterm congressional elections. The Republicans were aware that aggressive questioning could backfire, so they brought in a female prosecutor to take evidence from Dr. Christine Blasey Ford. They knew that women's support for Trump was dropping and that public interest in the hearing was high, especially among women who identified with the #MeToo movement and were fearful about the fate of *Roe v. Wade* in a conservative Supreme Court. Over twenty million people would tune in to watch the hearing live. Trump had personal reasons to be interested in the case; he knew what it was like to be accused of sexual misconduct.

Following Ford's testimony, on Fox News, Judge Andrew Napolitano commented, "Dr. Ford is exceptionally credible," and Chris Wallace called her "a disaster for the Republicans."[23] The answer to undermining Ford's performance was the Trump TV playbook. When the nominee gave his statement, he appeared almost consumed with rage, his face red, his fists clenched. It was a counterpunch strategy mainly directed to the president but also intended to challenge the dignity and decency of Dr. Ford. Kavanaugh placed blame for these false accusations on familiar Republican targets: the Democrats could not get over losing the 2016 election; it was revenge by the Clintons, a circus, a grotesque character assassination fueled by a frenzy on the left.[24] Senator Lindsey Graham also erupted in anger at the subsequent questions, his role as victim in Trump world made clear: "I know I'm a single white male from South Carolina and I'm just supposed to shut up!" The patriarchy was striking back. The committee eventually allowed a short time for further FBI investigations before a final vote. The Justice Department ensured it was not very thorough.

In the meantime, Fox News began its attacks on Dr. Ford. On September 27, Laura Ingraham mocked the psychology professor as a "combination of Rosa Parks and Joan of Arc—the heroine of all time." On October 1, Joseph diGenova, noted conspiracy theorist and frequent Fox guest, called her "a very disturbed woman with clear emotional and psychological problems." Fox portrayed the nominee as the victim of a Democratic hit job: Ford had memory problems. At a rally in Mississippi on October 2, Trump ridiculed her testimony to the television cameras and a cheering crowd. Sarah Sanders, in a White House press briefing on October 3, explained that "the Democrats exploit all women who have come out to make any kind of allegation."[25] Kavanaugh was confirmed fifty votes to forty-eight.

The Russia Investigation, Robert Mueller Testimony, House Intelligence Committee, July 24, 2019

Ten months later came another key hearing. The Mueller report on Russian interference in the 2016 election took two years to complete and was a grave danger to the president. Although Trump claimed total exoneration, high expectations were attached to the testimony of Robert Mueller before the House Intelligence Committee. He was known as America's straightest arrow, a highly decorated Vietnam veteran, post-9/11 director of the FBI, and a man whose Republican credentials were well-known. (He was even played by Robert DeNiro on *Saturday Night Live*; NBC, 1975–.) Mueller did not want to appear in the public spotlight and came reluctantly in response to the Democrats' subpoena. He insisted that he would say little beyond the written record and looked very uncomfortable as he faced the cameras and the interrogation of Trump surrogates. Devin Nunes (R-CA) spoke disdainfully of the Democrats wanting to "create a TV moment." In reality, Nunes was rehashing highlights from Fox News–trending conspiracy theories.[26] The job of the loyal and combative Republicans on the committee was to undermine the legitimacy of Mueller's investigation and testimony by providing alternative facts and narratives. They reinforced the president's main talking point that this was a hoax investigation fueled by "dirty cops" who hated him.

That this was viewed as congressional reality TV was confirmed in the networks' reviews of the proceedings. Chuck Todd of MSNBC called it "an optics disaster" without "pizzazz." Brian Williams also observed a "no caffeine" moment. Fox's Tucker Carlson called Mueller "a daft old man blinking in the sunlight." Louis Gohmert (R-TX) claimed that Democrats had exploited the special counsel for sound bites on CNN. Trump's opinion was that Mueller "couldn't perform well, no material." Reportage as TV review was found by some critics to be further debasing the political process.[27]

Mueller was not just visibly aging but of an older TV time: Perry Mason meets WWE. The Trump army, if it had stopped barracking the witness and interjecting off-the-point comments, might have facilitated a factual exchange. But that was not the point. If Trump came alive in the red light, Mueller seemed to be close to expiring. The White House called it an "epic embarrassment" for the Democrats. When television exposed Mueller as incapacitated, it sidelined the critical testimony that Trump was not exonerated and confirmed the triumph of image over substance in congressional TV.[28]

The Impeachment Hearings, Marie Yovanovitch and Fiona Hill, House Intelligence Committee, Mid-November 2019

The Democrat-controlled House of Representatives held hearings in the wake of revelations about the president's potentially impeachable actions concerning the suspension of Ukraine military aid in exchange for a politically charged investigation of Joe Biden and his son Hunter. In these hearings, career diplomats and civil servants were called in open session to answer questions on what they knew. The Republicans were hoping that this testimony would be so boring that the audience would quickly tune out and change channels. What emerged over these five days, however, was a surprising number of compelling witnesses and presidential reactions that could not be contained. Both Lieutenant Colonel Alexander Vindman and Ambassador Gordon Sondland offered important insights into the motivation of President Trump in his interactions with Ukraine's President Volodymyr Zelensky. I would like to concentrate, however, on the women, particularly Ambassador Marie Yovanovitch and Dr. Fiona Hill, who were well placed to channel decency in their responses to the hostile questioning of the Trumpian/McCarthyite Republican members.[29]

Ambassador Yovanovitch was the most senior woman in the diplomatic corps, with a thirty-three-year unblemished record in some of the toughest postings for the United States abroad and with a reputation for fighting corruption and holding nonpartisan views. She came into the room, however, having been fired from her post and subjected to pressure and smears from the president and his allies, providing echoes of McCarthy's notorious hounding of State Department diplomatic experts on Russia and China.[30] The committee chair, Adam Schiff, knew he needed a good performance from the ambassador. Marie Yovanovitch was a composed and highly focused witness against the Republicans' patronizing and arguably sexist questioning. The Democrats were sympathetic and respectful. Representative Mike Quigley (D-IL) said her firing was "like the end of a bad reality show," done by someone who "knows a lot about that."[31] While Yovanovitch was describing how it felt to have Trump say she would "be going through some things," the president tweeted, "Everywhere Marie Yovanovitch went turned bad. She started off in Somalia, how did that go? Then fast forward to Ukraine where the new Ukrainian president spoke unfavourably about her in my second phone call with him. It is a U.S. president's absolute right to appoint ambassadors." Schiff was quick to claim witness intimidation, and even Fox reported a bad lapse of judgment on the president's part. This was the clearest confirmation to date of how Trump TV had produced a reality-TV hearing. Ambassador Yovanovitch, declared heroine of the drama, was given a standing ovation when she left the committee room.[32]

Fiona Hill was the witness who was saved for last in these crucial impeachment hearings. She was the top Russia expert on the National Security Council and had worked closely with Trump's former national security adviser John Bolton. She had also written an acclaimed biography of Vladimir Putin. Like Vindman and Yovanovitch, Hill had chosen to become a US citizen and still retained her northern English accent. The press acclaimed her "steely directness, self-confidence and moral earnestness," which had made a distinct impression on the committee and the viewing audience.[33] Even Fox News had to admit that she was clearly an expert, albeit one misled by the Democrats. It selectively used her testimony to bolster its own reporting.[34] The mainstream media celebrated Dr. Hill as a feminist hero for testifying to the difficulty that men have with women's anger and for the grit she showed even as a young girl. She was outspoken in defense of Yovanovitch and the disgraceful way she had been treated. The committee also heard of the intimidation, smears, and death threats that both women received for testifying. Both Hill and Yovanovitch had been accused by the Right of being moles for George Soros, a favorite thinly veiled anti-Semitic trope. For many women watching, she was the antidote to Trump, standing with Dr. Blasey Ford, former acting attorney general Sally Yates, Marie Yovanovitch, and others to resist the president's "You're fired" in "The Apprentice: White House Edition."[35]

Saturday Night Live satirized the hearings as a daytime soap opera, with Jim Jordan shouting, "My job is yelling at a woman."[36] Hill's appearance brought a range of TV references. She was the woman detective of police procedurals: Helen Mirren's *Prime Suspect* (Granada, 1991–2006), *Vera* (ITV, 2011–), or other Brit Box offerings like *Line of Duty* (BBC, 2012–). Twitter came alive with praise for strong British women, a disapproving nanny crossed with Thatcherite steeliness. Hill had put "pizzazz" back into the proceedings. The *New York Times*' Zerlina Maxwell tweeted while watching Hill, "Is there a Fiona Hill fan club? Where do I sign up?" Hill acquired a fan base in a single day. She was the star, not Trump.[37]

Conclusion

By putting the current congressional version of political TV into a historical context, some conclusions about the phenomenon of Trump TV can be drawn. Comparisons to the demeanor and behavior of earlier demagogues on television and past televised hearings can point in different and contradictory directions. While in many ways Trump via Roy Cohn is McCarthy, he cannot visibly own this discredited figure, preferring instead to attach witch hunts to the opposition. Once television entered Congress in the 1950s, the debate began over its impact. It was hoped that opening up government operations would provide a public service, but the nature of the medium left it open to the distortion of dramatization and political opportunism, even in the unfiltered programming of C-SPAN. Neil Postman's prophecies of television's distractions undermining serious public discourse may be materializing.[38] Trump TV's infiltration of congressional proceedings is a catalogue of distractions countering responsible dialogue. There have been occasions when witnesses have risen above the spin, notably the women who have been extraordinary examples of decency in some dark times. The performances of Christine Blasey Ford, Marie Yovanovitch, and Fiona Hill display the forceful integrity that many expected of Robert Mueller. The red light did not intimidate or confuse them.

Cable television, in particular Fox News, with its niche audiences and symbiotic relationship with the former president, now reflects and directs the Republican stars in the committee room. The more Trumpian the performance of congressmen (rarely women), the better chance of positive exposure on Fox News and reelection. The Fox audience would rather watch fan favorite Jim Jordan insulting Adam Schiff than revelations on the impeachment case.[39] In *Audience of One*, James Poniewozik argues that changes in the delivery and content of television in the United States since the 1980s, in particular the evolution of Fox News, have created the audience (voters) and the reality star (candidate Trump) to which we can now add congressional TV. In fairness, all cable and mainstream TV networks have contributed to the prioritizing of performance over substance in political broadcasting.

One can expect too much, however, of television and its powers for good or for ill. Just as it was not the only element in McCarthy's downfall, and it certainly did not end organized crime, revelations without entertainment value in today's hearing rooms have difficulty in generating sustained outrage or even interest in a large section of the public. The United States has had a history of populist demagogues, and TV exposure is as likely to support them as to unmask their antidemocratic tendencies. Much of it is about reading the changing audience. Kefauver exploited the public's fascination with crime and the history of gangsters onscreen; McCarthy was able to intimidate the public by threatening witnesses until he pushed it too far; and Joseph Welch found his moment to summon a public sense of decency. In the Trump TV era, he has been the director of the drama, encouraging the Roy Cohn school of acting, while accusing his enemies of McCarthyism. When the action in the hearing room became too dull or threatening to his interests, he either interfered directly with a tweet or let his Republican surrogates know that they needed to act up and distract the viewers. The fear of perjury made it too dangerous for him to appear in person. The impeachment trial in the Senate, which pitted Democratic House members against Trump's lawyers (a number selected from TV), was the clearest evidence yet that the Republican base and its senators have decided to "see no evil."[40]

It is not likely that any Republican members of the current Congress will win an Emmy for public service. Trump programming only speaks to that portion of the country that constitutes his voting base. With such a polarized public, there is no longer an agreed set of eyes and ears to serve. This makes the search for a transformative televised decency moment in our time almost impossible. Public outrage has been fractured by politics and the media. The president needed another Roy Cohn, and Adam Schiff is not the Godfather or Joseph Welch. The women in this piece, both decent and clearly competent, had their influence in the moment countered by Fox News and the Trump camp. The president knew then and now that the audience is his voter and his jury. It is too late to turn off the television, and it may be too late to turn actors back into responsible public servants. Despite Trump's departure, his playbook continues to provide a script for the Republican opposition in Congress. Only time and ratings will tell how influential Trump TV has been in the reshaping of government institutions and the public performance of congressional actors.

Notes

1   Joel Rubin, "Devin Nunes and the Benghazi Boys Are Back—but Now They See No Evil," *Daily Beast*, November 15, 2019, https://www.thedailybeast.com/devin-nunes-and-the-benghazi-boys-are-backbut-now-they-see-no-evil-with-trump-ukraine-and-impeachment.

2   George Packer, "The Mafia Style in American Politics," *Atlantic*, October 3, 2019, https://www.theatlantic.com/ideas/archive/2019/10/roy-cohn-mafia-politics/599320/.

3   Ellen Schrecker, "Trumpism Is the New McCarthyism," *Nation*, May 21, 2018, https://www.thenation.com/article/archive/trumpism-is-the-new-mccarthyism/.

4 Douglas Kriner and Eric Schickler, *Investigating the President: Congressional Checks on Presidential Power* (Princeton, NJ: Princeton University Press, 2016), 14–17.

5 Richard Gid Powers, *Not without Honor: The History of American Anticommunism* (New Haven, CT: Yale University Press, 1995), 124–29.

6 Robert Shogan, *No Sense of Decency: The Army-McCarthy Hearings: A Demagogue Falls and Television Takes Charge of American Politics* (Chicago: Ivan Dee, 2009), 56.

7 Ira Shapiro, *Broken: Can the Senate Save Itself and the Country* (Lanham, MD: Rowman and Littlefield, 208), 18.

8 Shapiro, 18.

9 Thomas Doherty, "Frank Costello's Hands: Film, Television, and the Kefauver Crime Hearings," *Film History* 10, no. 3 (1998): 366–67.

10 Quoted in Eric Burns, *Invasion of the Mind Snatchers: Television's Conquest of America in the 1950s* (Philadelphia: Temple University Press, 2010), 136.

11 Michael Rosenwald, "Real Life Drama," *Washington Post*, April 10, 2018, https://www.washingtonpost.com/news/retropolis/wp/2018/04/10/real-life-drama-when-a-senator-won-an-emmy-for-grilling-witnesses-at-a-televised-hearing//.

12 Shogan, *No Sense of Decency*, 273.

13 David Nichols, *Ike and McCarthy: Dwight Eisenhower's Secret Campaign against Joseph McCarthy* (New York: Simon and Schuster, 2017), 113.

14 Nichols, 288.

15 Marie Brenner, "How Donald Trump and Roy Cohn's Ruthless Symbiosis Changed America," *Vanity Fair*, August 2017, https://www.vanityfair.com/news/2017/06/donald-trump-roy-cohn-relationship.

16 James Poniewozik, *Audience of One* (New York: Norton, 2019), 11.

17 Nichols, *Ike and McCarthy*, 234.

18 Poniewozik, *Audience of One*, 195–235.

19 Shogan, *No Sense of Decency*, 255; Philip Bump, "If Trump Shot Someone Dead on Fifth Avenue Many Supporters Would Call His Murder Trial Biased," *Washington Post*, March 14, 2019, https://www.washingtonpost.com/politics/2019/03/14/if-trump-shot-someone-dead-fifth-avenue-many-supporters-would-call-his-murder-trial-biased/.

20 Poniewozik, *Audience of One*, 249.

21 Elise Viebeck, Mike DeBonis, and Rachel Bade, "Bunch of Brawlers," *Washington Post*, April 23, 2019, https://www.washingtonpost.com/politics/bunch-of-brawlers-judiciary-panels-most-aggressive-members-ready-to-rumble-in-impeachment-probe/2019/12/03/a3750326-15da-11ea-9110-3b34ce1d92b1_story.html.

22 Matt Fuller, "Trump's Strongest Allies in Congress Don't Care How History Will Remember Them," *Huffington Post*, December 13, 2019, https://www.huffpost.com/entry/trump-allies-congress-history_n_5defdc34e4b0a59848d161dd.

23 Grace Panetta, "Trump Said He Found Kavanaugh Accuser Christine Blasey Ford's Testimony Compelling," *Business Insider*, September 28, 2018, https://www.aol.com/article/news/2018/09/28/trump-said-he-found-kavanaugh-accuser-christine-blasey-fords-testimony-compelling-and-called-her-a-very-credible-witness/23545198/; Nick Givas, "Napolitano 'Surprised' by Remarks from Kavanaugh Accuser's Lawyer, Says Matter Could Warrant Investigation," Fox News, September 5, 2018, https://www.foxnews.com/media/kavanaugh-ford-accuser-abortion-napolitano.

24 Benjamin Wallace-Wells, "Brett Kavanaugh's Angry, Partisan, Trump-Like Opening Statement," *New Yorker*, September 27, 2018, https://www.newyorker.com/news/current/brett-kavanaughs-angry-partisan-trump-like-opening-statement.

25 Alex Leary, "Trump Mocks Christine Blasey Ford at Mississippi Rally," *Wall Street Journal*, October 2, 2018, https://www.wsj.com/articles/trump-mocks-kavanaugh-accuser-christine-blasey-ford-at-mississippi-rally-1538535385; Aaron Rupar, "Fox Goes All In on Smearing Dr. Christine Blasey Ford," *Think Progress*, September 28, 2018, https://archive.thinkprogress.org/fox-news-goes-all-in-on-smearing-dr-christine-blasey-ford-984d8347a67d/.

26 Aaron Rupar, "Devon Nunes' Behavior during the Mueller Investigation Was Bizarre—Unless You Watch Fox News," *Vox*, July 24, 2019, https://www.vox.com/2019/7/24/20726353/mueller-hearing-devin-nunes-collusion-democrats; Eric Levitz, "The Five Biggest Lies Republicans Told at Mueller's Hearing," *New York*, July 24, 2019, https://nymag.com/intelligencer/2019/07/robert-mueller-hearing-testimony-5-gop-lies-steele-gohmert-fact-check.html.

27 Maria Bustillos, "MSNBC Public Editor: The Chuck Todd Show," *Columbia Journalism Review*, July 24, 2019, https://www.cjr.org/public_editor/msnbc-chuck-todd-mueller-testimony.php; Adam Serwer, "The Press Has

Adopted Trump's Reality-Show Standards," *Atlantic*, July 26, 2019, https://www.theatlantic.com/ideas/archive/2019/07/press-tires-russiagate/594874/.

28 Todd S. Purdum, "Robert Mueller and the Tyranny of Optics," *Atlantic*, July 25, 2019, https://www.theatlantic.com/politics/archive/2019/07/mueller-testimony-congress-optics/594676/.

29 Lauren Gambino, "Absolute Fearlessness: Women Take Impeachment Spotlight and Speak Truth as Trump Fumes," *Guardian*, November 22, 2019, https://www.theguardian.com/us-news/2019/nov/22/impeachment-hearings-women-donald-trump.

30 William J. Burns, "The Demolition of US Diplomacy," *Foreign Affairs*, October 14, 2019, https://www.foreignaffairs.com/print/node/1125007; Miriam Elder, "Marie Yovanovitch Is Not a Victim," *BuzzFeed*, November 15, 2019, https://www.buzzfeednews.com/article/miriamelder/marie-yovanovitch-congress-impeachment-victimhood-women.

31 Emily Nussbaum, "The Search for Pizzazz at the Impeachment Reality Show," *New Yorker*, November 21, 2019, https://www.newyorker.com/culture/cultural-comment/the-search-for-pizzazz-at-the-impeachment-reality-show.

32 Molly Jong-Fast, "Why Trump Attacked Marie Yovanovitch," *Atlantic*, November 16, 2019, https://www.theatlantic.com/ideas/archive/2019/11/why-trump-attacked-marie-yovanovitch/602134/.

33 James Poniewozik, "The President Bursts through the Virtual Courtroom Doors," *New York Times*, November15, 2019, https://www.nytimes.com/2019/11/15/arts/television/trump-tweet-hearing.html; John Cassidy, "The Extraordinary Impeachment Testimony of Fiona Hill," *New Yorker*, November 22, 2019, https://www.newyorker.com/news/our-columnists/the-extraordinary-impeachment-testimony-of-fiona-hill.

34 Charles Creitz, "Latest Impeachment Hearing Was the Fiona Hill Show," Fox News, November 21, 2019, https://www.foxnews.com/media/chris-wallace-it-was-the-fiona-hill-show-today-as-ex-nsc-aide-gave-compelling-impeachment-inquiry-testimony.

35 Jennifer Rubin, "Fiona Hill and David Holmes Tell It like It Is," *Washington Post*, November 21, 2019, https://www.washingtonpost.com/opinions/2019/11/21/fiona-hill-david-holmes-tell-it-like-it-is/; Andrew Sullivan, "Fiona Hill: The Antidote to Trump," *New York*, November 1, 2019, https://nymag.com/intelligencer/2019/11/andrew-sullivan-fiona-hill-is-the-antidote-to-trump.html.

36 Amanda Wickes, "SNL Gives the Impeachment Hearings the Soap Opera Treatment," *Atlantic*, November 17, 2019, https://www.theatlantic.com/entertainment/archive/2019/11/snl-impeachment-hearings/602146/.

37 Jessica Hinckley Mendoza, "Impeachment's Rock Stars: Powerful Women," *Christian Science Monitor*, November 21, 2019, https://www.csmonitor.com/USA/Politics/2019/1121/Impeachment-s-rock-stars-Powerful-women.

38 Neil Postman, *Amusing Ourselves to Death* (New York: Methuen, 1987), 135–39; David Kaiser, "How Early Warnings about the Effect of Television on American Politics Came True," *Time*, May 23, 2018, https://time.com/5211267/warning-television-american-politics/.

39 Ezra Marcus, "How Republican Congressmen Feed the Fox News Alternate Reality Machine," *Mic*, October 23, 2019, https://www.mic.com/p/how-republican-congressmen-feed-the-fox-news-alternate-reality-machine-19260595.

40 Thomas Doherty, *Cold War, Cool Medium* (New York: Columbia University Press, 2003), 213.

PART II

Fact, Fiction, and Critique

THE POLITICAL IS PERSONAL

DISTURBING FORM, REVISITING LIBERALISM, AND RESISTING TRUMP'S AMERICA IN *THE GOOD FIGHT*

Karen McNally

In May 2019, *New York Times* columnist Michelle Goldberg described *The Good Fight* (CBS All Access, 2017–)[1] as "the only TV show that reflects what life under Trump feels like for many of us who abhor him." Reflecting on the show's cultural significance, she continued, "When historians look back at this ghastly moment—if there are still historians when it's over—this fizzy, mordant cult series is likely to be one of its richest artifacts."[2] Developed as a "derivative" of the seven-season, critically acclaimed CBS legal drama *The Good Wife* (2009–16), *The Good Fight* emerged as unquestionably a Trump-era show,[3] the filming of its pilot taking place in the midst of the 2016 election and the first season commencing shortly after the new president's inauguration. The legacy of its predecessor was that of a legal and politically liberal-leaning setting with female-centered story lines that drew on contemporary political and cultural issues, accompanied by a surprising quirkiness provided by idiosyncratic characters and random injections of humor. While *The Good Fight* was intended as a close streaming-service relative rather than a direct replication of the earlier show, the election of Donald Trump steered *The Good Fight* straight into a turbulent era of United States politics that launched the narrative imperative of its drama. The legal arena becomes not so much associated with politics as consumed by it.

The Good Fight explores the political context of the Trump era through narratives that address the disruptive nature of the Trump presidency as it tramples on the foundations of the law and threatens to undermine the tenets of US democracy. At the same time, the characters become enmeshed in the wayward temper of the times, drawn into both the misogyny and racism exposed by the attitudes embraced and promoted by the president and forced to renegotiate the political role and operating practices of a once-Black, now diverse law firm established in the legal battleground of police brutality against Black Americans. Moreover, the show's characters either embody the chaotic lawlessness of an unruly administration or find themselves repeatedly assailed by challenges to their understanding of a democratic nation. Just as *The Good Fight* conveys these tensions with disruptions to form that set unruliness against the documenting of facts, the personalized impact of politics represented in the show occurs, I argue, within a historically shifting climate of political movement away from nation and party to the individual and toward the personalization of politics. For the central protagonist, Diane Lockhart, played by Christine Baranski, her expression of the educated white liberal's experience of a media-driven celebrity presidency sees her personal and professional worlds infected by its dangerous absurdity and her own investment in a lawful liberal democracy tested. What *The Good Fight* essentially lays out for the audience is American life when politics and the law go rogue.

The Political Is Personal

The feminist activist Carol Hanisch first popularized the phrase "the personal is political" in an essay published in 1970 that confronted prevalent thinking about second-wave feminism and female resistance as the psychological illness of individual women. Hanisch argued that a woman's recognition of her experience of gender-specific societal inequalities—often relayed in what came to be known as "consciousness-raising" sessions—was political expression and might translate into group action. As she put it, "Women are messed over. Not messed up!"[4] Rather than evidence of a need for therapy for an illness that could be cured, Hanisch argued, "Personal problems are political problems. There are no personal solutions at this time. There is only collective action for a collective solution."[5]

The acknowledgment of structural inequalities and the call to political action sounded by Hanisch was echoed in the various protest movements of the 1960s and 1970s and simultaneously drew on the positioning of the Republican and Democratic Parties as emblems of an elite political class whose power required disruption. The slow processes toward change for women and minorities effected by traditional political forces combined with grass-roots political action to promote personal experience as the inspiration for group political action. More recently, political scientists have identified a shift in the contemporary political culture of the United States and other Western democracies that conversely situates political activity and its impact in personal terms. The decline of parties as brokers of power and the rise of the individual politician, alongside the increasing significance of mass media, have created a symbiotic relationship between politicians, television, and, more recently, social media, where political leaders can frame themselves as the individual able to furnish the voters' needs and desires and even group protest movements function around various notions of individualism. As Kenneth H. Tucker Jr. argues, "Entrepreneurial, expressive, aesthetic, and networked modes of individualism now provide a shared language for Americans, no matter their political preference."[6]

In the United States, political campaigns have increasingly emphasized the appeal of the candidate over policies, as potential leaders utilize personal narratives to make a connection with voters who are simultaneously individualized by the media as representative US citizens. During the 2008 McCain-Palin Republican campaign for the presidency, for example, Samuel Joseph Wurzelbacher was transformed into a temporary celebrity as "Joe the plumber" and presented as a symbol of the middle-class small businessman following an unproductive encounter with the Democratic candidate, Barack Obama. Wurzelbacher, in turn, went on to exploit personality politics with various media interviews during the campaign, a failed run for Congress as a Republican candidate in Ohio in 2012, and a stint as a conservative activist and Trump-supporting commentator during the 2016 election.[7]

The strategy of personalization at the heart of US politics was affirmed by Donald Trump's first election campaign. Trump was initially reluctant to fully align himself with the Republican Party as a candidate and threatened instead to run as an independent if he failed in the primaries, suggesting, "I'll have to see how I'm being treated by the Republicans."[8] Trump's confidence in his options emphasized his intent to run as the myth of Donald Trump—celebrity, businessman, self-publicizing subject of the gossip columns—rather than as the political representative of the conservative program of the party to which he would later attach himself. The subsequent response of Republican politicians to discard a traditional conservative platform and instead board the "Trump train"—a term used during the campaign by loyalists such the former *Apprentice* contestant Omarosa Manigault Newman as a rallying cry to supporters—has led continuously to the accusation that the party has been usurped by the cult of "Trumpism," or what the cult expert Steven Hassan has referred to as "The Cult of Trump."[9] Trump's use of Twitter as a means of bypassing the structured practices and checks of government—evinced in his audacious fourth-wall-breaking tweet noted by committee chair Adam Schiff during Marie Yovanovitch's impeachment hearing testimony in November 2019[10]—remained part of an attempt to forge a direct relationship between Trump and the voters, particularly those identifiable as his base, prior to Twitter's permanent suspension of his account in January 2021. Televised campaign rallies and the press conferences held during the COVID-19 global pandemic crisis have similarly provided spaces for Trump to perform with off-script remarks that identify policies—formed or unformed—directly with the now-former president. Franklin Delano Roosevelt's radio "fireside chats" set a historical precedent at once amplified and distorted by Trump's arguable motivation of self-interest, indelibly made manifest by the January 6, 2021, "Save America" rally that prompted the storming of the Capitol building.

Trump is far from the first celebrity president of the Republican Party, to which General Dwight D. Eisenhower and Ronald Reagan attest, and while the Democrats' encounters with celebrity politics have been arguably more palatable, with examples such as John F. Kennedy's Hollywood-friendly 1960 campaign, their contemporary political game is frequently being played through the exploitation of personal experience. During a July 2019 debate in the race for the Democratic Party nomination before the two candidates' respective ascents to vice president and president, Senator Kamala Harris confronted former vice president Joe Biden about his history of opposition to school busing in the 1970s by relating her own positive experience: "There was a little girl in California who was a part of the second class to integrate her public schools and she was bused to school every day. And that little girl was me."[11] In an interview the same month with Harris and her sister and campaign chair, Maya Harris, the candidate acknowledged the requirement in contemporary politics to address policies and her candidacy through a personal lens. She explained, "I was raised that you don't talk about yourself. . . . But I've also realized that in order to form the relationships, it's important to let people know about my people." Harris was convinced, the article suggests, by her failure in the early months of the campaign to connect with voters. As her sister explained the change in strategy: "I've been trying to get her to tell more stories."[12] Attempts at policy change have also frequently been driven by revealing to those in power the experiences of individuals affected by those policies. A number of female Democrat representatives, for example, testified to the House Oversight and Reform Committee in July 2019 about conditions at Texas border facilities by repeating individual experiences related to them by women during their visit. As Congresswoman Ayanna Pressley put it, "Every person has a voice, but our institutions do not always listen. So today I do not speak on behalf of anyone, but I make space for the stories our nation so desperately needs to hear in this moment."[13]

The Politics of *The Good Wife*

The Good Wife, also helmed by showrunners Michelle and Robert King, centered on the personal and professional life of Alicia Florrick, played by Julianna Margulies, whose contented existence as a stay-at-home mother in the Chicago suburbs is shattered when the press releases a sex tape of her state's attorney husband, Peter Florrick (Chris Noth), with prostitutes. The subsequent exposure of a corruption scandal leads to her husband's resignation at a press conference, which forms the opening scene of the show and immediately positions the drama in the arena of contemporary politics. Recalling familiar television news moments of humiliated wives standing by their disgraced political husbands, from the president of the United States Bill Clinton to the governor of New York Eliot Spitzer and New York congressman Anthony Weiner, *The Good Wife* instantly establishes a critical perspective on US politics. The pilot's visual emphasis on Alicia Florrick's experience and her anger, demonstrated in the post-press-conference slap she dishes out to her husband, spotlight its female character and her arc of empowerment as the subject of the show's narrative.

Alicia's return to work as a lawyer to support her two teenage children while her husband serves a prison sentence and a narrative following her professional career, personal relationships, and an unsuccessful run for the office of state's attorney prompted interpretations of the show as variously feminist and postfeminist, with an unusually flawed woman at its center. Describing Alicia Florrick in *Time* magazine as "one of television's few complicated heroines," Eliana Dockterman suggests that her distinctiveness lay in the sense that "the show made us both love and hate Alicia, while other television writers fretted over their heroines being 'likable.'"[14] At the same time, *The Good Wife*'s politicized use of fashion was both a network challenge to the male-centered dominance of cable as "quality" or "peak" TV aimed at drawing a similar demographic of educated, middle-class Americans as its audience and key to characterizing the show's professional women as self-assured Obama-era feminists.[15] First Lady Michelle Obama wearing one of Alicia Florrick's Michael Kors suits to the State of the Union address in 2015 seemed only to confirm the political element of the characters' representation.[16]

The Good Wife's narrative thread connecting its characters to broader politics is pervasive, from Peter's eventual run to become the Democrats' nominee for president to appearances by the political strategist Donna Brazile and then–MSNBC host Chris Matthews that locate the characters in a semifictional world of the party machine and media promotion. Elsewhere, the show's engagement with political issues of contemporary resonance occurs through the firm's legal cases that draw on topics including gay marriage, campus rape, immigration, gun control, new technology, and social media companies, as well as the continuous monitoring by the National Security Agency (NSA), which explores the privacy-versus-national-security dynamic throughout. Raffaella Coletti argues that *The Good Wife* works as a key example of contemporary US TV shows that combine narrative innovation with real-world authenticity and portrayals of politics that outline its complexities, while nevertheless focused on a dominant white America.[17] *The Good Fight*'s development of style and form takes this innovation and nuance further as it establishes a constantly uneasy setting for its diverse universe of characters as they negotiate the impact of their immersion in the troubling political culture of a Trump administration.

Narrative and Form in *The Good Fight*'s Trump World

The conclusion of *The Good Wife* in May 2016 set the scene for the repositioning of its derivative in what was to be a very different political sphere. Departing the security and comfort of a Democratic liberalism that was both traditional and progressive, the liberal characters who move into the narrative world of *The Good Fight* are confronted by the seismic political shift that occurred with the election of Donald Trump in November 2016.

The show's heredity is signaled by the transfer of Christine Baranski's Diane Lockhart as its lead alongside Lucca Quinn, played by Cush Jumbo, and a multitude of returning guest characters, as well as clear thematic links to the earlier drama that include articulating the modern woman's experience. As cocreator Michelle King indicated in a 2017 interview, "That was the DNA of the series, that we wanted to see women at different points of their lives having to rebuild and what that meant. So that was presidential politics aside."[18] The pilot episode therefore depicts the rupture to Diane's plan of blissful retirement in Provence, when she becomes the unwitting victim of a Bernie Madoff–style Ponzi scheme, and her struggle to regain a space in a legal world resistant to the whiff of scandal around an older woman. The election-night result, revealed as the pilot was being filmed, however, shifted *The Good Fight* into explicitly political territory, gestured by the drama's opening, as its lead watches in horror the new president's inauguration on television ("Inauguration" 1.1). Her professional landing as a partner at the African American law firm Reddick, Boseman & Kolstad (later to become Reddick, Boseman & Lockhart)—to the quip from managing partner Adrian Boseman (Delroy Lindo) that she represents their "diversity hire"—positions Diane's story firmly within a narrative that will enmesh itself in the cultural mood of a Trump presidency and address the political landscape that emerges.

Unsurprisingly, the characters' legal universe is persistently drawn into "the new normal": a case to ban threats and abuse on Chummy Friends (Facebook) and Scabbit (Reddit) is confronted by the Alt-Right Milo Yiannopolous–style character Felix Staples (John Cameron Mitchell; "Social Media and Its Discontents" 1.6); a television network is under threat of a lawsuit if it runs a #MeToo story on a sexual assault allegation against a movie star ("Day 436" 2.5); the firm pitches to the Democratic strategist Ruth Eastman (played by Margo Martindale) readying the party for a Trump impeachment ("Day 450" 2.7); a Stephen Miller stand-in responsible for the southern border immigration strategy of child separation becomes a target of a liberal resistance group ("The One Where the Sun Comes Out" 3.9); Lucca wins a promotion against a "Historical Law Society" (Federalist Society) lawyer by revealing that he prepped Brett Kavanaugh for his Senate Judiciary Committee confirmation hearing ("The One Inspired by Roy Cohn" 3.2); a Russian student claims to have the infamous "pee tape" capturing Trump with prostitutes in a Moscow hotel room ("Day 464" 2.9);

and Lucca ponders whether the unidentified celebrity on the telephone requesting divorce advice is Melania Trump ("The One With the Celebrity Divorce" 3.6).

In a 2018 article in the *New Yorker*, the TV critic Emily Nussbaum remarks of Michelle and Robert King as showrunners, "Their brand might be summarized as 'Looks like 'L.A. Law,' tastes like 'The Wire.'"[19] In the close-to-synchronous setting of *The Good Fight*'s narrative, the show creates a distinctive tone and mood through stylization and disruptions to form that speak to the uncommon temper of the times in which the characters' stories are framed. Characters therefore have monologues, like Lucca discussing with her sleeping baby whether to go for a promotion ("The One Inspired by Roy Cohn" 3.2) and Liz Reddick-Lawrence (Audra McDonald) explaining to Diane the history of Black disenfranchisement from the democratic process ("The One Where Diane and Liz Topple Democracy" 3.7); fantasy moments occur, such as Diane's imagined dystopia of the disruptive lawyer Roland Blum (Michael Sheen) singing "I'll Be There" before images of US nationhood ("The One Where Diane Joins the Resistance" 3.3); and nature symbolizes unstable forces as birds crash against windows when Maia Rindell (Rose Leslie) is interviewed by the FBI ("Self Condemned" 1.9) and the city of Chicago succumbs to "The Great Chicago Flood" as the FBI walls close in on Diane ("The One Where the Sun Comes Out" 3.9).

The show additionally plays with form in its depiction of the collision between fact and fiction promoted by a Kellyanne Conway–termed "alternative facts" world and a presidency conducted in the form of a television show, indicated by the characters' constant TV news watching and the title sequence's exploding televisions with images of Trump, Vladimir Putin, Attorney General Bill Barr, and Fox News host Sean Hannity. In the book *Audience of One: Donald Trump, Television, and the Fracturing of America*, the *New York Times* television critic James Poniewozik tracks Trump's ascendency to the United States' highest office alongside the development of American television and the nation's political and media culture. The president's television obsession has been so all-consuming, he suggests, that "Trump's own staff created TV events to placate, control, and persuade him. Things were more real to Trump if he saw them on TV. *People* were more real if he saw them on TV—even people he saw, in person, every day."[20] *The Good Fight* both displays and exploits for its tone the persistent sense of incongruity created by this consumption and presentation of a mediated reality as actuality. Michelle King's response to a "TimesTalks" audience question in 2019 about marrying reality and stylistic innovation in what is ostensibly a legal drama was, "We're not 5 percent off a traditional law show at this point. I'd say we're at least 30 percent off, so you know, tonally, I think, a lot more becomes easy to accept."[21] The show's genre-stretching style therefore both reflects and confronts the no-rules chaos of the Trump era in a number of fourth-wall-breaking moments that both blur the boundaries between fact and fiction and position the characters and audience in the same shadowy locale. In a direct address to the audience, the firm's African American investigator Jay Dipersia (Nyambi Nyambi) puts the case for why "it's time to punch a few Nazis" when he and Lucca are attacked by white nationalists while observing voting in a special election ("The One Where a Nazi Gets Punched" 3.5). When Jay finds himself in ICE custody due to the FBI's political targeting of the firm, and the team has his citizenship confirmed through the Einstein visa strategy used by Melania Trump, his whistling of *The Good Fight*'s theme on his release simultaneously crosses the diegetic and nondiegetic worlds and celebrates the successful exploitation of lawlessness against a lawless administration ("Day 485" 2.12).

Attempts to reassert the primacy of facts against a fictional media circus flow through the show's interruptions to narrative form, with, for example, written explanations of Alt-Right acronyms such as "SJW: social justice warrior: slang for progressives" and "Cucks: the Alt-right's term for co-opted conservatives" ("Social Media and Its Discontents" 1.6). More consistently, the show inserts musical animated video shorts similar to the *Schoolhouse Rock!* educational shorts for children that originally ran on ABC between 1973 and 1985. Addressing topics and people in the Trump universe explored and characterized in the narrative, the shorts take an appropriately timed break from the fictional world to clarify the kind of facts that are frequently denied in "alternative facts" politics. Animated moments summarize the facts on topics from impeachment ("Day 450" 2.7) to nondisclosure agreements (NDAs; "The One About the Recent Troubles" 3.1), fake news ("The One Where Diane Joins the Resistance" 3.3), Russian troll farms ("The One Where Kurt Saves Diane" 3.8), and the biography of Roy Cohn ("The One Inspired by Roy Cohn" 3.2). So generically innovative and politically confrontational are these insertions that the Kings have expressed doubt that a network (as opposed to CBS's streaming sister) would have sanctioned their inclusion.[22] Indeed, one short, titled "Banned in China," which addressed companies' self-censorship for the sake of China's global market, was banned even by CBS All Access and replaced by eight seconds of text stating, "CBS HAS CENSORED THIS CONTENT" ("The One Where Kurt Saves Diane" 3.8). The resolution was a salve to the showrunners, who had threatened to quit the show as a response to such ironic creative censorship by its streaming service.[23] The disruptive power of these animated shorts, which pierce the fictional world with facts and play Trump at his own media game, seems more than demonstrated by such nervous corporate action.

Personifying Chaos

The Good Fight's disturbance of form, which emphasizes the leaky borders between fact and fiction in the Trump era, works alongside a mood of chaos and performance to distinguish the aberrant nature of contemporary politics. In the 2018 book *Fear: Trump in the White House*, Bob Woodward says of the first years of the Trump administration, "Despite almost daily reports of chaos and discord in the White House, the public did not know how bad the internal situation actually was. Trump was always shifting, rarely fixed, erratic. He would get in a bad mood, something large or small would infuriate him."[24] A presidency reliant on constructed media imagery, the breaching of which led to Trump's multiple Twitter meltdowns, illuminates the short-termism prompted by self-interest alongside a disdain for normative conventions through which presidential politics was conducted within the Trump administration. *The Good Fight* establishes this mood of chaotic unpredictability with startling, violent narrative events: lawyers are repeatedly murdered in a violent purge described as a "plague"; an envelope arrives at the offices of Reddick, Boseman & Lockhart containing a powder they suspect is Ricin ("Day 422" 2.3), and Adrian Boseman is shot by a white policeman seeking to close down the case against himself for shooting a Black undercover colleague ("Day 471" 2.10).

In a continuance of its mirroring of form and theme, the show addresses the disorder created by repeated assaults on legislative norms, exemplified by the president's attempts to appoint judges rated "not qualified" by the American Bar Association, Attorney General Barr's multiple interventions in legal cases brought against Trump and his allies, and the various attempts to have courts and state officials overturn results in the 2020 election amid Trump's unsubstantiated allegations of fraud.[25] The narrative conveys the absurdity of this rule-breaking political culture as characters are faced with a variety of unqualified and exploitable Trump-appointed judges ("Day 457" 2.8; "The One About the End of the World" 3.10) and Adrian and Julius outclass a committee formed of the host of "Ted and Friends" (a clear play on *Fox and Friends*), a singing drama teacher, and a Trump-appointed judge ("Day 492" 2.13). The show's fourth season hinges on the existence of Memo 618, a fictional metaphor alluding to the ability of the powerful and wealthy to manipulate and abuse the justice system with the aid of government. Without equality in the law, Diane warns, "the country breaks down. . . . It's over, we're done." ("The Gang Is Satirized and Doesn't Like It" 4.4) Moreover, *The Good Fight* explores the thread between abuse of the law, media celebrity, Trump, and Washington through its stylized characterization of Roland Blum, whose extravagant persona and lawlessness embody the rules-busting illegality of the Trump era.

Constructed as a mythical, Dionysian figure of excess, Blum consumes food, alcohol, drugs, and sex with appetite and makes performance art of his profession, bellowing legal arguments in court and launching into a rendition of "Too-Ra-Loo-Ra-Loo-Ral." The characterization, however, is firmly rooted in the Trumpian world, as a figure drawn around Roy Cohn, the lawyer to Joseph McCarthy and mentor to Trump. Robert King explains, "Roy Cohn is the connecting line between the blacklist and McCarthyism and Trump—he is the umbilical cord. We were trying to suggest that umbilical cord is still alive today with this character, Roland Blum."[26] Simulating Roger Stone's tattoo of Richard Nixon, Blum sports an image of Roger Stone on his back, makes an unsubstantiated allegation of murder against a public prosecutor, suborns perjury by a witness, and uses the GOP tactics of the Brooks Brothers riot during the 2000 election to protest his innocence, all underwritten by an unremitting stream of lies.[27] The *Washington Post* calculated in its January 20, 2020, edition that as president, Donald Trump had made 16,241 "false or misleading claims."[28] Robert King describes the thematic significance of Blum's introduction into the narrative in its third season: "One of the themes of this year is storytelling beats facts every time. [Blum] is a walking example of someone who believes narrative convinces juries, not facts."[29]

Blum's first appearance in the third season's second episode notably occurred just two months after Roger Stone was taken into custody by the FBI in January 2019 in relation to the special counsel's Russia investigation.

When Maia Rindell spots a photograph of Blum alongside Roy Cohn and Roger Stone on the wall of Blum's Xanadu-inspired apartment, he describes his Cohn-driven philosophy as "whoever tells the best story goes home with cash and prizes." Heralding Cohn as the Euphrates River from which he springs, Blum outlines the political and legislative influence of Cohn on sites of power in the Trump era, telling Maia, "His spirit lives on in me, in the White House" ("The One Inspired by Roy Cohn" 3.2). Through the course of the season, Blum unashamedly draws attention to his contempt for the truth by calling a witness named Enid Blyton to lie on the stand and confronting the charge of suborning perjury with a T-shirt declaring, "Roland Blum Did Nothing Wrong," referencing Roger Stone's version of the same following his arrest. If Trump's famous cry "Where's my Roy Cohn?" will remain unanswered by the combination of Roger Stone and Bill Barr, *The Good Fight* suggests, this parallel netherworld between fact and fiction provides an alternative in the form of Roland Blum.[30]

"Now It's Personal"

In the opening shot of the pilot episode of *The Good Fight*—streamed one month after the inauguration—Diane Lockhart's look of disbelief as she watches Trump being sworn into office positions the lead character as the representative of white, educated, liberal America and its reaction to the Trump presidency. Diane's navigation of Trump-era politics, as she veers between shock, resignation, and resistance, becomes the show's narrative imperative, moving the character beyond the comfortable liberalism of *The Good Wife*. In the earlier show, Diane's politics play an integral but relatively innocuous role in her professional life and are only minimally disturbed by her eventual marriage to the ballistics expert and National Rifle Association supporter Kurt McVeigh (Gary Cole). The shock and horror of Trump's election, then, smashes this complacency, as Diane becomes consumed by the Trump show, its cultural impact spurs the legal cases taken by the firm, and her response becomes increasingly politicized. As Hannah Giorgis wrote in the *Atlantic* in 2019, prior to the season 4 opener that imagines a Hillary Clinton–led United States, "Where a Hillary-era Diane might have been most concerned about her own professional legacy, the Trump-era Diane weighs the events of her own life against much larger social dynamics. She is perennially plugged in."[31] Rather than discovering a way to politicize her personal life,

Diane rediscovers political engagement when politics comes for her and the liberal world in which she exists. As she shifts at least temporarily from the legislative strategies that would mark the Hillary Clinton presidency she envisioned, her enticement into the unlawful and radical becomes a reflection on the nation's transformed politics under Trump, its endangering of democracy, and its effects on the individual. For Diane in *The Good Fight*, the political becomes personal.

Diane's political go-to of feminism articulates the shift that occurs as the new cultural climate explicitly enters her professional life. The #MeToo movement becomes a focal point when the firm acts for a reality-TV-show contestant suing a network that allowed her to be raped (modeled on the *Bachelor in Paradise* allegation; "Day 422" 2.3) and advises a network planning to broadcast a Ronan Farrow–style exposé accusing a major Hollywood actor of sexual harassment ("Day 436" 2.5). Such references to the exposure of a widespread culture of sexual harassment and abuse simultaneously allude to the accusations of abuse made by numerous women against the president himself and the NBC *Access Hollywood* taped evidence of his "grab 'em by the pussy" attitude toward women's sexual autonomy. However, when Diane tells a millennial feminist berating her for effecting the legal removal of an "Assholes to Avoid" website, "Women aren't just one thing, and you don't get to determine what we are" ("Day 478" 2.11), she condemns lawlessness and alternative constraints on female identity and preserves her Emily's List brand of feminism in the midst of an online "cancel culture."

At the same time, Diane's full immersion in a political climate that is unrecognizable in both philosophy and style to both what has preceded it and what she expected leads to the temporary unraveling of a character who was previously described as "ferocious, professional and powerful."[32] As she constantly channel-hops, landing on ever-more outlandish Trump-related news stories, begins microdosing the hallucinogen psilocybin ("Day 408" 2.1), and has a one-night stand with the bartender and anarchist Tully Nelson (Tim Matheson) while estranged from husband, Kurt ("Day 429" 2.4), the careful exactitude with which her personal and professional lives have been lived comes undone. The bizarre images that Diane—perhaps—sees of a couple donning Trump masks, dancing, and having sex in the office building opposite convey again the sense of a world that merges the real and the imaginary, suggesting the absurdity of the political landscape and Diane's own personal disorientation in an unrecognizable America.

Diane is fittingly awoken from the despair that she describes to Liz Reddick as a "dark night of the soul" ("Day 415" 2.2) by the arrival of presidential politics in the offices of Reddick, Boseman & Lockhart. When Ruth Eastman, a consultant to the Democratic National Committee, invites the partners to pitch their prosecution strategy in a case for the envisioned impeachment of Donald Trump, Diane backs Liz's offensive approach centered on narrative—fact-based or otherwise—as she animatedly counters the accusation from the Republican partner Julius Cain (Michael Boatman) that her position constitutes "Trump derangement syndrome" and departs from Obama-era politesse:

> I'm tired of "when they go low, we go high." Fuck that. When they go low, we go lower. . . . If it's one thing that we've seen this past year, it's that lies persuade. Truth only takes you that far, and then you need lies. . . . I'm just done with being the adult in the room. I am done with being the compliant and the sensible one, standing stoically by while the other one picks my pockets, while the other side gerrymanders Democrats out of existence—a three-million-person majority and we lost the presidency, a Congress that keeps a Supreme Court justice from being seated because he was chosen by a Democratic president. . . . I have spent the last few months feeling fucking deranged, like I'm living in some bad reality show, going numb, all Trump, all the time, what's real, what's fake? Well, you know what, I just woke up.

Diane's awakening, in which she confronts the politics of unfair play, false narratives, and a media presidency and which is symbolized by her switch from mind-healing aikido classes to aggressive axe-throwing ("Day 450" 2.7), represents a determination to take on Trump and the Republican Party at their own game. The impact of the contemporary political culture on her mental health and behavior personalizes the politics Diane had previously been able to maintain at a comfortable distance due to its familiarity. As Michelle King describes the evolution of the show through the third season, the question becomes "whether you can fight an opposition that you see as dirty without becoming sullied yourself."[33]

Diane's fight of the good fight plays out through her involvement with an underground female resistance group called the "Book Club," whose rules imitate those of their target: "Move fast. Be smart. Attack. Lie. Don't get caught" ("The One Where Diane Joins the Resistance" 3.3). In a 2018 article in the *Atlantic* following that year's congressional elections and the success of a number of leftist candidates, the journalist and political commentator Peter Beinart notes both the historical impact of movements outside the Democratic Party on shifts in its ideological perspective and how such contemporary influences might lead to alternative strategies in the event of 2020 electoral success in the presidential race. Beinart suggests that confronting or using the strategies of the Republicans, such as the filibuster or packing the Supreme Court, might be the demonstrative effect of leftist influence. "Perhaps most important," he argues of this wing of the party, "they're more willing to challenge entrenched norms of fair play to forge a more equal country."[34] In *The Good Fight*, the Democratic Party appears already in this space, with the strategist declaring to Liz, "Democrats need to stop being such pussies" ("Day 492" 2.13). The Book Club occupies the alternative space of a resistance group, a radical example of Kenneth Tucker's description of political movements that use "languages of the self," social media, and "visual aesthetic politics" to create an autonomous arena for political engagement.[35] The tactics of the Book Club include outing the transitioning sister of a country music star in order to have the singer publicly condemn the Alt-Right and promote the vote ("The One With Lucca Becoming a Meme" 3.4) and "swatting" Trump's Miller-like border policy adviser, which results in his death ("The One Where the Sun Comes Out" 3.9). Such strategies create a parallel between the rule-breakers of Trump's administration and those of the resistance, trapping Diane in a contradiction of aims and methods that fundamentally challenges her personal and professional integrity and, by extension, that of the liberalism she represents.

Reflecting on both the media landscape in which contemporary politics is being played and the equivalences being drawn with Watergate, the show simultaneously frames Diane's political journey within an *All the President's Men*–style (Alan J. Pakula, 1976) narrative. Just as accusations of corruption and possible impeachment become obvious throwback connections to the era of President Nixon, the closing episode of season 2 explicitly evokes the forensic investigation of facts by the journalists Bob Woodward and Carl Bernstein that the film celebrates as both an exemplar of professional prowess and a service to the nation's democracy ("Day 492" 2.13). From the opening clacking of typewriter keys that establishes the date, Diane becomes a fact-finder of Trump's misdeeds after the FBI targets her with a charge of conspiracy to assassinate the president due to her brief relationship with left-wing radical Tully. When she finds an anonymous note in her bag after aikido class, she puts a flowerpot in the window of her office and meets her "Deep Throat" in an underground parking lot. Diane's informant is less FBI mole, more Stormy Daniels–style porn-star-turned-director, guiding her to "follow the women"—the prostitutes, extramarital lovers, and a "love child" who represent Trump's Achilles' heel and through whom justice for Diane and the country might be found. Indeed, Trump's downfall will be achieved, the show suggests, more likely through various forms of female active opposition than through the unraveling of male institutional monetary power that was the marker of Watergate. The FBI's invasion of Diane's marriage through Kurt makes clear the personal nature of the political forces waged against her. The couple's alliance, illustrated in a conversation typed out in their apartment to the accompaniment of classical music to combat possible bugging devices—a *President's Men* scene parallel in all but the contemporary switch to a laptop—indicates how one more political intrusion on her personal world necessitates Diane's pursuit of justice. As Diane explains to her "Deep Throat" the reason she should break her NDA, "We need to fight . . . because now it's personal" ("The One About the Recent Troubles" 3.1).

Race and the Intersectional Experience

For Diane Lockhart, the political becomes personal when her political haven is embattled and her belief in democratic and legal strategies fragments. However, the show simultaneously explores the alternative lived experience of its Black characters as it dramatizes the impact of history, America's racial divisions, and intersectionality on their perspectives on the contemporary political climate and their responses to a democracy whose rules have continuously worked against them. When Diane flinches at the Book Club's "undemocratic" plan to hack voting machines, Liz reminds her, "We share a lot of things, but we do not share histories." Citing contemporary examples, both national and personal, of the disenfranchisement of Black voters, Liz argues for rule-breaking as an appropriate response to a society that legislates structural inequality: "One person hits a few buttons and suddenly Black voters are reenfranchised. That means something very different to me than it does to you" ("The One Where Diane and Liz Topple Democracy" 3.7). As Liz cites incidents of friends and family being denied their voting rights in America's democracy alongside contemporary statewide strategies, her experience is revealed as both personal and historical and informs her perspective on a contemporary United States that, unlike for Diane, represents a continuum of inequality. When Jay's retaliation against the racial insults and physical attacks of a group of "Red Jackets" (a reference to groups such as the Proud Boys) is to punch Nazis, he explains his actions as a confrontation of the idea of equality of speech when it enables the white nationalist Richard Spencer to be interviewed on the day of Trump's inauguration ("The One Where a Nazi Gets Punched" 3.5). The suggestion of a monolithic Black response is simultaneously repeatedly avoided, including when the DNC's solicitation of advice on strategizing for the Black vote in 2020 provokes division on the topic of reparations among the firm's group of liberal and conservative associates and partners, and DNC chairman Frank Landau (Mike Pniewski) departs in confused frustration ("The Gang Gets a Call from HR" 4.3).

A historically weighted and racially defined perspective is repeatedly highlighted in the show as the Black characters both experience the political maelstrom and react to the failings in their professional liberal world. When Lucca notes in a discussion of police shootings of Black men that only the Black members of the firm are able to cite the names of those killed, she is essentially asking not only whether Black lives matter enough not to be killed but moreover whether they matter enough to be remembered by white liberals, pointing to the exclusiveness of national memory ("The One With Lucca Becoming a Meme" 3.4). Marissa's upset at the insinuation of racism, and Diane's later furious memorizing of the victims' names suggest that the white liberal acknowledgment of dissimilar experiences is more acquired than instinctive and can be shaken by the discomfort of such conversations. In a January 2020 *Washington Post* article, professor of political science Jeanne Theoharis likens the self-satisfaction of white liberals to the attitudes of northerners who were repeatedly called out by Martin Luther King Jr. for their abhorrence of southern segregation and violence while displaying a reluctance to address local racism. Citing the August 2017 events in Charlottesville and Trump's promotion of racial divisions, Theoharis suggests, "It is easy to focus on the crassest forms of racism infecting our nation," but "we also must reckon with [King's] long-standing critique of the 'polite' racism of his liberal allies, of the language and the policies they employed to excuse and perpetuate racial injustice."[36] Politeness breaks out into hostility and racial divisions on *The Good Fight* when Jay tackles the firm's inequalities by releasing confidential employment records, sparking arguments about pay, promotion, and offices. As professional and personal relationships are unsettled and Maia is fired in an effort to maintain an image of racial equity for the firm, the show suggests the ruffling of the status quo that emerges as the subject of inequality moves local ("The One With Lucca Becoming a Meme" 3.4).

The complexities opened up by structured inequalities in a firm established as a Black enterprise and Adrian's stance from a business rather than racial perspective are expanded on by the intersectional experience of African American women, articulated through the show's Black female characters. A 1989 essay by the legal scholar Kimberlé Crenshaw identified the particular brand of discrimination suffered by Black women, who, she argued, "often . . . experience double-discrimination—the combined effects of practices which discriminate on the basis of race, and on the basis of sex. And sometimes, they experience discrimination as Black women—not the sum of race and sex discrimination, but as Black women."[37] Reddick, Boseman & Lockhart become embroiled in the #MeToo movement in legal defense of white women but more closely when several revelations about the firm's founder, Carl Reddick (Louis Gossett Jr.), expose the sexually abusive past of Liz's recently deceased father ("The One About the Recent Troubles" 3.1). The narrative events bring into play the writing out of Black women from the #MeToo story and from a movement initiated by the African American activist Tarana Burke in 2006 to support women of color. As the narrative reveals Reddick's victims of sexual abuse and rape, the issues raised circulate around the reconciliation of Reddick's civil rights leadership with his identity as a sexual abuser and the social contract assumed by Black women to protect Black men from public censure in a discriminatory United States.[38] The refusal of one victim to condemn Reddick or accept a financial settlement and the response of another—notably at the urging of her daughter—to accept the money offered for silence point to the alternative individual perspectives even within this intersectional framework. For Liz, the situation requires a negotiation of personal trauma, professional responsibility, and sisterhood with both the victims and her female allies. When Liz specifically targets the investigative assistance of Marissa, who assures her, "Hey, we're in this together," it becomes an attempt to disturb a racial dynamic that has alienated women of color from feminism and the #MeToo movement and that was fueled further by the reported 47 percent of white women who voted for Trump in 2016.[39]

Lucca's various professional and personal interactions explore further the intersectional juncture of race and gender that informs the reception of women of color in the contemporary United States. Her heritage of a white mother and Black father, relationship with a white US attorney, Colin Morello (Justin Bartha), with whom she has a child, and friendships with white colleagues Marissa and Maia bring additional complexities to the character's representation and the context in which she exists. Lucca's visit to the palatial home of Colin's parents, during which party guests are at pains to demonstrate their Trump-hating, antiracist credentials, the comedic tone of which prefaces Lucca more disturbingly being described as "the hot Black girlfriend" asset of her boyfriend's possible Senate run, all points to the race and gender essentialism through which her identity is framed in the exclusive setting of wealthy white liberalism ("Reddick v. Boseman" 1.8). In a professional setting, the partners discuss Lucca's image as what Marissa describes as "not Black enough" for the firm's brand and therefore for a partnership. When Jay suggests that her image is similar among the Black associates due to her friendships, Lucca's resistance mirrors Diane's attack on young feminists' attempts to restrict women's identities, with Lucca having to combat the added critique of being a "traitor to the race": "You know, I do not have to prove myself to anyone, or perform what they think Black should look like. This is 2019. I'm not playing this stupid fucking game" ("The One About the End of the World" 3.10). While Diane has won her case, however, Lucca is denied a partnership.

Outside the professional and personal environments in which Lucca's working identity often shields her from explicit racism beyond unconscious microaggressions (despite their conspicuousness to the recipient), she is subjected to the kind of racism experienced by Black Americans and repeatedly highlighted by camera-filmed footage in the Trump era. Lucca's visit to the park with her child becomes a viral incident when a bystander films her encounter with a young white mother who first assumes that Lucca must be the nanny to her child before accusing her of kidnapping and then summoning the police. The online racial and misogynistic abuse that follows the posting of a video of Lucca "mothering while Black" characterizes the underlying attitudes toward Black womanhood that inspire such incidents in the real world and that have historical roots in the privileging of white motherhood, despite women of color often assuming the mothering role in white families.[40] Cush Jumbo's emotional retelling of her own similar experiences while living in New York as both a woman and mother of a child of mixed heritage—with Audra McDonald noting that she also had been mistaken for the nanny of her child—reinforces the contemporary authenticity of the show's narrative events and the heightened racial divisiveness of the Trump presidency on which it draws.[41]

Conclusion

As "entertainment for the resistance," *The Good Fight* depicts more directly than any of its television contemporaries the profound impact of the Trump presidency on the US climate.[42] Conveying the turbulence of an extraordinary political era, the show dramatizes the relentless barrage of TV news and events, the pervasiveness of sexual and racial abuse and inequality exposed, and the repeated assaults on political norms and the justice system that became the Trump's administration's means of doing business in the White House. The legal world in which *The Good Fight*'s narrative exists provides the show with a framework in which to explore the multiple ways that the period from the 2016 election has fundamentally altered the United States. Setting the accusations of impeachable behavior, interventions in the justice system, and Trump's media circus alongside the #MeToo and Black Lives Matter movements and the increasing importance of social media and television in the political conversation, the show confronts the challenges to democracy and equality that have occurred or been given succor and the places where resistance is to be found.

This professional ground also becomes a sphere in which to consider the impact on the individual of the contemporary political climate. Just as Trump's presidency is partly defined by its amplification of the personalized style of politics, the political becomes personal for these characters, affecting both their professional lives and personal relationships. The liberal, racially diverse arena of a majority-Black law firm sets the scene in which liberals are prompted to confront the limits of their recognition and understanding of the experience of Black Americans, and the alternative experiences and perspectives of the show's Black characters signal the broader historical and contemporary experience. The immersion of *The Good Fight*'s central protagonist, Diane Lockhart, in the Trump era, moreover, displays a character journey that is emblematic of the educated white liberal's response to America's extraordinary times. After the "fake news," reality-TV nature of the nation's politics leaves the character suspended between the real and imaginary worlds, the challenges to the contemporary political anomaly through radical illegality, which she ultimately rejects, point to the necessity of the exploitation of norms for their very restoration.

The show displays and confronts the mood of unrestrained chaos that afflicts the characters' universe with the character of Roland Blum, whose performed excess, illegality, and links to historical strategies of political maneuvering place him metaphorically in the Trump White House. At the same time, the show's disturbance of form, with the interjection of musical shorts, fourth-wall-breaking moments, monologues, and the merging of the diegetic and nondiegetic worlds, aims to connect the characters and audience in a shared experience of unrestrained chaos and to reassert the primacy of facts into the understanding of contemporary politics. As *The Good Fight*'s narrative and style locate the characters amid the turbulence of the contemporary era, its reflections on the cultural and political issues it addresses consistently avoid simplistic resolutions, taking the characters and their stories instead into a nuanced actuality in which intersectionality, personal relationships, business imperatives, and individual life experiences crisscross the borders of how they might be defined and determine their responses to the events that occur.

The fourth season of *The Good Fight* begins with Diane, having passed out following the descent of a SWAT team on her apartment, imagining herself celebrating a historic win for Hillary Clinton in the 2016 election ("The Gang Deals with Alternate Reality" 4.1). The illusory United States that unfolds in this reversal of the season 1 opener fails to provide Diane's nirvana, leading instead to the consequences of no #MeToo movement, Harvey Weinstein still in place, and Reddick, Boseman & Lockhart taking him on as a client. The show's continuing representation of the messiness that surrounds any search for resolution in a flawed political and cultural landscape points to its central imperative of dynamic and critical engagement with the political impact of Trump. As the 2020 election result and a post-Trump presidency steers the show's future direction, *The Good Fight*'s innovative depiction of the ties that bind the political and the personal sets challenges for its audience to contemplate, just as its characters are destined to encounter them onscreen.

Notes

1   CBS All Access was rebranded as Paramount + in March 2021.
2   Michelle Goldberg, "The Only TV Show That Gets Life under Trump," *New York Times*, May 3, 2019, https://www.nytimes.com/2019/05/03/opinion/the-good-fight-trump.html.
3   "'The Good Fight' Cast and Showrunners Conversation at 92Y," YouTube, February 4, 2017, https://www.youtube.com/watch?v=PW6d92TqJCU&t=981s.
4   Carol Hanisch, "The Personal Is Political," in *Radical Feminism: A Documentary Reader*, ed. Barbara A. Crow (New York: New York University Press, 2000), 113.
5   Hanisch, 114.
6   Kenneth H. Tucker Jr., "The Political Is Personal, Expressive, Aesthetic, and Networked: Contemporary American Languages of the Self from Trump to Black Lives Matter," *American Journal of Cultural Sociology* 6, no. 2 (2017): 361.
7   Spencer Neale, "Whatever Happened to Joe the Plumber?," *Washington Examiner*, December 21, 2019, https://www.washingtonexaminer.com/news/whatever-happened-to-joe-the-plumber.
8   Tessa Berenson, "Trump Threatens to Run as a Third Party Candidate," *Time*, July 23, 2015, https://time.com/3969382/donald-trump-third-party-candidate/.
9   Virginia Heffernan, "Column: Call Trumpism What It Is: A Cult," *Los Angeles Times*, January 10, 2020, https://www.latimes.com/opinion/story/2020-01-10/donald-trump-cult-steven-hassan-moonie.
10 Michael D. Shear, "With a Tweet, Trump Upends Republican Strategy for Dealing with Yovanovitch," *New York Times*, November 15, 2019, https://www.nytimes.com/2019/11/15/us/politics/trump-tweet-yovanovitch.html.
11 Matt Stevens, "When Kamala Harris and Joe Biden Clashed on Busing and Segregation," *New York Times*, July 31, 2019, https://www.nytimes.com/2019/07/31/us/politics/kamala-harris-biden-busing.html.
12 "Meet the Woman behind Kamala Harris's Campaign: Her Sister, Maya," *Lily News*, July 29, 2019, https://www.thelily.com/meet-the-woman-behind-kamala-harriss-campaign-her-sister-maya/.

13 Nik DeCosta-Klipa, "Ayanna Pressley Gave a Powerful Speech Describing What She Saw inside Border Detention Facilities," *Boston.com*, July 12, 2019, https://www.boston.com/news/politics/2019/07/12/ayanna-pressley-border-facilities-speech.

14 Eliana Dockterman, "How *The Good Wife* Changed Feminism and Politics on TV," *Time*, May 8, 2016, https://time.com/4322155/good-wife-finale-feminism-politics/.

15 Taylor Cole Miller, "The Fashion of Florrick and FLOTUS: On Television, Gender Politics, and 'Quality Television,'" in "*The Good Wife* and Broadcasting Quality: Re-centering Feminist TV Studies," special issue, *Television & New Media* 18, no. 2 (2017): 155.

16 Lindsay Putnam, "'Good Wife' Costume Designer on Why Michelle Obama Was Right to Channel Alicia Florrick," *New York Post*, January 21, 2015, https://nypost.com/2015/01/21/good-wife-costume-designer-on-why-michelle-obama-was-right-to-channel-alicia-florrick/.

17 Raffaella Coletti, "*The Good Wife*'s (Geo)Politics between Originality and Stereotypes: A New Wine or Just a New Bottle?," *Geopolitics* 23, no. 1 (2018): 50–66.

18 "'Good Fight' Cast and Showrunners."

19 Emily Nussbaum, "The Incendiary Verve of 'The Good Fight,'" *New Yorker*, May 28, 2018, https://www.newyorker.com/magazine/2018/06/04/the-incendiary-verve-of-the-good-fight.

20 James Poniewozik, *Audience of One: Donald Trump, Television, and the Fracturing of America* (New York: Norton, 2019), 265.

21 New York Times Events, "TimesTalks The Women of 'The Good Fight,'" interview by Melena Ryzik with Christine Baranski, Audra McDonald, Cush Jumbo, and Michelle King, YouTube, March 12, 2019, https://www.youtube.com/watch?v=gWy-Mwg3rMU.

22 Joy Press, "*The Good Fight*'s Show-Runners on (Not) Impeaching Trump and the Nature of Evil," *Vanity Fair*, March 12, 2019, https://www.vanityfair.com/hollywood/2019/03/the-good-fight-interview-showrunners-robert-michelle-king.

23 Laura Bradley, "CBS Censored *The Good Fight*, So Its Show-Runners Threatened to Quit," *Vanity Fair*, May 8, 2019, https://www.vanityfair.com/hollywood/2019/05/the-good-fight-censorship-cbs.

24 Bob Woodward, *Fear: Trump in the White House* (New York: Simon and Schuster, 2018), 18.

25 Li Zhou, "Senate Republicans Were Laser-Focused on Confirming Judges in 2019—Even the Unqualified Ones," *Vox*, December 23, 2019, https://www .vox.com/policy-and-politics/2019/12/23/21031430/senate-republicans -judges-american-bar-association-unqualified-mitch-mcconnell-donald -trump; Paul Rosenzweig, "Why Bill Barr Got Rid of Geoffrey Berman," *Atlantic*, June 21, 2020, https://www.theatlantic.com/ideas/archive/2020/ 06/why-bill-barr-got-rid-geoffrey-berman/613339/; Ann Gerhart, "Election Results under Attack: Here Are the Facts," *Washington Post*, March 11, 2021, https://www.washingtonpost.com/elections/interactive/2020/ election-integrity/.

26 Press, "*Good Fight*'s Show-Runners."

27 Michael E. Miller, "'It's Insanity!': How the 'Brooks Brothers Riot' Killed the 2000 Recount in Miami," *Washington Post*, November 15, 2018, https:// www.washingtonpost.com/history/2018/11/15/its-insanity-how-brooks -brothers-riot-killed-recount-miami/.

28 Glenn Kessler, Salvador Rizzo, and Meg Kelly, "President Trump Made 16,241 False or Misleading Claims in His First Three Years," *Washington Post*, January 20, 2020, https://www.washingtonpost.com/politics/2020/ 01/20/president-trump-made-16241-false-or-misleading-claims-his-first -three-years/.

29 Press, "*Good Fight*'s Show-Runners."

30 Caroline Fredrickson, "Donald Trump Wanted Another Roy Cohn. He Got Bill Barr," *New York Times*, December 12, 2019, https://www.nytimes.com/ 2019/12/12/opinion/trump-bill-barr-.html.

31 Hannah Giorgis, "Christine Baranski Leads the Best #Resistance Show on Television," *Atlantic*, March 12, 2019, https://www.theatlantic.com/ entertainment/archive/2019/03/the-good-fight-season-3-christine -baranski-leans-in/584608/.

32 Amy Roberts, "Diane Lockhart Deserves That 'Good Wife' Spinoff," *Bustle*, May 13, 2016, https://www.bustle.com/articles/160726-diane-lockhart-has -deserved-a-good-wife-spinoff-for-a-long-time.

33 New York Times Events, "TimesTalks Women of 'The Good Fight.'"

34 Peter Beinart, "Will the Democrats Go Too Far?," *Atlantic*, December 2018, https://www.theatlantic.com/magazine/archive/2018/12/democratic-party -moves-left/573946/.

35 Tucker, "Political Is Personal," 376.

36 Jeanne Theoharis, "Martin Luther King and the 'Polite' Racism of White Liberals," *Washington Post*, January 17, 2020, https://www.washingtonpost.com/nation/2020/01/17/martin-luther-king-polite-racism-white-liberals/.

37 Kimberlé Crenshaw, "Demarginalizing the Intersection of Race and Sex: A Black Feminist Critique of Antidiscrimination Doctrine, Feminist Theory and Antiracist Politics," *University of Chicago Legal Forum* 1989, no. 1 (1989): article 8, 149.

38 Rebecca Leung and Robert Williams, "#MeToo and Intersectionality: An Examination of the #MeToo Movement through the R. Kelly Scandal," *Journal of Communication Inquiry* 43, no. 4 (2019): 349–71.

39 Pew Research Center, "An Examination of the 2016 Electorate, Based on Validated Voters," August 9, 2018, https://www.pewresearch.org/politics/2018/08/09/an-examination-of-the-2016-electorate-based-on-validated-voters/.

40 Brandon E. Patterson, "It's Time We Had a Talk about White People Calling the Cops on Black People," *Mother Jones*, May 17, 2018, https://www.motherjones.com/crime-justice/2018/05/its-time-we-had-a-little-talk-about-white-people-calling-the-cops-on-black-people/.

41 New York Times Events, "TimesTalks Women of 'The Good Fight.'"

42 Goldberg, "Only TV Show That Gets Life."

ON THE VALUE OF UNCERTAINTY IN UNCERTAIN TIMES (OR, "PAY ATTENTION, YOU ASSHOLES!")

DONALD TRUMP, DAVID SIMON, AND
THE PLOT AGAINST AMERICA

Simon Stow

On Monday June 1, 2020, amid nationwide protests following the police kill-ing of George Floyd, an unarmed Black man, in Minneapolis, Minnesota, Donald Trump concluded a speech at the White House by declaring himself "your President of law and order and an ally of all peaceful protesters," before announcing that he was "going to pay [his] respects to a very, very special place."[1] Trailed by multiple administration officials, Trump walked out of the White House gates, across Lafayette Square, to St. John's Episcopal Church, where he posed for a photo holding a Bible. His supporters saw this as a sym-bolic triumph of Churchillian proportions, while his critics focused on the aggressive police action used to clear legally gathered protestors in order to facilitate the photo op. Trump's actions led many commentators to return to a question asked frequently during his political rise: Is Trump a fascist?[2]

Less than three months earlier, the cultural polymath David Simon offered an intervention into the debate: a television adaptation of Philip Roth's 2004 novel *The Plot Against America*, a book depicting an interlude of alternative history in which the aviator Charles Lindbergh is elected pres-ident promising to keep the United States out of World War II. In keeping with Lindbergh's anti-Semitism, his fictional correlate enacts policies that appear to undermine American Jews. On its publication, and despite Roth's denial, the book was widely seen as a commentary on George W. Bush's presidency.[3] It divided critics along political lines: the conservative Jonathan Yardley condemned the book, while the liberal James Wolcott celebrated its perceived critique.[4] Revived as a lens for understanding the Trump years, the novel produced a similar political division. Majid Shirvani argued that "Trump's amazing triumph . . . must be regarded through the lens of *The Plot Against America*," and Brittany Hirth said that "Roth's anticipation of contemporary political life . . . is downright uncanny," while Frank Rich wrote that it "may yet be viewed as a rather optimistic fairy tale. Charles Lindbergh's effort to impose America First fascism . . . end[s] with the restoration of democratic order. We cannot vouchsafe that Trump's unchecked plot against America will have that salutary an ending."[5]

Roth, however, appeared to reject at least some of these parallels: "There is surely one enormous difference between the political circumstances I invent there for the U.S. in 1940 and the political calamity that dismays us so today. . . . Lindbergh . . . may have been a genuine racist and an anti-Semite and a white supremacist sympathetic to Fascism, but he was also—because of the extraordinary feat of his solo trans-Atlantic flight at the age of 25—an authentic American hero. . . . Trump, by comparison, is a massive fraud."[6] As with Roth's denial of the Bush parallels, his seeming rejection of the posited Trump parallel cannot necessarily be taken at face value: he was well aware that Simon saw his miniseries as a commentary on Trump.[7] Disingenuity and/or evasiveness is, moreover, a hallmark of Roth's characterization of the relationship between the written world of his fiction and the unwritten world in which it is produced.[8] At times, Roth seemed committed only to the literary and the aesthetic, asserting, "At their best, writers change the way that readers read. That seems to me the only realistic expectation."[9] Simultaneously, however, Roth also identified moments in which the written world of fiction offered the basis for an intervention into the unwritten world beyond it.[10] This tension is heightened by Roth's compulsive playfulness about his authorial identity.

Philip Roth in Fact and Fiction

Roth's *Plot* is presented as a memoir written by a fictional—or "semi-fictional"—Philip Roth about his childhood.[11] The Roth family in the written world of the novel take their names from the Roth family of the unwritten world. They live in a written-world version of the unwritten world house and neighborhood in which the unwritten world author was raised. This "habit of presenting the author as a fictional character in his own books is," writes Paul Berman, "an old trick of Roth's, not to say a mania."[12] In Roth's novel *Operation Shylock*, for example, the narrator "Philip Roth" encounters another "Philip Roth," who may or may not be an imposter. Neither is, however, necessarily the "Philip Roth" who wrote the novel in which these other Roths appear. Berman's "mania" might, however, be better thought of as the author's attempt to disrupt "knowing" readings of his texts: readings that reduce his work to the expression of a specific position invariably reflecting the views of the critic in the manner of Yardley and Wolcott.[13]

The desire of critics—both lay and professional—to say what a text means in a definitive fashion is strong and much in evidence among those who assert that Roth's *Plot* should be understood as a commentary on George W. Bush or Donald Trump. Roth's elusiveness is playful but far from frivolous. As Catherine Morley notes, it cultivates, or seeks to cultivate, an uncertainty in the reader.[14] It is in such uncertainty, in such unknowingness, that critical thinking begins. As the novelist Milan Kundera observed in an interview with Roth, "The stupidity of people comes from having an answer for everything. The wisdom of the novel comes from having a question for everything. . . . The novelist teaches the reader to comprehend the world as a question. There is wisdom and tolerance in that attitude. In a world built on sacrosanct certainties, the novel is dead."[15]

Donald Trump, not known to be a reader,[16] has an answer for everything: he never admits mistakes and never apologizes, and the list of subjects on which he has claimed expertise—including hurricanes, forest management, drones, windmills, science, and steam-powered catapults—is dizzying.[17] It is, perhaps, unsurprising that given totalitarianism's commitment to rank certainty, Trump might be surrounded by a miasma of fascist suspicion. This is not to suggest that there is something about reading that necessarily saves readers from fascism.[18] Nor is it to mock Trump and/or his supporters for his and their strident anti-intellectualism; it is rather to draw a distinction between their commitment to certainty and the ethos embraced and potentially cultivated by the ambiguities in Roth's fiction. For it is when Simon best embodies contingency and uncertainty that his *Plot* offers its most effective engagement with Trump and the powerful and persistent forces in American history that Trump might be thought to embody. Indeed, the frequently made claim about Trump—"this is not normal"—is misleading: Trump, as Simon shows us, is anomalous only in brazenness, degree, and style, not in substance. Cultivating a Rothian ambiguity within a highly realist televisual format that seeks a paradoxical historical authenticity within a uchronia, Simon offers viewers a critical perspective essential to identifying and fighting fascism and other forms of oppression. Simon moves beyond the polemical to cultivate a way of seeing that both alerts viewers to the fragility of democracy and offers them resources for renewing democratic practice.

As the experience of Alvin Levin, played by Anthony Boyle, suggests, however, fighting Nazis solely with art and good intentions is likely to be unsuccessful: the drawings of a heroically depicted Lindbergh by Alvin's cousin Sandy Levin (Caleb Malis) show how the promiscuous power of the aesthetic can be employed in the service of what William Connolly has called "aspirational fascism."[19] It will, nevertheless, be suggested that Simon offers a valuable resource for such conflict, one that can productively inform possible political violence. It is an approach predicated on what John Keats called "negative capability," the capacity to exist without certainty.[20] It is then somewhat problematic that so much criticism of Simon's *Plot* saw so little contingency in its approach.

Beware Your Own Footprint

In a largely negative review of Simon's adaptation, Robert Lloyd identifies parallels between Simon's *Plot* and Trump's America. Arguing that "Simon's politics are easy to read. . . . It's difficult not to read this [*Plot*] as a memo to Trump," he seeks an unwritten world referent for almost every aspect of the show. Observing that the character of Walter Winchell asks, "How long will Americans remain asleep while their cherished Constitution is torn to shreds by the fascist fifth column of the Republican right?" he suggests, "You could tweet that any day of the week and it wouldn't feel anachronistic at all." Perhaps immune to Nabokov's critical dictum—"Ask yourself if the symbol you have detected is not your own footprint"[21]—Lloyd complains, "Spoken aloud, and loudly, Roth's (and Simon's and Burns') political points can come across a little too explicitly, obviously, heavily."[22] The comment is echoed by the more balanced Charles Bramesco: "Trump parallels come early and often, and while the writing occasionally prints its subtext in font a couple of sizes too large, it's all in order to make the point that much more forcefully."[23] At the other end of the political spectrum, however, there were those who were keen to discredit Simon's allegorical use of Roth.

The libertarian Glenn Garvin identified several of the "show's political missteps," asserting that the overly idealized Roosevelt in fact "spent a good bit of his spare time plotting schemes to keep Jews out of a postwar America" and pointing to the show's underplaying of the efficacy of Lindbergh's spying on the Luftwaffe and its ignoring of Canada's refusal of Jewish refugees from Europe. Such errors, he argues, undermine "both its dramatic and its political credibility."[24] Sharing Garvin's concerns about "the troubling record towards the Jewish people of President Franklin D Roosevelt," Melanie Phillips suggests that the pro-Lindbergh rabbi Lionel Bengelsdorf—played by John Turturro—should best be understood as a parallel to "Rabbi Stephen Wise, the community leader who acted as Roosevelt's cheerleader and thus sanitized his . . . acquiescence in the extermination of Europe's Jews."[25] Echoing the description of Herman Levin (Morgan Spector) by Evelyn Finkel (Winona Ryder) as "narrow-minded and frightened" and Sandy's assertion that his parents are "narrow-minded ghetto Jews," Phillips distinguishes between those "reason[ed]" and informed Jews who support Trump and those who express an "irrational hatred" toward someone considered by many Jews to be the most pro-Israel and pro-Jewish US president ever. Such unhinged hatred, she suggests, is "an undercurrent in the six-part TV adaptation of the Philip Roth novel," a manifestation of "Simon's highly-selective indignation."[26]

For many critics, then, the relationship of Simon's *Plot* to Trump—as Roth's *Plot* to Bush—is a matter of great clarity: with almost every event in the written (or filmed) world having its referent in the unwritten world, or something of a Rorschach test in which they find and dismiss all the supposed Trump parallels. Some, however, offered a more subtle appreciation of political allegory. Gabe Friedman calls *Plot* "the scariest show I've seen," pointing to the very ordinariness of its characters as making their experiences all the more terrifying and to the sense of uncertainty cultivated in the viewer. Indeed, he suggests, the "tension of being on that dividing line, between safety and a lack of it, filled me with dread as I watched [and] made the show more powerful than a gut-wrenching Holocaust film that shows

Jews being violently abused and murdered."[27] It is in this space between certainties—between "is" and "is not" Trump, between "is" and "is not" fascist—that Simon's *Plot* finds its aesthetic efficacy and critical-political leverage.

Simon certainly sees both his and Roth's *Plot* as "startling[ly] . . . allegorical to our current political moment," but his understanding of allegory is more nuanced than that of many of his critics or would-be champions.[28] Simon has compared Alvin's subplot to Shakespeare's *Julius Caesar* and the overthrow of a tyrant. The parallel suggests how the show's allegorical aspects might best be understood: as a lens through which to view the politics of the unwritten world, rather than as key to mapping correspondences, real or imagined, between fictional and nonfictional events.[29] A 2017 Shakespeare in the Park production of *Julius Caesar* featured a suit-wearing Caesar whose overly long tie evoked Trump. While the parallel was sufficiently upsetting to prompt two Trump supporters to interrupt a performance, the power of the allegory lay in the suggestion of similarity, rather than in nailing down whether Brutus was, say, Jeff Sessions.[30] Simon can, to be sure, be something of a polemicist.[31] Nevertheless, it is by letting Roth's story play out and by not overemphasizing the allegorical aspects of the show that Simon best captures what is at stake for democracy in the Trumpian moment. It is in these more questioning moments that he offers his viewers a possible political pedagogy in an anti-intellectual time.

Plot as Democratic Pedagogy

Simon's *Plot* begins with a focus on the family, religion, and civil society. The Levins' Shabbat meal identifies them as Jews, but the appearance of Hasidic Jews collecting for Palestine marks them out as non-Orthodox. Over the dinner table, Alvin briefly raises Hitler's persecution of Jews, but the conversation is dominated by a baseball. Juxtaposing Jewishness and Americanness, Simon establishes the Levins as assimilated American Jews. The subsequent scene in which they visit a house—in a non-Jewish neighborhood—that Herman wants to buy, situates them within the American Dream. Thereafter, however, Herman and his wife, Bess (Zoe Kazan), establish a dynamic that runs throughout the show: his optimistic belief in America and her more cautious engagement with the world beyond her household. This tension offers an always ongoing dialectic that drives the dramatic pedagogy of Simon's piece, one evident in the next scene, in which the Levins engage with the state.

It is, perhaps, a little too on the nose that the first overt evidence of the show's political pedagogy occurs in the classrooms of Philip (Azhy Robertson) and Sandy Levin, but the subtlety of the presentation rescues the complexity of the position. Simon juxtaposes two scenes in which Sandy and then Philip recite the Pledge of Allegiance—underlining their American identity—cutting from Sandy to Philip following the line "for which it stands," a phrase then repeated by Philip's class. It is an embodiment of Herman's beliefs: Jewish at home and American beyond it. There is, nevertheless, much to trigger Bess's suspicion. First, the bizarreness of the pledge as a form of programming: the overlapping recitations suggesting repetition as indoctrination. Likewise, there is the wording of the pledge. The recitation, absent "under God," may jar on modern ears. The addition of this phrase in 1954 was seen as a Cold War counterblast to communist godlessness. Simon's presentation suggests the contingency of US values, which can so easily be rewritten in the face of threats real and imagined. More telling is Simon's depiction of the students with hands over their hearts. This scene is set in 1940. Until 1942, however, the pledge was marked by the "Bellamy Salute," a straight-armed gesture identical to the Nazi salute.[32] It is not clear whether Simon's anachronism is deliberate or simply a mistake. Either way, an awareness of the problematic undercurrents in the ceremonial assertion of allegiance to the flag suggests the validity of Bess's suspicions. It is not that Herman is wrong and Bess right, nor its opposite, but rather that both perspectives are to be embraced at once, and in so doing, the viewer might recognize the contingency of their perspective and, thus, the "stupidity" of embracing a final position in the manner of totalitarian states.

This tension between Herman and Bess is evident during their trip to Washington, DC, with Herman's insistence that they visit the nation's capital and reclaim America's symbols for themselves and Bess's desire to visit Canada to reconnoiter an escape route. Simon's pedagogy is evident in the family's two encounters with the police as representatives of the state. In the first, with the family holding up traffic as they search for their hotel, a motorcycle cop assists them, directing them around traffic and leading them to their hotel. For Herman, this is evidence of the American decency; for Bess, a source of considerable anxiety. "But how do you know where he is taking us, Herman?" she asks, wiping away tears. In the second instance, the police enforce apparent anti-Semitism when the Levins are ejected from their hotel.[33] When the desk clerk threatens to call the police, Herman's belief in American institutions is such that he welcomes their summoning. Nevertheless, one of the officers sneeringly refers to Herman as "*Levin*," suggesting that his sympathies lie with the hotel and not its customer and that, in this moment at least, it is Bess who best understands the mechanisms of US bigotry.

The Herman-Bess dynamic is likewise repeated in the family's interaction with their tour guide, Mr. Taylor (Michael Cerveris). Herman consults Bess about the possibility of hiring him, with Bess's response—"I don't know. Who sent him?"—offering a counterpoint to Herman's trusting nature. Once again, the viewer is presented with two entirely plausible viewpoints, with Simon never choosing between them. Taylor remains something of a cipher: he does exactly what he says he will do and serves as an effective tour guide to the nation's capital; but equally, there is, perhaps, something that is unnerving about his affect and diction that makes Bess's anxieties seem justified. It is, nevertheless, Taylor who facilitates the family's trip to the Lincoln Memorial.

In Roth's *Plot*, the family visit the Memorial during the daytime; in Simon's, at night. The Lincoln Memorial and the Washington Monument are illuminated, the architectural embodiments of US ideals. Confident in these ideals, Herman engages in a testy exchange with a middle-aged couple. After Herman questions the woman's paralleling of Lincoln and Lindbergh, the man calls him "a loudmouth Jew." As the family gaze on the inscribed Gettysburg Address, Herman expresses anger about the slur being used against him in a shrine to Lincoln, demanding that Philip read the words. As Philip, sharing Bess's anxiety, fails to speak, Herman asserts, "'All men are created equal.' It's as plain as day," leading Bess to exclaim, "Herman, I can't go on like this."

The Herman-Bess dialectic between righteous idealism and the fear of seeking to make good on those ideals is echoed in the iconography and history of the Lincoln Memorial. Dedicated in 1922 before a segregated audience, it serves as a reminder of the ways in which the United States' alleged commitments have never been incompatible with racial oppression. Once again, however, the complexity and the contingency of these issues—which refuse ultimately to come down on either Bess's or Herman's side—are suggested by the way in which Lincoln rewrote the Constitution at Gettysburg, incorporating into it the Declaration of Independence and its commitment to equality.[34] Lincoln reworked the nation's ideals in response to a crisis: the same method employed—to different ends—by Eisenhower with the Pledge of Allegiance. Simon reveals how the manipulability of ideals can be employed to multiple ends, further suggesting the contingency of the nation and its values and, thus, the usefulness of the Herman-Bess dialectic as a mechanism for understanding its politics. Such juxtaposition is a persistent trope in Simon's *Plot*. It is, perhaps, telling that the unsettling encounter at the Lincoln Memorial is followed by the Levins' ejection from the hotel for what seem to be—though not unequivocally—anti-Semitic reasons. As the Levins depart, the hotel's name is briefly glimpsed over Herman's shoulder. That their visit to the Lincoln Memorial is followed by their ejection from the Douglas Hotel suggests the way in which the nation to which Herman is dedicated has possibly been turned upside down, with the Lincoln-Douglas debates being won not by the forces of right but by Stephen Douglas's far less noble commitments.

Lindbergh and Ambiguity

In March 2020, *Salon* illustrated a story with a famous photograph of Lindbergh giving a straight-arm salute at an America First Committee rally, captioned, "Charles Lindbergh . . . giving the Nazi arm salute during a rally on October 30, 1941."[35] A. Scott Berg nevertheless argues that the picture was taken during the Pledge of Allegiance.[36] That Lindbergh's 1941 audience made unequivocal Nazi salutes does little to resolve the question of whether the pilot—who espoused anti-Semitic tropes—was a Nazi. His cipher-like state in Roth's fiction, and in Simon's adaptation of it, likewise fails to resolve the question in the written world. "Everyone sees what he is," declares Herman of Lindbergh, but it would be more accurate to say that everybody sees what they *think* he is: hero pilot; fascist president; American savior. Nobody in Simon's production can, however, see Lindbergh (Ben Cole) at all: he is largely filtered through the media. When he does appear, he is seldom the focus of the scene. His stump speech is short and scripted. His politics remain elusive. Herman asserts that Lindbergh is a fascist, while Rabbi Bengelsdorf offers repeated assurances that Lindbergh is far from anti-Semitic. There is no way for the viewer to judge who, if anybody, is offering a full understanding.[37] Even the viewer's tendency to side with the more sympathetic Levins over the creepy Bengelsdorf is less than reliable. Herman's reverence for Alvin's sometime boss, Abe Steinheim (Ned Eisenberg)—in the face of Alvin's account, and Simon's depiction, of Steinheim's odious behavior—suggests that any propensity to side with Herman should be resisted.

The theme of persistent misrecognition repeats itself throughout the series, such as when Philip mistakes the body of Seldon's father for his own. Similarly, with the character of Mrs. Finkel (Eleanor Reissa), Bess and Evelyn's mother, whose dementia makes her confused and prone to misperception, Simon employs her confusion about her circumscribed world as a metaphor for the similar confusion of those in the broader world of the show and of an audience unable to make sense of the Trump years. Similarly, Simon's decision to abandon the (unreliable) single narrator of Roth's novel and to employ another Rothian mechanism, "refracting his narratives through the voices of people who only know part of the story," serves to further the uncertainties faced by the characters and their audience.[38] That "everyone's point of view is comprehensible, if not necessarily sympathetic," adds to the sense of uncertainty pervading the show.[39]

A similar dynamic is evident in the names of the government programs that punctuate the narrative. "Just Folks," a summer program that sends Jewish children to rural America, seems wholesome and insidious in equal measure. "Homestead 42" and "The Office of American Absorption" are similarly ambiguous and equally unnerving. It is this aspect of Simon's *Plot* that Lloyd misses when he declares, "Factoring out the speculative aspects of the story, one is left with a moderately diverting drama of a family under pressure, arguing about whether what looks like trouble is really trouble. (It really is.)"[40] The critic's certainty is not Simon's certainty; it is not the characters' certainty, nor, perhaps, is it meant to be the audience's certainty. Embodying Kundera's maxim about an answer for everything, Lloyd misses the value of Simon's democratic pedagogy predicated on the recognition of contingency and the cultivation of uncertainty.

Art and Democracy

The philosopher Jason Stanley recounts the story of his grandmother Ilse, who worked for the Jewish underground in 1930s Berlin, "venturing into the Sachsenhausen concentration camp, dressed as a Nazi social worker, rescuing from death hundreds of Jews confined there, one by one." She recounted, Stanley observes, "the disparity between the extremes she witnessed in the concentration camp and the denials of the seriousness of the situation, its normalization, by the Jewish community of Berlin." She "struggled to convince her neighbors of the truth: A concentration camp, for those on the outside, was a kind of labor camp. . . . There was no comprehension of the tragic reality." For Ilse Stanley's Jewish brethren, the relative normality of their lives prevented them from seeing the dangers, repeatedly misperceiving their circumstances. "We were still able to leave the country; we could still live in our homes; we could still worship in our temples; we were in a Ghetto, but the majority of our people were still alive. For the average Jew, this seemed enough."[41] As Ilse Stanley's experience suggests, alerting people to the political dangers they face can be an impossible task, even with firsthand testimony. Simply telling, Ilse Stanley's story suggests, is insufficient, hence Walter Benjamin's assertion about the necessity of responding to fascism "by politicizing art."[42] This is not, however, necessarily the same as engaging in polemic: an artistic form of the problematic telling that Ilse Stanley found so ineffective. While some critics have suggested that Simon's *Plot* is indeed a polemic, this might be a manifestation of the polarized political moment in which the show appeared.[43]

The function of art, argued Alfred C. Danto, is the "transfiguration of the commonplace," the ability to reveal something about the world that could not hitherto be seen.[44] In a time of political uncertainty, when it is not clear whether assaulting of protestors is the momentary transgression of the law or something more sinister and systematic, it might be argued that seeking to cultivate uncertainty in the citizenry is redundant, artistically *and* politically. There is, perhaps, already enough uncertainty to go around. Nevertheless, as Ilse Stanley's experience suggests, it is all too easy to ignore not just what one is told but what one feels: the sense of uncertainty that might alert one to the possible abnormality of the moment in which one finds oneself. The persistent trope—"this is not normal"—about the Trump presidency serves, according to Jason Stanley, a valuable political purpose. "Normalization," he writes, "means precisely that encroaching ideologically extreme conditions are not recognized as such because they have come to seem normal."[45] Simon's capacity for polemic is suggested by his assertion that Roth's message in *Plot* was, "Pay attention, you assholes."[46]

It may be, however, that it is in Simon's attempted cultivation of uncertainty in his audience by never resolving the uncertainty faced by his characters that he better achieves his goal of prodding his viewers to pay attention. Such uncertainty works against the normalization as a mechanism of, if not necessarily fascism, then "fascist tactics."[47] It is an approach that also works against the certainties offered up by what Connolly calls Trump's "aspirational fascism," in which "definitive assertion takes priority over extended justification."[48] Such an approach seeks to cultivate an attitude and ethos conducive to a pluralism in which there are no final answers, only an always ongoing debate about issues of concern.[49] The potential benefit to democratic politics is threefold. First, it cultivates an eternal vigilance against the normalization of any abhorrent deviation. Second, it offers the potential to generate in the citizenry an ethos essential to meaningful democratic practice, what Connolly calls a "bicameral orientation to political life . . . straddling two or more perspectives to maintain tension between them."[50] Third, the turn to the aesthetic over the polemical offers the capacity for the critical evaluation of alleged abnormality, drawing attention to the way in which the "not normal" may actually be its opposite.

Uncertainty and Democracy

The dialectic of uncertainty best evinced between Herman and Bess is omnidirectional: it interrogates everything with which it comes in contact. Thus, the genealogy of the Pledge of Allegiance and the palimpsest at work in the Gettysburg Address suggest the ways in which the supposedly eternal principles of the American republic can be reworked in good and bad ways. In *Plot*, Lincoln's positive palimpsest serves as a counterpoint to the anti-Semitic graffiti scrawled on the gravestones in the Jewish cemetery or to the swastikas superimposed on Philip's stamp collection in his nightmare. Simon's *Plot* captures the contingency of America and the contingency of democracy. "Our moral clarity regarding identities or forms of life that were once but are no longer excluded is a product of political victories," observes Bonnie Honig. "Victorious political actors *created* post hoc the clarity we now credit with having spurred them on to victory ex ante." Nevertheless, she suggests, "Things could have gone another way. They may yet do so."[51]

The most obvious example of the contingency that Simon depicts and seeks to cultivate occurs in the show's finale. In the novel, Lindbergh's disappearance is followed by the reelection of Roosevelt, and an attack on Pearl Harbor draws the United States into World War II. For some, Roth's ending was too neat, seeming to reduce the Lindbergh presidency to an unfortunate interlude in US history.[52] While there is something to be said for this reading, Jason Siegel suggests a more compelling account of the novel's conclusion: "Roth's overly contrived resolution to his counter-history emphasizes the mere contingency by which we do not find ourselves living in a fascist state to argue that the potential for American fascism remains present."[53] Simon weaves his similar understanding into an alternate ending. Concluding with an undecided election, Simon reemphasizes the contingency of American democracy. "Democracy," he observes, "is precious, and it's something that has to be attended to, like an orchid."[54] Indeed, inadvertently perhaps echoing Sheldon Wolin's work on the "fugitive" nature of democracy, Simon declares, "Democracy, and freedom . . . can never be completely won. Every day is a quotidian struggle. . . . You're never going to finish the job. There's never a moment where you dust off your hands and say, 'Well, there it is. That's our republic. It's perfected.' It's struggle. It's the hardest form of government there is, is to attempt self-governance, and it's utterly imperfect. But freedom can be lost and lost quickly, and all you have to do is stop fighting for it."[55]

The cultivation of uncertainty might, nevertheless, be considered an inadequate response to Donald Trump—fascists, aspirational or otherwise, are not known for the commitment to nuanced critical thinking—especially given the violence that has bubbled under, and to the surface of, his politics. Tear gas, rubber bullets, and stun grenades will, in the short term at least, inevitably triumph over Connolly's "bicameral orientation." A commitment to contingency does not, however, preclude the use of violence, neither in Simon's fictional world nor in the world in which it opposes the political forces embodied by Trump and his followers. Simon embodies Angela Davis's demand "not to lay down the gun, but to learn how to set the sights correctly, aim accurately, squeeze rather than jerk and not be overcome by the damage": a call for any political violence against oppression to be informed by critical thought rather than unthinking reaction.[56] When Alvin and his friends assault two patrons of a German beer garden in an ostensible retaliation for an attack on their friend, there is no indication that their targets were responsible for the assault. It is telling, then, that Simon intersperses the assault with scenes of Nazi violence and Japanese atrocities.

What could be seen as a justification for Alvin's attack might better be understood as a paralleling of Alvin's assault with fascistic violence: when one of Alvin's accomplices says that their targets look drunk and asks if their proposed actions are fair, the question of justice is instantly dismissed. The subsequent violence of which Alvin is a part tellingly draws no such questions or parallels from Simon. Indeed, what appears to be Alvin's role in Lindbergh's disappearance is bloodless and dispassionate: the execution of a violent act informed by careful thought. Simon's commitment to contingency reveals, then, a problematic violence at the heart of American life. Alvin's attack becomes a microcosm of Native American clearance, slavery, lynching, and colonialist expansion—violence underpinned by attitudes that make Trump's politics not just possible but endemic to the American experiment. Simultaneously, however, Simon demonstrates how violence might be employed in the fight against such politics without becoming that to which it is opposed.

Conclusion: Contingency, Democracy, and Political Action

"In its own history," observes Jason Stanley, "the United States can find a legacy of the best of liberal democracy as well as the roots of fascist thought (indeed, Hitler was inspired by the Confederacy and Jim Crow laws)."[57] This acknowledgment demands a recognition that, far from being "not normal," "Donald Trump was produced by America."[58] Trump's abnormality, Simon suggests, is a matter of style not substance: a fundamental brazenness in a dog-whistle age. This understanding only emerges from a recognition of the contingency of US democracy: its history, its problematic present, and what Roth calls its "relentless unforeseen" future.[59] By cultivating an awareness of US contingency and seeking to inculcate contingency as a democratic ethos and perspective in the viewer, Simon's *Plot* constitutes an intervention into the present political moment—concerned with protecting American democracy in the face of the manifold threats against it—that also offers to go beyond that moment. It is a perspective in which Donald Trump is the embodiment of both a potentially fleeting and, simultaneously, possibly permanent historical moment. The suggestion is not that Trump is a toothless figure who poses little threat to the republic but rather that if, as Roth asserts, the artist's job is not "the solution of the problem" but "the correct presentation of the problem," the contingency depicted and cultivated by Simon does the latter, alerting viewers to the multiple dimensions of Trump's politics and thus enabling them to engage in informed action in the face of it.[60] Simon's reworking of Roth's conclusion was partly inspired by an HBO executive who noted that the show would air during the 2020 election cycle and would "speak directly to . . . what's at stake."[61] By ending his *Plot* with the contingency of an undecided election, Simon turns over the potential political import of the series to his audience, inviting them to engage in action themselves, informed by their contingent perspective. It is a truly democratic act in undemocratic times, suggesting with Sheldon Wolin that "the possibility of renewal draws on a simple fact: that ordinary individuals are capable of creating new cultural patterns of commonality at any moment."[62]

Notes

The author is enormously grateful to Brittany Hirth and Catherine Morley for sharing their work during the COVID-19 lockdown when library closures made interlibrary loans unavailable.

1   Donald J. Trump, "Statement by the President," White House, June 1, 2020, https://trumpwhitehouse.archives.gov/briefings-statements/statement-by -the-president-39/.

2   Ishaan Tharoor, "Is It Time to Call Trump the F-Word?," *Washington Post*, June 3, 2020, https://www.washingtonpost.com/world/2020/06/03/trump -protests-fascism/.

3   Philip Roth, "The Story behind 'The Plot Against America,'" *New York Times*, September 19, 2004, https://www.nytimes.com/2004/09/19/books/ review/the-story-behind-the-plot-against-america.html.

4   Jonathan Yardley, "Homeland Insecurity," *Washington Post*, October 3, 2004, https://www.washingtonpost.com/wp-dyn/articles/A63751 -2004Sep30.html; James Wolcott, "The Counter Life," *Nation*, November 4, 2004, https://www.thenation.com/article/archive/counter-life/.

5   Majid Shirvani, "Deconstructing Roth's *The Plot Against America*: The Making of the President Donald Trump," *Rethinking Social Action Core Values in Practice: Lumen Proceedings* 1, no. 1 (2017): 813; Brittany Hirth, "'An Independent Destiny for America': Roth's Vision of American Exceptionalism," *Philip Roth Studies* 14, no. 1 (2018): 89; Frank Rich, "Trump's

Plot against America," *New York Magazine*, July 18, 2020, https://nymag
.com/intelligencer/2018/07/frank-rich-trumps-plot-against-america.html.

6　Charles McGrath, "No Longer Writing, Philip Roth Still Has Plenty to Say,"
New York Times, January 16, 2018, https://www.nytimes.com/2018/01/16/
books/review/philip-roth-interview.html.

7　Matthew Dessem, "*The Plot Against America*'s Showrunners on Why They
Changed the Ending," *Slate*, April 20, 2020, https://slate.com/culture/2020/
04/the-plot-against-america-finale-david-simon-ed-burns-interview.html.

8　Simon Stow, "Written and Unwritten America: Roth on Reading, Politics,
and Theory," *Studies in American Jewish Literature* 23 (2004): 77–87.

9　Philip Roth, *Reading Myself and Others* (New York: Vintage, 2001), 147.

10　Roth, 158.

11　Stow, "Written and Unwritten America," 79.

12　Paul Berman, "*The Plot Against America*," *New York Times*, October 3, 2004,
https://www.nytimes.com/2004/10/03/books/review/the-plot-against
-america.html.

13　Simon Stow, "The Politics and Literature of Unknowingness: Philip Roth's
Our Gang and *The Plot Against America*," in *A Political Companion to Philip
Roth*, ed. Lee Trepanier and Claudia-Franziska Bruehwiler (Lexington:
University Press of Kentucky, 2017), 71.

14　Catherine Morley, "Memories of the Lindbergh Administration: Plotting,
Genre, and the Splitting of the Self in *The Plot Against America*," *Philip Roth
Studies* 4, no. 2 (2008): 148.

15　Philip Roth, *Shop Talk: A Writer and His Colleagues and Their Work* (New
York: Vintage, 2002), 100.

16　Hillel Italie, "Does Trump Read? If So, What? Fiery 2005 Letter Shines
Light on His Relationship with Books," *Chicago Tribune*, February 15,
2018, https://www.chicagotribune.com/entertainment/books/ct-trump
-letter-literature-20180215-story.html.

17　Shawna Chen, "Donald Trump, Expert," *Politico*, September 13, 2019,
https://www.politico.com/magazine/story/2019/09/03/donald-trump
-expert-227997.

18　Jeremiah P. Conway, "Compassion and Moral Condemnation: An Analysis
of the Reader," *Philosophy and Literature* 23, no. 2 (1999): 289.

19　William E. Connolly, *Aspirational Fascism: The Struggle for Multifaceted
Democracy under Trumpism* (Minneapolis: University of Minnesota Press,
2017).

20 John Keats, *Selected Letters of John Keats*, rev. ed. (Cambridge, MA: Harvard University Press, 2002), 61.

21 Vladimir Nabokov, *Strong Opinions* (New York: Vintage, 1990), 66.

22 Robert Lloyd, "'The Plot Against America' Depicts a Familiar Crisis. That Doesn't Make It Great TV," *Los Angeles Times*, March 16, 2020, https://www.latimes.com/entertainment-arts/tv/story/2020-03-16/hbo-plot-against-america-philip-roth-david-simon.

23 Charles Bramesco, "'It Can't Happen Here': The Horrifying Power of 'The Plot Against America,'" *Guardian*, March 30, 2020, https://www.theguardian.com/tv-and-radio/2020/mar/30/the-plot-against-america-philip-roth-tv-hbo.

24 Glenn Garvin, "*The Plot Against America* Is Not about Trump, Even If the Comparisons Are Inevitable," *Reason*, March 13, 2020, https://reason.com/2020/03/13/the-plot-against-america-is-not-about-trump-even-if-comparisons-are-inevitable/.

25 Glenn Kessler, "The 'Very Fine People' at Charlottesville: Who Were They?," *Washington Post*, May 8, 2020, https://www.washingtonpost.com/politics/2020/05/08/very-fine-people-charlottesville-who-were-they-2/.

26 Melanie Phillips, "Mining for Hate in 'The Plot Against America,'" *JNS: Jewish News Syndicate*, March 19, 2020, https://www.jns.org/opinion/mining-for-hate-in-the-plot-against-america/.

27 Gabe Friedman, "I Cover Anti-Semitism. 'The Plot Against America' Is the Scariest Show I've Seen," *Times of Israel*, April 18, 2020, https://www.timesofisrael.com/i-cover-anti-semitism-the-plot-against-america-is-the-scariest-show-ive-seen/.

28 "In 'The Plot Against America,' David Simon Finds Present Day in an Imagined Past," NPR.org, March 13, 2020, https://www.npr.org/transcripts/814602908.

29 Dessem, "*Plot Against America*'s Showrunners."

30 Michael Paulson, "Two Protesters Disrupt 'Julius Caesar' in Central Park," *New York Times*, June 17, 2017, https://www.nytimes.com/2017/06/17/theater/julius-caesar-central-park-trump-protesters.html.

31 Charles McGrath, "'The Plot Against America' Imagines the Rise of an Intolerant Demagogue," *New York Times*, March 5, 2020, https://www.nytimes.com/2020/03/05/arts/television/plot-against-america-hbo-david-simon.html.

32 Richard Ellis, *To the Flag: The Unlikely History of the Pledge of Allegiance* (Lawrence: University Press of Kansas, 2005), 118, 137.

33 Stefanie Boese, "'Those Two Years': Alternate History and Autobiography in Philip Roth's *The Plot Against America,*" *Studies in American Fiction* 41, no. 2 (2014): 286.

34 Garry Wills, *Lincoln at Gettysburg: The Words That Remade America* (New York: Simon and Schuster, 2006); see also Simon Stow, "Pericles at Gettysburg and Ground Zero: Tragedy, Patriotism, and Public Mourning," *American Political Science Review* 101, no. 2 (2007): 195–208.

35 Candace Fleming, "Charles Lindbergh's Unapologetic Bigotry: How He Became the Face of the America First Committee," *Salon*, March 29, 2020, https://www.salon.com/2020/03/29/charles-lindbergh-america-first-racist/.

36 A. Scott Berg, *Lindbergh* (New York: Berkley Books, 1999), 515.

37 T. Austin Graham, "On the Possibility of an American Holocaust: Philip Roth's *The Plot Against America,*" *Arizona Quarterly: A Journal of American Literature, Culture, and Theory* 63, no. 3 (2007): 143.

38 Charles McGrath, "'The Plot Against America' Imagines the Rise of an Intolerant Demagogue," *New York Times*, March 5, 2020, https://www.nytimes.com/2020/03/05/arts/television/plot-against-america-hbo-david-simon.html.

39 Judy Berman, "HBO's Philip Roth Adaptation *The Plot Against America* Is Essential Viewing for All Americans," *Time*, March 13, 2020, https://time.com/5802828/plot-against-america-hbo-review/.

40 Lloyd, "'Plot against America' Depicts a Familiar Crisis."

41 Jason Stanley, *How Fascism Works: The Politics of Us and Them* (New York: Random House, 2018), 188.

42 Walter Benjamin, *Illuminations* (New York: Mariner Books, 2019), 195.

43 Garvin, "*Plot Against America* Is Not about Trump."

44 Arthur C. Danto, *Transfiguration of the Commonplace: A Philosophy of Art* (Cambridge, MA: Harvard University Press, 1983).

45 Stanley, *How Fascism Works*, 190.

46 Dessem, "*Plot Against America*'s Showrunners."

47 Stanley, *How Fascism Works*, 190.

48 Connolly, *Aspirational Fascism*, 56.

49 Connolly, 84, 92.

50 William E. Connolly, *Pluralism* (Durham, NC: Duke University Press, 2005), 4.

51 Bonnie Honig, *Emergency Politics: Paradox, Law, Democracy* (Princeton, NJ: Princeton University Press, 2009), 47, 49.

52 Timothy Parrish, "Philip Roth: *The Plot Against America*," *Philip Roth Studies* 1, no. 1 (2005): 98.

53 Jason Siegel, "'The Plot Against America': Philip Roth's Counter-Plot to American History," *MELUS* 37, no. 1 (2012): 148.

54 Dessem, "*Plot Against America*'s Showrunners."

55 Dessem.

56 Bettina Aptheker, *The Morning Breaks: The Trial of Angela Davis* (Ithaca, NY: Cornell University Press, 2014), 210.

57 Stanley, *How Fascism Works*, xviii.

58 David Denby, "The Plot Against America: Donald Trump's Rhetoric," *New Yorker*, December 15, 2015, https://www.newyorker.com/culture/cultural-comment/plot-america-donald-trumps-rhetoric.

59 Philip Roth, *The Plot Against America* (Boston: Houghton Mifflin, 2004), 113.

60 Roth, *Reading Myself and Others*, 50.

61 Dessem, "*Plot Against America*'s Showrunners."

62 Sheldon Wolin, *Fugitive Democracy and Other Essays* (Princeton, NJ: Princeton University Press, 2018), 212.

From Political Depression to "Satiractivism"

Late-Night in the Tribal Era of Trump

Dolores Resano

In one of the early episodes of *Saturday Night Live* (NBC, 1975–) after the election of Donald Trump as president of the United States in 2016, Alec Baldwin appeared in his much lauded and criticized impersonation of Trump addressing fictional journalists at a fictional preinauguration press conference, which he opened with the following lines: "I'd like to start by answering the question that's on everyone's mind: Yes, this is real life. This is really happening. On January 20, I, Donald J. Trump, will become the forty-fifth president of the United States."[1] By unambiguously addressing the feeling of shock, disbelief, and despair that was pervasive among large sectors of the American public after the improbable election—most certainly, the liberal sector of the audience—the skit was continuing a line of argument started on the November 20 postelection show, when, in a brilliant exercise of parodic self-awareness, *SNL* had aired the skit "The Bubble," which was the name of a closed community-housing project where "life continues for progressive Americans as if the election never happened."[2] What *SNL* was making evident is that it was not only shock that liberal America felt but that it acknowledged that its little bubble existed and that it had burst.

To say that the election of Trump and the four years of the embattled Trump presidency were divisive for the United States is an understatement. Even if divisiveness has been a feature of US politics since well before the

2016 campaign, which many people locate back in the 1990s and Newt Gingrich's tenure as Speaker of the House, Trump's years in office, his policies, and his rhetoric arguably intensified an adversarial logic in a country that was already split along the lines of partisan-based politics. It has become common in political analysis to speak of "tribalism," a term that Amy Chua excellently explores in *Political Tribes* as the desire to belong to a group of people who are or think like you, something that goes beyond the notions of group, party, or affiliation and that has turned democracy "into a zero-sum group competition."[3] As George Packer has argued in a piece for the *New Yorker*, "American politics today requires a word as primal as 'tribe' to get at the blind allegiances and huge passions of partisan affiliation. Tribes demand loyalty, and in return they confer the security of belonging. They're badges of identity, not of thought."[4]

In this tribal dynamic, society is divided into mutually exclusive poles that, crucially, have their own systems for legitimizing facts and knowledge. Even if we acknowledge that motivated reasoning and confirmation bias are inescapable processes in human judgment—regardless of ideology, education, or party affiliation—the United States of Trump is characterized by what David Roberts has aptly called "tribal epistemology," in which the acquisition and validation of knowledge are framed within an "us vs. them" logic.[5] In this sense, the true "shock" of the Trump presidency is that it has opened up a new type of epistemic crisis, one in which "truth isn't truth," according to Trump's TV lawyer and former mayor of New York Rudy Giuliani, and in which the presentation of objective falsehoods can be defended as "alternative facts," in the coinage of Trump senior adviser Kellyanne Conway.[6] From this point onward, the noncompliant media becomes the "enemy of the people," and every negative or unflattering story is dismissed as "fake news," which does not mean "false news" anymore but "news I don't like" or "news I perceive as attacks against me."[7]

The problem with political tribalism is that it contributes to the erosion of the public sphere—understood in simple and nonspecialist terms as a common space for the deliberation of ideas, where the "public conversation" takes place—and to the reinforcement of information bubbles and siloed communities that, as the expert in online conspiracy theories Renee DiResta suggests, "experience their own reality and operate with their own facts."[8] There is an argument to be made that social networks have become a new public sphere, or at least a very influential part of it, but it is also true that social media as a public space is extremely conditioned by affinity filters and recommendation engines, the famed algorithms that present users with a "public conversation" that is already aligned with their ideological positions, lifestyles, affiliations, interests, demographic, and so on. In other words, and as DiResta argues, "the Internet doesn't just reflect reality anymore; it shapes it," and the erosion of the public sphere as a common space seriously undermines the very notion of a *shared*, objective reality.[9]

In this context, *SNL's* admission of its audience's liberal bias raises important questions regarding the social and political effect that ironic and satirical humor on television may have, especially, and in the first place, when "the other side" may not be watching. This chapter looks at the political possibilities of late-night television in a context where the shifting dynamics of the postnetwork era may actually be contributing to the reinforcement of information bubbles and siloed communities. As William Howell notes in a recent article, the emergence of cable networks in the 1990s enabled the cultivation of narrower audiences that could be targeted with specifically tailored contents, as a result of the transition from the limited and hence "hyper-democratic" options of broadcast television to the wide variety of channels offered on cable and, more recently, satellite television.[10] Nowadays, audiences are narrowed even further when "narrowcasting" is combined with the exponential rise of social media and digital platforms, which play a pivotal role in the dissemination and consumption of TV materials, as increasingly more people get access to TV clips through sharing in social media than by actually watching live television. Taking Henry Jenkins's notion of convergence culture further, scholars have been referring to this recent phenomenon as "social television," which can be loosely defined as the intersection of TV viewership and social media participation, a type of dissemination that, besides informative, recreational, and emotional uses, has the potential to create "a sense of collective belonging."[11]

Moving into the terrain of late-night humor, it is worth noting how the shift from broadcasting to narrowcasting and the community-building capacities of social networks and social television have effectively enabled the making of an "identity-based satire" that "reinforces unifying group attributes," especially when the type of humor that late-night engages in is already ideologically selective.[12] This may be one of the contributing factors why US late-night television tends to be disparaged as a stronghold of liberal views (or at least left of center) and as the exclusive realm of "'the irony demo': the coastal, college-educated cadre of young viewers who get much of their political analysis in the form of satire."[13] Even if conservative networks like Fox News have attempted to break into the late-night scene, for example, with the creation of *The 1/2 Hour News Hour* (Fox News Channel) in 2007, efforts at right-wing satire have not been successful.[14] Experts in conservative humor like Alison Dagnes and Saul Austerlitz have analyzed the phenomenon and suggested that conservatives are not too fond of the inherently subversive quality of political satire. As they point out, "there's something about conservatism that makes the idea of poking fun at our leaders, or the ruling ideas of the day, as being inappropriate or out of bounds," as anathema to a conservative mind that is more deferential to the status quo.[15] This does not mean that conservatives do not enjoy or engage in humor; in fact, conservative talk-show hosts seem to thrive in radio, among them Rush Limbaugh and Alex Jones, and some people have suggested that Trump himself is a great conservative comedian.[16] It seems evident, though, that the satirical nature of late-night in itself conditions the ideological affiliations of its audience, which tends to be more progressive.[17]

In other words, in a media landscape that is already ripe for "homophilous sorting" (that is, the formation of clusters of like-minded people), the subversive type of humor of late-night satire seems to further select the audience, making these shows effective "liberal strangleholds."[18] And the narrower this audience becomes, Howell notes, the more the satirist can move from humor and mobilization toward "celebrating their shared righteousness and enlightenment, enabling a cathartic reaction in place of laughter."[19] The potential to build communities of social television can indeed help to promote democratic values and participation, but it can also breed cynicism, a sense of superiority, and a further removal from those "others" whom we are meant to comprehend. In this context, where the audience of late-night functions, in effect, as an information silo and ideological bubble, does political satire really have the ability to promote an ideological change in its audience, as the scholarship on political satire repeatedly argues?[20] Or is this capacity weakened when audiences are so narrowed, in a culture where the art of deliberation is seriously imperiled, if not already defunct? Is satire's sole function to effect "cathartic release"?[21] If late-night hosts are perceived as "limousine liberals shouting into the void," does their satire have the power to mobilize its audience to action, or do they run the risk of plunging viewers into "political depression," exacerbating the negative feelings of a community that despairs at the "theater of the absurd" of current politics, as CNN host Van Jones recently called it?[22]

This chapter problematizes the usual trend in humor studies to argue for the positive effects of late-night political satire and draws attention instead to the existence of an increasingly narrow and targeted audience that significantly lowers the impact of those alleged positive effects. It speculates about the possibility that this type of politically engaged humor may actually contribute to strengthening political tribalism and a culture of "political depression"—the notion that Lauren Berlant and Ann Cvetkovitch have conceptualized as a certain cynicism about the state of political affairs—the real possibilities of sociopolitical change, and a further withdrawal from political participation. A culture of political depression involves, in Cvetkovitch's phrasing, "the sense that customary forms of political response, including direct action and critical analysis, are no longer working either to change the world or to make us feel better."[23] In other words, humor can break apathy, but it can also breed a detached attitude toward contemporary politics. And as Berlant has argued in both *The Queen of America Goes to Washington City* (1997) and *Cruel Optimism* (2009), affects like political depression can constitute, together with feelings of numbness, lag, allegiance to normativity, and distant promises and expectations of change, a "technology of patience," those mechanisms by which people "seem to consent to, or to take responsibility for, their painful contexts," thus remaining stuck in the very circumstances they wish to avoid.[24] This, in turn, enables the logic of cruel optimism, the continued desire for things that, in the process of trying to obtain them, actually impede our flourishing.[25] In this light, and if we consider that these increasingly politicized late-night shows may have a role to play in civic life, whether denunciation, parody, catharsis, or calls to action, this chapter asks several questions: Is it possible that they may also be contributing to an affective instance that actually keeps subjects engaged either in the fantasy that sociopolitical change is viable or, alternatively, in the conviction that there is nothing to be done? Can the humorous transgressions of late-night satire become merely part of the "rhythm" of disaffection that reinforces the status quo? Do they promote cynicism as a response that accepts "that nothing will ever change and that collective political efforts are meaningless"?[26] Or do they delude viewers into thinking that denunciation and outrage can bring political change?

Late-Night Reacts to the Election of Trump

An interesting way to address these questions is to examine the reactions of late-night hosts after the election of Trump in November 2016. Visibly shocked and surprised, many of them delivered sobering monologues that included some dose of self-examination and attempted to transmit some hopeful, positive message to their audiences. Stephen Colbert signed off his special, live election broadcast with a sentimental, at times funny, and overall awkward monologue, in which he wondered, "How did our politics get so poisonous?" and suggested that perhaps we had "overdosed... drank too much of the poison."[27] Seth Meyers, who had famously said at the 2011 Correspondents' Dinner that he thought Donald Trump "was running as a joke," acknowledged that he had been wrong about Trump's chances and, in a highly emotional speech, reflected on how best to deal with his own feelings of sadness, anger, and fear: "I am hopeful for President Trump, because hope is always the best possible path to take."[28] SNL's cold open was replaced by a rendition of Leonard Cohen's "Hallelujah" by Kate McKinnon, who also exhorted viewers, "I'm not giving up, and neither should you."[29] In the same show, the stand-up comedian Dave Chappelle declared, "I'm wishing Donald Trump luck, and I'm going to give him a chance. And we, the historically disenfranchised, demand that he give us one, too."[30] A few days later, Trevor Noah of The Daily Show (Comedy Central, 1996–) published an op-ed in the New York Times under the title "Let's Not Be Divided. Divided People Are Easier to Rule."

However, as Caitlin Flanagan argued in early 2017, these well-intentioned calls for understanding, "the saintly appeal for reaching out to the other side," were short-lived, or, at least, they soon had to coexist with "the excoriating, profanity-strewn, ad hominem tirade against the president (and by extension against anyone who might agree, in any small measure, with his actions)."[31] Trump's improbable victory turned the temporary shift toward more political content in 2016, a presidential election year, into increased and permanent political coverage after 2017, and those shows that have become more overtly political and adversarial have been rewarded with improved ratings, to the detriment of lightweight comedy shows that persist in a blander type of humor. A good indicator is the fact that The Late Show with Stephen Colbert (CBS, 2015–) managed to surpass, for the first time, The Tonight Show Starring Jimmy Fallon (NBC, 2014–).[32] In fact, Fallon came under intense scrutiny for his jokey, playful approach to politics after his widely criticized interview of Trump in September 2016, during which he tousled the candidate's hair and for which he was accused of "normalizing" and "humanizing" Trump. Although Fallon admitted, "I was devastated. I didn't mean anything by it. I was just trying to have fun," the fallout attests to the "broader shift to a more partisan, more openly anti-Trump late-night" and how difficult it is to navigate the limit between making jokes about "serious" things and making light of them.[33] In this respect, it is worth mentioning Bill Maher as a stand-alone in liberal late-night, a self-professed liberal who launches scathing attacks both on the Right and on the Left in his weekly show *Real Time with Bill Maher* (2003–) on HBO. The difficulty in classifying Maher according to the stereotype of the liberal late-night host is replicated in the field of humor studies, where there is very little scholarship on Maher's brand of satirical humor (articles abound, however, on the thorny issues that Maher usually brings up in his show: freedom of speech, political incorrectness, secularism, agnosticism, etc.). James Caron offers what could be, in my view, a possible explanation for this lack of attention, when he suggests that Maher's comic speech tends to upset the necessary balance between political and laughable, in favor of the former.[34]

As I have argued elsewhere, interrogating the role of humor and speculating about the death of irony and satire is a recurrent trope at moments of crisis,[35] and the 2016 election was such a shocker that comedians were soon called to reflect on the challenges that a Trump presidency would pose for the exercise of comedy and satire and for their shows in particular. A few months into the presidency, Meyers suggested that the challenge for comedians would be having to compete with a "White House [that] has the best writers' room in comedy," while cultural critics suggested that one of the main challenges would be "to strike the right balance with Trump, both in how to satirize events that are close to satirical on their own and how to find something new to say."[36] Meyers denied any concerted effort on comedians' part to engage in gratuitous presidential bashing and suggested that "the day he stops giving us stuff to talk about, we will move on to something else"; in the meantime, "we put on CNN and just wait."[37] Accused by Comcast of being a "professional presidential critic" bordering on treasonous,[38] Meyers defended his continuous coverage of Trump because the actions of the US president have an impact in the world; he lamented that Trump "gave us so much content that we had to turn into a content machine in order to get through it all" and at the same time admitted that there was a risk that his show could worsen tribalism.[39]

The view that late-night television has an important role to play in civic society is shared not only by the vast amount of scholarship on the subject but also by late-night satirists themselves, and Meyers has suggested that he believes his task is to "point out how insane it all is" and that this, in turn, could help viewers (and himself) to stay "sane."[40] In this view, there is nothing dismissive in laughter; it is cathartic and may actually help those who may be "stressed out or depressed" by the news. Meyers conceives of his show as a nice "companion piece" or supplement to the news that reminds the audience that "it's stressful and depressing, but here are also nine to twenty jokes . . . which maybe make it go down a little easier."[41] Especially since 2016, he believes that his show's role is to combat what I have been referring to as "political depression": reminding people who are "fed up with politics, or who want to burn it all down or vote for an outsider, that politics matters, that it matters who is in power, that who is president matters . . . that ultimately counting on an idea like impeachment is a far less likely outcome than just showing up and voting."[42] His hope is that people who watch his show will be inspired to go and vote; otherwise, Meyers does not believe that his show can change public policy or opinion.

From Political Depression to "Satiractivism"

But what if he could? In the first airing of *Last Week Tonight* (HBO, 2014–) after the 2016 election, John Oliver shared in the political exhortations of fellow comedians, but he also warned that good intentions and hope were not enough: "This is a moment that calls not just for sobriety but for all-out activism. . . . We're going to have to actively stand up for one another," Oliver said. "And it can't just be sounding off on the internet or sharing think pieces or videos like this one that echo around your bubble."[43] Implicitly referring to what has been derogatorily called "clickactivism" or "slactivism" (slacker + activism), Oliver seemed to be calling for a different type of action, one for which I will borrow Sophia McClennen's coinage "satiractivism." Satiractivism "almost always combines political activism with satirical commentary," and because it occurs in the context of a twenty-first-century media ecosystem, it tends to rely heavily on social media and digital platforms, not necessarily as the site of production but as the means for distribution, action, and viralization.[44]

As McClennen argues, these forms of humorous action can have "significant political impact," replacing the type of political action that older generations are used to engaging in (and who then refer to these newer forms in derogatory terms, such as "slactivism").[45] Satiractivism shares in many ways the underlying philosophy of "laughtivism," a term coined by CANVAS (the Center for Applied Nonviolent Action and Strategies, established in 2004 in Belgrade) "to describe the use of humor in nonviolent struggle" that aims to raise awareness about social and political issues. As one of the founders of CANVAS, Srđa Popović, notes, this type of activism uses humor in a clever way "to mock and undermine the authority of autocrats."[46] While it is not my intention to liken the type of political conflicts and actions that CANVAS engages in with the actions of a host on late-night television, I wish to draw attention to how both are an engaged type of humor that aims to intervene in the political debate. This is a key distinction from other types of ironic humor that are usually perceived as disaffected, detached, and ineffectual. Scholars like Heather Lamarre, for example, prefer to use the term "satirical political activism" to describe this kind of "entertainment-based political commentary," which is a performative "hybrid between political parody and real world activism" that transcends the normal boundaries of political comedy on television and effectively colludes with reality.[47]

Indeed, late-night hosts have long been using their notoriety and influence to try to appeal to lawmakers and to have an impact on public policy: Jon Stewart's continued campaigning for the passing of the Zadroga Act in 2010, which secured health benefits for first responders who had served during 9/11, is a well-established case, and his campaigning for its renewal continued in 2015 and 2019, which included crashing Stephen Colbert's show dressed as Trump. Leaving humor temporarily aside, late-night hosts have sometimes made public appeals and brought about material changes to conversations and, sometimes, to policy. Jimmy Kimmel's emotional speech in 2017 calling on Congress not to limit health-care access to people with preexisting conditions (through a proposed amendment to the Affordable Care Act) was extremely powerful and personal, given his newborn son's health condition, and was successful in forcing the Senate not to pass the bill.

However, there is something different in what Oliver is doing, keeping the tricky balance between the serious and the laughable and moving his audience to action, to the extent that he is considered the undisputed "chief comedy news influencer."[48] Cultural critics and scholars alike have discussed the "John Oliver Effect," which refers to Oliver's ability to break down an issue to explain it to his audience, in segments that last what is an eternity in television (twenty minutes), and his imaginative appeals to the audience to take a specific action. As Terrance Ross notes, "Sometimes the action is audacious or silly, but it's still action."[49] While not all of Oliver's shows include a call to action, his long segments dedicated to a single issue have often elicited response from governments, politicians, and company spokespeople, and not always positively. This occurred, for example, when the coal magnate Bob Murray, CEO of the largest private coal company in the United States, sued HBO and Oliver for defamation; when Chinese authorities blocked HBO's website in China days after Oliver's segment criticizing President Xi Jinping; and when Thailand denounced "John William Oliver" in an official military document after one of his long segments had made fun of Thailand's crown prince.

But other times, his segments have a notable effect on policy: the John Oliver Effect is credited with the relaxation of bail requirements in New York City after the airing of a segment that denounced how bail requirements disproportionately affected nonviolent and poor offenders who could not afford the bond set and showed with facts and figures how pretrial services were more effective, fairer, and cheaper.[50] The level of detail offered in Oliver's topical segments is higher than one would find in an ordinary news article, and some commentators have noted how the show's success is almost oxymoronic, because "*Last Week Tonight* is a show for the nerds, for people who like having income inequality or prisoner reentry explained to them in an accessible way, but with a side of dick jokes and a heavy dose of exasperation from Oliver that validates their frustration with the state of things."[51] An alum of Stewart's *The Daily Show*, Oliver does indeed display an angry tone, strong opinionating, and "unwavering, bombastic, belittling, humiliating screeds against Donald Trump," having called the president everything from "con man" to "scumbag" to "shitweasel."[52] However, as Megan Garber notes, this should not detract from the fact that Oliver "has long been dissatisfied with anger and indignation alone."[53]

The most successful instances of the John Oliver Effect have always counted on the complicity of the audience to reach its goals, and his two campaigns in favor of net neutrality in 2014 and 2017 are perhaps the most notable. After explaining net neutrality in depth and how the Federal Communications Commission (FCC) was planning to roll back its regulations, effectively allowing the existence of paid "internet fast lanes," Oliver's call to action led to change in regulations in 2014 and to the crash of the website of the FCC in 2017 (although the FCC disputes that this was a result of viewers' actions). In the first instance, Oliver asked viewers to send emails to the FCC, calling on them to focus their "indiscriminate rage in a useful direction" and encouraging them to "seize your moment, my lovely trolls."[54] Forty-five thousand emails were sent. In 2017, Oliver set up the URL gofccyourself.com, which directed users straight to the comments form on the FCC website (which was otherwise very difficult to find) and asked viewers to file complaints: "This is the moment you were made for, commenters," Oliver harangued, as inspirational, cheesy music started sounding in the background.[55] More than a million and a half comments were posted, and the FCC website crashed twice. Even if the FCC is to be believed that the crash was not a result of Oliver's call, it is evidence of Oliver's influence when he focuses on specific issues. Successful in 2014 under the Obama administration, the campaign was not, however, successful in 2017 under Trump, and the FCC proceeded to roll back net neutrality regulations.

In 2019, Oliver launched a third campaign against the FCC, denouncing its bland approach to regulating "robocalls," automated phone calls made by a computerized autodialer that deliver prerecorded messages, usually used for telemarketing and political campaigns, and that in 2018 saw a 57 percent increase and were the cause of 60 percent of the complaints lodged to the FCC.[56] In its usual resort to irony, Oliver's campaign against robocalls involved autodialing each of the five FCC commissioners every ninety minutes with a prerecorded message that urged them to take action to stop robocalls. The message said, "Hi, FCC. This is John from Customer Service. You've just won a chance to lower robocalls in America today. [*Laughs*] Sorry, but I am a live person! Robocalls are incredibly annoying, and the person who can stop them is you! Talk to you again in ninety minutes. Here's some bagpipe music: [*Bagpipe music*]." This action did not involve getting viewers to call the FCC themselves because, as Oliver said, "thanks to the miracle of robocalling, I can do it all by myself." But it was still a good example of how, in this case, one citizen can find ingenious and humorous ways to channel frustration into pressuring for change.[57]

Other examples of Oliver's satiractivism include the spike in donations to the Society of Women Engineers, an action he encouraged after learning that the Miss America pageant claimed to be the "world's largest provider in scholarships for women."[58] Incensed (or pretending to be) by the fact that this affirmation was indeed true, Oliver dedicated one of his topical segments to the matter and mentioned other organizations that also provided scholarships for women, after which the Society of Women Engineers received in two days a sum that represented 15 percent of its annual donations. More recently, Oliver promoted the publication of the children's book *A Day in the Life of Marlon Bundo*, which is a parody of *Marlon Bundo's Day in the Life of a Vice President*, a book tribute to the Pence family's pet rabbit written by the vice president's daughter, Charlotte Pence, and illustrated by his wife, Karen Pence. Oliver announced the publication of his own version of *Marlon Bundo* after a long segment deriding Mike Pence's controversial stance on LGBTQ issues, thus justifying his own version of the book, which revolves around Marlon's same-sex romance with another rabbit, named Wesley. The spoof was released before the Pence book was meant to be launched; it became a best-seller and reached number one in sales on Amazon on the day following the show. Furthermore, the producer of *Will & Grace*, Matt Mutchnik, considered it such "a poignant story about how love and community can rise above intolerance" that he donated copies of the book to every public-school library in Indiana (Pence's home state).[59]

While not all campaigns can be successful, they may also serve the purpose of energizing the community of viewers: such was the case of the campaign to use the hashtag #GoGetThoseGeckos on Twitter and Instagram, meant to pressure Russia to retrieve a number of geckos that it had put in a satellite as part of a sex experiment in space and with which it had lost contact. While Oliver later jokingly admitted that control of the satellite was regained even before the show was broadcast, he took the opportunity to uplift the audience and launch a second campaign under the hashtag #WeGotThoseGeckos, even if no credit was due. More recently, Oliver focused his attention on WrestleMania 35, the main event of the World Wrestling Entertainment (WWE), and on the WWE's treatment of its workers as regards social benefits. He encouraged fans in MetLife Stadium, where the event would take place, to chant for "retirement accounts, workers' comp, and family and medical leave."[60] There is no evidence that this call to action was successful, and the WWE responded in a statement saying, "Prior to airing, WWE responded to his producers, refuting every point in his one-sided presentation. John Oliver simply ignored the facts," and then invited the host to attend the event. However, the segment served to put issues of social justice in the spotlight.

To conclude, Oliver's combination of information, humor, pranks, and activism is not the norm in late-night television, but we may be seeing how other popular formats of entertainment, like podcasting, are also starting to combine activism with information and entertainment. For instance, the political podcast *Pod Save America*, hosted by the former Obama staffers Jon Favreau, Dan Pfeiffer, Tommy Vietor, and Jon Lovett, combines entertainment and information with calls to specific political action, having sprung from the hosts' shock and soul-searching after Hillary Clinton's electoral defeat (and their complacent, ad hoc campaign podcast *Keepin' It 1600*, in reference to 1600 Pennsylvania Avenue, the address of the White House). Besides their weekly discussion of US politics and their breaking down of the news, from a liberal perspective that they do not conceal, they also promote initiatives like "Fuck Gerry(mandering)," "Fair Fight 2020," "Get Mitch or Die Trying," "Vote Save America," and "Unify, or Die," while selling merchandise that goes from trolling Republican lawmakers to creating a sense of community—the "Friends of the Pod" logo. While their initiatives are more conventional in political terms than Oliver's and are aimed at political institutions and processes, both activist attitudes are examples of a response that avoids falling into political depression, cynicism, and detachment.

As Cvetkovitch has shown, political depression is usually considered a negative affect, but it can be depathologized if we acknowledge that political disappointment and failure can also be enabling and lead to effective action and transformative work. The affective implications of political depression, like apathy, indifference, and a feeling of dispossession or powerlessness, can also become the "sites of departure for new community formations."[61] As I have tried to show in these pages, satiractivism is one such communal and positive response that can foster positive feelings at a time when a large majority feels that "the news is demoralizing enough already" and wonders, "Why flip on a comedy show to be further incensed and depressed?"[62] At a time of tribal allegiances, it seems unlikely that the "other side" can be reached, and perhaps, then, we have to admit that there is little political satire and late-night television can do with regard to convincing those in the "other tribe." Perhaps all that can be hoped for is a better and more informed understanding, including of one's own ideological limitations and biases. To borrow Michalinos Zembylas's phrasing, "a depressive position is not the end of the story, but rather the point of departure for responding productively."[63] Perhaps satiractivism is such a way of turning political depression and disaffection into transformative action, avoiding the logic of cruel optimism and critically engaging with current conditions of inequality, injustice, and the highly manufactured quality of contemporary politics.

Notes

This work has received funding from the Irish Research Council under the Government of Ireland Postdoctoral Fellowship program GOIPD/2018/11 and the European Union's Horizon 2020 research and innovation program under the Marie Sklodowska-Curie grant agreement No. 894396.

1 "Press Conference," *Saturday Night Live*, NBC, January 15, 2017.
2 "The Bubble," *Saturday Night Live*, NBC, November 20, 2016.
3 Amy Chua, *Political Tribes: Group Instinct and the Fate of Nations* (New York: Penguin, 2018), 177.
4 George Packer, "A New Report Offers Insights into Tribalism in the Age of Trump," *New Yorker*, October 12, 2018.
5 David Roberts, "Donald Trump and the Rise of Tribal Epistemology," *Vox*, May 19, 2017.
6 "Giuliani: 'Truth Isn't Truth,'" interview with Chuck Todd, *Meet the Press*, NBC, August 19, 2018, video, https://www.nbcnews.com/meet-the-press/video/giuliani-truth-isn-t-truth-1302113347986; "Kellyanne Conway: Press Secretary Sean Spicer Gave 'Alternative Facts,'" interview with Chuck Todd, *Meet the Press*, NBC, January 22, 2017, video, https://www.nbcnews.com/meet-the-press/video/conway-press-secretary-gave-alternative-facts-860142147643.
7 In the 2008 essay "And Now . . . the News? Mimesis and the Real in *The Daily Show*" (in *Satire TV: Politics and Comedy in the Post-Network Era*, ed. Jonathan Gray, Jeffrey P. Jones, and Ethan Thompson [New York: New York University Press, 2008], 85–103), Amber Day discussed the term "fake news" and how it was used to refer to satirical shows that parodied the format of news shows, like *The Daily Show* or the segment "Weekend Update" on *Saturday Night Live*, and how these shows' treatment of

the news was sometimes more "real" than that in traditional news shows, exerting a more "careful examination of political reality." Jonathan Gray, Jeffrey P. Jones, and Ethan Thompson, introduction to *Satire TV*, 29. A decade later, the term has acquired very different connotations.

8 Renee DiResta, "Social Network Algorithms Are Distorting Reality by Boosting Conspiracy Theories," *Fast Company*, May 11, 2016.

9 DiResta.

10 William Howell, "Judgments, Corrections, and Audiences: Amy Schumer's Strategies for Narrowcast Satire," *Studies in American Humor* 5, no. 1 (2019): 70–92.

11 Henry Jenkins, *Convergence Culture: Where Old and New Media Collide* (New York: New York University Press, 2006); Donatella Selva, "Social Television: Audience and Political Engagement," *Television & New Media* 17, no. 2 (2016), 159.

12 Howell, "Judgments, Corrections, and Audiences," 76.

13 Michael Learmonth, "The Lure of Latenight," *Variety*, September 3, 2006.

14 Jake Nevins, "Why Can't Rightwing Comics Break into US Late-Night TV?," *Guardian*, September 27, 2017.

15 Nevins.

16 Nevins.

17 See also the recent volume by Dannagal Goldthwaite Young, *Irony and Outrage: The Polarized Landscape of Rage, Fear, and Laughter in the United States* (Oxford: Oxford University Press, 2019).

18 Nevins, "Rightwing Comics."

19 Howell, "Judgments, Corrections, and Audiences," 79.

20 See, for instance, the volume *Satire TV: Politics and Comedy in the Post-Network Era*, ed. Jonathan Gray, Jeffrey P. Jones, and Ethan Thompson (New York: New York University Press, 2008), and the recent special issue of the journal *Studies in American Humor*, "Satire Today," ed. James E. Caron, 5, no. 1 (2019).

21 Howell "Judgments, Corrections, and Audiences," 91.

22 Nevins, "Rightwing Comics"; CNN, "Seth Meyers Explains Why He's Tough on Trump," interview on *The Van Jones Show*, YouTube, June 16, 2018, https://www.youtube.com/watch?v=vKAPPTw9uS8.

23 Ann Cvetkovitch, *Depression: A Public Feeling* (Durham, NC: Duke University Press, 2012), 1.

24 Lauren Berlant, *The Queen of America Goes to Washington City* (Durham, NC: Duke University Press, 1997), 222.

25 Lauren Berlant, *Cruel Optimism* (Durham, NC: Duke University Press, 2011), 1.

26 Robbie Duschinsky and Emma Wilson, "Flat Affect, Joyful Politics and Enthralled Attachments: Engaging with the Work of Lauren Berlant," *International Journal of Politics, Culture and Society* 28 (2015): 184, https://doi.org/10.1007/s10767-014-9189-4.

27 *Stephen Colbert's Live Election Night Democracy's Series Finale: Who's Going to Clean Up This Sh*t?*, Showtime, November 8, 2016.

28 "Seth Meyers Shares Remarks on Donald Trump's Presidency," *Late Night with Seth Meyers*, NBC, November 9, 2016.

29 "Cold Open," *Saturday Night Live*, NBC, November 12, 2016.

30 "Dave Chappelle Monologue," *Saturday Night Live*, NBC, November 12, 2016.

31 Caitlin Flanagan, "How Late-Night Comedy Fueled the Rise of Trump," *Atlantic*, May 2017.

32 John Koblin, "Stephen Colbert's 'Late Show' Tops 'Tonight Show' in Total Viewers," *New York Times*, February 7, 2017. For a follow-up, see also Koblin's "Colbert Beats Fallon for First Time in Key Ratings Demographic," *New York Times*, March 5, 2019.

33 Dave Itzkoff, "Jimmy Fallon Was on Top of the World. Then Came Trump," *New York Times*, May 17, 2017.

34 James E. Caron, "The Quantum Paradox of Truthiness: Satire, Activism, and the Postmodern Condition," *Studies in American Humor* 2, no. 2 (2016): 153–81.

35 A classic example is 9/11. See Dolores Resano, "Of Heroes and Victims: Jess Walter's *The Zero* and the Satirical Post-9/11 Novel" (PhD diss., Universitat de Barcelona, 2017), 101–57.

36 Jim Rutenberg, "Colbert, Kimmel and the Politics of Late Night," *New York Times*, September 24, 2017; Matt Viser, "Democrats and Activists Punish Trump with a New Strategy: Ignoring Him," *Washington Post*, January 17, 2019.

37 CNN, "Seth Meyers Explains Why He's Tough on Trump,"

38 CNN.

39 Dave Itzkoff, "Seth Meyers Confronts the Trump Era on 'Late Night,'" *New York Times*, January 25, 2017.

40 CNN, "Seth Meyers Explains Why He's Tough on Trump,"

41 New York Times Events, "TimesTalks: Seth Meyers," interview by Frank Bruni, YouTube, May 20, 2019, https://www.youtube.com/watch?v= uwpAzQhggdQ.

42 New York Times Events.

43 "President-Elect Trump," *Last Week Tonight with John Oliver*, HBO, November 13, 2016.

44 Sophia McClennen, "What's Wrong with Slactivism? Confronting the Neo-liberal Assault on Millennials," *Workplace* 30 (2018): 298–99.

45 McClennen, 299.

46 Srđa Popović, "Laughtivism: The New Activists Will Spread Democracy—with a Cheeky Smile on Their Faces," Princeton University, 2013, 99. http://www.princeton.edu/~slaughtr/Commentary/13%20Wired%20world%20in%202013%20%28dragged%29%201.pdf.

47 Heather Lamarre, "When Parody and Reality Collide: Examining the Effects of Colbert's Super PAC Satire on Issue Knowledge and Policy Engagement across Media Formats," *International Journal of Communication* 7 (2013): 394.

48 Alissa Wilkinson, "5 Years In, HBO's *Last Week Tonight* Is a Lot More than 'Just Comedy,'" *Vox*, February 17, 2019.

49 Terrance F. Ross, "How John Oliver Beats Apathy," *Atlantic*, August 14, 2014.

50 "Bail," *Last Week Tonight with John Oliver*, HBO, June 7, 2015.

51 Wilkinson, "5 Years In."

52 Flanagan, "Late-Night Comedy."

53 Megan Garber, "John Oliver, Activist," *Atlantic*, November 14, 2016.

54 "Net Neutrality," *Last Week Tonight with John Oliver*, HBO, June 1, 2014.

55 "Net Neutrality II," *Last Week Tonight with John Oliver*, HBO, May 7, 2017.

56 "Robocalls," *Last Week Tonight with John Oliver*, HBO, March 10, 2019.

57 "Robocalls."

58 "Miss America Pageant," *Last Week Tonight with John Oliver*, HBO, September 21, 2014.

59 Max Mutchnick (@MaxMutchnick), "Blown away by @iamjohnoliver's new book, A Day in the Life of Marlon Bundo," Twitter post, March 30, 2018, https://twitter.com/MaxMutchnick/status/979834647365349376?s=20.

60 "WWE," *Last Week Tonight with John Oliver*, HBO, March 31, 2019.

61 Michalinos Zembylas, "Political Depression, Cruel Optimism and Peda-
    gogies of Reparation: Questions of Criticality and Affect in Human Rights
    Education," *Critical Studies in Education* 59, no. 1 (2018): 5.
62 Tim Grierson, "The Year in TV: How Late-Night Hosts Became the Resis-
    tance," *Rolling Stone*, December 6, 2017.
63 Zembylas, "Political Depression," 14.

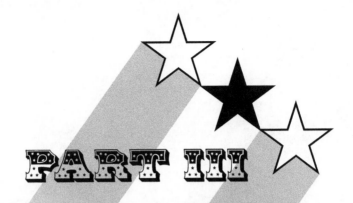

PART III

Genre, Style, and Reception

STAR TREK: DISCOVERY AND CONTROVERSY

"THE WAR WITHOUT, THE WAR WITHIN"

Teresa Forde

Star Trek: Discovery (2017–), a CBS All Access series and part of the *Star Trek* franchise,[1] has become a site of contention due to a variety of issues. These include its status as a prequel to *Star Trek: The Original Series* (*TOS*, NBC, 1966–69), issues of diversity, political commentary, and the need for a subscription in order to watch it on its streaming service. Since its initial broadcast in 2017, the show has been accompanied by statements made by the showrunners and cast about the current political and cultural climate and Donald Trump's presidency. Talk of the boycotting of and backlash against *Discovery* has taken various forms and emerged most virulently leading up to and during the show's initial broadcast in the wake of Trump's election as president in 2016. Showrunner Aaron Harberts describes *Discovery*'s inception: "The allegory is that we really started working on the show in earnest around the time the election was happening."[2] The issue of diversity has become a problematic development in the evolution of the series as critics of the show reject what is seen as a "forced" diversity agenda. A number of negative responses have lamented the loss of Gene Roddenberry's original vision in favor of a "political correctness" that, it is argued, is anathema to the *Star Trek* universe. Also, running the show on CBS All Access, which is a subscription channel, has angered fans who wish the series were freely accessible.

Science fiction as a genre has long been ascribed cultural relevance, and its dystopic tendencies have been interpreted as a commentary on current events, as well as being viewed as a projection of what might happen in the future. *Discovery* is one of two prequels, situated in the timeline between *Star Trek: Enterprise* (*Enterprise*, UPN Network, 2001–5) and *TOS*. Within the *Star Trek* franchise, *TOS* is retrospectively understood in relation to the exploration of liberal ideas in the 1960s, and *Star Trek: The Next Generation* (*TNG*, UPN, 1987–94), *Star Trek: Deep Space Nine* (*DSN*, UPN, 1993–99), and *Star Trek: Voyager* (*Voyager*, UPN, 1995–2001) have also been interpreted in relation to issues of representation and a more ethical approach to space travel. Some of these shows have been criticized as controversial or progressive, whether politically regarding representation or in relation to canon. This chapter explores the extent to which *Discovery* became embroiled in a "culture war" within social media in the United States during the run-up to and broadcasting of its first series amid the election of Donald Trump. The producers and actors claim that *Discovery* is offering a message of diversity and is a direct challenge to Trump's politics, creating the show as a form of social and political critique. Wisely avoiding the unfortunate acronym "STD," an abbreviation often used by critics of the show, *Discovery*'s fandom nickname is *Disco*, which evokes the spirit of the music and cultural movement celebrating diversity of gender, race, and sexual identity. Although there have been changes to production and collaborations, the overall focus of the show, I argue, has seen a commonality of purpose established in direct response to the wider political and social climate under the Trump administration.

Science Fiction and Utopia

As a response to the contemporary political climate, *Discovery* has established an overtly political position through both its celebration of its cast and crew and its showrunners' intentions. Andrew Milner explores the relationship between science fiction and society as an "implied connection" with the real: "The whole point of utopia or dystopia is to acquire some positive or negative leverage on the present."[3] In addition, Lincoln Geraghty suggests that the *Star Trek* franchise provides a particular form of utopian aspiration and an opportunity to express utopian ideals: "*Star Trek* is not just any utopia. It is a specific American utopia, which may appear to be a contradiction in terms, for a utopia is not a place. But *Star Trek* is a place and space in the American imagination, and as such it embodies that which is missing, lacking, and absent in America."[4] Geraghty implies that *Star Trek* can provide a utopian challenge to contemporary American society in emphasizing ideals that need to be either established or, potentially, reinvoked. Set up as a prequel to *TOS*, *Discovery* also informs what will happen next in the *Star Trek* universe. As Bruce Issacs recognizes in his analysis of "*Star Trek* as myth," "Utopia exists on board the *Enterprise*, in which the crew of the Starship offers a new multiculturalism of a united Federation of Planets, free of the prejudice of race and sexuality."[5] *Discovery* conforms to the utopian aim of the Federation of Planets, even though the first season depicts a war between the Klingons and the Federation that precedes their later alliance. Both *TOS* and *Discovery* work toward utopian ideals yet break with protocol and the Prime Directive of noninterference with other cultures, often fueling the narrative drive in the process.

Discovery has experienced a number of seasonal showrunner changes: Bryan Fuller initially left amid production issues; then replacements Gretchen Berg and Harberts moved on due to issues with their approach to budgeting and casting; they were subsequently replaced by the executive producer and cocreator Alex Kurtzman, who was then joined by Michelle Paradise. In each case, however, the showrunners have been vocal about what they feel the show means and what it brings to contemporary social and political debates within the United States. Kurtzman describes *Discovery* being in the tradition of *Star Trek* as a "mirror to the world we live in." This concept of science fiction is somewhat of a simplification, although it does reflect a tradition of interpreting science fiction as a commentary on contemporary events. Kurtzman specifically refers to isolationist politics and references the border wall between the United States and Mexico: "We live in a world now where we're talking about building walls around ourselves, literally, to keep people out, and I think that's not in keeping with the vision of *Star Trek*. What are the freedoms that we're giving up in making choices to protect ourselves? How does that chip away at our essential understanding of Starfleet doctrine, and what it means to assume diversity? Why do we need to keep people out?"[6] Kurtzman cites Starfleet doctrine as a guide to how we should behave in order to ensure social progress and implies that the values enshrined within the franchise directly conflict with the Trump administration's divisive politics. He is both invoking core principles of Starfleet and aligning *Discovery* with the *Star Trek* universe, while also criticizing Trump's political program of building a wall between the United States and Mexico to keep Mexicans out of the country. This approach by Trump to the border wall is generally set in contrast to previous administrations, which argued that they were trying to legitimize and control immigration as opposed to seeking the exclusion of Mexican immigrants. Kurtzman also suggests a dual function in the relationship between the characters within the *Star Trek* universe and the choice of the *Discovery* cast, telling NBC News, "We are creating a world that we would like to see. . . . We're creating it in the literal world that we surround ourselves with the cast, the crew and the writers and we're creating it on screen and we're hoping that people can follow."[7] This description of the production of *Discovery* as a kind of utopian haven highlights the broadening of diversity of the cast onscreen as it aims to follow the Starfleet doctrine within the show.

Discovery and Diversity

The original vision for *Discovery* was to ensure diversity of representation, for example in the ways in which casting offers a challenge to the status quo. Harberts wanted to maintain Fuller's vision and enhance *Star Trek*'s diversity as a franchise: "The show stars an African-American female lead, an openly gay couple and a Pakistani-British lieutenant."[8] Establishing such a focus has become a clear challenge to both staunch Republican views and *Star Trek* fans who profess a dislike for "political correctness" in its representation of diversity. As Ethan Sacks suggests, the production of *Discovery* offers a specific voice and alternative message to what is happening within US society: "Airing in the Trump era—with all of its political divisions, international crises and the looming existential threat of climate change— . . . can seem even further away than Alpha Centauri. Especially for a cast and crew that wear their progressive views on their sleeve as proudly as the Starfleet insignia on their chests."[9] The introduction of a female, African American lead into the canon in the figure of Michael Burnham (Sonequa Martin-Green), as well as a Malaysian actor to play Captain Philippa Georgiou (Michelle Yeoh), has been extremely problematic for some long-standing *Star Trek* fans. Executive producer Harberts sees such changes as fundamental to this vision: "I'm very proud of all of the diversity on the show. Gender identity, sexual orientation, race and it is really just a representation of what the world is."[10] He also implies the need for an audience to accept an agenda of diversity when watching the show, despite any criticism of "virtue signaling" regarding the intentions of showrunners or the cast.

A number of criticisms of *Discovery* focus on the lack of white male leads on the show, Rebecca Williams has found: "Examples of disgruntled and hostile tweets incorporated #WhiteGenocide to criticise the issue of diversity and the influence of characters who are championed by 'social justice warriors' (SJW)."[11] Williams recounts that these critics implied that SJWs were not "real fans" and probably did not even watch the series, even though some themselves had refused to watch it due to their distaste for its diversity. These comments regarding the lack of white characters and a diversity agenda are often conflated, and SJWs are criticized for prioritizing a diversity agenda. For example, one fan's tweet in May 2017 reads, "Star Trek Discovery: The only white males are a Vulcan a-hole and a wimpy helmsman. This show appears to be fully SJW converged."[12] A tweet regarding the candidate for the 2016 Republican presidential nomination Jeb Bush that incorporated the hashtag #WhiteGenocide in its handle was retweeted by Donald Trump in 2016, further aiding its legitimacy.[13]

As Katryn Alessandri argues in relation to the *Star Trek* franchise, "Considering that the show has continued to shatter boundaries for decades, it is baffling that anyone could limit this franchise . . . as only significant for a white space cowboy."[14] Nevertheless, diversity and inclusion have been perceived as threatening in the contemporary US climate. As Manu Saadia recognizes, "This being the United States in 2017, Internet trolls are accusing 'Star Trek: Discovery,' the newest incarnation of the sci-fi franchise, due to début on television in the fall, of white genocide."[15] Although the tweeters using the hashtag #WhiteGenocide are a minority of social media critics, their inflammatory terminology has garnered them wider media attention. These criticisms constitute a backlash that is symptomatic of a fear of change. As Saadia indicates, some critics have also "dubbed the show 'Star Trek: Feminist Lesbian Edition.'"[16] Similar attitudes have been used to criticize other science fiction franchises with female leads, such as *Star Wars*.

Klingons on the Starboard Bow?

A significant theme that *Discovery* is addressing is the conflict between the Klingons and Starfleet depicted within season 1. As Keith Wagstaff describes it, "a charismatic leader, T'Kuvma . . . rallies the Klingons together around a common enemy: the Federation, a cesspool of multiculturalism that threatens Klingon identity and purity," which makes the Klingons seem "a little too real in the age of Trump."[17] However, the initial warlike representation of the Klingons, established at the start of season 1, develops into a more intricate and redemptive story by the end of season 2. Some criticism of the Klingons representing Trump supporters partly arose due to Harberts's referencing of the political outlook of Trump's presidency. He hinted strongly, for example, that the initial representation of the Klingons as warlike enemies and the Federation's response raised issues of racism and bigotry that are currently evident within the United States: "It's a call to isolationism. It's about racial purity, and it's about wanting to take care of yourself. And if anybody is reaching a hand out to help you, it's about smacking it away. . . . That was pretty provocative for us."[18] Even the Klingon cry of allegiance, "Remain Klingon," was envisaged as a play on the "Make America Great Again" (MAGA) slogan. Consequently, CBS felt the need to deny the claim that *Discovery* was being critical of Trump supporters in its portrayal of Klingons.[19] The conflation of Klingons with Trump supporters was further fueled by merchandising such as a cap emblazoned with the phrase "Make the Empire Glorious Again," a Klingon war cry evocative of the MAGA caps worn by Trump supporters.[20]

The analogy between Trump supporters and the Klingons illustrates the sensitivity to criticism of representation within a science fiction show, compounding the relevance of *Discovery* to contemporary politics, and also points to how a show's narrative tensions might be interpreted in alignment with political antagonism in the United States. In a discussion of the polarization of attitudes, showrunner Gretchen Berg commented on connections between *Discovery*'s political concerns and the combative relationship between the Trump administration and North Korea, illustrated by the warlike atmosphere and sense of threat between the Klingons and the Federation within the first season: "North Korea is in our thoughts as we finish the series. What began as a commentary on our own divided nation—in terms of Trump supporters and non-Trump supporters—[is] actually right at the place where Starfleet finds itself in episode one and we couldn't have anticipated that happening. But how do you end conflict when both sides have such strong opinions?"[21] So Berg suggests that the initial conflict with the Klingons in *Discovery*'s first season, which was seemingly irreconcilable, directly echoes the conflict that emerged within the United States between pro- and anti-Trump supporters, dividing a nation and affecting wider political relationships. She implies a correlation between a political divide and the narrative in *Discovery*. As Saadia argues, "Each successive 'Star Trek' cast has been like a model United Nations. . . . The franchise's claim to fame, its central premise, is its advocacy for science, non-belligerence and, above all, multiculturalism."[22] Therefore, this series needed to address the divisions affecting the Federation and seek to build bridges onscreen in a way that may not be possible within the country.

Acting and Actorvism

The producers and actors of *Discovery* have explicitly argued that it is offering a message of diversity on- and offscreen and acts as a direct challenge to Trump's politics. Martin-Green expresses her role as one of both responsibility and obligation. She refers to the cast and crew's commitment to "actorvism," which, as a form of "art activism," encapsulates a sense of duty and purpose: "You can't help but feel a little undeserving of the endowment," Martin-Green says of joining the historical ranks of *Trek* leads: "I certainly believe that art is service, and it's been tremendous to be able to be a part of the legacy. It's what you dream about as an actor is to be a part of something that has this kind of impact."[23] The decision to have a female African American lead in casting Martin-Green was decisive and significant. It is also somewhat of a departure to make the lead someone other than a Starfleet captain, allowing Burnham's character to break the rules and avoid protocol outside the confines of the captain's role in order to establish a challenge to the status quo, although Starfleet captains also regularly flout the rules.

The importance of female and Black characters within *Discovery* is recognized by critics such as Casey Cipriani, whose article in *Bustle* describes how "the women of Star Trek 'Discovery' took control in the season 1 finale & it was a perfect ending," as actors including Martin-Green and Michelle Yeoh, as well as Mary Chieffo (L'Rell), Mary Wiseman (Sylvia Tilley), and Jayne Brook (Vice Admiral Katrina Cornwell), go on to discuss their roles in relation to feminism. As Chieffo explains, "I genuinely dreamed that I could be a part of something that did have this many strong women and have a message that I believe in. It's such a feminist piece."[24] Diverse and well-rounded female characters suggest such a feminist stance. Tilley has a particularly interesting story line when she travels to the Mirror Universe and takes the place of her more assertive and warlike alter ego. Concerns regarding representation within media have emerged from the #TimesUp and #BlackLivesMatter movements that have identified the lack of positive Black and female representation and experience within film and television, which can be mitigated by women taking on more leading roles both in front of and behind the camera. Tamara Deverell took the helm of production design on *Discovery* partway through 2017 and was the first woman to have this position within the *Star Trek* franchise.[25] Within a science fiction series in which set design is such an intrinsic aspect of the show, such a role is particularly significant.

In *TOS*, Lt. Uhura (Nichelle Nichols) challenged televisual representations in the 1960s and has been cited by Martin-Green as an inspiration. Nichols famously considered leaving the show, only to be persuaded to continue by Martin Luther King Jr., as her role was a significant prime-time presence onscreen.[26] The first season of *Discovery* included six women writers, and female actors on the show have described it as an inspirational experience. In particular, Martin-Green, as lead Michael Burnham, discusses the "privilege" of working on *Discovery*: "It makes me want to do better as a human being. It causes me to want to rise up and be better because I feel like I need to live up to the story that we're telling."[27] This form of positive representation is part of *Discovery*'s commentary on and reaction to contemporary politics of exclusion and disempowerment. Martin-Green asserts, "We've come to a point where representation alone isn't enough. Positive representation is necessary."[28] In addition, one of *Discovery*'s returning characters, Philippa Georgiou (played by Michelle Yeoh), is due to reemerge in a spin-off series about a secret Federation intelligence organization (working title *Section 31*). Both characters follow on from the franchise's first female captain, Kathryn Janeway (Kate Mulgrew), in *Voyager* during the 1990s. Burnham, in particular, also follows *Trek*'s first African American captain, Benjamin Sisko, from *Deep Space Nine*.

Despite the issue of positive representation in casting and characters, however, the show's story lines are not always as sanguine as might be claimed. There is, for example, the discovery of alien exploitation in the use of the spore drive, as this is shown to create unforeseen destruction and lead to an ethical quandary over its use and in what manner. Equally, Mirror Universe characters are sometimes initially ethically dubious, such as Philippa Georgiou's alter ego, the xenophobic Terran Emperor, who goes on to serve the Federation. These aspects of the narrative reinforce the point that *Discovery* is an entertainment show that needs conflict to fuel narrative, despite striving toward utopia. Later series, such as *TNG*, claim to have abolished poverty and achieved peaceful world relations yet still must encounter aggressive enemies and challenging foes.

Discovery's cast members have also commented on the negative influence of Trump within a wider context. Wilson Cruz (Dr. Hugh Culber) set up a petition in response to his local gym being linked to an advocate of Trump, arguing that the gym does not share the kinds of ideals to which he aspires and that Trump's lack of inclusivity has worked against the gay community. Cruz suggested, "We believed it was a safe space for people like us. We believed that we were supporting a company that was inclusive, accepting and celebrating our diversity and supporting our physical and mental health as a community."[29] Cruz's call for inclusivity echoes the way in which *Diversity* has been discussed by showrunners and cast, extending this to the gay community. Dr. Culber's relationship with Lt. Paul Stamets (Anthony Rapp) is the first explicitly gay relationship of two main characters within the *Star Trek* universe and epitomizes the ways in which *Discovery* seeks to be seen as progressive and inclusive. As season 1 emerged during Trump's first year as president, the focus was on the ways in which it would provide social commentary, and the show's cast and producers engaged with the show with Trump's policies in mind.

Captains of Disco

The first season of *Discovery* was viewed as quite disruptive and volatile in relation to the canon, introducing warlike Klingons and casting Burnham as a criminal at the outset. Captain Georgiou is initially the Starfleet captain, but the season develops with Burnham serving under Captain Lorca (Jason Isaacs) and his rogue crew. Lorca epitomizes the unreliable enemy within, as he does not adhere to Starfleet's principles and appears to have no scruples whatsoever. Isaacs has been vocal in his response to Twitter comments about *Discovery*, saying, "I hope [Trump] puts his phone down for a while and watches the show."[30] As Kurtzman has remarked on the significance of season 1 airing six months after Trump came into office, "We recognized how important it was for the core message of 'Trek' to be amplified after the election," highlighting the ways in which the show was both responding to and leading on issues that were politically pertinent.[31] Where *Star Trek* differs most in comparison with *Discovery*, according to Bruce Isaacs, is in how "the modes of utopia occurring in *Star Trek* emphasize the dream aspect of the utopian vision rather than the imperative for social political agency."[32] Within season 2 of *Discovery*, the issue of political agency is further enhanced by the break with the Prime Directive of noninterference in order to encourage the active emancipation of the Kelpiens on Kaminar. The latter is the home planet of Saru (Doug Jones), an interim captain of USS *Discovery* and the first alien to captain a Starfleet ship. Saru's former Kelpien passivity diminishes in his time on the ship as he becomes braver and more proactive, leading to the eventual liberation from subjugation of the Kelpien race. It is later revealed that this intervention in Kelpien culture and the Kelpiens' newfound bravery may unwittingly have worked to USS *Discovery*'s advantage, as the Kelpiens later come to its aid to fight the technological enemy Control, a form of artificial intelligence, acting alongside *Discovery* and previously unlikely allies, the Klingons.

As a cast member in season 1, Jason Isaacs has remarked on his desire to star in the show because of its commentary on the "Trump-Brexit era"; that commentary involves "presenting a vision of the world that's full of drama but also full of resolution and unity."[33] His character, the unscrupulous Captain Gabriel Lorca from the Mirror Universe, appeared in season 1 and was anathema to the principles of previous Starfleet captains due to their adherence to most Starfleet protocols and an ethical and altruistic approach to their responsibilities. Outside of the show, Isaacs criticized the Trump administration and made analogies between Trump and Lorca. Referencing the #TakeTheKnee protests at American football games in support of the Black Lives Matter movement, Isaacs tweeted, "In the spirit of Gene Roddenberry—If I could take one knee on the bridge I would."[34] Isaacs's actorvism has a media platform through his comments on events alongside his interpretation of Lorca as a Trump-like adversary. Isaacs's comments about President Trump evoked responses that decried him as, for example, a "#HollywoodLiberal," a clear criticism of those who position themselves as anti-Trump and who challenge a right-wing platform.[35]

In season 2, a return to some of the more recognizable traditions of the *Star Trek* franchise emerged on *Discovery*, with the inclusion of Captain Pike (Anson Mount), forerunner to Captain Kirk on the *Enterprise*, as he was the original captain at the beginning of *TOS*. This season also brought a sense of legitimacy to *Discovery*, particularly as Pike would be seen as an already recognizable Starfleet captain who was ultimately supportive of Burnham and the crew. Pike filled what has been described as a "leadership vacuum," as Mount has discussed his character's role in the show, alongside the change in season 2 to focus on weekly issues: "'Let's tackle racism; let's tackle the unknown.' They wanted to be able to get back to those big questions, and they wanted the audience to feel safe. So that was another thing that went into selecting an already established character."[36] In this account, Mount recognizes that Pike becomes a reassuring character from the *Star Trek* narrative and draws the show further toward the canon. The argument is that wider cultural issues are more easily addressed when the crew is established and working in harmony, which was a part of Gene Roddenberry's initial vision as original producer of the show. A selfish and egotistical captain at the helm is not conducive to effective leadership, making this change an implied criticism of Trump's presidential style.

Conclusion

Critics of *Discovery* argue that it is not subtle in its representations and that it is politically biased: "Since you started producing this set of episodes, over 90% of our Media have been on direct or sideways attack of President Trump and all of those who want him as President."[37] This approach conflates the impact of *Discovery* with a whole range of media and seems to imply a political program of biased representations that directly challenge Trump's presidency. In a follow-up response to an article on the depiction of the Klingons, there is disdain from one fan, who argues, "The Federation is forcing multiculturalism onto every planet in the galaxy while playing different species against each other."[38] Although most new iterations of *Star Trek* have been criticized when entering the universe, the lack of subtlety of the messages in relation to *Discovery* has also been raised. As recognized by Jonathan Holmes in his comparison of *Discovery* with *The Orville* (Fox, 2017–), "In the age of Trump, such issues are fraught. Discovery-detractors frequently complain about how 'unsubtle' its progressive messaging has become. It's an odd point. Star Trek has never been a subtle show."[39] Both *The Orville* and *Discovery* have explored contemporary issues such as gender and sexuality in thoughtful ways. As Harberts has noted, "It's been interesting to see how the times have become more of a mirror than we even thought they were going to be."[40] Considering the expressed opinions of the cast and crew, *Discovery* seems to be both emblematic of and a conduit for contemporary issues. Season 3 is set over nine hundred years in the future, when the remaining crew seek to overcome the influence of the AI adversary Control, as they extend the world of *Star Trek* and respond to the ramifications of history.

Following on from *Discovery*, *Star Trek: Picard* (2020–) has broadcast on CBS All Access through audience subscription and has been described as "firmly grounded in our troubled political present, centering on a disillusioned Picard who's removed himself from Starfleet, disgusted by the Federation's move toward isolationism in response to a refugee crisis."[41] In *Picard*, which is set during a later period in the *Star Trek* universe than the initial seasons of *Discovery*, the Federation itself has become intolerant of difference. Jean-Luc Picard (Patrick Stewart), formerly captain in *TNG*, must act as a renegade to challenge this regime. Patrick Stewart has also been vocal in his political views, and the show has been interpreted as critical of the contemporary political climate and Trump's politics. This critique seems similarly intentional and illustrates the extent to which *Discovery* heralded a science fiction challenge to the politics of the Trump era.

Notes

1 CBS All Access was rebranded as Paramount + in March 2021.

2 James Hibberd, "*Star Trek: Discovery* to Tackle Trump-Era Political Divide," *Entertainment Weekly*, September 7, 2017, https://ew.com/tv/2017/09/07/star-trek-discovery-trump-political-divide/.

3 Andrew Milner, "Reading Utopia and Science Fiction (1978): Editor's Introduction," in *Tenses of Imagination: Raymond Williams on Science Fiction, Utopia and Dystopia*, ed. Andrew Milner (Oxford, UK: Peter Lang, 2010), 93.

4 Lincoln Geraghty, "Eight Days That Changed American Television: Kirk's Opening Narration," in *The Influence of "Star Trek" on Television, Film and Culture*, ed. Lincoln Geraghty (Jefferson, NC: McFarland, 2008), 19.

5 Bruce Issacs, "A Vision of a Time and Place: Spiritual Humanism and the Utopian Impulse," in *"Star Trek" as Myth: Essays on Symbol and Archetype at the Final Frontier*, ed. Matthew Wilhelm Kapell (Jefferson, NC: McFarland, 2010), 12.

6   Andrew Whalen, "'Star Trek: Discovery' Is against Building Trump's Border Wall: Kurtzman Argued That Is against the Values of Star Trek," *Newsweek*, August 1, 2019, https://www.newsweek.com/star-trek-discovery-season-2 -build-wall-trump-spock-klingons-1284387.

7   Ethan Sacks, "'Star Trek: Discovery' Keeps Progressive View of Future in the Trump Era," NBC News, January 13, 2019, https://www.nbcnews.com/ pop-culture/tv/star-trek-discovery-keeps-progressive-view-future-trump -era-n957956.

8   Farnoush Amiri, "'Star Trek: Discovery' Cast, Crew Reveal Why Trump Should Watch Diverse Take on Franchise," *Hollywood Reporter*, October 9, 2017, https://www.hollywoodreporter.com/live-feed/star-trek-discovery -cast-crew-reveal-why-trump-should-watch-diverse-take-franchise -paleyfest-ny-2017-1046847.

9   Sacks, "'Star Trek: Discovery' Keeps Progressive View."

10   Amiri, "'Star Trek: Discovery' Cast, Crew."

11   Rebecca Lewis, "A Star Trek Fan Reveals SJW Fears and Why He Can't Stand the Words 'Diversity and Tolerance,'" *Metro*, May 26, 2017, https:// metro.co.uk/2017/05/26/a-star-trek-fan-reveals-sjw-fears-and-why-he -cant-stand-the-words-diversity-and-tolerance-6664284/.

12   Rebecca Lewis, "Star Trek Fans Decry Discovery's Diversity, Forgetting Gene Roddenberry's Vision of Inclusivity," *Metro*, May 25, 2017, https://metro.co .uk/2017/05/25/star-trek-fans-decry-discoverys-diversity-forgetting-gene -roddenberys-vision-of-inclusivity-6660755/?ito=cbshare.

13   Tal Kopan, "Donald Trump Retweets 'White Genocide' Twitter User," CNN.com, January 22 2016, https://edition.cnn.com/2016/01/22/politics/ donald-trump-retweet-white-genocide/index.html.

14   Katryn Alessandri, "Tuesdays with Malfoy: The Pain of Sharing Fandoms," in *Fan Phenomena: Harry Potter*, ed. Valerie Frankel (London: Intellect, 2019), 201.

15   Manu Saadia, "For Alt-Right Trolls, 'Star Trek: Discovery' Is an Unsafe Space," *New Yorker*, May 26, 2017, https://www.newyorker.com/tech/annals -of-technology/for-alt-right-trolls-star-trek-discovery-is-an-unsafe-space.

16   Saadia.

17   Keith Wagstaff, "Klingons on 'Star Trek: Discovery' Feel a Little Too Real in the Age of Trump," *Mashable*, September, 25, 2017, https://mashable .com/2017/09/24/klingons-star-trek-discovery-trump-supporters/?europe =true.

18 Matthew Rosza, "'Star Trek: Discovery' Creators: Our Klingons Are Secretly Trumpsters," *Salon*, September 22, 2017, https://www.salon.com/2017/09/22/star-trek-discovery-creators-our-klingons-are-secretly-trumpsters/.

19 Carli Velocci, "Klingons in 'Star Trek: Discovery' Not Based on Trump Supporters, CBS Says," *Wrap*, September 11, 2017, https://www.thewrap.com/star-trek-discovery-klingons/.

20 James Whitbrook, "You Can Buy an Official Star Trek: Discovery MAGA Hat, Because Apparently We're in the Mirror Universe," *Gizmodo*, June 3, 2018, https://io9.gizmodo.com/you-can-buy-an-official-star-trek-discovery-maga-hat-1823551736.

21 Matt Miller, "*Star Trek: Discovery* Will Tackle American Politics in a Way the Show Has Never Done Before. There's No Escape from Trump in the Vastness of Space," *Esquire*, September 8, 2017, https://www.esquire.com/entertainment/tv/a12199522/star-trek-discovery-politics-trump/.

22 Saadia, "Alt-Right Trolls."

23 Casey Cipriani, "The Women of 'Star Trek: Discovery' Took Control in the Season 1 Finale & It Was a Perfect Ending," *Bustle*, February 12, 2018, https://www.bustle.com/p/the-women-of-star-trek-discovery-took-control-in-the-season-1-finale-it-was-a-perfect-ending-8189702.

24 Cipriani.

25 Bill Desowitz, "'Star Trek Discovery': How They Designed the Mirror Universe and the Klingon World," *IndieWire*, May 16, 2018, https://www.indiewire.com/2018/05/star-trek-discovery-production-design-below-the-line-emmys-1201964968/.

26 Margaret A. Weitekamp, "More than 'Just Uhura': Understanding Star Trek's Lt. Uhura, Civil Rights, and Space History," in *"Star Trek" and History*, ed. Nancy Reagin (New York: Wiley, 2013), 28.

27 Neela Debnath, "Star Trek Discovery Season 3 Release Date, Cast, Trailer, Plot: When Is New Series Out?," *Express*, January 21, 2019, https://www.express.co.uk/journalist/122436/Neela-Debnath.

28 Sacks, "'Star Trek: Discovery' Keeps Progressive View."

29 Vic Parsons, "Gays Boycotting Equinox and SoulCycle over Investor's Trump Fundraiser," *Pink News*, August 8, 2019, https://www.pinknews.co.uk/2019/08/08/lgbt-boycotting-equinox-soulcycle-donald-trump-fundraiser/.

30 Amiri, "'Star Trek: Discovery' Cast, Crew."

31 Amiri.

32 Bruce Isaacs, "A Vision of Time and Place: Spiritual Humanism and the Utopian Impulse," in *"Star Trek" as Myth: Essays on Symbol and Archetype*, ed. Matthew Wilhelm Kapell (Jefferson, NC: McFarland, 2010), 191.

33 Daniel Holloway, "Can 'Star Trek: Discovery' Help CBS Boldly Go into a Streaming Future?," *Variety*, August 29, 2017, https://variety.com/2017/tv/features/star-trek-discovery-preview-cbs-all-access-sonequa-martin-green-1202540540/.

34 Jamie Lovett, "'Star Trek: Discovery' Star Invokes Gene Roddenberry in Support of #TakeTheKnee," *Comicbook.com*, September 24, 2017, https://comicbook.com/startrek/2017/09/24/jason-isaacs-take-the-knee-rodenberry-star-trek-discovery/.

35 Douglas Ernst, "Jason Isaacs, 'Star Trek Discovery' Star, Mocks Angered Fans as 'Closeted Humans' after Trump Rants," *Washington Times*, September 26, 2017, https://www.washingtontimes.com/news/2017/sep/26/jason-isaacs-star-trek-discovery-star-mocks-angere/.

36 Amiri, "'Star Trek: Discovery' Cast, Crew."

37 Jeff Webb, comment on Velocci, "Klingons in 'Star Trek Discovery.'"

38 Horus, comment on Velocci.

39 Jonathan Holmes, "Sci-Fi's Social Justice Wars: Why Do Star Trek: Discovery Fans Hate The Orville?" *Telegraph*, May, 7 2019, https://www.telegraph.co.uk/tv/0/sci-fis-social-justice-wars-do-star-trek-discovery-fans-hate/.

40 Amiri, "'Star Trek: Discovery' Cast, Crew."

41 Emma Dibdin, "Patrick Stewart Has Always Been an Activist. That's Why *Star Trek: Picard* Is a Bold Political Statement," *Esquire*, March 5, 2020, https://www.esquire.com/entertainment/tv/a31141189/patrick-stewart-star-trek-picard-interview-politics-donald-trump/.

PARANOIA, THE HIVE MIND, AND EMPOWERED SISTERHOOD

AMERICAN HORROR STORY'S TRUMP-HAUNTED WORLD

K. Scott Culpepper

Ryan Murphy and Brad Falchuk's anthology horror series *American Horror Story* (*AHS*, FX, 2011–) has showcased America's deepest fears and social anxieties since the inception of the series. *American Horror Story* joins a rich literary and media heritage of capturing everyday fears in supernatural metaphors that take audiences to the brink of human depravity. The show broke some interesting new ground in its first season, *American Horror Story: Murder House* (2011), by giving viewers a happy ending for at least some of its ghostly characters. Murphy and Falchuck's blend of horror, hope, and hysterical quirkiness has sustained a loyal following for nine seasons. Four of those seasons have so far been produced since Donald Trump's election in 2016 and loss to Joe Biden in 2020, with the most recent, *Double Feature*, airing in 2021. It seems inevitable that a show titled *American Horror Story* would address the United States' existential crisis symbolized by Trump's ascendancy and the social divisions that made it possible. *AHS* did not disappoint, treating viewers to stories that delved into the hive mentality endemic in too much contemporary political discourse, feminism and the power of collective sisterhood, the subversive influence of tech conglomerates in a digital age, and the difficulties of breaking cycles of oppression without becoming yet another oppressor. This chapter explores how these themes were developed by *American Horror Story* through characters and scenarios that embodied the traumatic fissures of Trump's America in graphic symbolism. Through the searing lens of the horror genre, *AHS* forced viewers to confront the worst and best of the United States in a time of division and soul-searching.

AHS: Cult and the Hive Mind

Ryan Murphy surprised fans in February 2017 when he announced that *AHS* would tackle the Trump moment head-on in its seventh season. "I don't have a title but the season that we begin shooting in June is going to be about the election that we just went through," Murphy said on Andy Cohen's *Watch What Happens Live* (Bravo, 2009–).[1] Subsequent reveals established that the seventh season would be titled *American Horror Story: Cult* and feature returning cast members Evan Peters and Sarah Paulson in the lead roles.[2]

Cult premiered on September 5, 2017, on the FX network and ran until November 14, 2017, just a week past the one-year anniversary of the election that inspired the season. The story broke the mold of previous *AHS* seasons by generally steering clear of supernatural elements. With the exception of some implied use of magic, the threats emerging in fictional Brookfield Heights, Michigan, stem from human obsessions, brokenness, and paranoia. The British scholar Derek Johnston has noted in his analysis of *American Horror Story* how the show follows gothic horror traditions by centering story elements around special events such as holidays or on the family structure, those elements that provide the framing for human experience.[3] The series's focus on "seasonality" that Johnston engages rises to a new level in season 7 with the focus on the election season, the most raucous and American of seasons. The family element highlighted in earlier entries in the series returns with two very unusual family units. The series begins with juxtaposed scenes of Ally Mayfair-Richards (Paulson) and her wife, Ivy Mayfair-Richards (Alison Pill), mourning Trump's election victory with friends while, across town, Kai Anderson (Peters) engages in a bizarre celebration that includes grinding Cheetos up in a blender and spreading them across his face to resemble Trump's orange skin tone. Kai's bright blue hair and his shouted declaration that revolution is coming keys viewers in to his foreshadowed role as leader of the titular cult. His creepy interaction with his sister, Winter (Billie Lourd), in which he compels her to share her disappointment about the election through a "pinky swear" ritual, underscores his seductive charisma ("Election Night" 7.1).

The themes of the season connect to current events as Kai establishes a clown-masked cult that raids suburban homes in a campaign designed to stoke fear. Kai seizes on that fear to raise support for his bid to secure a seat on the city council. Meanwhile, Ally's world plunges into chaos. She is already beset by a variety of phobias, including coulrophobia, or fear of clowns, and her ability to cope crumbles as she feels helpless to protect her son, Oz (Cooper Dodson), and suspects that Ivy may be tiring of dealing with her constant paranoia. Their already-struggling marriage receives a further blow when Ally reveals that she voted for the third-party candidate Jill Stein, a betrayal that Ivy finds unforgivable. The first half of the season portrays Kai's increasing influence, both in the light as a candidate and in the shadows as a secret cult leader, while Ally's world shatters along with her sanity.

Murphy and Falchuck infuse *American Horror Story* and its characters with Dickensian exaggerated eccentricity that often makes the show as funny as it is scary. *AHS: Cult* satirizes the hive mentalities at all ends of the political spectrum, poking fun at some of the treasured tropes of all sides. In "Election Night," the progressive millennial Winter complains, "What is wrong with CNN for not giving us a trigger warning when they announced the results?" Harrison Wilton (Billy Eichner), the Mayfair-Richardses' eccentric neighbor who moves into the house next door after the former occupants are murdered, reveals a massive arsenal of weapons in his garage to Ally. His wife, Meadow Wilton (Leslie Grossman), comments, "He's been storing guns since Obama got elected," as Harrison rifles through an armory capable of subduing a small army ("Don't Be Afraid of the Dark" 7.2). Meadow herself plays the part of ditzy neighbor and neglected wife until she expresses her growing romantic obsession with Kai, who recruits her to stage a mass shooting at one of his rallies. She convinces Ally that she has turned against the cult right up to the moment she unleashes her violent endgame and literally leaves Ally holding the gun following Meadow's suicide ("Mid-Western Assassin" 7.6). Kai's henchman Gary (Chaz Bono) encapsulates the stereotype of the MAGA-hat-wearing Trump disciple amped up ten decibels. Ivy and Winter chain Gary to a fence the night before the election as retribution for his attempted sexual harassment of Ivy. Gary remains chained to the fence throughout election day. With only an hour left before the polls close, Kai appears and offers Gary a saw, with which he severs his own hand so that he can go to the polls and vote for Donald Trump ("11/9" 7.4).

Ally experiences an inversion of her own tribal affiliations when she accidently shoots a Hispanic restaurant worker sent by Ivy to check on her during a blackout. The incident creates a public backlash against the couple, with protestors picketing outside their restaurant. The Wiltons, themselves professed advocates of immigration restrictions, arrive at Ally's front door wearing sombreros and tossing Taco Bell coupons at her. Ally finds herself labeled as a racist by the very progressive allies that constitute her tribe. Kai seizes the opportunity to insinuate himself into her life, dispelling the protestors and seeking to make her feel that he offers protection ("Neighbors from Hell" 7.3). While Kai appears draped in the trappings of Trumpism at the beginning of the series, his goals are revealed to be more complex as the story unfolds. Kai's flexible tribalism serves as a means to the creation of a hive mind in his minions, rather than as an end.

The hive-mind metaphor features prominently throughout *AHS: Cult* and in all the promotional materials that advertised the season. The cover art for DVD and Blu-ray releases of the season portrays a figure with an exposed brain. The brain consists of honeycomb. Television and internet trailers featured images of bees, as did the opening credits of the season. Murphy and Falchuck display examples from all ends of the political, social, and cultural spectrum to demonstrate that the line between tribe and cult is always thin. Kai's growing group of clown killers and neo-Nazi minions provide only one example of how the hive mind shapes collective consciousness. The show further illustrates how the hive mentality works in recent history with chilling re-creations of the shooting of the artist Andy Warhol by the radical feminist Valerie Solanas in 1968 and the Tate-LaBianca murders carried out by Charles Manson's cult in 1969 ("Valerie Solanas Died for Your Sins Scumbag" 7.7; "Charles Manson in Charge" 7.10).

Kai constructs the hive mind on a foundation of fear and maintains it by stoking more fear. When Winter confesses that she is afraid in the wake of Trump's election, Kai responds with a sinister smile, "Everyone is" ("Election Night" 7.1). Kai says in an address to the city council, "Above all, humans love fear, the fear that, over time, we have honed and polished and built up, brick by brick, until it stands before us every day as tall as the Trump Tower." He expresses his core conviction with the line, "Fear is currency. It has value." Winter displays her own indoctrination by Kai when she teaches Oz, "People are going to believe what they want to believe. The trick is figuring out what they want to believe and giving it to them" ("Don't Be Afraid of the Dark" 7.2).

Fear cultivates the hive mentality by driving people to seek certainty and security in an uncertain and insecure world. Harrison Wilton explains the virtues of the hive mentality to the Mayfair-Richardses as he cares for his own bees while dressed in full beekeeper's garb: "To answer your question from before . . . a hive is the perfect natural community, because every single member of the community is devoted 100 percent to a singular task. There's no arguments, there's no complaints, there's no me. I admire them." Kai combines fear with humiliation to prompt a sense of outrage and entitlement in the minds of the oppressed. He tells Ally, "You see . . . you need to give a humiliated man some way to redeem himself in his own eyes, or else he's at risk to be drawn into darkness, like Germany after World War I." Kai's historical allusion speaks also to the composition of his followers, a collection of misfits and cast-offs who have found meaning in a common messianic delusion.

Ally's collection of phobias serves as a metaphor for all the irrational fears that threaten to control people's lives. Sociopathic narcissists like Kai enjoy the advantage of being free from the fear and self-doubt that more rational human beings experience every day. Like Ally, humans' ability to achieve freedom and flourishing depends on their refusal to let fear dictate their perspectives and choices. Ally's refusal to let fear determine her reality provides the turning point in the middle of the season as she begins her own long game to save her son and defeat Kai.

Empowered Sisterhood

American Horror Story engineers a twist in every season that turns the story in new, surprising directions. That twist emerges in *Cult* as Ally herself leaves an asylum following her arrest for the mass shooting that Meadow actually carried out. Meadow revealed that Ivy was part of Kai's cult, recruited by Winter after their meeting the day before the election and their revenge plot against Gary. Ally's realization that the cult has been playing on her fears using the inside information provided by Ivy liberates her from bondage to those fears. Having recognized that her strings are being pulled and by whom, the puppet now becomes the puppet master. She convinces Kai of her loyalty by revealing a traitor in his cult and joins the cult despite Ivy's objections.

Bebe Babbitt (Frances Conroy) contacts the female members of Kai's cult claiming to be the former lover of the radical feminist Valerie Solanas (Lena Dunham) and warning them not to trust Kai. The horror genre scholar Conny Lippert highlights the way previous seasons put the "American" in *American Horror Story* by focusing on historical events that invoke the traumas afflicting the American psyche, such as slavery, racism, and persecution of the other.[4] The psychic trauma inflicted on women due to misogyny takes a prominent role in *Cult*. The introduction of Solanas highlights a period in the late 1960s when the feminist movement was wrestling with the extent of the reforms women were seeking. Solanas represented the radical fringe of feminism with the publication of her *SCUM Manifesto* in 1967. The *SCUM Manifesto* advanced Solanas's argument that men were responsible for degrading society and that women alone could fix society. Solanas called for the removal of the male sex and the formation of an organization named SCUM to work toward that goal.[5] There were early suggestions that SCUM was an acronym that stood for "Society to Cut Up Men," an allegation that Solanas later denied despite her creation of a *Village Voice* ad that contained the phrase in 1967.[6] Dunham's version of Solanas quotes the manifesto throughout the episode.

SCUM never existed in the real world except in Solanas's imagination. The fictional Bebe Babbitt reveals to Winter, Ivy, and the journalist Beverly Hope (Adina Porter) that an underground movement based on the *SCUM Manifesto* has existed in the world of *American Horror Story* for decades. *American Horror Story* casts a different story for Solanas, focusing on her dread that her attempted murder of Andy Warhol will be her only legacy. This fictional Solanas was responsible for executing the series of murders attributed to the Zodiac killer as a means of destabilizing society. Babbitt plays a double game as she urges the women of the cult to betray Kai while also leading Kai to believe that she is orchestrating the whole scenario for his benefit. The double game becomes a triple one as Ally discovers both plots and uses the conflict to advance her own.

Two themes emerge from the final episodes of *Cult* that continue to resonate throughout all three seasons of *American Horror Story* released during Trump's presidency. Those themes involve the strength of empowered sisterhood and the struggle to break cycles of oppression. Even as the women who betrayed Ally fall to her plan, she cultivates new allies. Ally works with the FBI to bring down Kai and his organization from the inside. Following Kai's arrest, Ally launches a campaign for the Michigan Senate. Kai escapes from jail by seducing a female guard and tries to shoot Ally at a televised campaign event. When he pulls the trigger, Kai realizes that the gun the guard gave him is empty. The guard appears, revealing that she was working with Ally the whole time. Beverly Hope, now Ally's campaign manager, shoots Kai before he can attack Ally. Ally wins the senate seat, in part because she secures a majority of the female vote. In the final segment of the season, Ally tucks Oz into bed as they discuss her victory. When Oz asks her what it means to lead, Ally says, "To take them to a better place, a better world. I want that for you, Oz—a world where you can be a better man than the ones who came before you" ("Great Again" 7.11). She informs Oz that the babysitter will be there with him because she has to go out for a meeting. When he asks whom she is meeting, Ally replies, "A group of powerful, empowered women who want to change the system." Ally returns to her room, where she dons a dark cloak similar to the one Valerie Solanas wore earlier in the season, and leaves for her meeting.

Empowered sisterhood has surfaced as a theme in previous seasons of *American Horror Story*, particularly in the third season, *AHS: Coven*. The specter of a president using flagrant sexist language and accused of multiple accounts of sexual misconduct lent an even greater urgency to this typical *AHS* theme. The women who survive *Cult* manage this feat by overcoming the barriers that men have erected to divide them. They pierce the veil of lies to embrace the truth that their power is found in united sisterhood and that united sisterhood is the thing the men who seek to control them fear the most. This theme returns in seasons 8 and 9.

The final shot of Ally dressed in black poses an ambiguous ending for *Cult*. As the title of the episode says, things seem "Great Again" (7.11). But here the viewer must pause and ponder the question of how one can break cycles of oppression. Has Ally found a means to tame the movement that Valerie Solanas founded and make it a force for good? Will they create a world where men can be better alongside women who strive together with them as their equals? Cycles of oppression have arisen throughout the series as characters abuse one another, only for the abused to return the mistreatment in kind after they finally achieve their own power and agency. Ally has dispensed violent retribution herself to Ivy, Kai, and other members of the cult. The final scene prompts viewers to ask if Ally has found a way to bring balance to all these forces, refusing to return evil for evil and thereby to break the cycle of oppression.

The Trump Era as Apocalypse

American Horror Story returned to form with its eighth season, titled *Apocalypse*. Televised on FX from September 12 to November 14, 2018, *Apocalypse* delivered on a long-standing promise from Ryan Murphy that he would craft a crossover season featuring the casts from the first-season story *Murder House* and the third-season story *Coven*. The resulting story incorporated more *Coven* characters, with the *Murder House* cast making cameo appearances in a couple of episodes. *Apocalypse* centered on the rise of an Antichrist character named Michael Langdon (Cody Fern), whose supernatural conception and birth were shown in *Murder House*. The world is devastated by a nuclear holocaust in the first episode, and the early episodes of the series focus on an eccentric group of survivors who have been given sanctuary in an underground bunker called "the Outpost." A mysterious group known as the "Cooperative" has arranged for the bunker and sends Langdon to determine which of the bunker residents are worthy to be invited to the Cooperative's central bunker, where they can be guaranteed survival.

The twist comes earlier than usual, in episode 3 ("Forbidden Fruit"), when the Supreme of the titular season 3 *Coven*, Cordelia Goode (Sara Paulson), and two of her fellow witches arrive at the Outpost. They resurrect three of the Outpost occupants who have been poisoned by Langdon along with the other occupants. These three women are revealed to be members of Cordelia's coven whose memories were suppressed so that they could infiltrate the Outpost incognito. One of them, Mallory (Billie Lourd), has shown indications through her magical skills that she will be the next Supreme. Mallory's coming ascendancy means that Cordelia will decline until she dies, keeping with the natural process of succession. Her full power will not manifest itself until Cordelia's death. The five witches confront Langdon at the end of the third episode, their conversation indicating that there is a more complex backstory.

That backstory traces Langdon's journey from his childhood with his grandmother Constance (Jessica Lange) to his discovery by a group of

Satanists led by the Church of Satan founder Anton LaVey (Carlo Rota), who appears as a character long after his actual death in 1997. Langdon has come to the attention of the warlocks, who have resented the greater power of the witches' Supreme for centuries. The warlocks believe in the legend of an "Alpha" warlock who will arise with greater power than the Supreme. They attempt to persuade Cordelia that Langdon is the Alpha. Despite Langdon's displays of power, Cordelia senses the evil in him and takes steps to prepare for his rise.

The conflict between the witches and warlocks ignites another battle between masculine and feminine agency in *Apocalypse*. The theme of empowered sisterhood takes on a more supernatural and mystical cast as former rivals among the witches must come together to defeat the greater threat of Michael Langdon. Once the leaders among the male warlocks realize that Langdon is something evil rather than their anticipated Alpha, they join the witches; however, Langdon destroys them, leaving the witches alone to resist on their own. The final battle wages between the witches and Langdon. Mallory attempts a time-travel spell that will take her back to a time before Langdon became strong so that she can prevent his ascent. As the battle continues, Mallory receives a mortal stab wound and teeters on the edge of death before she can complete the spell. Cordelia faces Langdon, who proclaims her failure and savors how much he is going to enjoy watching Cordelia die. Cordelia reaches out magically to draw Langdon's knife from his hand to her own, saying, "You still don't get it, do you? Even now. You think there's only winning and losing, success and failure. But failure is when you've lost any semblance of hope. You will get to watch me die, but you won't find it satisfying. Satan has one son, but my sisters are legion, motherfucker" ("Apocalypse Then" 8.10). Cordelia stabs herself and activates Mallory's full powers as Supreme due to the symbiotic connection between them. Mallory revives as Cordelia dies, and she completes the spell that takes her back in time to kill Langdon before he can achieve his full strength. This moment serves as the emotional climax of the story and illustrates the concept of united empowered sisterhood with the most vivid metaphor possible as Cordelia's personal sacrifice literally feeds the life force of her coven sister.

Mallory achieves a reset of the destructive events that began the season by running over Langdon with a car as Constance watches. Constance allows him to die because she also has witnessed the depths of his evil. Murphy and

Falchuck offer the fantasy of a total reset in which a series of fatal errors are reversed by eliminating a single despotic figure, a tantalizing thought for a United States growing weary of the endless spectacle of Trumpian dysfunction in the second year of his presidency. The haunting coda at the end of the final episode provided a final chilling reminder. Timothy and Emily (Kyle Allen and Ash Santos), two young people who were chosen for the Outpost in the original timeline, are shown meeting and marrying in the newly established timeline. A few years later, Anton LaVey appears again, with the same companions who revealed themselves to Langdon in the original events, to take the couple's child, a child who has displayed psychotically violent tendencies by murdering his babysitter. Murphy and Falchuck allow their fans to imagine a world where the emissary of evil can be overthrown, only to remind them that there is always another emissary of chaos waiting in the wings. The struggle continues. Freedom and flourishing cost those who would enjoy them the responsibility of constant vigilance.

Another Trump-era issue that arises in *Apocalypse* is the influence of tech companies and social media on public discourse. Flashbacks reveal that Langdon has received aid from two tech billionaires, named Jeff Pfister (Evan Peters) and Mutt Nutter (Billy Eichner), who specialize in robotics ("Sojourn" 8.8). The eccentric pair echo traits of Bill Gates and Mark Zuckerberg, representing the pervasive and potentially destructive influence of big tech on politics and society at just the time that new revelations were emerging regarding the role of social media platforms such as Facebook in Russian election interference.[7] Jeff and Mutt sold their souls to Satan. They were awaiting the coming of Langdon and preparing the way by devising the apocalypse plan that devastates the world. All the technical aspects of the plan were theirs, including the creation of the Outpost. Langdon unites their technical prowess with his Satanic minions and the Cooperative, a cover for the mythical Illuminati, to unleash the apocalypse that only the united empowered sisterhood of Cordelia's coven can overcome.

The Trump Era as Reversion

Falchuck and Murphy's ninth season of *American Horror Story* returned to the 1980s from September 8 to November 13, 2019, with the simple title *1984*. The season was presented as a nostalgic return to 1970s and 1980s slasher films such as *Friday the 13th* (Sean S. Cunningham, 1980). Set in a parallel to that film's Camp Crystal Lake, called Camp Redwood, the story follows a group of counselors who are tasked to open Camp Redwood after over a decade of inactivity due to a mass murder carried out by a former camp caretaker named Benjamin "Mr. Jingles" Richter (John Carroll Lynch) in the 1970s. The new director of the camp, Margaret Booth (Leslie Grossman), survived the massacre that night with only the loss of her ear, which alludes to Mr. Jingle's reported fetish for taking the ears of his victims ("Camp Redwood" 9.1). The season begins with a typical 1980s horror plot that shows Jingles escaping from an asylum and engaging in a series of revenge killings at Camp Redwood. The twist for the season occurs in episode 6 ("Episode 100"), which also doubles as the one hundredth episode of the series. Events flash forward to 1989 as the characters from the original 1984 horrors are drawn back to Camp Redwood, where the ghosts of those who were killed there in the past await them. The plots woven throughout the season are resolved in the shadow of an attempt by Margaret to spark renewed killings. Those resolutions occur in violent ways in some cases and in surprisingly redemptive fashion in others. The season magnifies the power of the past to accentuate the characterization of figures in the present, noted by the scholar of horror Rebecca Janicker in her analysis of *Murder House*.[8] Like a series of interlocking Russian dolls, revelations of past events ranging from the early 1970s, 1984, and 1989 provide texture and substance for understanding the complex cast of characters.

1984 appears on the surface to stick to its superficial guise as a campy nostalgia trip. Yet that very nostalgia trip makes a searing political statement. So much of the Trump era exudes 1980s nostalgia, in part because it is supported by a Religious Right whose origins lie in the late 1970s and early 1980s. Though the Trumpian promised land lies in a mythical version of 1950s America, that myth was forged in these later decades with entertainment such as *American Graffiti* (1973) at the movies and *Happy Days* (ABC, 1974–84) on television. The worldview embraced by Trump's most enthusiastic followers adopts the simplified dichotomies of good and evil featured in 1980s entertainment without weighing the cultural and social complexities of the era. Some contemporary Americans of a more conservative bent are invested in the same social, historical, and cultural revisionism in regard to the 1980s that earlier generations performed on the 1950s. Murphy and Falchuck delight in revealing the contradictions of 1980s culture that enlighten, fascinate, and repel at different points.

Leslie Grossman plays Margaret Booth to chilling perfection. Margaret personifies the traumatized survivor who has found faith in Christ and purpose through redeeming the most horrifying experience of her life. She scolds the counselors for their stereotypical sexual promiscuity and partying. Margaret speaks in Religious Right shibboleths from the era:

> I am aware of the decadence of our era: women's underwear that shows the buttocks, pornography in your own home, Van Halen. I have been fighting the Lord's fight against filth around the world for years. Charles Keating is a dear friend. I was right by his side in Cincinnati during that Larry Flynt trial. And that is why, while still grieving my sweet husband Walter's untimely death, I took a small portion of the large fortune he left to me to buy this camp and create a safe, pure, godly, and decent place for the children of this country to escape for the summer. ("Camp Redwood" 9.1)

Charles Keating engaged in antipornography activism, leveraging his platform as a successful attorney and businessman. Appointed by President Richard Nixon to lead the President's Commission on Obscenity and Pornography in 1969, Keating embodied muscular Christianity as a swimming champion who learned to love the sport during his days at Catholic summer camps.[9] Jerry Falwell formed the Moral Majority political action group in 1979 and claimed credit for helping to elect Ronald Reagan as president in 1980.[10] Keating supported the Ohio prosecution of *Hustler* publisher Larry Flynt in 1976 for peddling obscenity, and Falwell later tangled with him as well.[11] Keating was prosecuted for criminal activity himself when he fell under indictment in 1990 and was convicted in 1991 on seventeen counts of conspiracy, fraud, and racketeering in connection with the failure of the Lincoln Savings and Loan Association.[12] The heirs of Keating and Falwell among evangelicals are counted among the strongest supporters of the Trump administration. Complex discussions have intensified in the wake of Trump's election and presidency regarding the sphinx-like character of politicized US evangelicalism, given the widespread support of American evangelicals for Donald Trump.[13] Was evangelical concern always more political and Machiavellian than moral in character? Were evangelicals and other Religious Right groups well intentioned people whose moral crusade was co-opted by their desperation to win? Is it appropriate to speak of "evangelical" as a political category? All of these questions have caused animated debates over religious support for Trump both within Christian circles and outside them. Margaret Booth offers an interesting, though exaggerated, example of the cultural piety that began the 1980s with a crusade for moral reform and ended the decade with a series of high-profile scandals centered around prominent Christian televangelists including Jim and Tammy Faye Bakker, Jimmy Swaggart, and Robert Tilton. Thirty years later, Jerry Falwell's heir and an ardent Trump supporter, Jerry Falwell Jr., would follow in their footsteps with financial and sex scandals of his own.

Margaret's piety runs thin below the surface. She prompts Mr. Jingles to remember that it was her, not him, who slaughtered her fellow campers in 1970. Margaret escapes from the 1984 massacre and establishes a successful business providing horror tours of sites where grisly events happened. Seeing a dip in business, she plans a 1989 concert at Camp Redwood to stimulate renewed interest in the site, hoping that the ghosts or hired serial killers will massacre the attendees ("Episode 100" 9.6). Margaret bills herself as the moral savior of the children who will come to the camp, but she is in reality the monster waiting to destroy both the counselors and kids if given the opportunity.

Empowered sisterhood also plays a role in *1984* as allusions are made to the stereotypical "final girl" of 1980s horror movies. Brooke Thompson (Emma Roberts) assumes the role of the virginal innocent girl at the start of the season, fitting nicely into the general "nice girl survivor" persona of 1980s slasher flicks. A twist ensues when Brooke is framed for the 1984 murders at the camp and sentenced to death by lethal injection. Brooke escapes her execution through the intervention of Dr. Donna Chambers (Angelica Ross), who is trying to make amends for releasing Jingles from the asylum and helping to start the bloodbath in 1984. Brooke and Donna set out for Camp Redwood to stop Margaret from creating another massacre. Brooke's innocence has been tempered by the 1984 massacre and her time in prison. She is determined to kill Margaret and believes that her quest will end as a suicide mission. Donna mentions the trope of the "final girl" and insists that Brooke will be the final girl of this story ("The Lady in White" 9.7).

That conviction wavers for both Donna and the audience when Brooke is shot during a struggle with Margaret. The ghosts of the camp kill Margaret, but Donna believes that Brooke has died as well. In 2019, Mr. Jingle's son, Bobby Richter (Finn Wittrock), contacts Donna as he tries to find his father, who disappeared at the camp in 1989. Bobby has received money from a mysterious benefactor for years and assumed that it was Donna. When Donna confirms that it is not her, they begin a search for the benefactor. They discover that the benefactor is, in fact, Brooke, who was helped by one of the ghosts that night in 1989 and survived her gunshot wound. Brooke tells Bobby that she knew the tendency of the camp to pull people back in who had a connection to it, and she wanted to give him a better legacy because his father inspired her by his efforts to try to move beyond the camp, breaking the cycle of oppression. She apologizes to Donna for not telling her that she had survived. Brooke says, "Donna, I hope someday you can forgive me. We're bonded for life. We're the ones that got away." To which Donna replies, "Yeah. I guess we're both the final girl" ("Final Girl" 9.9). The theme of feminine strength in unity resonates in yet another *AHS* story in a Trump era in which the gains of the women's movements have met challenges in US culture. Brooke and Donna represent the two female characters in *1984* who put their personal rivalries aside for the common good. Their bond as survivors and sisters transcends the barriers of tribe and petty personal differences. Instead of a single survivor, *AHS: 1984* ends with two "final girls" who survive only because they work together.

Breaking Cycles of Oppression

Ryan Murphy and Brad Falchuck ended their first two seasons created after the 2016 election with more ambiguous notes. Viewers hope that Ally has shattered the cycles of oppression to bring real healing in her small part of the world, but the slightest hint of uncertainty lingers. The world is restored after *Apocalypse*, and all seems well with the main characters; but the presence of a budding Antichrist waiting in the wings reminds viewers that the battle between stability and chaos, love and hate, never ends. The ending that the showrunners crafted for *1984* harks back to the hopeful conclusion of *Murder House* by emphasizing the possibility of healing hatreds and restoring broken families.

A complex backstory for Mr. Jingles unfolded when it was revealed that Jingle's mother, Lavinia (Lilly Rabe), worked at the camp when he was a boy. His brother, Bobby, drowned when Jingles was supposed to be watching him. Jingles's mother blamed him and went insane, murdering people at the camp and dying in an aborted attempt to kill Jingles. Jingles returns to the camp in 1989 to protect his infant son from Richard Ramirez (Zack Villa), the infamous "Night Stalker," who in the world of *AHS* becomes a satanically empowered supervillain. Jingles kills himself to gain the ghostly power to defeat Ramirez, confining him to the camp ("Rest in Pieces" 9.8). Jingles's son Bobby, named after his little brother, returns to the camp to find out what happened to his father. He discovers that the ghosts have trapped Ramirez at the camp, and they work to protect Bobby from Ramirez when the Night Stalker tries to escape for one last attempt. Bobby meets his father, his grandmother, and his namesake uncle among the other ghosts. The final scene of the season has Bobby fleeing from the camp as the ghosts hold Ramirez down. The deceased aerobics instructor Montana Duke (Billie Lourd) calls after him, "Get out of here and never come back. But don't forget us. Tell our ghost stories to your children, and we'll live on forever. The '80s will never die" ("Final Girl" 9.9). Bobby looks back when he gets beyond the boundary of the camp to see his family reunited in death and smiling at him, while "The Living Years" by Mike and the Mechanics plays over the closing scene. The cycles of oppression that have haunted the camp and Bobby's own family have been broken. The nostalgia that prompted destructive actions can also inspire acts of forgiveness and charity as people remember the real, historically verifiable, noble aspects of the past.

For all of Ryan Murphy and Brad Falchuck's exploration of the horrors of the human condition, they tend to also create small moments of hope that suggest humans can be better than their worst selves. The reunion of a family fractured by hatred, death, and misunderstanding at the end of *1984* creates a powerful image in an age when Americans are wondering if there is any repairing of the fractured world they are experiencing. While it is more correct to say that Trump's presidency has revealed those fractures in their stark reality and exacerbated them rather than created them, the excesses of his personality and presidency have presented the dysfunctions of the American psyche in their most horrific, exaggerated form. The Trump era resembles *American Horror Story* in that regard. *American Horror Story* amplifies our vices and virtues through exaggerated eccentricity in settings that represent our rawest existential fears. The Trump era has laid bare both the ugliest and the most inspiring realties of US culture and human nature. Can nobler traits such as reconciliation, breaking cycles of oppression, personal sacrifice, and empowered united sisterhood lead us to a better humanity? In keeping with the best conventions of the horror genre, *American Horror Story* reminds that the scariest monsters we must conquer lie within.

Notes

1 Wade Sheridan, "'American Horror Story' Season 7 to Explore 2016 Presidential Election," UPI, February 16, 2017, https://www.upi.com/ Entertainment_News/TV/2017/02/16/American-Horror-Story-Season-7 -to-explore-2016-presidential-election/5521487247178/.

2 Alex Stedman, "'American Horror Story' Season 7 Title, Teaser Revealed," *Variety*, July 20, 2017, https://variety.com/2017/tv/news/american-horror -story-season-7-title-ryan-murphy-1202500519/#.

3 Derek Johnston, "Seasons, Family, and Nation in *American Horror Story*," in *Reading "American Horror Story": Essays on the Television Franchise*, ed. Rebecca Janicker (Jefferson, NC: McFarland, 2017), 45–63.

4 Conny Lippert, "Nightmares Made in America: *Coven* and the Real *American Horror Story*," in Janicker, *Reading "American Horror Story*," 182–99.

5 Breanne Fahs, *Valerie Solanas: The Defiant Life of the Woman Who Wrote SCUM (and Shot Andy Warhol)* (New York: Feminist Press, 2014), 15–24, 100–137.

6 Sharon L. Jansen, *Reading Women's Worlds from Christine de Pizan to Doris Lessing: A Guide to Six Centuries of Women Writers Imagining Rooms of Their Own (New York: Palgrave Macmillan, 2011), 159–60*.

7 Brett Molina, "Facebook and Russian Election Interference: Some Americans Say Facebook Should Be Fined," *USA Today*, February 18, 2018, https://www.usatoday.com/story/tech/news/2018/02/18/robert-mueller -investigation-some-americans-want-facebook-fined-over-meddling/ 349270002/.

8 Rebecca Janicker, "'There's a Power in It. A Power We Can Use': Perpetuating the Past in *Murder House*," in Janicker, *Reading "American Horror Story*," 128–44.

9 Michael Binstein and Charles Bowden, *Trust Me: Charles Keating and the Missing Billions* (New York: Random House, 1993), 77.

10 George Marsden, *Religion and American Culture: A Brief History*, 3rd ed. (Grand Rapids, MI: William B. Eerdmans, 2018), 245–49.

11 Binstein and Bowden, *Trust Me*, 80–98.

12 Robert D. McFadden, "Charles Keating, 90, Key Figure in '80s Savings and Loan Crisis, Dies," *New York Times*, April 2, 2014, https://www.nytimes .com/2014/04/02/business/charles-keating-key-figure-in-the-1980s -savings-and-loan-crisis-dies-at-90.html.

13 John Fea, *Believe Me: The Evangelical Road to Donald Trump* (Grand Rapids, MI: William B. Eerdmans, 2018), 1–42; Thomas Kidd, *Who Is an Evangelical? The History of a Movement in Crisis* (New Haven, CT: Yale University Press, 2019), 144–50.

TEACHING DEMONS AND EATING NAZIS

MORALITY IN TRUMP-ERA FANTASY COMEDY

Hannah Andrews and Gregory Frame

Despite the myriad scandals that dogged his campaign, Donald Trump won the US presidential election in November 2016. From the openly racist remarks Trump made on the campaign trail to the *Access Hollywood* recording in which he bragged about sexually assaulting women while host of *The Apprentice* (NBC, 2004–17), Trump's bad behavior was tacitly accepted (if not endorsed) at the ballot box. That he was not punished in 2016 by electoral defeat is, in keeping with the spirit of the times, shocking but not surprising. Trump's approach to politics and business is underpinned by the (im)moral values of the times in which he has enjoyed his greatest prominence: the age of globalized, neoliberal capitalism. That his aggressive individualism, narcissism, and selfishness were no impediment to securing the presidency suggests the normalization, indeed valorization, of these characteristics in Western societies.

Much of the television fiction that has emerged from this sociopolitical context engages in a liberal backlash to the hardening of the political Right emblematized by Trump's presidency. A significant portion of these shows presents thinly veiled political allegories in alternate realities in shows like *Black Mirror* (Channel 4 / Netflix, 2011–), *The Handmaid's Tale* (Hulu, 2017–), and *The Man in the High Castle* (Amazon, 2015–19). The task of critiquing the moral bankruptcy of the neoliberal political settlement and challenging viewers to reconsider their own ethical standards has fallen to the critically marginalized genres of fantasy and comedy. *The Good Place*

(NBC, 2016–20) and *Santa Clarita Diet* (Netflix, 2017–19) feature sympathetic, albeit flawed characters in fantastical scenarios that require them to consider ethical options carefully and make life changes for the collective good. *Santa Clarita Diet* features a successful, white, middle-class couple, Sheila and Joel Hammond (Drew Barrymore and Timothy Olyphant), whose ordinary lives as suburban realtors are turned upside down when Sheila contracts a mysterious, zombie-like virus and must consume human flesh as her sustenance. With help from their daughter, Abby (Liv Hewson), and her friend Eric (Skyler Gisondo), they conduct an impossible search for sustainable sources of food by eating only victims who "deserve it," a hyperbolic parable of the struggle for ethical consumption. *The Good Place* similarly portrays its protagonists negotiating a morally complex terrain. It tells the story of Eleanor Shellstrop (Kristen Bell), who, having been a selfish, unkind person in life, is sent in error to the Good Place, a paradisiacal afterlife intended only for the most morally deserving. Along with three other souls who do not belong there—the chronically indecisive professor Chidi Anagonye (William Jackson Harper), the depthless socialite Tahani Al-Jamil (Jameela Jamil), and the childlike petty criminal Jason Mendoza (Manny Jacinto)—Eleanor must prove, by engaging with philosophical ethics, that she has the moral fiber necessary to earn her place in heaven.

This chapter explores how these shows handle moral questions and offer them simultaneously as comic narrative material and implicit critiques of the culture from which they emerge. We begin by exploring how the generic frameworks in which the shows are positioned create a space in which contemporary ethics can be interrogated. By analyzing the relationship between comedy and ethics in the shows, we demonstrate how both commonsense morality and metaethical philosophy become the butt of jokes. We then consider how these shows manufacture fantastical situations in which moral dilemmas may be tested, providing a safely sequestered space for ethical experimentation. This develops into an examination of the ways in which both shows engage in specific political critiques. Both shows question the pursuit of instant gratification that characterizes the neoliberal ideal and examine how globalization has created a society where even good behavior can have unintended negative consequences. We conclude with a synoptic example of an issue that persistently arises in both series as the moral pursuit that defines our times: the politics of environmentalism. Ultimately, we argue, both *The Good Place* and *Santa Clarita Diet* offer primers on what constitutes being good in the neoliberal Trump era, confirming that ethics and morals still matter, despite significant evidence to the contrary.

Genre

The Good Place represents an explicit and *Santa Clarita Diet* an implicit examination of contemporary Western morality and its performance (and improvement) under extreme circumstances. As we shall see, the fantasy premises of the shows provide the narrative contexts in which these explorations can take place. But these are also comedies. The comic register of the shows contains their sophisticated analysis of contemporary ethics within an audience-friendly address. Comedy also fulfills its customary ability to comment on the culture from which it emerges. Andrew Stott argues that jokes "emerge from within the social framework and necessarily express the nature of their environment, which means that all jokes are necessarily produced in a relative relationship to the dominant structures of understanding and the epistemological order."[1] In the case of *Santa Clarita Diet* and *The Good Place*, this epistemological order is one in which there is a basic, communal, and commonsense morality. Many of the jokes in these series depend on an unspoken assumption that this broad ethical framework is shared by characters and viewers, even if the protagonists' behavior frequently breaches it. The shows assume a position of social liberalism and tolerance, demonstrated especially, as we will discuss, in their attitudes to environmentalism. Formulating this moral baseline enables these series to satirize it, making fun of the many contradictions in contemporary moral life and our limited ability to live by even rudimentary ethical standards.

In *Santa Clarita Diet*, the Hammonds are carefully framed as epitomizing the average suburban, middle-class family. They are highly invested in their nonexceptionality, attempting to maintain their self-identity as nice people despite their murderous activities. The primary driver of comedy in the show is the absurd contrast between the mundanity of their everyday life and the extremity of their crimes. For example, a moment of slapstick occurs in the opening of "Strange, or Just Inconsiderate?" (1.8) when Sheila and her friend Alondra (Joy Osmanski) have a humorously dull conversation in the kitchen while, through a window in the background, Joel can be seen struggling to move his neighbor's freshly murdered corpse over the fence. Amy Elyse Gordon points out that the Hammonds are motivated by a desire to avoid being "assholes," which she interprets as a healthy regard for their duty to others around them, even when the stakes are relatively low.[2] It also evinces their emotional intelligence and social intuition, which is key to their success as realtors, the frequent butt of jokes in the series (and not only because they comically mispronounce "realtors" every time it is spoken). As Sheila observes, operating successfully as a realtor requires her to be "demure and chipper" ("Pasión!" 2.6), a difficult ask for a woman with newly limited impulse control. The assumption that realtors are nice, normal people is suggested in lines of dialogue such as, "We're realtors, so killing people and stuffing them into freezers doesn't come naturally" ("No Family is Perfect" 2.1). The Hammonds' ordinariness is conceived as synonymous with moral neutrality, enabling a comic contrast to the extraordinary moral and pragmatic choices they are obliged to make.

An equivalent of this insistence on normalcy can be found in *The Good Place* in Eleanor's frequent assertion that she is a "medium person," therefore deserving of a "medium place" in the afterlife. Her desire for moral equilibrium is unsurprising because the level of moral goodness required to gain access to the Good Place is unrealistically high. The points system by which humans are judged is a confusing mixture of metaethical principles. The afterlife architect Michael (Ted Danson) explains in the opening episode of the series that every human action causes "some amount of good or bad" and that the accumulated moral worth of one's actions is used to determine entry into the Good or Bad Place ("Everything Is Fine" 1.1). So far, so utilitarian. However, actions are assigned an absolute points value, implying instead a deontological approach. Bad actions are presented in a comically litotic framing, with minor transgressions, such as "ruin opera with boorish behavior," incurring negative points, though not on the scale of, say, genocide, a points value of −433115.25. When the humans visit the Bad Place, they encounter a museum in which immoral actions on Earth are displayed for the amusement of demons alongside the punishment earned ("The Burrito" 2.11). One of the exhibits is called the Hall of Low Grade Crappiness, which shows actions as trivial as flossing in an open-plan office. Acts of casual thoughtlessness or that are simply annoying, such as "using Facebook as a verb," accumulate negative points that will result in eternal torture. Presenting minor infractions as the making of bad people assumes a shared attitude of mild contempt for these actions, while simultaneously inviting the viewer to recognize and find humor in their own weaknesses.

The idea that the Good Place is populated by those who have "lived the best lives," and that a corrupt motivation for good actions invalidates them, also implies that virtue ethics is in play. Aside from Eleanor, Chidi, Tahani, and Jason, the residents of the Good Place are caricatures of goodness, excessively altruistic and adopting unachievable ethical standards. Eleanor is initially unconvinced that any of the residents are "really that much better" than she is but is dismayed when she meets a lifelong human-rights activist, a land-mine campaigner, and a man who donated both his kidneys to a stranger at the cost of his own life. The requirement of supererogatory actions for access to the Good Place produces a comically large gap between what can reasonably be demanded of ordinary people and what is required to be a good person. It is little wonder, therefore, that the show's favored work of moral philosophy, frequently cited and even used for an episode title (1.6), is T. M. Scanlon's *What We Owe to Each Other*, a work of contractualist ethics that advocates for mutual agreement on ethical rules between rational agents. It is unlikely that in this reasonable scenario we would demand that other people continually risk their own lives in order to save ours. A more likely result is the production of "morally medium" people.

Comedic framings of ethical quandaries are a means to keep the seriousness of these shows' moral economies at a remove from the viewer. Both series also use fantasy premises as a distancing device. As Greta Christina points out, one of the effects of this is to set the moral stakes higher, which is a framework for jokes in the series, particularly the absurd juxtaposition between trivia and eternity that is central to the litotic mode.[3] However, as scholars of fantasy are keen to emphasize, the mode is not entirely separate from reality but is determined by the social context from which it emerges. Fantastic texts cannot help but refer to "reality," whether as its opposite or through metaphorical representation. Indeed, according to scholars of the fantastic, to equate it with an *escape* from reality or to assume that it dupes us into ideological complicity that reinforces structures of power is to mistake its nature. Rather, "by both evoking and disturbing sociocultural verisimilitude, the fantastic . . . is understood to offer new (and potentially subversive) perspectives on society."[4] Rosemary Jackson coins the term "paraxis" to refer to the place of the fantastic next to the "real," implying an inextricable link between them that enables fantasy to "shade and threaten" the real.[5] In these fantasy-comedies, the paraxic link between real and fantasy opens an arena of ethical experimentation, where the hypothetical situations that often arise in moral philosophy can be given narrative expression and greater emotional weight than if they remain merely thought experiments.

The best example of this process in *The Good Place* is in "The Trolley Problem" (2.6). In this episode, Michael is having difficulty with the consequentialist moral philosophy that Chidi teaches the group, because he finds it too obscure. He also notes that the existence of the points system for entry to the afterlife invalidates abstract thinking, because moral behavior is given concrete value. Like many freshman students, he is frustrated by the lack of a right answer to philosophical questions. Unlike these students, he is a powerful demon and capable of literalizing the thought experiment Chidi has given them. This is Philippa Foot's 1967 "Trolley Problem," which questions the morality of switching tracks so that a runaway trolley kills one person, as opposed to taking no action and allowing it to kill five. Michael clicks his fingers, and Chidi suddenly finds himself literally in charge of this trolley. His indecision brings the five people to a grisly death, their viscera spraying him in the face as they violently expire. By turning the problem into a gruesomely verisimilar scenario, Michael demonstrates the real consequences of Chidi's failure to act. The Trolley Problem is an exploration of the moral distinction between killing and letting die. *Santa Clarita Diet*'s version of the same issue plays out in an episode in which the Hammonds' professional rival Christa (Maggie Lawson) has erroneously been identified as a target by the Knights of Serbia, a group ritually committed to the extermination of undead people and the virus that infects them ("We Let People Die Every Day" 3.3). Joel and Sheila quickly realize that they would be morally responsible for Christa's death, even if they are letting her die rather than killing her, an activity that they are, by now, rather practiced at. In both episodes, abstract philosophical scenarios are played out literally, in a brief conceit and as part of a broader narrative arc. Fantasy scenarios provide a testing ground on which philosophical abstraction and real-life morality collide.

In the fantastic premises of these shows, reality is sequestered, kept at a safe remove from the narratives, which take place in an imaginary afterlife or a hyperreal version of a genuine location. Yet reality constantly threatens to resurface in these stories, whether through the flashbacks in *The Good Place* that show the activities of the afterlife residence prior to their deaths or via fleeting dialogical references to extratextual political and social reality. For example, the afterlife's Judge (Maya Rudolph) blames Michael's meddling in human affairs for a range of events that have taken place in recent years, such as Brexit and the seemingly inexplicable success of *The Greatest Showman* (Michael Gracey, 2017; "The Brainy Bunch" 3.2). These unlikely and (it is implied) unwelcome occurrences are the unintended consequences of supernatural intervention. This provides ironic commentary on the strangeness of the Trump-era times. Contemporary reality is so extreme, so perturbing, that only supernatural intervention can truly explain it. Reality is the unconscious of these fantasies, a comedic inversion that enables them to comment effectively on our times.

In *Santa Clarita Diet*, diegetic everyday reality constrains Sheila's undead whims. Her activities put her at risk, since she and Joel are untrained and unskilled as killers, a fact that he frequently remarks on: "Killing people is hard. I used to think that was a good thing" ("Going Pre-med" 2.5). To facilitate their activities, they hire out a storage unit and kit it out with plastic covering and tools, such that Joel remarks that it looks like it is from a "kill-room catalogue." This references another text in which the protagonist carefully and methodically selects and kills his victims: *Dexter* (Showtime, 2006–13). Dexter (Michael C. Hall) is, like Sheila, a "moral" serial killer motivated by an unassailable compulsion to kill but following an ethical code.[6] The Hammonds have nothing as systematic as Dexter's "Code of Harry," a set of guidelines developed by his adopted father for how to select murder victims whose deaths will accomplish more moral good than harm, a broadly utilitarian approach to extrajudicial capital punishment. They do share with Dexter the fact that the moral ambiguity they present to the viewer is "purchased at the price of a complete lack of ambiguity regarding the victims."[7] Like Dexter, Sheila wishes to kill only those who "deserve" it. Here, the generic framing of the series comes into play. *Dexter*'s placement between police drama and thriller enables it to display victims as deserving of their fate: we follow Dexter investigating their crimes, assuring himself and the viewer of their inherent immorality, and only then exacting vigilante "justice."

Such opportunities are not available to the protagonists of *Santa Clarita Diet*, since the comedy-fantasy hybrid does not provide narrative excuses for such detailed exposure of Sheila's victims. Instead, the show experiments with what might constitute moral deviancy sufficient to excuse murder. Examples of Sheila's victims include a homicidal drug dealer, a sexual harasser, a misogynist bully, and a carer who steals from her vulnerable clients, though rejected targets also include a woman who allows her dog to defecate on their lawn and Abby's obnoxious but ultimately harmless school principal. This suggests that the Hammonds' vision of morality broadly aligns with liberal values of gender equality, sexual consent, and care for the community but does not permit them to kill those who merely insult or inconvenience them. Sheila describes her ideal target as a "young, single Hitler" ("We Can Kill People" 1.3). In season 2, the Hammonds find their holy grail: a softball team comprising neo-Nazis. The timing of this discovery in relation to the production history of the show is not accidental. Made in 2018, the episode evokes the alarming rise of the Far Right during the first two years of the Trump presidency in the relative ease with which Sheila finds a sustainable source of "young, single Hitlers." The revitalization of fascist ideology has unexpectedly positive consequences for Sheila as moral serial killer, a paraxic link between the fantasy of the undead in our midst and contemporary political reality, in which moral and cultural polarization is stark and, as it is put in *The Good Place*, there are "Nazis again, somehow" ("Chidi Sees the Time Knife" 3.11).

Politics

Beyond the two shows' comedic treatment of specific elements of the Trump era, *The Good Place* and *Santa Clarita Diet* articulate broader critiques of the corrosion of morality in contemporary politics. As shows produced in the aftermath of the 2008 global financial crisis, they exist in a period in which the system of neoliberal capitalism (low regulation, low tax, debt-fueled consumption, and the fixation with profit at the expense of all else) has come under severe scrutiny but has thus far avoided meaningful structural reform.[8] Instead, both shows contend with a society that has outsourced the ethical quandaries that the system has created to individuals who, largely through their consumer choices and workplace behavior, became responsible for giving neoliberal capitalism a (largely superficial) ethical makeover. In the absence of the reform or replacement of capitalism, individuals and organizations must "self-regulate" to resolve the problems of the market, charging them with the location of ethical solutions within narrow ideological limits. *The Good Place* and *Santa Clarita Diet* therefore explore the struggle to be good—an unselfish, community-minded, ethical citizen-consumer—in a neoliberal society that seems to reward the precise opposite.

Following Sheila's contraction of the mysterious zombie-like virus, she changes into an embodiment of the neoliberal ideal. She is more confident, assertive, and dynamic, tending to her individual needs and desires (initially) without compunction. She survives with next to no sleep, one aspect of our humanity that has thus far remained impervious to "the voraciousness of contemporary capitalism."[9] Unburdened by conventional human weaknesses, Sheila is better placed to become a risk-taking, self-motivated entrepreneur. Sheila's transformation speaks to the impact that neoliberalism has had on the human nervous system. As Mark Fisher argues, neoliberalism demands of us a capacity to respond to unforeseen events and live in conditions of total instability.[10] Joel laments the sudden imposition of precarity on their previously stable and simple middle-class lives and consistently expresses frustration when his plans—eating out, getting a haircut, or building his own bookshelves—are derailed. He expresses their continuous dilemma thus: "Our life is precarious. Every day, we're one mistake away from losing everything" ("Knighttime" 3.2), giving voice to a fundamental truth for most of society under neoliberal capitalism. Yet Sheila's obligations to her family mean she is unable to give in to her neoliberal id entirely.

Sheila therefore remains tethered to society, seeking to protect her daughter from the violence that she must now undertake to survive, and through Joel's efforts to uncover the origin of her illness, she seeks to prevent the disease from spreading. In order for Sheila to compensate for the ethical disruption she has caused her family and wider society, she devotes some time to pursuing superficially selfless activities. In volunteering for Meals on Wheels, which brings hot food to the old and infirm, she performs a conventional aspect of neoliberal selfhood: an apparently altruistic act that functions as a salve for her conscience. As Jean says, "You think you can come and help an old lady three days a week and do whatever you want the rest of the time" ("Belle and Sebastian Protect the Head" 3.5). Sheila also learns to manage her impulses over the course of the series. From buying a Range Rover and murdering a colleague who sexually harasses her in the first episode, she gradually masters self-discipline and denial. *Santa Clarita Diet* articulates a struggle commonly endured: the pursuit of a neoliberal ideal that demands of us actions, choices, and behaviors that could potentially alienate or destroy other aspects of human life for which we yearn. This valorization of family, community, and stability represents a riposte to neoliberalism's prioritization of self-interest whatever the cost.

The Good Place is more explicit in its articulation of the impossibility of consistent moral goodness in the neoliberal era. In season 3, Michael discovers that nobody has been admitted to the Good Place in 521 years ("Janet(s)" 3.9). This is because, under capitalism, even the choices people make with good intentions eventually have negative consequences: for example, the flowers you purchase for your mother have been picked by slave labor and flown halfway around the world, poisoning the atmosphere. Michael realizes that when humans think they are making one choice, they are actually making dozens of unconscious choices. Even Doug Forcett (Michael McKean), the person who most accurately described the Good Place in a drug-induced hallucination while on Earth and subsequently led his life according to a very strict ethical code, is likely to end up in the Bad Place. Doug's relentless focus on his carbon footprint and absurd self-sacrifice to preserve mere shreds of happiness in others is revealed to be inadequate ("Don't Let the Good Life Pass You By" 3.8). *The Good Place* thus satirizes the "folk-political" responses to neoliberalism that advocate a retreat into the local, organic, and authentic as a means of resisting its overwhelming force.[11] It exposes the confidence trick at neoliberalism's heart: the production of ethical subjects who believe they are helping to ameliorate the worst effects of capitalism by self-regulating their personal and consumer behavior. In condemning all humans to the Bad Place despite the best intentions of some of them, *The Good Place* reveals that even the willingness and desire to make ethical choices is inadequate against the social and environmental wreckage wrought by neoliberalism.

Environmentalism as a moral cause is a motif that preoccupies both shows and therefore represents a useful means by which to synthesize the debates we have explored in this chapter. Discourses of sustainability and ethical consumption are understood in *The Good Place* and *Santa Clarita Diet* as straightforwardly correct. References to environmentally conscious attitudes are common and fleeting, visible for example in recurring jokes about Chidi's agony over his use of unsustainable almond milk or Joel's fixation with his family's carbon footprint. The characters' concern for environmental issues speaks to the way responsibility for managing and overcoming the climate emergency has been outsourced from the corporate entities that are most responsible for it to individuals who are looking to effect ethical reform of neoliberal capitalism. Even the term "carbon footprint" was popularized by BP as part of a 2005 public-relations campaign designed to distract consumers from its lack of progress on environmental issues, as well as to shift the impetus for change from the corporate to the individual level.[12] These worries speak to Peter Bloom's suggestion that neoliberalism has consolidated its power by convincing citizens to assume moral and ethical responsibilities that will ultimately help the industries that are most culpable for environmental damage to avoid accountability for it.[13] Despite this, environmentalism represents the political unconscious of both shows, particularly in their insistence on showing the damage that the individual's selfish or inconsiderate actions can have on their immediate surroundings. As products of the Trump era, in which the effects of ecological breakdown are accelerating and Trump, as president, led the United States to withdraw from global efforts to address its causes and consequences, these shows engage with these issues in both their fantastical and realist registers.

In *Santa Clarita Diet*, Joel's concern for the environment evinces itself as metaphor through his determination to ensure the undead disease does not spread. He locates its origins in a batch of infected clams that he and Sheila aim to destroy (although ultimately it is not they who succeed in doing so but the Knights of Serbia). The intention to use the undead infection as a metaphor for the wreckage that human activity has caused to the environment is signaled in the very first episode, as Eric observes drily, "We're the real zombies: consuming everything we want, regardless of consequences" ("So Then a Bat or a Monkey" 1.1). *The Good Place* develops this aspect of its critique in more detail, with immediate environmental impacts as the result of personal indiscretion used as a metaphor for global climate change. As Eleanor seeks to disguise the fact she does not belong in the Good Place in the show's first few episodes, the consequences of her presence reveal themselves in a series of catastrophes that beset the neighborhood: flying shrimp, a giant frog and ladybug, and huge, rampaging giraffes that wreak chaos and destruction. When she later abandons the cleanup task that she and Chidi have volunteered for in favor of the more enjoyable activity of flying, the garbage rains from the sky. When she destroys a cake to distract everyone before Jason reveals himself also to be a fraud, a giant sinkhole opens up, a common consequence of the environmental damage caused by fracking. The environmental chaos caused by Eleanor's presence, and her surly attitude to cleaning up the neighborhood, echoes her rudeness to the environmental activist she encountered outside the supermarket immediately before she died. Eleanor's hostility toward environmental concerns is the most extreme example of her thoughtlessness and lack of care for the people around her, though there are many others. In her relentless pursuit of her own gratification, the show is at pains to construct Eleanor as representing the kind of selfishness that is characteristic of the neoliberal era and its "reification of conventionally morally castigated values of greed and even gluttony."[14] When Eleanor is returned to Earth, becomes a vegetarian, and volunteers at the environmental organization of which she had been so dismissive, these changes are used as an index of her moral growth. In her concern for a cause bigger than herself, Eleanor begins to prove her moral virtue.

While Joel and Sheila are environmentally conscious at a superficial level in their everyday life, Abby takes a more direct approach. Inspired by her mother's increased boldness and in her desire to do something "more intense than a tweet," Abby undertakes to sabotage a fracking site that is being developed close to Santa Clarita. In so doing, she unwittingly becomes an ecoterrorist, which she only realizes later by the presence of the FBI investigating the explosion. Whereas environmentalism had previously been an unspoken moral anchor for the series, in this action, it becomes the justification for extrajudicial activity. Fracking is an assault on the environment seemingly equivalent to the overt and comically exaggerated badness of Sheila's victims, such that the show tacitly approves of Abby's extralegal remedy for it. Neither her parents nor, it is presumed, the viewer offer a genuine reproach to Abby for these actions. The suggestion is that she has retained the moral high ground and acted for her community, rather than illegally vandalized private property (the sanctity of which remains an ideological totem of US capitalism). Not only this, but her protest works, and the fracking company disbands from the area. The show thus provides moral justification and implied support for direct action in a way that is quietly radical. The fantasy premises of these shows set the moral stakes higher than a social realist program may, but they do not abandon a sense of the increased urgency of ethical issues in contemporary sociopolitical life. This manifests itself in presenting care for the environment as an ever-present moral imperative that cannot be avoided and a responsibility that can no longer be shirked.

Conclusion

As the seasons of *The Good Place* and *Santa Clarita Diet* progress, references to extratextual sociopolitical reality become more regular and more pointed.

It is tempting to view this as a direct response to the daily assault on everyday morality coming from the Trump White House. From climate-change denial to tolerance of neo-Nazism to alleged collusion in foreign election tampering, breaches of generally accepted ethics became regular occurrences at the top of US politics in the Trump era. The response of these morally focused shows has been a more overt exploration of the complexities and contingencies of ethical decision-making in daily life. It is no accident that the third season of both shows invests narrative energy in a specific exploration of the meaning of morality for their protagonists. Produced in 2018–19, the middle of Trump's term, their critique of selfish, short-termist, or unethical behavior becomes more urgent. By *The Good Place*'s fourth season, a thinly veiled avatar for Trump is introduced to an experimental neighborhood, designed to test whether the human capacity for moral growth invalidates the afterlife's points system. Brent (Benjamin Koldyke) is an entitled, condescending, bigoted businessman with no self-awareness, and his chances of ethical improvement seem laughably slim.

Despite the shows' obvious intentions to critique the moral vacuum at the heart of capitalistic ideology, though, *Santa Clarita Diet* and *The Good Place* reveal themselves to be implicated inevitably in the structures of neoliberalism itself. The Hammonds' answer to Sheila's inability to tolerate her sexist boss, who is unable to recognize her worth or respect her opinions, is not to address these institutional issues but to extricate themselves from them by creating their own company. Operating precisely within the ethical framework of neoliberalism, the Hammonds become entrepreneurs. This inability to escape the neoliberal imaginary is also illustrated by the points system in *The Good Place*. In its visualization as akin to stocks and shares, it is realized as a capitalistic metaphor, with points earned through good deeds and lost through bad ones, a system underpinned by a machinery of confounding accountancy represented in season 3. There is no doubt that in its ethos of "loyalty, love and empathy" ("Employee of the Bearimy" 4.5), *The Good Place* seeks to offer an alternative to the ruthless individualism and selfishness advocated by neoliberalism, but its prescription for the cure ultimately reinforces Bloom's argument that neoliberalism has so successfully convinced us of its permanence and immutability that it is up to us to "self-regulate" to resolve the problems of the market.[15] As Jim McGuigan suggests, under neoliberalism, "individuals are now compelled to make agonistic choices . . . and also they are required to take sole responsibility for the consequences of their choices."[16] *The Good Place* takes this to an extreme conclusion by suggesting that failure to be good at a personal level results in eternal damnation. By individualizing the struggle through the stories of Eleanor, Chidi, Tahani, and Jason and their attempts to save their own souls, *The Good Place* reinforces neoliberalism's creation of ethical subjects. Obliging individuals to take personal responsibility enables neoliberalism to avoid accountability for the economic and social damage it has caused and to perpetuate itself.

Fantasy and comedy have been theorized as imbuing texts with an enhanced ability to comment on the society and culture from which they derive. Their combination in *The Good Place* and *Santa Clarita Diet* enables these series to represent a search for moral rightness in a context in which it has been all but abandoned by the controlling elite. The fantastical premises of these series allow them to incorporate moral questions at the heart of their narratives, and though we are invited to laugh at the moral quandaries faced by these characters, they are never treated as trivial or meaningless. The shows address an audience that is presumed to share the care that these characters show to each other and the world around them. Despite these shows' failure to suggest an alternative to or escape from the neoliberal trap, they invoke the moral intuitions of their audience to present a determined critique of a political leadership that depends on a populace that is indifferent, distracted, and confused. In doing so, they represent relief to an immoral political culture, providing an optimistic balm for the despair that it can engender.

Notes

1   Andrew Stott, *Comedy* (Abingdon, UK: Routledge, 2005), 10.

2   Amy Elyse Gordon, "*Santa Clarita Diet* and Moral Imperfectionism," *Prindle Post Online*, April 30, 2019, https://www.prindlepost.org/2019/04/santa-clarita-diet-and-moral-imperfectionism/.

3   Greta Christina, "Pop Culture and Suspension of Disbelief: *The Good Place*," *Humanist* 78, no. 2 (2018): 38.

4   Catherine Johnson, *Telefantasy* (London: BFI, 2005), 8.

5   Rosemary Jackson, *Fantasy: The Literature of Subversion*, 2nd ed. (London: Routledge, 2003).

6   Simon Riches and Craig French, "The Ethics of a Serial Killer: Dexter's Moral Character and the Justification of Murder," in *Dexter: Investigating Cutting Edge Television*, ed. Douglas L. Howard (London: I. B. Tauris, 2010).

7   David Schmid, "The Devil You Know: *Dexter* and the 'Goodness' of American Serial Killing," in Howard, *Dexter*, 139.

8   Peter Bloom, *The Ethics of Neoliberalism* (Abingdon, UK: Routledge, 2017), 19.

9   Jonathan Clary, *24/7: Late Capitalism and the Ends of Sleep* (London: Verso, 2014), 10.

10 Mark Fisher, *Capitalist Realism: Is There No Alternative?* (Ropley, UK: O Books, 2009), 34.

11 Nick Srnicek and Alex Williams, *Inventing the Future: Postcapitalism and a World without Work* (London: Verso, 2016), 11.

12 William Safire, "Footprint," *New York Times Magazine*, February 17, 2008, https://www.nytimes.com/2008/02/17/magazine/17wwln-safire-t.html; Gregory Solman, "BP: Coloring Popular Opinion," *Adweek*, January 14, 2008, https://www.adweek.com/brand-marketing/bp-coloring-public-opinion-91662/.

13 Bloom, *Ethics of Neoliberalism*, 74.

14 Bloom, 9.

15 Bloom, 48.

16 Jim McGuigan, "The Neoliberal Self," *Culture Unbound* 6 (2014): 237.

FIRST AS FARCE, THEN AS TRAGEDY

THE HILARIOUS NIHILISM OF THE TRUMP-INFLUENCED FINAL SEASON OF *VEEP*

Michael Mario Albrecht

The first line that Selina Meyer utters in the recap of previous seasons that introduces the seventh and final season of *Veep* (2012–19) is, "I hate this country." Meyer, portrayed masterfully by Julia Louis-Dreyfus, began the first season of the show as the titular "veep," who has over the course of the first six seasons run three unsuccessful campaigns for president, although briefly ascending to the office due to a presidential scandal. She was not reelected. In several moments in "Iowa," the seventh season's premiere, Meyer offers nihilistic lines that give insight into the writers' thinking in the final season, the only one written after Donald J. Trump was elected president of the United States. Meyer is writing a speech to kick off her fourth presidential campaign in Iowa and soliciting from her staff answers to the question of why she should want to run for president. For the first six seasons of the show, Meyer has represented an empty vessel who is adept at reciting platitudes without substance, but sincerity eludes her. When she asks a staff member sincerely why she would want to be president, the staff member quips (perhaps sarcastically), "So I could nuke America." Meyer responds, "That's actually not bad." At another point in the episode, she remarks, "This entire country is getting more disgusting by the second."

If the first six seasons of the show found their humor in the absurdity of the political system, season 7 takes a much more nihilist turn that reflects satire reaching its limits of critique. *Veep* was never an optimistic show, and its titular lead was an insipid, vapid, power-hungry politician who had a less-than-thinly-veiled disdain for her constituents; and yet her character seems downright likable compared to the man who won the White House in 2016.

In this chapter, I situate *Veep* within discussions of satire that have emerged in the past twenty years and ultimately suggest that the Trump era has offered a challenge for traditional satirical strategies. *Veep* ran up against the limits of satire in its final season and ultimately took a dark and nihilist turn in the era of Donald J. Trump. In *Political Satire, Postmodern Reality, and the Trump Presidency*, the political scientist Mehnaaz Momen notes that "the rise of Trump in the political world and the prioritization of entertainment in the media reflect similar trends where the retrospective political and cultural theaters value performance over any other values, and real issues become swamped in the celebration of ritualistic and symbolistic gestures. We are more aware yet more helpless, boxed in by the paradoxes and bolstered by postmodernism."[1] Alan Kirby takes it a step further and suggests that the tenets of postmodernism have collapsed, providing us with a framework of the "apparently real," which "affords an intensity of 'reality' which is greater and more engulfing than any other, including unmediated experience."[2] If postmodernism still allowed a space for critique, the digimodernist collapse allows no such space. The first six seasons of *Veep* offered a horrific, nihilistic version of politics that served as satirical hyperbole in the context of a Washington that exhibited only some of those qualities. Upon the election of Donald J. Trump, any notion that the nihilism was hyperbolic became absurd, as the truth of the nihilist impulses of Trump and his supporters was greater than any plot that the writers of *Veep* could imagine.

When *Veep* premiered on HBO in April 2012, Selina Meyer, who had run for president and lost in the primaries, was handpicked for the vice president position because she was nonthreatening. In the show's first season, she and her staff in the VP office are always hoping to get a meeting with the president and rarely achieving their aim. The joke is that the vice presidency is a powerless job, and Meyer treats it with the utmost disdain. The cast comprises a motley crew of power-hungry Washington insiders with foul mouths and dubious ethics, and Meyer reigns supreme as the most power-hungry, foul-mouthed, and ethically dubious member of the bunch. For six years, the writers and showrunner worked to create a politician and staff whose vulgarity and disregard for ethical or political norms was so over-the-top as to be unbelievable; its humor relied on satire by hyperbole. When Donald Trump was elected, Selina Meyer not only was entirely believable but seemed tame in comparison to the president of the United States. Any hyperbole that once existed was rendered moot. In an April 2017 *New York Times* article, Mike Hale notes that *Veep* had to pull some jokes from season 6 (which was written and filmed before Trump was elected but aired after his inauguration) because they were too close to some actual rumors about a potential Trump scandal. Specifically, the show pulled some urine jokes because of the rumors of Trump's dalliances with watersports alleged in the Steele Dossier. Hale laments that "when real life exceeds some of the show's most over-the-top imaginings, it also takes some of the life out of the show's satire."[3] I would be more specific and suggest that *Veep*'s satire relies on hyperbole. When an administration refuses to allow writers to imagine a politician whose actions would be "over-the-top," then hyperbolic satire can no longer function.

Selina Meyer embodies the out-of-touch politician dripping with disdain for the average American. She concisely sums up her reason for being in office and her relationship to her constituents in "Election Night" (4.10), the finale of season 4: "You do your best. You try to serve the people, and then they just fuck you over. And you know why? Because they're ignorant and they're dumb as shit. And that, ladies and gentlemen, is democracy." In 2015, that kind of disdain for the people from a politician seemed so beyond the pale as to be obvious satire. In the era of Trump, the hyperbole was no longer self-evident, as Trump regularly seemed to exhibit that kind of disdain. After the Nevada caucuses in 2016, Trump gloated about winning with the "poorly educated" and then quipped, "We love the poorly educated."[4] He provided demeaning nicknames to his political opponents, labeled the press as "fake news" and "enemies of the people," and suggested that a journalist might be angry due to her menstrual cycle when she challenged him during a debate.[5] Selina Meyer loses her edge when juxtaposed with Trump's crassness. For *Veep*'s first six seasons, the show was able to sustain its momentum by consistently showing the myriad hypocrisies of Washington politics and the frustrating patterns through which those with the most questionable ethical frameworks often reach the greatest heights. As Michael Young explains, "When *Veep* first aired in 2012 we were initially afforded the chance to laugh at the inane workings and missteps of a warped version of the American body politic with a casual and dismissive cheek-iness. The show was funny because things couldn't really [be] that bad in Washington, so it was ok to laugh at the foibles of the characters who were running the country."[6] However, everything changed on November 8, 2016, when a character won the election who was arguably more incompetent, less empathetic, and more contemptible than even the brilliant writing team at *Veep* could have created.

Satire and Politics

In *Strange Bedfellows*, an examination of late-night comedy, Russell Peter-son notes that "satire nourishes our democracy."[7] This is a bold claim about the power of comedy, but it is one shared by others. In "The State of Satire, the Satire of State," Jonathan Gray, Jefferey P. Jones, and Ethan Thompson explain further: "Political comedy, satire, and parody all provide important narrative critiques that enable democratic discourse and deliber-ation. Satire's lessons often enable people—as an audience, a community, a polity—to recognize the naked emperor and, through their laughter, begin to see realities that have been obscured. In that regard, satire provides a valu-able means through which citizens can analyze and interrogate power and the realm of politics rather than remain simple subjects of it."[8] For Gray et al., satire makes manifest an underlying reality that political discourse hides. In the case of *Veep*, the characters exhibit the qualities of political characters not to the letter but to the extreme; as such, the terrible characteristics that pervade Washington become easily identifiable when they exist as carica-tures of their "real-life" counterparts.

Anshuman Mondal provides a framework for thinking about the rela-tionship between satire and democracy. In "Taking Liberties?," he explains that satire is a certain kind of performance that is "above all a moral performance, one based on the distance between things as they are and as they *should be*."[9] In this schema, the satirical humor of *Veep* (at least for its first six seasons) came from our knowing that the show presented things as they *should not be* and its offering the possibility of imagining a better world by *not* following the example set by Selina Meyer, her staff, or really anyone else on the show. That distance provided the conditions of possibility for satire to meaningfully effect change in democracy. In a Panglossian endorsement of a functioning demo-cratic system, Russell Peterson notes that "democracy depends on the devotion of its followers to sustain it. Some of the people, some of the time, must keep on believing that our electoral choices matter, that if we speak out our voices must be heard, that our representatives truly represent our interests."[10] *Veep* may have had a nugget of that optimism, even though it showed the world as it should not be in order to convey it.

The later Bush and Obama years were in fact halcyon days for folks who believed in the power of satire to effect change in a democracy, and *Veep* premiered in the midst of this heyday. However, these salad days of satire were preceded by the events of September 11, 2001, after which many pundits prophesized that the attacks would bring about the end of irony and would usher in a new age of sincerity. Two weeks after the attacks of 9/11, Roger Rosenblatt penned a famous article for *Time* magazine titled "The Age of Irony Comes to an End." He begins the piece by gloating, "One good thing could come from this horror: it could spell the end of the age of irony. For some 30 years—roughly as long as the Twin Towers were upright—the good folks in charge of America's intellectual life have insisted that nothing was to be believed in or taken seriously. Nothing was real."[11] Rosenblatt can barely contain his glee that the "chattering class," with their "giggles and smirks," will no longer have irony at their disposal as a tool to look down on the "slobbering bumpkins" who might actually believe in something sincerely.[12] For Rosenblatt and many other critics, the gravity of 9/11 was so enormous as to erase decades in which irony and satire had pervaded as a primary mode of engagement, not only for comics but also for the culture writ large. In the immediate wake of the 9/11 attacks, late-night comics suspended production, *Saturday Night Live* (NBC, 1975–) broadcast only reruns, and even *The Onion* ceased creating new content.

Once comics started producing content again, they were careful to tread lightly, and those who failed to read the country's temperature were under censure. As David Gurney contends in his essay "Everything Changes Forever (Temporarily)," "the boundaries of acceptable discourse were tightened and vehemently policed post-9/11, and even the imitation of transgression became unacceptable."[13] Gilbert Gottfried was booed at a Friars Club roast of Hugh Heffner for making a joke about the 9/11 attacks, and Bill Maher was famously fired from his ABC show *Politically Incorrect* (1993–2002) for suggesting that participating in suicide bombing was braver than launching missiles from remote locations. However, in *A Decade of Dark Humor*, an investigation of humor after 9/11, Ted Gournelos and Viveca Greene suggest that, while in the days immediately following 9/11 speech was heavily policed, satirical comedy was one of the ways that people were able to negotiate the post-9/11 political and media landscape. In their introduction to the edited collection, Gournelos and Greene maintain that "humor, irony, and satire were not only shaped *by* 9/11 and its aftermath, but were also pivotal in shaping responses to the events—especially as their practitioners combated the foreclosure and silencing of discourse and (re)opened and reinvigorated an active, contested public sphere."[14]

Published two years before the election of Donald J. Trump, Sophia McClennen and Remy M. Maisel's *Is Satire Saving Our Nation* became dated almost as soon as it was published. At the height of satire activism, they are extraordinarily optimistic about the possible ramifications for satire in a strong and vibrant democracy. Focusing on the period between 2001 and 2014, they maintain that "satire emerged as one of the strongest voices of critical thought and democratic deliberation. With its witty mix of humor, critical thinking, and speaking truth to power, satire transformed our withering democracy into a robust *demockracy*."[15] McClennen and Maisel trace the period emerging in the wake of September 11, paying particular heed to the rise of Jon Stewart and Stephen Colbert. They are especially interested in the ways in which these comics were able to create more active engagement in democratic citizenry through their programs. The authors point to Stewart's work on Capitol Hill with 9/11 first responders; Colbert's Super PAC, Americans for a Better Tomorrow, Tomorrow; Colbert's appearance before Congress; and their joint "Rally to Restore Sanity and/or Fear" at the National Mall. For McClennen and Maisel writing in 2014, "Satire is saving our nation. It is correcting the misinformation of the news, holding politicians accountable, and helping reframe citizenship in ways that productively combine entertainment and engagement."[16] As quaint as their argument may have seemed in the Trump era, and as vitriolic as *Veep* was from the beginning, it did emerge in the cultural milieu in which political satire not only was widely prolific but was seen as effecting change in democracy. *Veep* may have been the most cutting of the political satires of the time, but it still resonated with a host of other political satires, some of which scholars were confident were saving the nation.

Veep ran conterminously with the Netflix show *House of Cards* (2013–18), which featured another power-hungry Washington insider who would do anything for power. In a *Pod Save America* podcast, Obama-era staffers interview *Veep*'s season 5 showrunner David Mandel, and in their conversation, they confide that they feel *Veep* is more realistic than either *House of Cards* or the Bush-era political drama *The West Wing* (NBC, 1999–2006).[17] Ironically, even before the Trump era, the Washington insiders found *Veep*, a show that obviously relies on comic hyperbole, to have more verisimilitude than shows that rely on dramatic realism.

Satire in which reality and performance might be confused was widely used as a source of comic material in the years between 9/11 and the Trump era. Michael Moore, Sacha Baron Cohen, Stephen Colbert, and the Yes Men, culture-jamming tricksters who use elaborate pranks to show the contradictions of corporate culture and media oligopoly, regularly tried to confuse their target to make a political point during this period. The savvy viewer was in on the joke, and the satire emerged from the ironic distance between who these men purported to be and who they actually were. In *Satire and Dissent*, an analysis of this form of satirical comedy, Amber Day warns of the danger inherent in this kind of performance. For Day, "They are always potentially threatening to their targets in that their parodic send-ups, satiric attacks, and ironic impersonations run the risk of becoming definitely real—of actually tripping up, revealing, or sabotaging. As performative satire, these forms have the potential to bring into being precisely that which they name or enact."[18] While *Veep* obviously operates in a different register from the vérité style of Moore or Cohen or the direct spoof performance of Colbert, watching the final season of *Veep*, one wonders if the writers felt as though they had brought into being that which they had named and enacted. The digimodernist style allows for *Veep* to circulate as if it were in the register of documentary and provides a framework for thinking about how the final season functions differently from the first six.

Digimodernism

Alan Kirby suggests that a new era of digimodernism (a term he coined) has emerged that represents as profound a paradigmatic shift as the one between modernism and postmodernism. In *Digimodernism*, he provocatively suggests, "Since its first appearance in the second half of the 1990s under the impetus of new technologies, digimodernism has decisively displaced postmodernism to establish itself as the twenty-first century's new cultural paradigm."[19] Digimodernism reflects the media shifts that have characterized the end of the 1990s and the first two decades of the twenty-first century, particularly those that have moved media involvement from the eyes to the hands. Kirby explains that digimodernism, "properly understood as a con- traction of 'digital modernism,' is a pun: it's where digital technology meets textuality and text is (re)formulated by the fingers and thumbs (the digits) clicking and keying and pressing in the positive act of partial or obscurely collective textual elaboration."[20]

One characteristic that Kirby ascribes to differentiate digimodernism from postmodernism is the notion of the "apparently real." For him, the postmodern model suggests that distinctions between the real and the con- trived are collapsed and that this distinction and collapse overflows with profundity. The apparently real "proffers what seems to be real . . . and that is all there is to it. The apparently real comes without self-consciousness, with- out irony, or self-interrogation, and without signaling itself to the reader or viewer. Consequently, for anyone used to the refinement of postmodernism, the apparently real may seem intolerably 'stupid': since the ontology of such texts seems to 'go without saying,' more astute minds may think they cry out for demystification."[21] If parody requires a distance between the said and the unsaid for both its humor and its social critique, then the digimodernist text is removing that distance.

When Fredric Jameson famously explained and lamented the prolifer- ation of postmodern texts in the 1980s, he went to great lengths to differen- tiate between true satire and pastiche, the latter of which would be the mark of postmodernism. According to Jameson, in the postmodern world of the 1980s, "parody finds itself without a vocation; it has lived, and that strange new thing pastiche slowly comes to take its place. Pastiche is, like parody, the imitation of a peculiar or unique, idiosyncratic style, the wearing of a linguistic mask, speech in a dead language."[22] However, for scholars like Jameson, agonizing over the difference between the parodic and the pastiche was a worthwhile endeavor. The digimodernist notion of the "apparently real," in which the real and the constructed exist on the same plane and that collapse does not register as profound, is what is novel about the new era.[23] If *Veep* did call into being Trump, that interpolation similarly is not profound, because everything exists in a digimodernist plane—distinctions between reality shows, scripted shows, "serious" presidents, and reality-TV presi- dents have all collapsed. That distinction between the parodic and the pas- tiche that Jameson was so concerned about no longer matters, as everything holds the same ontological status in the realm of the apparently real. If parody relies on a gap between the world as it should be and the world as it is for its effect, it loses any edge when divisions between those worlds collapse.

In "After Politics / After Television," Joe Conway draws on Kirby's notion of digimodernism to describe shows like *Veep*, which "enshrines 'the apparently real' as its dominant aesthetic."[24] He explains that digimodernist texts "mimic nonfictional forms to project a world that *is* just as it *appears*."[25] In so doing, he aims to differentiate the digimodern from the postmodern: "While postmodern texts gesture to some historical consciousness through ironic techniques of pastiche or parody, the digimodernist text operates as if there has never been any time except for the immediately streaming now." Conway suggests that digimodernist texts allow for both the neo-vérité style of shows like *The Office* (NBC, 2005–13) and *Parks and Recreation* (NBC, 2010–15), and what he refers to as the "neo-Shakespearean camp" of shows like *Veep* and *House of Cards*.[26] In all of these cases, Conway points to a relationship between the text and its audience that no longer requires an ironic distance. The characters on those shows are always looking directly at the viewer, and the viewer is positioned as being in the show rather than viewing it from afar. The viewer is positioned as part of the assumed documentary that is already in progress and consequently part of the digimodernist media landscape. For Conway, any space for critical critique that might have been made possible by the ironic space that satire allowed is stifled in the digimodernist text as the distance between the text and the viewer collapses.

Conway dubs this new form "satire vérité" and maintains that "one of the political consolations of satire vérité, it seems, is that its anti-aesthetic aesthetic allows viewers accustomed to the hypermediated spectacle of government to experience fictional political events in an apparently real, apparently depoliticized way, as if they were glimpsed for the very first time."[27] For Conway, the complete absurdity and incompetence of all of the players on *Veep*—the politicians, staff, voters—amount to a depoliticized absurdity. He laments that "the only 'real' of the world that *Veep* is able to either visualize or verbalize seems to be an obscene and scatological one."[28] He closes the article by following Kirby's logic, suggesting that any gap between parody and pastiche is meaningless in a digimodernist mediascape. For him, "digimodernist dystopia is one where the knowing pastiches and parodies of postmodernism cease to register because they require a broad foundation of past cultural knowledge that has been leveled into nonmeaning."[29]

Conway was writing in 2016, before Donald J. Trump was elected and before the final season of *Veep* was conceived. I am not necessarily sure I agree with his assessment of seasons 1 to 6 of *Veep*, but his analysis is prescient and spot-on for season 7. If the first six seasons of *Veep* were dystopic, the final season was downright nihilistic.

The Nihilism of Season 7

An article in *Variety* that was published two episodes before the finale of *Veep* seems myopically naïve in light of how the finale turned out. In "How the Trump Era Wrecked *Veep*," Daniel D'Addario explains that "*Veep* used to sit somewhat astride the politics of the time. Now, chasing currency, it's become a product of them, filled with a gross loathing that's available just about anywhere else."[30] D'Addario is correct that *Veep* used to avoid politics in the sense that Selina Meyer is decidedly centrist; she hates taking any position for fear that it might alienate potential voters. Rather, for the first six seasons, the show mocked the absurdity of the system. In the era of Trump, that no longer became feasible. D'Addario laments that the characters came to resemble too closely the Trump administration and consequently became too unlikable. With two episodes remaining, he is cautiously hopeful that the series will end without taking a fully dystopian turn. D'Addario writes, "With two episodes left, there's a chance the show will reclaim its characters—not redeem them, just show a baseline understanding of who they are and what they want that does something more interesting than directly map onto Trump administration figures."[31] D'Addario did not get his wish, as the show's finale was extraordinarily dark, even for a show that was consistently dark.

Throughout the final season, Meyer foreshadowed the nihilist finale with quips about the troubled state of the United States in the Trump era. I suggest that these bon mots reflect the writers' pessimistic perspective about the current state of the United States. In "Discovery Weekend" (7.2), Meyer goes to a retreat with a billionaire to woo him and his campaign dollars. When Meyer remarks about the irony that "the next president of the United States is being chosen by a closeted ex-record producer," an aide retorts that "the Electoral College hasn't exactly been hitting it out of the park." In "Pledge" (7.3), after the press and voters laud Meyer for winning a debate with her new egregiously misogynist slogan "Man Up," she quips, "God bless

America for hating women almost as much as I do." Both of these comments seem to be direct jabs at the 2016 election, when Donald Trump beat Hillary Clinton in the Electoral College, though not in the popular vote, and misogyny was widely touted as one of the reasons why she lost. Lest there be any doubt about Meyer's contempt for democracy, in "Oslo" (7.6), she is detained by the prime minister of Finland for potential war crimes that Meyer committed when she was president. The Finnish prime minister tells her, "I'm sorry, Selina, I have a commitment to the principles of truth and justice." Meyer simply pushes the prime minister out of her way and exclaims, "As the former president of the United States, truth and justice can gargle my balls."

In the series finale, "Veep" (7.7), Meyer finally achieves her goal of winning the presidency, but to do so, she has to abandon any inkling of integrity she may have ever possessed. The *Daily Beast*'s Kevin Fallon describes the finale as "harrowingly bleak, nihilistic, and so dark it nearly veered on glib."[32] The episode starts in media res at Meyer's convention, which is deadlocked, with five candidates having a shot at the nomination. Meyer knows that she will have to maneuver wisely, use her political capital, and completely sell out to gain the nomination. In order to secure a key endorsement, Meyer abandons the party's platform on same-sex marriage, even though her daughter is a happily married lesbian. When she explains the sellout to her daughter, she gets in a jab at the US democratic process, explaining, "It is just the party platform. It's like a to-do list of things we're not gonna do. Restore faith in democracy? I mean, we couldn't do that even if we wanted to." For the entire convention, she promises the veep slot to John Devito (played by Ian Roberts), an honest and loyal war hero who has supported her from the beginning. In order to secure delegates, she dumps Devito at the last minute for Jonah Ryan (Timothy Simons), a reprehensible demagogue who infected crowds because of his antivax policies and who ran with a policy against algebra because it was "Muslim math." To rub it in, Meyer steals Devito's speech for her nominating address. During her earlier brief stint as president, she was able to "free Tibet" at the convention, and she makes a deal with China that if she wins her nomination, the Chinese will fix the general election to make sure she wins. Finally, as a coup de grâce, she throws her most loyal staffer, Gary (Tony Hale), under the bus for a corruption scandal, which he knew nothing about, with the result that Gary spends several years in jail. She does all of this without blinking an eye, and she seems to relish the Machiavellian power grab that she is able to perform at the election. The audience does not get to see a softer side of Meyer or of any of the staffers who surround her. The show depicts all of them, and the Washington milieu out of which they emerge, as worthy of disdain and scorn. Meyer's opening line of "I hate this country" is the theme of the season, as expressed by the characters, as well as, presumably, the producers of the show. No longer is there a space for satirical critique; there is just a bleak rendition of the United States in the Trump era.

In a 2019 retrospective, the *Politico* writer Joanna Weiss suggests that the nihilistic political shows of the decade presaged the nihilistic political climate at the turn of 2020. In "How TV Predicted Politics in the 2010s," she contends, "Today's real-life sweeping nihilism about politicians' motives, the widespread hatred of the 'swamp,' the notion that the process is flawed and the rules of engagement themselves might not be worth following, was, if not created by television, then at least predicted by it."[33] Rather than trying to ascertain a chicken-or-egg causality, I suggest that Kirby's notion of digimodernism provides a framework for thinking of the particular media moment in which the distinction between entertainment politics and politics as such is collapsed. Collapsing the distinction between the separate spheres removes the possibility for satirical critique and allows for nihilism to fester, as no space can exist between what is and what should be. When *Veep* became indistinguishable from reality, when truth became stranger than fiction, it was no longer able to operate as a biting satire and instead transformed into hilarious nihilism. As the *Rolling Stone* reviewer Rob Sheffield writes, when Trump ascended to the presidency, "it was as if that 1938 *War of the Worlds* radio broadcast got interrupted by an actual Martian invasion."[34] When the writers could no longer explore the difference between the world as it *is* and the world as it *should be*, what remained was a dark space in which the show represented both the world as it *is* and the world as it *should not* be. This nihilism was unsustainable, and *Veep* ultimately had to burn itself to the ground, albeit in a darkly hilarious manner.

Notes

1 Mehnaaz Momen, *Political Satire, Postmodern Reality, and the Trump Presidency: Who Are We Laughing At?* (Lanham, MD: Lexington Books, 2019), 143–44.

2 Alan Kirby, *Digimodernism: How New Technologies Dismantle the Postmodern and Reconfigure Our Culture* (New York: Continuum, 2008), 149.

3 Mike Hale, "On Season 6 of *Veep*, Satire Meets Its Match," *New York Times*, April 14, 2017, https://www.nytimes.com/2017/04/14/arts/television/veep-season-6-tv-review.html.

4 Josh Hafner, "Donald Trump Loves the 'Poorly Educated'—and They Love Him," *USA Today*, February 24, 2016, https://www.usatoday.com/story/news/politics/onpolitics/2016/02/24/donald-trump-nevada-poorly-educated/80860078/.

5 Philip Rucker, "Trump Says Megyn Kelly 'Had Blood Coming out of Her Wherever,'" *Washington Post*, August 8, 2015, https://www.washingtonpost.com/news/post-politics/wp/2015/08/07/trump-says-foxs-megyn-kelly-had-blood-coming-out-of-her-wherever/.

6 Michael P. Young, "Such Schadenfreude—Unpacking the Medley of Caustic Humor and Politics in *Veep*," *AM: Journal of Art and Media Studies* 20 (2019): 67.

7 Russell L. Peterson, *Strange Bedfellows: How Late-Night Comedy Turns Democracy into a Joke* (New Brunswick, NJ: Rutgers University Press, 2008), 23.

8 Jonathan Gray, Jeffrey P. Jones, and Ethan Thompson. "The State of Satire, the Satire of State," in *Satire TV: Politics and Comedy in the Post-Network Era*, ed. Jonathan Gray, Jeffrey P. Jones, and Ethan Thompson (New York: New York University Press, 2009), 16–17.

9 Anshuman A. Mondal, "Taking Liberties? Free Speech, Multiculturalism and the Ethics of Satire," in *Comedy and the Politics of Representation: Mocking the Weak*, ed. Helen Davies and Sarah Ilott (Cham, Switzerland: Palgrave Macmillan, 2018), 33 (emphasis in original).

10 Peterson, *Strange Bedfellows*, 9.

11 Roger Rosenblatt, "The Age of Irony Comes to an End," *Time*, September 24, 2001, http://content.time.com/time/magazine/article/0,9171,1000893,00.html.

12 Rosenblatt.

13 David Gurney, "Everything Changes Forever (Temporarily): Late-Night Television Comedy after 9/11," in *A Decade of Dark Humor: How Comedy, Irony, and Satire Shaped Post-9/11 America*, ed. Ted Gournelos and Viveca Greene (Jackson: University of Mississippi Press, 2011), 13–14.

14 Ted Gournelos and Viveca Greene, "Introduction: Popular Culture and Post-9/11 Politics," in Gournelos and Greene, *Decade of Dark Humor*, xii (emphasis in original).

15 Sophia A. McClennen and Remy M. Maisel, *Is Satire Saving Our Nation? Mockery and American Politics* (New York: Palgrave Macmillan, 2014), 6.
16 McClennen and Maisel, 175.
17 Tim Molloy, "Obama Aides Say *Veep* More Accurate than *West Wing, House of Cards*," *Wrap*, April 14, 2017, https://www.thewrap.com/obama-aides-say-veep-accurate-west-wing-house-cards/.
18 Amber Day, *Satire and Dissent: Interventions in Contemporary Political Debate* (Bloomington: Indiana University Press, 2011), 187.
19 Kirby, *Digimodernism*, 1.
20 Kirby, 1.
21 Kirby, 140.
22 Fredric Jameson, *Postmodernism, or, The Cultural Logic of Late Capitalism* (Durham, NC: Duke University Press, 1992), 17.
23 Kirby, *Digimodernism*, 139.
24 Joe Conway, "After Politics / After Television: *Veep*, Digimodernism, and the Running Gag of Government," *Studies in American Humor* 2, no. 2 (2016): 182.
25 Conway, 185.
26 Conway, 187.
27 Conway, 187.
28 Conway, 200.
29 Conway, 203.
30 Daniel D'Addario, "How the Trump Era Wrecked *Veep*," *Variety*, April 29, 2019, https://variety.com/2019/tv/news/trump-wrecked-veep-hbo-1203196732/.
31 D'Addario.
32 Kevin Fallon, "The *Veep* Series Finale Was Darker than *Game of Thrones*—and Way More Satisfying," *Daily Beast*, May 13, 2019, https://www.thedailybeast.com/the-veep-series-finale-was-darker-than-game-of-thronesand-way-more-satisfying.
33 Joanna Weiss, "How TV Predicted Politics in the 2010s," *Politico*, December 28, 2019, https://www.politico.com/news/2019/12/28/how-tv-in-the-2010s-predicted-politics-089916.
34 Rob Sheffield, "Hail to the *Veep*: How HBO's Political Comedy Made History," *Rolling Stone*, May 13, 2019, https://www.rollingstone.com/tv/tv-features/veep-series-finale-rob-sheffield-832302/.

PART IV

Power and Gender

FOSSE/VERDON AND THE #MeToo MOMENT

Steven Cohan

The limited series *Fosse/Verdon* (first shown in the United States on the cable network FX from April 9, 2019, to May 28, 2019) pivots between two genres. On the one hand, it can be viewed as a backstager focusing primarily on the Broadway milieu of the two protagonists, Bob Fosse (Sam Rockwell) and Gwen Verdon (Michelle Williams); on the other hand, it is just as viewable as a melodramatic biopic portraying the couple's complex and progressively dysfunctional relationship. The series is ambitious about who constitutes its intended audience, too. While addressing a theatrically literate viewer able to recognize the many passing allusions to details about the Great White Way and its people, *Fosse/Verdon* also aims for the more general television viewer who has probably seen *Cabaret* but is unfamiliar with the assortment of Broadway players populating the series. Minor figures in the biographical story, such as Harold Prince, Cy Feuer, George Abbott, Michael Kidd, Joan McCracken, Jack Cole, and Leland Palmer, come and go in episodes that are themselves nonlinear in their structure. While the rich texture implies the former viewer, the time frame of the series seems meant for the latter one. *Fosse/Verdon* builds episodes around the films and musicals that a television audience of a certain age would be most familiar with—*Sweet Charity* (1969), *Cabaret* (1972), *Lenny* (1974), and *All That Jazz* (1979) and the stage hits *Pippin* (1972–77) and *Chicago* (1975–77)—so, aside from *Damn Yankees* (1955–57), it forgoes giving much due to the shows from the 1950s that established Verdon as a major star whose name alone could ensure a show's profitable run, while Fosse was more slowly earning his reputation as a choreographer of note and striving to take on the director's hat.

This omission, I argue, complicates the #MeToo context for the series, which both the promotion in the trades and reviews emphasized, for it exposes the main contraction inherent in the project, namely, that while it professes to be about *both* Fosse and Verdon, the series is still mostly fascinated by *him*. In this respect, the series was inescapably bound to its moment of production in the Trump era, with the feminist intent of acknowledging Fosse's sexism and giving equal credit to Verdon colliding with the patriarchal mystique of a charismatic but toxic masculinity.

#HimToo

Pitching the series at the Television Critics Association several months prior to its airing, the production team asserted that "the #MeToo era is just the right time" for their treatment of Fosse and Verdon. While recognizing the comparability with Fosse's autobiographical film *All That Jazz*, the show-runner and cocreator Steven Levenson claimed, "The FX's project amends that movie to correct the record, reinserting Verdon into a storyline Fosse wrote her out of to a great degree."[1] In a *Variety* interview at the time the series began to air, Levenson reiterated, "What we know about Fosse, a lot of that is actually Verdon as well. She has been left out of that narrative. Part of it is about reclaiming the story for her and reclaiming her place in the work." Although he and the cocreator and director Thomas Kail had been talking about the project for two years, when #MeToo happened, Levenson said, "it suddenly felt like, oh that's the reason to do this story. Before then we had wondered how to tell the story of this man who had a bit of a complicated relationship with women, to say the least. . . . We decided to steer right into it. That is the story."[2] A month before the Emmys, Levenson further explained in the *Hollywood Reporter*, "The more we learned about Bob Fosse and delved into his psyche, we saw troubling behavior there. He did a lot of bad things with his power. . . . But as the [#MeToo] movement happened, it felt like we had to tell this story." The movement afforded "an opportunity, especially factoring in Gwen, to talk about how men like this can thrive in the entertainment industry and the kind of culture that encourages and allows them to behave that way."[3]

Factoring Verdon into the narrative enables the writers to depict the couple's professional collaboration and personal relationship as a codependency, but one responding to different needs, since "the story" recounts

Fosse's "complicated relationship with women" and the "bad things [he did] with his power." As James Poniewozik put it in his *New York Times* review, "This is their unequal burden; he seems never to think beyond himself, she can never stop thinking of everything and everyone."[4] A rather selfless, if passive aggressive, Verdon, increasingly aware that she is aging past her career as the series progresses, comes off as Fosse's enabler; she interprets his inarticulate direction, using her body and the precision of her own movement to illustrate what he tries to tell his dancers. And Fosse comes off as a joyless creator, suspicious of his success, recklessly promiscuous, addicted to Seconal and Dexedrine, fascinated by death, and, at least due to Sam Rockwell's grim performance, lacking the impish sparkle for which he was known. From an unsympathetic perspective, then, the #MeToo movement appears to have given Levenson and his team license to dwell on Fosse as a sexual predator, but without glamorizing his behavior (which may explain the grimness of Rockwell's performance). Jessica Yu, who directed episode 4, "Glory," explained what she, Levenson, Kail, and the scriptwriter Joel Fields "talked about when researching this particular part of Bob's life": "a lot of women who had gone through that time said, 'Oh, it was just a different time.' So we tried to contextualize it without condemning the entire era."[5]

In the series's characterization of Fosse, *Fosse/Verdon* follows the template of Sam Wasson's 2013 biography of the man.[6] In Wasson's book, chapter titles count down to the moment of Fosse's death in Verdon's arms. The series repeats this trope with recurring chyrons, some of which similarly count down to his fatal heart attack in the street, while others establish gaps in time from one hit or major award to the next, identify the moment and setting of a new scene to effect a transition, or note how long it has been since Verdon's last Tony Award. What following Wasson so closely also means, though, is that the series's narrative stops when Fosse dies; his life, not Verdon's (who died in 2000), determines the timeline. The series therefore ignores what subsequently happened to her. Would it not have been worthwhile at least to recap in a scene or two or a montage how she had a secondary career acting in films and television and also served as artistic adviser on the 1999 Tony Award–winning *Fosse*, which Ann Reinking codirected? The series misses an opportunity for a coda, one consistent with the declared #MeToo mission, that could encourage viewers to think about how and why two women, Verdon and Reinking, who loved Fosse and put up with his infidelities and self-destructive behavior, would keep alive his legacy after his death.

As Levenson explained to the *Hollywood Reporter*, the 1970s is "the show's home base," for that was the decade when Fosse and Verdon's art was "most revolutionary," and "it's also the time period when their marriage really collapsed and then collapsed again." The creative team decided not to show "things like Bob's early years in Hollywood or Gwen's time with Jack Cole" except in "fragments," Levenson added, "because ultimately the tree trunk of the show was Bob and Gwen."[7] In short, the series aims not to recount the lives of Fosse *and* Verdon but to posit the hyphenate personality as indicated by the title, *Fosse/Verdon* as a single entity, although the slash can as easily be read as placing Fosse, the Romantic genius whose personal demons drove his "revolutionary" art, over the selfless Verdon in importance.

After all, Fosse left a body of work on film, and the revival of *Chicago* (1996–present)—which Reinking, who played Roxie Hart in the show after Verdon left and repeated the role in the revival, staged in his "style"—still runs on the Main Stem after nearly twenty-five years, whereas Verdon had only a reputation. As Poniewozik stated about the series in his *Times* review, "It has the feel of a Fosse story in which the '/Verdon' was appended."[8] The impetus, then, is to dramatize how "Fosse" became a famous brand in the 1970s. By comparison, Verdon's celebrated performances in *Can-Can* (1953–55), *Damn Yankees, New Girl in Town* (1957–58), *Redhead* (1959–60), and *Sweet Charity* (1966–67) were, with the exception of her starring role in the film version of *Yankees*, ephemeral though still legendary during the 1970s, just as her fame as a major Broadway star is now pretty much forgotten, except in the minds of old-timers. So although the series begins with the New York reviewers lamenting the absence of Verdon in the film version of *Sweet Charity*, thereby acknowledging her greater fame in 1969, the series ultimately shows how Fosse surpassed her with his prominence as a film and stage director, a trajectory that runs in counterpoint to Verdon's desperation to go back to work onstage after *Charity*, despite the industry's ageism. Similarly, Fosse's many excesses and self-destructive behavior contrast with Verdon's normality as a woman, monogamous lover, and mother of their daughter, Nicole (who also served as one of the show's executive producers). Reflecting this imbalance and ignoring the ephemerality of Verdon's great stage successes, one hostile reviewer even called Michelle Williams's Verdon "a second-tier showbiz figure whom nobody would be thinking about, much less making a series about, if she hadn't been married to Fosse"; and this reviewer attributed the series's reluctance just to focus on Fosse, "a genius who left an indelible mark on both Broadway and film," to the #MeToo movement.[9]

Even reviews of the series that found a lot to like in *Fosse/Verdon*—the central performances, attention to period detail, the capturing of the theater milieu, the re-creation of famous musical numbers—evaluated its flaws in the light of #MeToo. Emily Todd VanDerWerff pointed out on *Vox*, "The series is certainly aware of the monstrous elements of Fosse's personality, particularly the way he would make sleeping with him a virtual requirement for young, pretty, would-be chorus girls. But it's never quite sure if it should say something damning his behavior or let the audience make up its own mind." At the same time, the series "flattens [Verdon's] life story into: 'She was every bit as talented and creative, but limited by a society that had little value for women.'"[10] Linda Holmes noted on National Public Radio that *Fosse/Verdon* is part of a contemporary TV and film genre focusing on "men who are brilliant geniuses but who are awful people because of their terrible pain." She could sense how the creative team behind the series—all Broadway veterans—are fascinated by Fosse but concluded, "It's supposed to be shedding light on something. It's just not clear what."[11] Offering some of the same criticism, Emily Nussbaum wrote in the *New Yorker* that *Fosse/Verdon* is "a #MeToo-era take, poking holes in the notion of the dysfunctional male genius—and, crucially, devoting equal time to Gwen Verdon." But comparing it unfavorably to *All That Jazz*—"one of the best portraits of workaholic creativity ever made," albeit "harder to make now" given its "bad boy" protagonist, a thinly disguised reflection of Fosse himself—Nussbaum felt that the series is "weighed down by good intentions. It's heavy, but mainly it's heavy-handed. . . . Too often, it's 'All That Jazz' backwards, in flats."[12]

Fosse

Possibly as a cue for focusing on the #MeToo melodrama of Fosse's self-destructiveness, addiction to numerous drugs, chain-smoking, and one-night stands or casual affairs, aside from a few standout scenes that I shall discuss later, not a lot of time is spent on showing the process by which he created dances, though attention is initially given to Verdon's input. The first episode, "Life Is a Cabaret," has her translating the inarticulate Fosse's direction to the dancers when blocking the "Big Spender" number of *Sweet*

Charity and suggesting that he cut one of the performers for the number's framing by the camera. (Wasson attributes the idea to Fosse, not Verdon.)[13] Although acclaimed onstage as Charity, Verdon was passed over for Shirley MacLaine, a bigger name, for the film. Nonetheless, Verdon shows no animosity about losing the part and travels with Fosse to Los Angeles to coach MacLaine and assist Fosse on set. As Wasson comments, "Though being Fosse's dramaturge and ubiquitous assistant seemed to many a sad and selfless position for Gwen to take, Gwen herself thought that, considering the alternative, it was very much a good deal for her. In addition to being the director's wife, she was now the guardian of his style—its oldest representative, its most expert practitioner. And having more of Fosse's work in her brain-body than anyone else, Verdon was an unbeatable back catalogue for him, poised to be essential to Fosse even after her dancer's body gave out."[14] Somewhat later in this episode, in West Germany, Verdon understands when no one else does what Fosse wants to do on the set of *Cabaret* as she smooths over the friction with producer Cy Feuer, selects costumes for star Liza Minnelli, and flies back to New York in search of a gorilla head for the "Meeskite" number, while Fosse beds his German translator, precipitating Verdon and Fosse's separation.

Following Wasson's biography, too, reiterated flashbacks to Fosse's days as a young teen dancer on the burlesque circuit hint at his molestation at thirteen by a group of strippers, and this trauma apparently determined the adult Fosse's predatory relations with women, his inability to commit to monogamy, and his fascination with the dark side of sexuality, as increasingly realized in his choreography. When making *Cabaret*, with a certain decadent look in mind for the Kit Kat Klub, he and his translator go to a brothel to cast women for the film. "When I was a kid I danced in places like that," he tells her. "What do you call a thirteen-year-old kid who gets screwed by a bunch of strippers?" Fosse later asks in a fantasy monologue modeled after the subject of his film *Lenny*, which he is frantically editing while preparing *Chicago*, until he suffers a heart attack. "The luckiest guy in the world," he replies in this sixth episode. "All I Care About Is Love," adding, as a riff on the stages of grief, "the Triangle of Shame," composed of "pleasure, confusion, and humiliation all at the same time." He concludes, it "screws up your relationships for the rest of your life." Fosse's anxiety about being impotent following his surgery interrupts the monologue. After he successfully orgasms with Ann Reinking (Margaret Qualley), he asks,

"What's the difference between sex and applause?" His answer: "You only applaud somebody you love."

Like Wasson's book as well, *Fosse/Verdon* characterizes the director's art through his fascination with the dark underside of the razzle dazzle of show business. As Kevin Winkler describes in his smart analysis of Fosse's work from his beginnings as a dancer to the end of his life, "At its darkest, Fosse's show business reflects his own conflicted feelings about it—how it robbed him of his youthful innocence or the way he could so easily manipulate audiences through dazzling staging."[15] At the same time, the series makes Fosse's art inseparable from his sexual relations with his female dancers. "Sex was a medium for Fosse," Wasson writes, psychologizing and rationalizing Fosse's predatory behavior as a kind of testing of his female dancers. The biographer's discourse catches the "free love" ethos of the 1970s but without the distance afforded by the present day.

> It was as much a physical act as it was an opportunity to learn about and merge with his female collaborators, a way of giving to them so they could give back more and better—that is, if they didn't break under the pressure or retreat in anger. As a means of communication, sex was an exclamation point, far better than the periods of regular life. Sex improved on respect and trust—for the dancers and for him. Sex brought him closer to the epicenter of talent, as if by dipping a hand to the geyser, he could steal back a drop for himself. And his effort brought him applause too.[16]

Wasson mentions the time a dancer in *Pippin*, in resisting Fosse's advances after rehearsal, "kicked him in the groin," a moment that happens in the fourth episode of *Fosse/Verdon*, "Glory."[17] Fosse's staging of a dance number in that show is then mediated by his anger at the dancer, which causes him to humiliate her in rehearsal and replace her with Ann Reinking, who, Verdon whispers to Fosse, is so good that she knows she does not have to sleep with him to get the spot. Subsequently, the reluctant dancer agrees to spend the night with Fosse, presumably to get him off her back.

Episodes do display the precision that characterized Fosse's choreography, as it made use of every muscle in a dancer's body to tell a story—hands, fingers, neck, torso, knees, feet—but the series does not dwell on the love and devotion he earned from his "family of dancers, gypsies he used over and over again."[18] Already by the 1960s, there was a discernible "'Fosse dancer': fiercely loyal, keenly aware of his legacy, and willing to work endlessly to help him achieve his vision and burnish their own skills."[19] In *Fosse/Verdon*, however, the more palpable moments of showing Fosse's art in process are not in the dance rehearsals, which seem mediated by the creative team's self-consciousness of #MeToo, but in the editing room, as he cuts *Cabaret* and *Lenny* and recuts and then recuts yet again, often a shot or a frame or two at a time. When editing, Fosse can assert his total control over the object, and we see the artful effect re-created on the screen in the editing room.

The series's other insight about what made Fosse tick as an artist focuses on his egoism and desire for total control as inseparable from his insecurity, especially about his producers, which colludes with his self-destructiveness; and here too one may see the connection to his predatory relation with his dancers outside of rehearsal, which amounted to his asserting his power over them as much as sexual gratification. Fosse's desire to control every element of his choreography is how he apparently understands his seduction of his dancers, as made clear in the power contests with the women he works with—with that female dancer who resisted his advances; with Verdon, who had contractual control over everything on *Chicago*, or even in his first combative meeting with her when each is shown inspecting the other for *Damn Yankees*; with the numerous times he makes Ann Reinking read the same lines in her audition for the character based on herself in *All That Jazz*.

"Glory" recounts the director's extraordinary trifecta in winning the Academy Award, the Emmy, and the Tony in a single year, 1973; yet ultimately, he finds all the acclaim unsatisfying. Severely inebriated, he brings the Oscar to Verdon's apartment and climbs into her bed while she is there with her boyfriend Ron; another time, he fantasizes jumping off a balcony; and finally, he imagines a suicide modeled on the finale of *Pippin* (when the title character is given the choice of boring normality or a celebratory suicide) with the cast, friends, and Verdon urging him on, but he pulls back, "choosing life" instead of "the only perfect act," his suicide. This episode ends with Fosse calling 911 and checking into the Payne Whitney Psychiatric Clinic.

Despite what the series shows about Fosse and Verdon's codependency through their collaborations, the title's slash increasingly comes to signify the tension in their working relationship during the 1970s. One thread of episode 5, "Where Am I Going?," has Verdon trying to convince Fosse, recovering from a heart attack, to direct her passion project, *Chicago*, instead of *Lenny*. In episode 7, "Nowadays," he wants her help when editing *Lenny*, which, angry that he is paying little attention to preproduction of *Chicago*, she refuses; he agrees to do *Chicago* out of guilt, although his heart is in *Lenny*. During rehearsals of *Chicago*, Fosse keeps simplifying Verdon's part in "We Both Reached for the Gun," implying that her body can no longer keep pace with his choreography, but the moment is dramatized as a power struggle between the star and her director. Then, when Fosse refuses to give Verdon "Nowadays" as a solo so that she will have the spotlight in the final moments of *Chicago*, insisting that it be a duet with Chita Rivera, Verdon claims to have been responsible for his career. "I picked you up on my back and I carried you . . . and you never forgave me for it." The episode neglects to mention the compromise reached—onstage Verdon sang the song's first chorus before being joined by Rivera, the first time in the show that the theater's two greatest dancers danced together; for that matter, there is no acknowledgment of Verdon's weak throaty voice at this point in her life, which required that she share the song "My Own Best Friend" with Rivera at the end of act 1, and this may have been a reason for Fosse's reluctance to have her do "Nowadays" as a longer solo.[20] Yet, earlier in the series, in "Where Are You Going?," Verdon tells Reinking that her job is to keep Fosse alive. "Is it worth it?" the younger woman asks. "He'll give you what he gave me," Verdon responds, and she means he gave her her career.

So who carried whom?

Verdon

In this respect, I think the series seriously missteps by ignoring the 1950s. In "Life Is a Cabaret," Fosse mutters at one point, "All I ever wanted to be was Fred Astaire." The line condenses his early ambition as a dancer, performing in a nightclub act and briefly on Broadway with his first wife, Mary Ann Niles, and then by himself at MGM, where he quickly learned he had the talents but not the looks wanted by the studio as his parts shrank in importance. Furthermore, showing more of Fosse's past might have given a stronger indication of how he professionally used his wives, strong dancers in their own right, who served as booster, instructor, and muse, until he left each for another and younger woman—Niles, Joan McCracken, Verdon, Reinking.

The film musicals apparently gave an uncredited Fosse a chance to choreograph some of his own dancing, supplying an archive in which one can
already see indications of his mature style; and they also introduced him
to a mentor in Stanley Donen, who directed him in *Give a Girl a Break*
(1953) and brought him to Hollywood to re-create his numbers from *The
Pajama Game* (1957) and *Damn Yankees*; a colleague in Carol Haney, who
partnered with him in *Kiss Me Kate* (1953) and had "Steam Heat," her own
star-making number, staged by Fosse in *Pajama Game* (1954–56), which
she repeated in the film; a classically trained dancer like Tommy Rall, with
whom Fosse danced in an exciting challenge dance in *My Sister Eileen*
(1955), the first musical for which Fosse received full choreographic credit
for all the numbers; and competitors like Gower Champion, his costar in
Give a Girl a Break, who became a celebrated director-choreographer on
Broadway at the same time that Fosse did. With the exception of Champion,
these were all people Fosse would work with again at some point, on film,
television, or the stage.

The reticence to include Verdon's 1950s career more fully is even more
significant for how the series views her in relation to Fosse, however. As
noted already, in Hollywood, he was a contract performer at MGM, but
after successes on Broadway, he returned to choreograph at Columbia and
Warner. Verdon was a member of Jack Cole's dance troupe in New York
and his assistant in Hollywood at Fox, where, without credit, she danced on
film with Danny Kaye in *On the Riviera* (1951) and Betty Grable in *Meet Me
After the Show* (1951) and *The Farmer Takes a Wife* (1953), as well as performing uncredited in several other films, and she instructed Marilyn Mon-
roe and Jane Russell how to move and dance for *Gentlemen Prefer Blondes*
(1953). Inclusion of both Fosse's and Verdon's early Hollywood careers could
have provided something of a ballast to their later careers in the late 1950s
and afterward through recognition of their comparable talents as dancers and instructors, while also showing their persistence as they fought to
become known for their special talents.

Aside from Verdon's show-stopping performance in *Can-Can* and
Fosse's sense of lost control during the tryout of *Damn Yankees*, when Harold Prince and George Abbott go behind his back in deciding to cut the
first-act closing number, despite Fosse's inclination to fix it, *Fosse/Verdon*
completely bypasses Verdon's other Tony-winning roles in *New Girl in Town*
and *Redhead*. Though Fosse choreographed all three hits and won Tonys for

his choreography for each, and Verdon insisted that he also direct *Redhead*, the shows ran on her name alone and not, as was the case with their later collaborations on *Sweet Charity* and *Chicago*, his as director-choreographer as well.

Today, with concept or catalogue musicals often sold on the basis of a composer, one may forget how Broadway in the 1950s was star driven, particularly by women who had a stage charisma that never registered with the same dazzling effect in their screen roles: like Verdon, Mary Martin and Ethel Merman had shows designed especially for them, and their names could guarantee profitable runs. Here is how Winkler describes Verdon at her peak:

> Verdon's blazing hair topped a delightfully animated face, with a wide mouth and sparkling eyes. It was a true stage face, one that registered every flicker of emotion to the farthest balcony seat. Verdon danced boldly and with athletic confidence and had the muscular legs of a [Jack] Cole dancer, but those legs supported a figure both luscious and delicate, with expressive, graceful arms and a fluid torso. . . . Her acting matched her dancing—direct, focused, and playful. Verdon's voice, which she had seldom been called upon to use, was the delicious topper: hoarse and crinkly, like cellophane, and with a throaty laugh that bubbled with innuendo. She was a sexpot with a sense of humor. The package was perfection.[21]

Including some reference to Verdon's fame in the 1950s as a star who could sing and act as well as dance would have strengthened one's impression of her equal footing (so to speak) with Fosse. As important, first tracing their separate career paths would establish what each brought to their partnership once they began to collaborate on *Damn Yankees*. "It was a joke they both knew and understood: sexuality leavened with humor, which gave it humanity and universality. Fosse's humor was a welcome antidote to Jack Cole's dour intensity, and Verdon's strength and versatility allowed Fosse to stretch as a choreographer."[22]

In the shows after *Damn Yankees*, Verdon and Fosse each expanded the other's talents. *New Girl in Town*, a musical version of Eugene O'Neil's *Anna Christie*, revealed Verdon's acting chops, though she studied with Sanford Meisner and had to audition for the part several times. Fosse's controversial "Red

Light Ballet," an erotic memory of Anna's of her past working in a brothel, which choreographs her disgust but also her pleasure in controlling men, was initially cut, then revised, then mostly restored because Prince and Abbott thought it was too filthy, thereby setting up a Fosse-Verdon-dancers camp in opposition to the producers' will; the number also forecast Fosse's later staging when he had full control. But the musical also depended greatly on Verdon; when she missed several performances during the Boston tryout, *four* women were needed to take her place: "one to sing and act, and the other three to perform her dances."[23] Her stamina at this stage of her career was so great, in fact, that "Essie's Vision" in *Redhead*, a lengthy dance number composed of five discrete sections, each different in tone and style, was "the ultimate showcase for Verdon's dance versatility and unflagging energy." By the long and very physical number's end, dancers remembered being "ready to vomit" from exhaustion, whereas an indefatigable Verdon called it "the greatest fun I've ever had."[24]

So dependent were *New Girl* and *Redhead* on Verdon's great talents that neither show has been revived, and both are remembered now mainly for their cast albums. Now I do recognize the need for some condensation due to time constraints, but, at the very least, showing Fosse and Verdon working together to bring *Sweet Charity* to Broadway would have been more compelling in establishing the impact of her absence from the film version than reciting the *Times* review lamenting that fact.

The series represents what Verdon and Fosse each found in the other in only a single scene, albeit a great moment as rendered, when star and choreographer warily test each other for *Damn Yankees*. In episode 2, "Who's Got the Pain?," Fosse stages the dance he has in mind for "Whatever Lola Wants," which became Verdon's signature song, and she joins in, elaborating, improvising, demonstrating to him what she can do in sync with his intention. Melding in the dance, they appear to be of one mind, one body; their initial combativeness and defensiveness gone, their mutual sexual attraction becomes apparent. Later the two hastily work out the choreography for the mambo "Who's Got the Pain?," as the replacement for the first-act finish, which was not working. However, their stage partnership, while important, still seems incidental to the episode's drama overall, which derives from their competition ("Bob and I aren't competing," Verdon says at the start of the hour); their starting an affair while doing *Yankees*; Fosse's anger at Prince and Abbot for going behind his back to cut the troubled number; Verdon's guilt because Fosse is still married to Joan McCracken, who is dying and whom she admires; and his later affairs in Germany while filming *Cabaret*. The episode concludes with a montage of three moments: her leaving him for good in Majorca after *Cabaret* has been filmed, the triumphant curtain call for *Damn Yankees*, and her knocking on Fosse's hotel-room door in Munich, gorilla head in hand, where we know what she will discover.

The series just hints at Verdon's backstory in episode 3, "Me and My Baby." Flashbacks—first occasioned by Verdon's finding Paddy Chayefsky babysitting Nicole in Fosse's hotel room, while Fosse is cavorting with his assistant editor—recount her being molested as a teen by a family friend, marrying him in a shotgun wedding, giving birth, divorcing him, interviewing Jack Cole, leaving her toddler son with her parents to join Cole's dance troupe, and finally getting the famous seven-minute, show-stopping ovation on the opening night of *Can-Can*. But the narrative of the episode is framed by Fosse's life in the present: it begins with his anxiety about editing *Cabaret*; he asks for Verdon's help on the film and on the opening number of *Pippin*, while she asks for his advice about a straight play she is doing as a comeback of sorts. She advises him on both projects; but he never has the time to attend a rehearsal of her play to give notes, and it closes on opening night. Furthermore, his advice after looking at the script is to suggest that she tell the writer to change the gender of a child in her big speech, which has been giving her great difficulty. "What do you know about raising a boy?" he asks rhetorically and thoughtlessly, no doubt having only Nicole in mind. Though Verdon did send for her son, put him in boarding school in the East, and maintained a relationship with him afterward, the series never mentions him again.[25]

Indicative of the extent to which the series erases Verdon, all the while appearing to give her equal billing, is its treatment of Ann Reinking (Margaret Qualley), whose own status as a dancer is overshadowed by her function in the narrative simply as Fosse's long-standing (for him) bed partner after his separation from Verdon. Indeed, Reinking's passivity in dealing with him echoes her character, Kate Jagger (based on herself), in *All That Jazz*. In *Fosse/Verdon*, Reinking's passivity enables Verdon to appear more defiant of her estranged husband in their later years, though he is still the dominant figure in her life, according to the series. What the series downplays, however, is the close friendship that developed between the two women, with Reinking ultimately looking up to Verdon as a teacher and maternal figure, the two working to preserve Fosse's legacy after his death.[26]

Instead, two scenes show Verdon asserting herself over a passive Reinking. "Where Am I Going?" establishes Reinking's close friendship with Nicole (a bonding represented in *All That Jazz*, too) when Fosse and Reinking, Verdon and Ron, Chayefsky and Neil Simon are all vacationing in Southampton. When the youngster throws up after smoking cigarettes in secret, Reinking goes to help, but Verdon, playing the mother card, tells her, "I will take care of it." Likewise, in episode 6, "All I Care About Is Love," which recounts Fosse's hospitalization after his heart attack, Verdon plays the wife card by sending Reinking home while Fosse undergoes surgery, telling her there is nothing she can do.

Additionally, Reinking's passivity in the series ignores what she apparently brought to Fosse's choreography as a dancer and muse: "For Fosse, Reinking was a new, highly trained dance muse," Winkler writes. "Her superb technical skills and the precise, elegant line of her dancing influenced a change in Fosse's choreography as he adopted a more lyrical, self-serious approach that his dance vocabulary was not always able to support. Reinking came to embody a new Fosse style, and many of his female dancers appeared to be cast in her image. Icy, earnest, unsmiling—these would increasingly be the touchstones of Fosse's dance style."[27] If Verdon's dancing could be as combustible as her flaming red hair, Reinking's was cooler and more restrained, and admittedly the passivity of her characterization in *Fosse/Verdon* might be trying to imply that personal tone, although we do not see it in dance terms. During Reinking's audition for *All That Jazz*, Fosse, no longer her lover at this point, punctures her reserve by having her repeat her brief scene many times; he repeats his alter ego's lines to get her angrier and angrier as she apparently relives the autobiographical moment in the script. When she completely lets loose, she gets the part.

Verdon/Fosse

But Fosse always wanted to be Fred Astaire. Until he grew too old for the role, he played the lead in summer stock and short-term revivals of *Pal Joey* at New York's City Center several times; his turning just to choreographing shows was something of a second career when he did not make it as a leading man in films or onstage; at least until his career as a director really took off, he seemed always to feel that disappointment about not making it as a dancer himself. When there was talk about opening *Redhead* in London, Fosse planned to play the role of the murderer, but the musical never made it across the pond. On the troubled production of *The Conquering Hero* (1961), Fosse, who was directing and choreographing until he was fired after several bust-ups with the writers and producers over his numbers, wanted to replace Tom Poston by playing the lead himself, which was the excuse for his getting fired; the show ended up opening (and closing) without a director or choreographer credit.[28]

In addition to Fosse's early musicals, a dancing Fosse twice appeared on film: as the sinewy snake in Donen's musicalized *Little Prince* (1974) and opposite Verdon in "Who's Got the Pain?" in the film version of *Damn Yankees*. This number reportedly uses the choreography of the stage version, for which Verdon received staging credit along with Fosse in the *Playbill*. Frequently excerpted to illustrate the couple's teamwork, it has since become iconic. The choreography is athletic and complex, albeit "built around small mambo steps, emphasizing hip and rib cage isolations," with "shimmies, a Chaplin walk, the use of hats," and a "swimming" traveling step.[29] What is interesting when re-created on film is that Verdon has a big smile through-out, showing her confidence in and the physical pleasure gotten from her dancing; she moves freely as if her joints had melted, whereas Fosse has a studied look on his face and his movement is a bit sharper and less effortless than hers. While their dancing is perfectly synchronized, if hers radiates joy and precision, his reflects mainly precision.

In the 1950s and 1960s, Fosse did television work too, choreographing numbers for Verdon for various variety shows and sometimes performing alongside her. The two danced together again on *The Garry Moore Show* on June 5, 1962, to "I Wanna Be a Dancin' Man," a number Astaire did in *The Belle of New York* (1952). Winkler notes in both his book and in com-ments in the documentary *Merely Marvelous: The Dancing Genius of Gwen Verdon* (2019) that in this number, a confident Verdon looks directly at the camera, while Fosse "cast[s] a look of endearment at his partner."[30] Verdon interjects "girl" as she and Fosse sing the title line, and he joins in; with a smile, he reiterates "girl" when they sing that line again. Possibly because the staging is simpler and more playful than "Who's Got the Pain?" (or because their marriage was on solid footing at this point?), the dancing here shows a greater warmth and intimacy, something generally missing from the series. As Verdon said in an archival interview included in the documentary, she and Fosse would have stayed together if they could have rehearsed all the time, for that was when they were most simpatico.

"I Wanna Be a Dancin' Man" was a number with special significance for Fosse. It opened act 2 of his dance musical *Dancin'* (1978–82) and was repeated in the Tony-winning tribute *Fosse* (1999–2001), where it was the finale of act 1. Reinking says that while the number was a tribute to Astaire, "the lyrics are very Bob," since they express both the ephemerality of dancing ("it's always footprints in the sand," as the lyrics state, "and it can get washed away by wind or the sea") and the importance "that it existed at all."[31] I assume from the credits on the Internet Broadway Database that the eight-minute number in *Fosse*, which is on YouTube, re-creates the staging in *Dancin'*. As done in *Fosse*, the ensemble of men and women are dressed identically in white three-piece suits, spats, striped bow ties, white gloves, and straw fedoras, and the unisex costume connotes a "dancin' man" and not a "dancin' girl." As the fifteen dancers do the trademark Fosse moves (jazz hands, bent arms and knees, snapping fingers, pelvis thrusts, and so forth, all isolating different parts of the body) in perfect unison, then break up to spotlight small groups of dancers, the effect is of watching multiple Fosses dancing.

The revue was designed as a tribute to Fosse, and Verdon was credited as artistic director; but when one recalls the earlier Fosse-Verdon duet to the song on the Moore show or how she was credited for the staging of "Who's Got the Pain?," his later art seems built on vacating her presence as a cocreator, muse, and perfect embodiment of his intentions. *Fosse/Verdon* seems to want to recognize how Verdon has been written out of the Fosse narrative, but it does not adequately show how much had been erased. Given Fosse's filmography and how his choreography has been re-created numerous times, the lyrics of "Dancin' Man," which reflect the temporality of stage art, apply much more to Verdon than to him. Ironically, however, though he forgot his choreography, as when he began work filming *Sweet Charity*, Verdon remembered every dance she ever did, which is why her input on that film proved so invaluable. Her absence from *Sweet Charity* was felt, but her presence was still there.

Notes

1   Lisa de Moraes, "'Fosse/Verdon' Explores Tortured Relationship of Dance Greats Bob Fosse and Gwen Verdon—TCA," *Deadline*, February 4, 2019, https://deadline.com/2019/02/bob-fosse-gwen-verdon-fx-michelle -williams-sam-rockwell-metoo-tca-1202549096/.

2 Amber Dowling, "'Fosse/Verdon' Boss on Exposing the 'Grit and Grime' of Bob Fosse in the Wake of #MeToo," *Variety*, April 8, 2019, https://variety.com/2019/tv/features/fosse-verdon-me-too-bob-fosse-premiere-interview-1203181805/.

3 Tara Bitran, "'Fosse/Verdon' Executive Producer on Conveying 'Troubled Behavior' Onscreen amid #MeToo Movement," *Hollywood Reporter*, August 2, 2019, https://www.hollywoodreporter.com/news/fosse-verdon-executive-producer-conveying-troubled-behavior-onscreen-1227779.

4 James Poniewozik, "Review: In 'Fosse/Verdon' a Portrait of the Artist as Problematic Fave," *New York Times*, April 8, 2019, https://www.nytimes.com/2019/04/08/arts/television/fosse-verdon-review.html.

5 Danielle Turchiano, "'Fosse/Verdon' Director Jessia Yu on Getting inside Bob Fosse's Mind, Tackling #MeToo," *Variety*, August 8, 2019, https://variety.com/2019/tv/awards/fosse-verdon-jessica-yu-glory-me-too-directing-pippin-fantasy-interview-1203285353/.

6 Sam Wasson, *Fosse* (Boston: Houghton Mifflin Harcourt, 2013).

7 Bitran, "'Fosse/Verdon' Executive Producer."

8 Poniewozik, "Review."

9 Kyle Smith, "*Fosse/Verdon* and the Dismal #MeToo Obsession," *National Review*, June 21, 2019, https://www.nationalreview.com/2019/06/fosse-verdon-hollywood-metoo-obsession/.

10 Emily Todd VanDerWerff, "FX's Fosse/Verdon Is Either a Masterpiece or a Disaster," *Vox*, April 9, 2019, https://www.vox.com/culture/2019/4/9/18303412/fosse-verdon-review-sam-rockwell-michelle-williams-fx-bob-fosse-gwen-verdon.

11 Linda Holmes, "'Fosse/Verdon' Wriggles and Kicks but Fails to Satisfy," NPR.org, April 9, 2019, https://www.npr.org/2019/04/09/711063555/fosse-verdon-wiggles-and-kicks-but-fails-to-satisfy.

12 Emily Nussbaum, "What Does It Take to Be a Female Genius?," *New Yorker*, April 8, 2019, https://www.newyorker.com/magazine/2019/04/15/what-does-it-take-to-be-a-female-genius.

13 Wasson, *Fosse*, 236.

14 Wasson, 234–35.

15 Kevin Winkler, *Big Deal: Bob Fosse and Dance in the American Musical* (New York: Oxford University Press, 2018), 103.

16 Wasson, *Fosse*, 191.

17 Wasson, 314.

18 Dennis McGovern and Deborah Grace Winer, *Sing Out, Louise! 150 Stars of the Musical Theatre Remember 50 Years on Broadway* (New York: Schirmer Books, 1993), 73.

19 Winkler, *Big Deal*, 110.

20 Getting *Chicago* to its opening was fraught, with Fosse emerging from his heart attack with a darker vision than others had wanted. Assistant choreographer Tony Stevens called Fosse "Prince of Darkness," and Fosse called him "Mary Sunshine," after a character in the show: Wasson, *Fosse*, 412. For the backstory of the production, see Ethan Mordden, *All That Jazz: The Life and Times of the Musical "Chicago"* (New York: Oxford University Press, 2018), 117–97.

21 Winkler, *Big Deal*, 48.

22 Winkler, 5.

23 Winkler, 66.

24 Winkler, 74.

25 Verdon apparently developed a loving relationship with her son, James Henagan Jr. While the child is absent from *Fosse/Verdon* after she joins Cole's troupe, and there may have been some estrangement when he was younger and placed in an East Coast boarding school, Henagan is a talking head in the documentary *Merely Marvelous: The Dancing Genius of Gwen Verdon* (dir. Ken Bloom and Chris Johnson, 2019), where he speaks knowingly and lovingly about her.

26 On Reinking's close friendship with Verdon, see Julie Miller, "*Fosse/Verdon*: Inside Ann Reinking and Gwen Verdon's Unlikely Friendship," *Vanity Fair*, May 5, 2019, https://www.vanityfair.com/hollywood/2019/05/bob-fosse-girlfriend-ann-reinking-gwen-verdon; and Michael Schulman, "Ann Reinking on Her Life as Bob Fosse's Muse, Lover, and Friend," *New Yorker*, May 28, 2019, https://www.newyorker.com/culture/culture-desk/ann-reinking-on-her-life-as-bob-fosses-muse-lover-and-friend.

27 Winkler, *Big Deal*, 167.

28 Winkler, 85.

29 Winkler, 51–52.

30 Winkler, 98.

31 Schulman, "Ann Reinking on Her Life."

"Grab Them by the Pussy"

The Sexual Politics of Touch
in *The Handmaid's Tale*

Donna Peberdy

Sales of Margaret Atwood's dystopian novel *The Handmaid's Tale*, originally published in 1985, soared in the run-up to the 2016 US election, featuring on numerous best-seller lists that year and the next. Countless journalists and news outlets attributed the novel's resurgent popularity to its "grotesque timeliness."[1] While the first season of the Hulu television adaptation was in midproduction during the election, Atwood has noted how those involved in the production woke up following Donald Trump's win to find "our show has just been framed."[2] In this chapter, I explore how a hate-fueled and divisive climate is played out and challenged in the television adaptation of *The Handmaid's Tale* (Hulu, 2017–) through what I refer to as the sexual politics of touch. In the drama, the regulation of touch becomes a controlling mechanism enforcing passivity and compliance. I consider how *The Handmaid's Tale*, as a social, cultural, and political analogy of our time, explores the politics of women's sexual agency through the act of touch. In doing so, it offers a commentary on the increasingly fragile human relations that characterize the contemporary Western world.

"You've Got to Push Back on These Women"

The Republic of Gilead, the fictional totalitarian state where much of *The Handmaid's Tale* is set, is a society whose sensory life is highly controlled and regulated. Like much of its population, Gilead's sensory life is sterile and barren: restricted, repressed, and markedly diminished. Fertile Handmaids,

whose sole function is to provide offspring for their designated Commanders and their Wives, are denied the ability to freely engage with their senses.
Oversized bonnets with wings narrow and limit their perspective, prevent-
ing them from looking at others and each other. Their dietary intake is regulated in order to make their bodies fit for pregnancy. Verbal communication
is restricted to sanctioned phrases and expressions lifted or repurposed from
the pages of the Bible. The silencing of women leads to auditory limitations
as news is delivered in hushed whispers, snatched murmurs, and covert gestures. Ceaselessly surveilled, Handmaids are forbidden from touch, bodily
contact, and tactile interactions, while others are forbidden from touching
them, with one exception.

The only permissible acts of bodily contact are those directly contributing to procreation. Sex is a predetermined and preordained scripted ritual,
drawn from the Genesis story of Jacob and Rachel, who have a child through
their handmaid Bilhah. Once a month, Handmaids must engage in the state-
sanctioned Ceremony: lying on their backs, their heads nestle in the lap of a
Wife, who holds the Handmaid's wrists while the Handmaid is penetrated by
the Commander. All three are fully clothed. Any other sensory engagement
(touch, eye contact) is prohibited, during the Ceremony or outside of it. Sex
in Gilead is sanctioned procreation; for the Handmaids, it is systematic,
institutionalized rape. Its function is for reproduction, never pleasure. Consequently, sex between people of the same sex is prohibited, and any "gender
treachery" is punishable by death or genital mutilation.

Atwood has recalled about writing the novel in West Berlin in 1984,
with the physical and ideological barrier of the Berlin Wall as her backdrop,
"I experienced the wariness, the feeling of being spied on, the silences, the
changes of subject, the oblique ways in which people might convey information, and these had an influence on what I was writing."[3] She finished writing
the novel in Tuscaloosa, Alabama, the same state that would, three and a half
decades later, pass the Human Life Protection Act—a near-total abortion
ban, even in cases of rape and incest. The year Atwood wrote *The Handmaid's Tale* was also the titular year of George Orwell's dystopian novel about
another totalitarian state governed by omnipresent surveillance and wom-
en's sexual oppression. "Orwell became a direct model for me," the Canadian
author has acknowledged.[4] *Nineteen Eighty-Four* joined Atwood's novel on
best-seller lists following the 2016 election, as readers apparently tried to
make sense of the turn of events that had allowed Trump to win the election.

The result, the *New York Times* reported, was "a stunning culmination of an explosive, populist and polarizing campaign that took relentless aim at the institutions and long-held ideals of American democracy."[5] Atwood has frequently noted that everything in her novel was based on something that had happened around the world—"No imaginary gizmos, no imaginary laws, no imaginary atrocities"[6]—and it is a rule that the television drama's showrunner, Bruce Miller, has stuck to. While Trump's election "didn't change consciously what we were doing," Miller notes, "it unfortunately made it easier to find examples, but also easier to find the language that people use to justify this kind of thinking."[7]

For the philosopher Alain Badiou, Trump's presidency is reactive, characterized by a "pathological relation to women" and an "ideological violence,"[8] evident in the ongoing consequences of his controversial family separation policy and his support for the antiabortion movement and "the Wall."[9] This ideological violence is played out in Trump's policies as well as in his performances, and it is palpable in his misogynistic rhetoric, full of "vulgarities and absurdities."[10] A clear case in point is the leaked video of Trump bragging to the *Access Hollywood* host Billy Bush about forcing himself on women: "I moved on her. . . . I moved on her very heavily, in fact," Trump said about the entertainment journalist Nancy O'Dell. "I moved on her like a bitch." He continued, "I just start kissing them. It's like a magnet. Just kiss. I don't even wait. And when you're a star, they let you do it. You can do anything. Grab them by the pussy. You can do anything."[11] The "grabber-in-chief," to borrow from the journalist and activist Naomi Klein, later excused his objectifying and aggressive language as "locker-room talk."[12] Billy Bush was subsequently fired by NBC; Donald Trump was elected the forty-fifth president of the United States.

Since Trump was elected, more than twenty historical accusations of sexual assault have been leveled against him, accusations the former president and his spokespeople are quick to "deny, divert, and discredit."[13] The "nasty women" accusing Trump and those men whom he defends have been mocked and insulted, their allegations met with demeaning language.[14] The "smackdown" is Trump's "brand of misogyny," the feminist philosopher Kate Manne notes, citing his "pig" and "dog" slurs directed at Rosie O'Donnell, Megyn Kelly, and Hillary Clinton as examples.[15] Such language and behaviors, Milena Popova argues, contribute to a "rape culture," that is, "a cultural environment . . . that enables sexual violence to thrive."[16] Trump's objectification and belittling of women did not abate in the context of the coronavirus pandemic in 2020. During a briefing while discussing mathematical modeling for projected deaths resulting from the virus, Trump used the opportunity to turn the devastating statistics into confirmation of his self-imagined sexual prowess: "The models show hundreds of thousands of people are going to die. You know what I want to do? I want to come way under the models. The professionals did the models. I was never involved in a model. But," he noted with a smirk and stroking his hands through the air as if outlining a curvaceous body, "at least this kind of model."[17] Yet, in Trump's United States, men are the ones living in "a very scary time," while "women are doing great."[18] "You've got to deny, deny, deny and push back on these women," Trump reportedly told the famed *Washington Post* investigative journalist Bob Woodward. "You've got to be strong, you've got to be aggressive. You've got to push back hard."[19] Trump's forcible rhetoric firmly situates the female body as a battleground on which demonstrations of power are acted out and won by men; the right to the female body is decidedly not in the hands of women.

Countering Trump's bullish belligerence, the figure of the Handmaid has been mobilized to highlight activism, becoming an international protest symbol, with hundreds of women donning red cloaks and white bonnets to stand against female oppression and threats to reproductive and civil rights.[20] As a protest symbol, their potency is in their striking blood-red color as well as their notable silence. "It's brilliant as a protest tactic because you're not making a disturbance," Atwood has commented. "You're not saying anything. You're sitting very silently and modestly."[21] It is a powerful subversion of the costume that marks the novel's Handmaids as highly visible and off-limits, to be seen but not heard, to be looked at but not touched.

The Deepest Sense

"Without touch there can be no other sense," Aristotle once wrote.[22] As a human requisite, touch has been described as "the most profound and philosophical" of the senses and "the foundation upon which all other senses are based . . . part of the fabric of everyday, embodied experience."[23] Touch "lies at the heart of our experience of ourselves and the world," the cultural historian Constance Classen observes in her consideration of what she refers to as "the deepest sense."[24] Touch connects us to others and, crucially, to ourselves. As Judith Butler speculates, drawing from the philosopher Maurice Merleau-Ponty, "If I cannot be touched, then there is no feeling, and with no feeling, there is no 'I'; the 'I' becomes unutterable, something unutterable to itself, unutterable to others."[25] For Butler, touch creates feeling, and feeling creates a sense of self and a sense of identity. The notion of an absence or lack of touch producing a loss of self is played out in the interactions of *The Handmade Tale*'s protagonist, Offred (Elisabeth Moss), and her perceptions of her life and purpose within Gilead. Gilead's Handmaids, with their tactile interactions policed and punished and their "deepest sense" denied, live a disembodied existence, disconnected from their past lives and present selves.

Atwood's novel is punctuated with references to touch throughout. Touch is denied, regulated, and coveted. "I hunger to touch something, other than cloth or wood. I hunger to commit the act of touch," thinks Offred, yearning to make bread with the Marthas, the low-status women who maintain the households of the Commanders.[26] She encounters a heavily pregnant Handmaid at the market: "Our fingers itch to touch her," she considers, articulating a shared yearning to make a connection with the sacred figure.[27] Contemplating her first illicit kiss with the Commander's driver, Nick (Max Minghella), she ponders, "Can I be blamed for wanting a real body, to put my arms around? Without it I too am disembodied. . . . I am like a room where things once happened and now nothing does."[28] Touch evokes memory, of the time before, of casual interactions once taken for granted and now resonant with meaning, of everyday objects that are now no more. Touch connects Offred with the past. Sliding into a bath recalls a trip to the aquarium with the daughter who was taken away from her. Placing her hand to another's pregnant belly transports her to the birth of her own daughter.

However, moments or references to touch in the adaptation—outside of the monthly Ceremony—are rare. This may, in part, be due to the differences across the two media and the necessity to drive the adaptation visually rather than solely to rely on first-person narration. The novel is a firsthand account from Offred's perspective narrated by interior monologue, a recounting, we later find out, that has been transcribed from cassettes recorded by Offred. While the adaptation retains Offred's voice-over narration, it does so sparingly. Much of what is articulated about touch in the novel is retained and amplified in performance, cinematography, and editing techniques: a lingering close-up of a hand on a shoulder, cross-cutting between one person's tactile gesture and another's. Moments of touch in the adaptation take on potent meaning as a result and are presented as sensory acts of significance, of defiance, activism, and hope.

Sensory Acts of Defiance

In the episode "Faithful" (1.5), four distinctly different sexual encounters involving Offred are depicted: the monthly Ceremony also involving Commander Waterford (Joseph Fiennes) and the Commander's Wife, Serena Joy (Yvonne Strahovski); a flashback to Offred's relationship with her husband, Luke (O-T Fagbenle), prior to the totalitarian regime of Gilead being established; and two sexual encounters with Nick, one initiated and observed by Serena and the other initiated by Offred. These four sex scenes allow a consideration of touch that complicates notions of consent, sexual agency, and sexual subjectivity. Linda Martín Alcoff argues that what is violated in sexual violation "is our sexual subjectivity, meaning our capacity for having sexual agency in our lives."[29] Across the episode, Offred experiences a reframing or renegotiation of sexual touch that involves the reclamation of her body. As a result, the television drama extends what the novel hints at toward its end by allowing Offred to reclaim her sexual subjectivity after, indeed alongside, its violation.

Across flashbacks, we learn that June (Offred's name, in the adaptation, from the time before Gilead) had an affair with Luke while he was married.[30] The first time they have sex, June says, "If we're only going to do this once, I like to go on top." June is presented as a woman with sexual agency who knows what she enjoys and is not afraid to ask for what she wants. These flashbacks are softly lit with warm lens flare, shallow depth of field, and extreme close-ups of kissing, clasped hands, touching each other's faces, and running hands over each other's bodies; the sex is explicitly consensual, and the pleasure is explicitly reciprocal. The scene is juxtaposed with Offred and Nick's first sexual encounter in Nick's annex apartment, made perverse in being watched by Serena, who has orchestrated it. Offred, on her back and fully clothed, scans her eyes across the sideboard as Nick rhythmically thrusts into her. Her face is vacant, bored even; she has learned how to present as indifferent, a participant in a perfunctory act, seemingly disengaged from her body. She catches Nick's eye, and he looks away, anguished. As he climaxes, Offred reaches her hand to fleetingly grasp hold of his elbow.

It is a gesture of sympathy and compassion but also forgiveness; Offred understands the position in which he has been placed. Prohibited, Offred's touch is a demonstrative gesture that confirms a deeper connection between the two, in spite of the coerced sexual act in which they have just taken part.

That evening, Offred is on her back again, this time for her Commander. Breaking protocol, Waterford maintains eye contact with Offred during the Ceremony and then places a hand on her thigh. Both actions are a violation of the unspoken agreement among the three, an agreement that keeps each in their "place" and maintains the order and ritual of the ceremony. Offred can only protest through internal monologue and pleading eyes: "Stop it. Stop it. Don't look at me like that. Please. Can she see him doing this? Can she feel him?" She is unable to physically or audibly resist; her internal monologue can be her only act of resistance.

Rather than a moment of being overcome by desire, Waterford's placing of his hand on Offred's thigh along with his held gaze present something more sinister: the suggestion that Waterford is not beholden to the rules and regulations. It is a moment of courting risk that disregards the potential consequences for Offred, something we encounter later in the series when Waterford takes Offred to the sex club Jezebels. When Waterford is later challenged by Offred in his office, he reasserts his power by pointing out what happens to Handmaids who depart from the expected script: referring to Offred's previous walking partner, Ofglen (Alexis Bledel), who is sentenced to "redemption" for gender treachery. The Commander tells Offred, "We had a doctor take care of the problem. It was such a small problem, truth be told." She has been subjected to genital mutilation. When Offred learns of the punishment, she seeks out Ofglen at the market; Ofglen has been posted to a new Commander and is now Ofsteven. Unable to comfort her with an embrace, Offred gently touches her gloved hand to Ofsteven's. It is a moment of solidarity and an act of defiance, a human gesture to respond to an act of barbarism. Ofsteven reveals that her real name is Emily. Moments later, Emily commandeers a car that has been left unattended at the market, driving around in circles and purposefully running over an armed Guardian before she is dragged from the car. It is a moment of acting out but also a moment of seizing control, of physical action and sensory rebellion, however temporary that might be. Handmaids are women without power or rights, but, for a moment, one is literally in the driving seat. Her actions subvert the power balance and rupture the status quo.

Offred's growing resistance is evinced in her small acts of sensory defiance—touching Nick's elbow, touching her hand to Emily's—that culminate in this episode in her seeking out Nick, without Serena as chaperone, and asserting her sexual agency. This assertion, a reclaiming of her body, requires a literal stripping away of the Handmaid's restrictive accoutrements: the heavy and capacious dress and cloak and expansive bonnet that enshroud her and present her as sexless, as forbidden and hidden, yet at the same time mark her as conspicuous: a blood-red beacon. She removes her hair covering, unclips her hair, takes off her dress, her underwear. It is then Offred who *undoes* Nick, removing his necklace, T-shirt; undoing his belt, trousers; unzipping his fly and lowering his trousers. The act of undoing is as important as the sex act that follows. It is an active and controlled undressing of herself and of her object of desire, a dismantling of conventions and the weight of expectation and control. The sex that follows is passionate, desiring, instigated and driven by Offred. She pulls Nick toward her, they kiss, and she leads him to the bed. Naked (except for Offred's socks, of course!), their limbs entwine, and hands run over each other's bodies. Offred's fingertips press into Nick's buttocks. It is a reciprocal exchange. Offred moves so she is on top of Nick. As she tips her head back, the last diegetic sound of the episode is her sexual moan. For anyone still unsure of Offred's sexual agency at this point, the soundtrack is taken over with Nina Simone's sensuous voice singing "I want a little sugar in my bowl."

Offred's assertion of sexual agency is framed against Emily's earlier apparent act of defiance at the market. The sex scene (and final five minutes of the episode) follow on from Offred's interior monologue in which she reflects on Emily's horrific punishment: "They didn't get everything. There was something inside her they couldn't take away. She looked invincible," appropriating a phrase that Luke had previously used to describe her. It is recognition of everything Emily risked in hijacking the car. Her invincibility is a refusal to be made passive, in spite of having her genitals mutilated. As a Handmaid, Offred is forced to renegotiate her sensory, and specifically haptic, existence in order to survive. She is frequently required to go into herself, refrain from physical contact to the point where she becomes disembodied and disconnected from herself. Yet with Nick, she initiates a reembodiment, asserting her ownership of her body and her sexuality.

You Leave Your Body

Two sex scenes frame the second-season episode "The Last Ceremony" (2.10), in which Offred's attempts to disconnect from the Ceremony sex act are called into question. In the first, a Ceremony takes place with an initially blurred Handmaid, who is revealed to be Emily—now Ofroy—Commander Roy, and the Commander's Wife. Offred's voice-over provides the commentary: "You treat it like a job. An unpleasant job to be gotten through as fast as possible. Kissing is forbidden. This makes its bearable. One detaches oneself. One describes. An act of copulation, fertilization perhaps. No more to you than a bee is to a flower. You steel yourself. You leave your body." The scene is framed mostly using overhead/overbed shots and close-ups of Emily's pained face intercut with close-ups of the Commander's straining face, which we initially read as physical exertion and pleasure, before he drops to the floor from a heart attack. There are also frequent close-ups on Emily's wrists being held by the Commander's Wife. The voice-over reframes earlier Ceremonies we have witnessed featuring Offred, where she has looked visibly bored, scanning the room or recalling memories to take her away from experiencing the rape. Here, the effect is more jarring and difficult to watch, as Offred's voice-over accompanies Emily's pained expression, suggesting that she is unable to detach herself, to leave her body.

A second scene in the episode is even more brutal. Heavily pregnant, Offred experiences contractions, which initiate an ostentatious birth ritual. It is a false alarm—Braxton Hicks—and Serena is left disappointed and humiliated. The Commander has also just had his power challenged, as Offred left him with the suggestion that the baby she is carrying is not his "own flesh." By way of a punishment, the Waterfords ominously conspire to help the baby along in "the most natural way." Serena invites Offred to sit next to her on her bed and then places her hand over Offred's. "We need to help the baby come out naturally," she whispers, as Fred comes in the room, shuts the doors, and takes off his jacket. Offred looks down at Serena's hand placed over her own as it moves to take her by the wrist. It is a small movement but affirms her intention to restrain Offred. Both Waterfords ignore Offred's shouts and proclamations as Serena moves over Offred in a dominating position that contrasts her usual ceremonial position behind her. Serena pins Offred to the bed as Fred recites the Bilhah story and forcefully penetrates her. As Offred's cries stop and her face is frozen in pained defeat, her earlier voice-over is repeated and extended: "You treat it like a job. One detaches oneself. No more to you than a bee is to a flower. Not me. Not my flesh. I'm not here." The camera remains focused on Offred's face. Fred grasps the bedpost at the moment of climax. It is an action we have seen him perform before, during previous Ceremonies, and one alluded to earlier in the episode when, experiencing a contraction, Offred grasps the bedpost for stability. She is aware of the irony then, removing her hand with disgust, and we are reminded of it again with this rape. The bedpost in this instance connects her touch to that of the Commander, an inanimate object on which meaning is attributed, no longer an item of furniture or sturdy support but a charged prop in the scene of Offred's serial sexual abuse.

Across these two scenes, Offred's voice-over is revealed to be wishful thinking, a self-preservation strategy rather than the lived experience. Her facial expressions contradict her will to detach, and the explicitly brutal rape asks us to revisit those earlier Ceremonies we witnessed, including the first time Nick has sex with Offred under Serena's watchful glare, and see them clearly as rape, confirming that any consent given is while under duress and therefore not consent. Voice and touch work together in these two scenes to highlight the contradictions of each. The voice-over narration, the inner voice, is not the truth but what Offred wishes to be the truth. It is a far cry from Offred's Ceremony voice-over in "Birth Day" (1.2), in which she says, dead-pan, "I wish he'd hurry the fuck up," an almost comical moment of defiance and resistance in a situation that is otherwise beyond her control. The writer of "The Last Ceremony," Yahlin Chang, has said that she wrote the scene with the intention of showing Offred's struggle to disassociate: "She hasn't [been subjected to] the ceremony in a long time," says Chang, "so she doesn't do us that favor of disassociating successfully before it starts. While it's going on, she's trying to disassociate, but she's having a hard time of it. She's out of prac-tice, and she's pregnant, and she's very much in her body."[31] More than this, the scene, along with the Ceremony scene from the start of the episode, suggests the Handmaids have never been able to disassociate. It is a horrific realization and a clear statement for anyone still contemplating Offred's and the other Handmaids' choice regarding their situation. The violent scene also confirms Fred's despotic egomania and Serena's sadism and complicity in the abuse of Offred, both deluded that they may be able to encourage the birth "naturally" through sexual force. Once the rape is over, Offred repeats the action she had been doing prior to being summoned by Serena: gently stroking the bump of her pregnant belly, a tactile action that is presented as reassuring to her unborn child but also to herself, a reconnection to a body that has been temporarily taken away from her and a body she now shares with her baby, who will soon also be taken away.

Unwanted Touch

In *Rape and Resistance: Understanding the Complexities of Sexual Violation*, Alcoff recognizes touch as central to sexual violation when she writes that "sexual violations occur in one form or another through the abrogation of physical intimacy, usually in the form of touch."[32] Drawing on the phenomenological approach taken by Edmund Husserl and Maurice Merleau-Ponty, Alcoff considers touch as a mode of communication through which our knowledge and understanding of ourselves and others is defined. Referring to Merleau-Ponty's consideration of touch as dialectical, Alcoff writes, "Being touched is always a touching alongside: in every encounter I touch that which touches me."[33] This dialectical nature is challenged in Offred's attempt to detach herself during the Ceremony in confirming her alienation as a victim of sexual abuse, at the same time as pointing to the impossibility of detachment. Offred's self-preservation strategy is in keeping with Alia Al-Saji's claim that "within a social field where it constantly risks unwanted and intrusive touch, feminine embodiment seems habituated to a certain defensive tactile self-containment."[34] The "Last Ceremony" episode highlights this strategy of self-containment and asks us to review what we have seen in the preceding episodes. It also reminds us that Offred's experience is a subjective experience and that we should not be too quick to conflate her experience with that of all Handmaids. The use of her voice-over, to accompany a Ceremony featuring first a different Handmaid and then herself, emphasizes that while there may be a desire or need to detach in order to make it bearable, the detachment fails.

Offred's attempts at self-containment can be considered alongside another tactile containment that is not self-imposed but is enforced as part of the Gilead regime. As the Handmaid indoctrinator Aunt Lydia (Ann Dowd) tells the Handmaids during a routine punishment for disobedience, "There is more than one kind of freedom. There is freedom to and freedom from. In the days of anarchy, it was freedom to. Now, you are being given freedom from. That is a gift from God. Do not underrate it" ("June" 2.1).

Aunt Lydia's comment refers to a shift in how women experienced freedom before the regime and following its implementation. In Gilead, women are protected from "unwanted and intrusive touch" due to its enforced prohibition. Aunt Lydia presents this as something the women should be grateful for, a burden they no longer need to carry. "We had choices then," Offred points out to Commander Waterford in the "Faithful" episode. "Now you have respect," he replies. "You have protection. You can fulfill your biological destinies in peace. . . . What else is there to live for?"

"Freedom from" might be welcomed in a culture where a man can make claims to grab women by the pussy and go on to become the president of the United States of America. What is not accounted for, however, is the extent to which the regulation of touch also means a restriction of touch that is wanted and, in fact, needed. Considering the significance of touch in *The Handmaid's Tale*, Atwood has herself described touch as "a very primal sense." The result of not being touched at all is being "isolated in the material world."[35] The theologian Cristina Traina also sees a threat to this primal sense in a contemporary culture that is becoming increasingly touch averse, which she attributes in part to increased reports of sexual abuse at the hands of politicians, teachers, pastors, and coaches. "Much of American society is a 'low touch' culture," she observes. "Against the backdrop of a ballooning presumption against touch, we have been satisfied with saying simply that good touch is no-touch, or touch that is not-bad."[36] And yet, Traina emphasizes, "touch is a condition of human flourishing," citing numerous studies that evince "the physical, psychological and spiritual need for a steady diet of touch."[37] By restricting and regulating touch, Gilead denies its subjects an essential human need, isolating them from each other as well as from themselves. "It is the goal of the regime to decree who can touch whom and how," Atwood explains. "All societies do this but totalitarianisms take it to an extreme."[38] The lack of touch makes for more pliable subjects, less likely to question their restricted choices.

I Didn't Choose This

The politics of touch, in the process of adaptation, undergoes a shift from negotiating and navigating language and the limits on choice and agency in the novel to a more deterministic approach to call out the Ceremony sex act as rape at key moments. In the novel, Offred struggles to know how to label the Ceremony sex act, noting, "My red skirt is hitched up to my waist, though no higher. Below it the Commander is fucking. What he is fucking is the lower part of my body. I do not say making love, because this is not what he is doing. Copulating too would be inaccurate, because it would imply two people and only one is involved. Nor does rape cover it: nothing is going on here that I haven't signed up for. There wasn't a lot of choice but there was some, and this is what I chose."[39] Confirming this sense of choice, Atwood has noted, "The Handmaids do have a choice—they can refuse to be Handmaids—but the alternatives on offer are less attractive. So they have in effect 'agreed.' Thus Offred struggles for a language that can accurately describe what she has in a way 'consented' to."[40] The less attractive alternatives that Atwood refers to here are to be sent to the Colonies—areas contaminated by radioactive waste to which infertile women, or other "unwomen," are sent to clean up as punishment and to atone for their sins—forced into prostitution at Gilead brothel, Jezebels; mutilated; or executed. Atwood's knowing use of scare quotes underscores this struggle for a language, distinguishing the novel's frame from that of the adaptation.

In the television drama, the Ceremony is framed as rape from the outset, although the word itself is not directly applied to the Ceremony until the sixth episode of the first season, "A Woman's Place." The term is expressed first to Nick when he tries to console Offred and then is heard a scene later when Offred reveals the truth of Gilead to a visiting female Mexican ambassador:

> I lied to you. This is a brutal place. We're prisoners. If we run, they'll try to kill us. Or worse. They beat us. They use cattle prods to try to get us to behave. If we're caught reading, they'll cut off a finger. Second offense, just the whole hand. They gouge out our eyes. They maim us in worse ways than you can imagine. They rape me. Every month. Whenever I might be fertile. I didn't choose this. They caught me. I was trying to escape. They took my daughter. So don't be sorry. Okay? Please don't be sorry. Please do something.

It is significantly at this point in the season, after we have already seen Offred seemingly give herself over to the Ceremony a number of times, that a more forceful certainty about consent, control, and sexual agency is articulated. The Mexican ambassador is an outsider to Gilead, a person—and woman—in power who has the ability and platform to speak out against the regime. The certainty of the language of rape in the television drama amplifies the uncertainty of the language of the novel. It also speaks to the shifting parameters of language in the #MeToo era and volume of historical sexual abuse and harassment accusations and cases being brought against men that date back to the 1980s and earlier. Shifting popular understandings of consent and sexual agency are key here. Offred's outpouring to the Mexican ambassador articulates an oppositional experience between us/Handmaids and them / the system of oppression that stretches far beyond her own encounters of brutality. The emphasis on a system is much more explicit than in the novel, which is more firmly tied to Offred's subjective experience as a result of its first-person recounting, and further complicates the Handmaid's agency and choice in taking part in the Ceremony. Agency and choice will always be in question, as Jeffrey Gaunthier notes, "when an oppressive system effectively defines the choice situation of the oppressed class."[41]

Reconfiguring Touch

The Handmaid's Tale has been widely received as a "political parable of our time" and "scarily relevant" in its depiction of the systemic and endemic oppression of women.[42] To examine this through the politics of touch not only reveals the constraints and containment that women are no longer tolerating, but it can also be read as a commentary on the increasingly fragile human relations that have begun to characterize the contemporary Western world since the publication of Atwood's novel. Writing just one year after the original publication of *The Handmaid's Tale*, the anthropologist Ashley Montagu wrote, "The world of western men has come to rely heavily for communication on the 'distance senses': sight and hearing and the 'proximity senses'—touch and taste—have been sidelined."[43] The consequences of Montagu's observation can be seen more recently in the arguments put forward by cultural critics such as Naomi Klein and George Monbiot. Both have discussed loneliness and detachment as the plague of our age, whereby our physical, social, and tactile interactions have become substituted or diminished and we have become increasingly disconnected from contemporary life and our selves.[44]

Touch connects us to our sense of self, our relations with others, and our culture, but this also works in reverse: our culture shapes our perception of, connection to, and relationship with touch. As Al-Saji notes, "Sociality, history and culture are not external to touch but configure its shape, texture and sense from within."[45] The act of touch has unquestionably become more politically charged in the wake of #MeToo and #TimesUp. With the spotlight on female oppression and unequal gender power relations, we are palpably experiencing a reconfiguration of the shape, texture, and sense of touch that is not rewriting but reframing earlier acts of touch. Calling out unwanted and intrusive touch has never been more prevalent, along with attempts to establish the parameters of sexual consent. "No more casual patting, it seems," Margaret Atwood has remarked, as the landscape of casual intimacy is redrawn, the language of consent is renegotiated, and the culture of touch is redefined.[46] In the time of the coronavirus pandemic, touch has been drastically restricted, with government-imposed quarantines, self-isolation, shielding, and social-distancing measures limiting touch to the parameters of one's household. Yet a worldwide surge in the reporting of domestic abuse and "intimate terrorism" serves to remind us that the *household* is not the safest space for everyone.[47] The third-season episode "Household" (3.6) plays on the double meaning of the term when Offred meets a Handmaid from a Washington, DC, household and learns that the face veil she wears—along with the other DC Handmaids—masks the horrific mutilation of her mouth, which has been sewn shut with rings through her lips. The silencing of women has been made permanent.

The television adaptation of *The Handmaid's Tale* plays out the reconfiguration of the shape, texture, and sense of touch. In Gilead's regulation of touch, we witness tactile containment taken to the extreme and the damaging consequences felt by women but also men, who are also subjected to proscriptive touch. The act of touching and being touched as depicted in *The Handmaid's Tale* is made all the more powerful when considered in the context of the Trump era and the brash, aggressive physicality that characterized Trump's politics and performance of politics during his presidency. Often lacking the approval of his own cabinet, Congress, and party, his has been a nonconsensual, neoliberal politics of impulsive demand and manipulative force, evident in his incendiary and puerile political enactments and pronouncements on the world stage. Touch, Alcoff writes, is "a structuring of the world beyond one's self." Thus, "a touch that is unwanted renders the self-other relation acutely perceptible, highlighting the separation of self from other."[48] In Trump's directive to "grab them by the pussy" and then his excusing it as "locker-room talk" and in his repeated refusal to wear a face mask in spite of the recommendations of the US health-protection agency, the Centers for Disease Control and Prevention (CDC), he has articulated a conscious and intentional separation, a denial of consent, an intentional abuse of power, a declaration of authority, of supremacy that, like Commander Waterford's thigh touching, has no regard for the boundaries of self.[49] It is this shift toward calling out unwanted touch—touch as sexual violation—that Trump was referring to in his comment about men living in "a very scary time," when actions, long since carried out, are brought back into the spotlight, their appropriateness previously taken for granted but now questioned. What many have struggled with, in particular, is that it is not that the culture has changed so that touch is now unwanted, but that kind of touch was never wanted in the first place.

Notes

I am greatly indebted to Margaret Atwood for generously giving her time to answer my questions about the novel and Hulu adaptation.

1   Emily Nussbaum, "A Cunning Adaptation of 'The Handmaid's Tale,'" *New Yorker*, May 15, 2017, https://www.newyorker.com/magazine/2017/05/22/a-cunning-adaptation-of-the-handmaids-tale.

2   Margaret Atwood, "Science Fiction and the Future: In Conversation with Margaret Atwood," interview by Caroline Edwards, *New Scientist Live*, October 1, 2017, https://www.newscientist.com/article/2215957-margaret-atwoods-the-testaments-anti-science-world-is-a-grim-warning.

3   Margaret Atwood, "Margaret Atwood on What 'The Handmaid's Tale' Means in the Age of Trump," *New York Times*, March 10, 2017, https://www.nytimes.com/2017/03/10/books/review/margaret-atwood-handmaids-tale-age-of-trump.html.

4   Margaret Atwood, "My Hero: George Orwell by Margaret Atwood," *Guardian*, January 18, 2013, https://www.theguardian.com/books/2013/jan/18/my-hero-george-orwell-atwood.

5   Matt Flegenheimer and Michael Barbaro, "Donald Trump Is Elected President in Stunning Repudiation of the Establishment," *New York Times*, November 9, 2016, https://www.nytimes.com/2016/11/09/us/politics/hillary-clinton-donald-trump-president.html.

6   Atwood, "Age of Trump."

7 Constance Grady, "Margaret Atwood and Bruce Miller Talk Handmaid's Tale, Pitch Tampon Names," *Vox*, June 7, 2017, https://www.vox.com/culture/2017/6/7/15736998/margaret-atwood-bruce-miller-handmaids-tale.

8 Alain Badiou, *Trump* (Cambridge, UK: Polity, 2019), 16, 18, 43.

9 See Maya Rhodan, "Here Are the Facts about President Trump's Family Separation Policy," *Time*, June 20, 2018, https://time.com/5314769/family-separation-policy-donald-trump; Sabrina Siddiqui, "'This Is the End-game': How Trump Has Helped Turn the Tide against Abortion," *Guardian*, May 18, 2019, https://www.theguardian.com/world/2019/may/18/trump-abortion-judges-appointments-culture-war-us; Julie Hirschfeld Davis and Michael D. Shear, *Border Wars: Inside Trump's Assault on Immigration* (New York: Simon and Schuster, 2019).

10 Badiou, *Trump*, 17.

11 Mark Makela, "Transcript: Donald Trump's Taped Comments about Women," *New York Times*, October 8, 2016, https://www.nytimes.com/2016/10/08/us/donald-trump-tape-transcript.html.

12 Naomi Klein, *No Is Not Enough: Defeating the New Shock Politics* (London: Allen Lane, 2017), 83–100.

13 Shannon Pettypiece, "Deny, Divert, Discredit: Trump Turns to His Scandal Playbook Once Again," NBCNews.com, September 20, 2019, https://www.nbcnews.com/politics/donald-trump/deny-divert-discredit-trump-turns-his-scandal-playbook-once-again-n1057181.

14 See Allie Malloy, Kate Sullivan, and Jeff Zeleny, "Trump Mocks Christine Blasey Ford's Testimony, Tells People 'Think of Your Son,'" CNN.com, October 3, 2018, https://edition.cnn.com/2018/10/02/politics/trump-mocks-christine-blasey-ford-kavanaugh-supreme-court; Michael D. Shear and Eileen Sullivan, "'Horseface,' 'Lowlife,' 'Fat, Ugly': How the President Demeans Women," *New York Times*, October 16, 2018, https://www.nytimes.com/2018/10/16/us/politics/trump-women-insults.html.

15 Kate Manne, *Down Girl: The Logic of Misogyny* (New York: Oxford University Press, 2017), 87.

16 Milena Popova, *Consent* (Cambridge, MA: MIT Press, 2019), 182.

17 Michael Ruiz, "President Trump Makes Joke about Dating Models While Discussing COVID-19 Models," FoxNews.com, April 3, 2020, https://www.foxnews.com/politics/president-trump-joke-dating-models-discussing-covid-19.

18 Jeremy Diamond, "Trump Says It's 'a Very Scary Time for Young Men in America,'" CNN.com, October 2, 2018, https://edition.cnn.com/2018/10/02/politics/trump-scary-time-for-young-men-metoo.

19 Bob Woodward, *Fear: Trump in the White House* (New York: Simon and Schuster, 2018), 175.

20 Peter Beaumont and Amanda Holpuch, "How The Handmaid's Tale Dressed Protest across the World," *Guardian*, August 3, 2018, https://www.theguardian.com/world/2018/aug/03/how-the-handmaids-tale-dressed-protests-across-the-world.

21 Andrew Anthony, "Margaret Atwood on Tyranny, Survival and Protest Tactics," *Noted*, October 1, 2019, https://www.noted.co.nz/currently/currently-profiles/margaret-atwood-handmaids-tale-author-tyranny-survival-protest-tactics.

22 Aristotle, *De Anima*, III.13.435a–436b, 602, in *The Basic Works of Aristotle*, ed. Richard McKeon (New York: Random House, 1941).

23 Denis Diderot cited in Élisabeth de Fortenay, *Diderot: Reason and Resonance*, trans. Jeffrey Melman (New York: Braziller, 1982), 157–58; Ashley Montagu, *Touching: The Human Significance of the Skin*, 3rd ed. (New York: Harper and Row, 1986), 4.

24 Constance Classen, *The Deepest Sense: A Cultural History of Touch* (Urbana: University of Illinois Press, 2012), xi.

25 Judith Butler, *Senses of the Subject* (New York: Fordham University Press, 2015), 46.

26 Margaret Atwood, *The Handmaid's Tale* (Toronto: McClelland and Stewart, 1985), 21.

27 Atwood, 36

28 Atwood, 113–14.

29 Linda Martín Alcoff, *Rape and Resistance: Understanding the Complexities of Sexual Violation* (Cambridge, UK: Polity, 2018), 111.

30 Offred's real name is never revealed in the novel, although readers have attributed "June" to her based on its being the only name whispered between the Handmaids at the Rachel and Leah Centre that never appears again. "That was not my original thought, but it fits," Atwood has conceded, "so readers are welcome to it if they wish." Atwood, "Age of Trump."

31 Josh Wigler, "Handmaid's Tale Writer Explains That 'Brutal' Ceremony Scene," *Hollywood Reporter*, June 21, 2018, https://www.hollywoodreporter.com/live-feed/handmaids-tale-season-2-episode-10-last-ceremony-explained-1122377.

32 Alcoff, *Rape and Resistance*, 71.

33 Alcoff, 71.

34 Alia Al-Saji, "Bodies and Sensings: On the Uses of Husserlian Phenomenology for Feminist Theory," *Continental Philosophy Review* 43, no. 1 (2010): 33.

35 Margaret Atwood, email correspondence with the author, December 2019.

36 Cristina Traina, "Touch on Trial: Power and the Right to Physical Affection," *Journal of the Society of Christian Ethics* 25, no. 1 (2006): 4.

37 Traina, 3, 6–7.

38 Atwood, email correspondence.

39 Atwood, *Handmaid's Tale*, 104–5.

40 Atwood, email correspondence.

41 Jeffrey A. Gauthier, "Consent, Coercion and Sexual Autonomy," in *A Most Detestable Crime: New Philosophical Essays on Rape*, ed. Keith Burgess-Jackson (Oxford: Oxford University Press, 1999), 85.

42 Leah Reis-Dennis, "A Parable for Our Time: Hulu's *The Handmaid's Tale*," *Nursing Clio*, April 25, 2017, https://nursingclio.org/2017/04/25/a -parable-for-our-time-hulus-the-handmaids-tale; Samira Wiley, quoted in Sandra Gonzalez, "'The Handmaid's Tale' Stars See Show as 'Scarily Relevant,'" CNN.com, April 26, 2017, https://www.cnn.com/2017/04/26/ entertainment/handmaids-tale-hulu/index.html.

43 Montagu, *Touching*, xiv.

44 Klein, *No Is Not Enough*; George Monbiot, *Out of the Wreckage: A New Politics for an Age of Crisis* (London: Bloomsbury, 2017).

45 Al-Saji, "Bodies and Sensings," 72.

46 Atwood, email correspondence.

47 Amanda Taub, "A New Covid-19 Crisis: Domestic Abuse Rises Worldwide," *New York Times*, April 6, 2020, https://www.nytimes.com/2020/04/ 06/world/coronavirus-domestic-violence.html.

48 Alcoff, *Rape and Resistance*, 72.

49 Anna North, "What Trump's Refusal to Wear a Mask Says about Masculinity in America," *Vox*, May 12, 2020, https://www.vox.com/2020/5/12/ 21252476/masks-for-coronavirus-trump-pence-honeywell-covid-19.

THE SOUND OF MONEY AND POWER

MUSICAL SCORING IN TRUMP-ERA TELEVISION DRAMA

Aimee Mollaghan

The Trump era witnessed a dissolution of the political status quo and traditional class structures that left liberal elites scrambling to understand their place within this new populist world order. This has culminated in dramas infused with dark comedic undertones, such as *Succession* (HBO, 2018–) and *The Good Fight* (CBS All Access, 2017–).[1] Playing on the taste and knowingness of the shows' liberal, educated audiences, the scores of both series directly reference seventeenth- and eighteenth-century orchestral music in an intentional and often bathetic manner. David Buckley's theme music for *The Good Fight*, for example, overtly draws on not only the stately conventions of Baroque music, such as a figured bass and counterpoint, but also the discord and emotion of Romanticism to create something that teeters on farcical in its extravagance and excess. Buckley states that he had to navigate between being comedic and serious in his score for the show. For *Succession*, the composer Nicholas Britell was tasked with establishing "a sonic palette of extreme, obscene wealth."[2] The musical theme, which recurs in different arrangements throughout the show, embodies the grandeur of old money and the disintegration of hegemonic complexes through its juxtaposition of classical instruments with electronic instrumentation and hip-hop beats.

The musical pastiche and allusions in these compositions can be intellectually understood by the shows' intended viewing demographics through the music's historical references, but audiences can also feel an emotional and structural unraveling through the musical form. Filled with the absurdity of history repeating itself, these scores are also underscored with tension and dissonance in their harmonic structures that reflect a societal unease. This chapter explores how series such as these utilize their musical scores to accentuate and embody the irrationality, chaos, and disruption of prevailing power and class structures during the Trump era.

Context and Commentary

The Good Fight, created by Michelle and Robert King, is deemed by the *New York Times* to be "the only TV show that gets life under Trump" and "entertainment for the resistance."[3] A spin-off of the CBS drama *The Good Wife* (2009–16), the show picks up the story of the liberal patrician lawyer Diane Lockhart (Christine Baranski) from where the earlier series leaves off as she negotiates life under the Trump presidency after losing her retirement fund in a Madoff-style investment scam. Lockhart, so liberal a lawyer that she keeps a photograph of herself with Hillary Rodham Clinton on her desk, joins Reddick Boseman, a traditionally African American law firm, along with her goddaughter, Maia Rindell (Rose Leslie), after they are both tainted among the blue-chip law firms by their association with the Rindell financial scandal. The show, like *The Good Wife* before it, grounds itself in the contemporary news cycle. This time, however, it expressly draws on events connected with the Trump presidency in order to demonstrate the preposterousness of life under Trump. The seasons are structured around the presidency, each episode literally counting down the days that have passed since Trump's inauguration. *The Good Fight* constantly blurs the lines between fact and fiction, between the real and surreal; an ambiguous figure, who may or may not be Melania Trump, sashays her way into the third season; a thinly veiled character based on the Alt-Right political commentator Milo Yiannopoulos blusters through the first and third; a copy of Trump's mythical golden-shower tape comes into the possession of Reddick Boseman in season 2. The Trump presidency is always in the background, creating an affective atmosphere, demarcating a world out of joint.

This societal unraveling becomes increasingly reflected in the structure of the program. Although it may begin with the financial downfall of the wealthy American 1 percenters, it quickly shifts toward comprehending the corrosion of US society under the Trump presidency. Diane, a stable voice of liberal sensibility in *The Good Wife*, gradually moves off-kilter as her moral barometer vacillates as *The Good Fight* progresses. She microdoses on psilocybin, takes up aikido and knife throwing, and joins an all-female liberal underground resistance group bent on undermining the Trump government by adopting many of the political and propaganda strategies previously abhorrent to her and other liberals.

The formal structure of the program becomes progressively disordered. By the third season, the show shifts to having a manifest pedagogical function, educating its audience on Trump-era concerns and strategies and offering a metacommentary on events. Beginning with the title sequence, it progresses to include 2-D animated explainers of legal and social terms connected to the Trump presidency, such as "nondisclosure forms." Fourth-wall breaks appear, where characters direct their thoughts to camera, increasingly infiltrating each other's seemingly private address. Even the weather in the third season comes to operate in pathetic fallacy with Trump-era society. Throughout the season, the weather becomes increasingly unstable, with lightning and torrential rain visible in the background of shots. This culminates in extreme weather conditions in the final episode of the season, which characters begin to connect to signs and symbols from the book of Revelations predicting the end of the world.

Buckley's theme music for *The Good Fight* serves to encapsulate the incongruity and destruction of the Trump era. The music is tied to a visual title sequence, also spectacular in its lavishness and extravagance, the music and image spurring each other to increasing excess, exploding the values and objects that symbolize Diane's pre-Trump life. Antique wooden desks are obliterated, expensive leather bags are torn asunder, wine glasses shatter, flowers explode. Buckley's music moves from the Baroque gentility of the viola da gamba to a cacophony of rage that teeters on farce as the percussion and full orchestra is joined by a screaming choir in triple fortissimo. There are changes in the arrangement of the title sequence across the first three seasons of the show, demarcating the increasing ludicrousness of the Trump era. The title sequence in season 2 features visual references to Putin, Trump, and the Alt-Right on exploding television screens. By season 3, the title sequence has taken a turn toward self-reflexivity in its self-consciousness and increased extravagance. Fine-china cups spin in concentric circles, enjoying the choreography of a Busby Berkeley dance number. There is a complete collapse of the moving image itself. At the point that the desk explodes in the season 3 title sequence, the entire set falls apart, and the black cyclorama and lights fall to reveal the set and the artifice of the sequence. The sequence and Buckley's music are high in energy and intensity yet nonetheless elegant in their richness and excess.

Succession, a satire of wealth and power created by the British screenwriter Jesse Armstrong, follows the fortunes of the super-rich Roy family members, each vying for control over the family's media conglomerate in the wake of the perceived imminent retirement of the elderly family patriarch, Logan. *Succession* draws on a number of families associated with media conglomerates as inspiration for the Roys, such as the Murdochs (News Corp. and Fox Corp.), the Redstones (ViacomCBS), and the Hearsts (Hearst Communications). A 2019 story in *Esquire* even maps the similarities between the Murdochs and the Roy family on the back of a *New York Times* exposé on the Murdoch family.[4] Echoing Orson Welles's family sagas *The Magnificent Ambersons* (1942) and *Citizen Kane* (1941), the show is even more opulent and baroque than *The Good Fight* in its locations, clothing, mise-en-scène and music. The term "stealth wealth" is frequently used about the series, particularly in relation to its use of costuming. The Roy family wear clothes that are sumptuous in fabrics and cut, without obvious branding. These are clothes for a cultured audience to read as expensive and tasteful. The film shot on 35 mm film, in an era in which most television drama, even *The Good Fight*, is shot digitally, further offers a subtle marker of taste, money, and refinement.

Quality Music for Quality Drama

Both *The Good Fight* and *Succession* are broadcast on subscription-based streaming services. They are for discriminating audiences, prosperous enough to afford subscriptions to CBS All Access or HBO in the United States or overseas alternatives. Unsurprisingly, they quickly became fodder for the chattering liberal classes, with weekly episodes dissected and scrutinized within Left-leaning quality-media platforms such as the *New York Times*, the *Guardian*, *Vulture*, the *New Yorker*, and the *Atlantic*. Dean J. DeFino asserts in his monograph *The HBO Effect* that existing ideas of "quality" television began to emerge when television networks first began to track audience data in the early 1970s. This led to the development of programming aimed at educated, professional, middle-class audiences with disposable income. HBO has made itself the poster child of quality television, becoming the yardstick by which other networks and platforms measure themselves. By virtue of using a subscription model, HBO has afforded itself greater autonomy than the major broadcast networks in the United States, which were dependent on the whims and caprices of advertisers as a source of revenue.

One of the principal ways HBO has marketed itself is as a selective service, available to an audience with the means to pay for its exclusive content. With HBO's move into original quality programming such as *Oz* (1997–2003), *Sex and the City* (1998–2004), and *The Sopranos* (1999–2007) in the late 1990s, its narrowcasting has proved increasingly enticing to a liberal, high-value demographic. DeFino points out that the subscription-based television model has long appealed to progressive liberals seeking an alternative to what was often viewed as the triviality of broadcast television. HBO bills itself as "Not TV," identifies itself as exclusive in relation to content and access, and positions itself as a desirable service for a discerning audience. As Jane Feuer suggests, "Although a cable service such as HBO has a very small audience of subscribers, much smaller than the equivalent audience for network quality drama, they happen to be the very upscale demographic willing to pay extra for more specialised and more highbrow fare."[5] HBO has long been identified as the catalyst for a new Golden Age of Television precipitated by its release of original series at the end of the twentieth century, following its prior association with sports programming, stand-up comedy specials, and self-produced movies. As DeFino posits, "HBO has always tried to distinguish itself from its competitors by offering what others could not."[6] Although at first this may have been through the inclusion of explicit content and graphic violence that were not acceptable on network television, it came to introduce across its original programming output a "level of narrative, character, and thematic sophistication that has spread across the channel spectrum."[7]

HBO has therefore had an impact on not just how quality television drama is watched but how it is made. Its model for producing innovative programming with high production values has become the standard that other services such as Showtime, Starz, AMC, FX, CBS All Access, and increasingly Netflix and Amazon Studios strive to emulate. Due to the freedom afforded creative teams, HBO has become an attractive home for television and film talent, providing writers and directors such as Steven Spielberg, Martin Scorsese, Adam McKay, and Alan Ball with a haven to explore longer-form subjects with the high production values and time more commonly associated with film production. This is especially apparent in the approach to scoring original series such as *Succession*. The Emmy-winning score for *Succession* is composed by Nicholas Britell, notable for his scores for critically well-received films such as *Moonlight* (Barry Jenkins, 2016), *The Big Short* (Adam McKay, 2015), and *If Beale Street Could Talk* (Barry Jenkins, 2019). Unusually, the second season of *Succession* had no temp score. This demonstrates an extraordinary level of freedom for the composer. Similarly, Buckley notes the liberty afforded him by Robert and Michelle King, the showrunners of both *The Good Wife* and *The Good Fight*.[8] Unlike prevailing scoring practices, both Buckley and Britell are long-term creative collaborators with the teams behind *The Good Fight* and *Succession*. Britell was brought onto *Succession* early on by Adam McKay. Likewise, Buckley began scoring *The Good Wife* during the fourth season and has continued to collaborate with the Kings on *The Good Fight* and their series *Evil* (CBS All Access, 2019–).

In *Tuning In: American Narrative Television Music*, Ron Rodman points out that once television programs came to look like films, there was a need for them to sound like films.[9] During the 1950s and 1960s, it was relatively common for composers such as Elmer Bernstein, Leonard Rosenman, John Williams, Henry Mancini, and Jerry Goldsmith, more associated with film music, to concurrently work in television. Rosenman was garnering Emmy Awards for his television scores while simultaneously being conferred Academy Awards for scoring critically lauded films such as *Barry Lyndon* (Stanley Kubrick, 1975). It is interesting that although there may be an increasing need for television music to sound like that of film, there nonetheless remain differences between scoring for the big and small screen, even with the deep pockets of subscription-based services. Leitmotifs in television dramas tend to differ from their counterparts in film by degree rather than nature. In classical film scoring, they represent short musical ideas, which come to be associated with characters, places, situations, or objects within a moving-image narrative through repetition and familiarity.[10] In contrast, due to the ephemerality of the television text, its leitmotifs tend to be more economical and draw more from the competencies of the audience to express meaning. Whereas a two-hour film has sufficient diegetic space to develop its models of demarcation, a television program "must rely on repetition of a limited number of musical leitmotifs for signification," its ascriptive nature "providing multiple modes of signification in a very short period of time."[11] This is something that the score for *Succession* eschews to a certain degree, extending the architecture of its score to encompass the entirety of a season. Indeed, both scores owe much to the Romanticism of classical Hollywood scoring.

Nonetheless, acknowledging the need to adapt to the vicissitudes of television and the audience that "quality" dramas attract, both scores mostly eschew attaching leitmotifs to the protagonists. Buckley—referencing his score for *The Good Wife* and the show's central protagonist, Alicia Florrick (Julianna Margulies)—poses the question, "I mean you—one has to ask oneself the question: If there is something called 'Alicia's theme,' what resonance and use would that have by episode 30?"[12] He makes a salient point, given the developmental arc of the protagonists across seasons. Providing characters with a fixed musical identity becomes somewhat redundant over the arc of multiple episodes. This does not mean to intimate that individual characters in *The Good Fight* do not bear their own leitmotifs on occasion. For example, the larger-than-life character of Roland Blum (Michael Sheen), who joins the third season of the show, is marked by a musical identity. Blum is a rapacious amalgam of Roy Cohn, Beau Brummel, and the Greek god Pan, and his leitmotif recurs with variations throughout the season, denoting his flamboyant appearance and Dionysian appetites. Buckley suggests that in a show that does not deign to lead its audience, it could perhaps be considered facile to provide each character with an individual theme. However, the themes associated with the protagonist, Diane, are, as he points out, associated with her interior states during significant moments of her life, whether this is reflecting her psychological processes while microdosing, her shifting relationship with her husband, Kurt (Gary Cole), or regaining her confidence and desire to continue "The Good Fight."[13] These themes return with variations in later episodes.

There is a similar approach in relation to the characters on *Succession*. There is no specific theme for individual members of the Roy family, for example, and Britell avers that in the first season, he was more concerned with "feelings and bigger picture concepts of the storyline and the world and the world in which these people find themselves and their relationships rather than individual characters."[14] Themes recur with variations throughout the first season to match scenes and character arcs. Although the original theme music returns in season 2, new melodic and harmonic ideas are introduced with the evolution of the narrative. Britell's variations can involve the use of different instruments, rhythms, time signatures, or classical forms.

The theme music recalls the type of "dark courtly classical music" that Britell considers the Roy family would imagine for themselves.[15] However, this marker of taste is thrown off balance by its arrangement. The opening is downbeat. It is in a minor key (C minor). The piano is dissonant, detuned, and often out of synchronization. The bass line is distorted. Extreme registers are used on the piano, underpinned by a low ostinato pattern of the two string layers. The high strings echo the piano motif. The sound of the hip-hop beat evokes a sense of historical New York hipness that Kendall Roy seems to strive for, while the incorporation of instruments such as sleigh bells hints to the ridiculous. Britell states, "The score for *Succession* has a similar duality that I think the show has, which is this combination of elements of absurdity and also a deep gravitas under the surface, because the show itself is dealing with very serious issues of concentrations of power and wealth in fewer and fewer people focused in the media industry, but at the same time there is a human side of the story, which focuses on some of the day-to-day absurdities and pettiness and strife among the cast of characters."[16] Listener expectations of the main theme's evolution are confounded to give an immediate sense of something erroneous: an expected C-minor chord with a B-natural note instead of a B-flat, accented dissonances that are not in the scale, jolting the music in a different direction. This reflects the skewed nature of the world of the Roys, the low-register chords buttressing the melody. Britell further upends audience expectations with the closing cadence of the piece. Rather than use the I-VI-ii-V chord progression that is often expected to signify the culmination of a minor-key piece of classical music, he uses a half diminished in a first-inversion V chord to upset the resolution. This is all underpinned by the hip-hop beat produced by 808 drum machines, which are controlling the rhythm of the melody and bass ostinato of the piano. Britell welds the rhythmical hip-hop beats of an 808 bass drum to the dissonant, detuned piano and layered strings, leading to an ambiguity of atmosphere, tone, period, genre.

The principle of theme and variation, used pervasively by Buckley and Britell, was a prevalent feature of seventeenth-century instrumental music. Although it was employed in Renaissance keyboard music, it became synonymous with the Baroque repertoire. A melody could be repeated with little or no change, with each melody being ornamented differently for each variation and the underlying harmonies typically remaining unchanged. The Baroque period precipitated a move toward a greater systemization and more defined structure in music, but there nonetheless remained a clear distinction between various styles of composition, with each regarded as distinct and enjoying its own social function and technical characteristics. Writing during this period became more idiomatic, with composers writing for particular instruments and incorporating affectation and ornamentation into their music as composers struggled to find "musical means for the expression of affections or states of the soul."[17] A vocabulary of devices and specific types of composition (the fugue, canzone) based on the principle of counterpoint emerged during this period to convey these states, which is why drawing on this historical musical idiom seems particularly apposite for these Trump-era dramas.

Buckley frequently references Renaissance, Baroque, and medieval music in his scores for *The Good Wife* and *The Good Fight*. This "homage to the past" is something that he first began to incorporate in *The Good Wife* in the fifth season.[18] The duality that Britell mentions in relation to his scoring of *Succession* is also signaled in Buckley's score for *The Good Fight*. Buckley, however, maintains that much of the dissonance comes from the collision between the "present tense" of the storylines and the anachronism of explicitly drawing on a musical vernacular rooted in sounds from the past. Buckley's score acts as a form of audiovisual counterpoint, or what Michel Chion might refer to as "dissonant harmony."[19]

There was also a question of fit with the dramatic and narrative mechanics of the show and the way in which liberal establishment figures like Diane in *The Good Fight* and, prior to that, Alicia in *The Good Wife* understand themselves and their position within society. This is connoted by the musical references in the score. Buckley suggests, "I think the justification for [the music] within the context of both *The Good Wife* and *The Good Fight*— the scenery, the environment, it looks rich, it looks plush, beautiful wooden panels rooms and leather, and Diane in all her refinery and Juliana Margulies back in the day—it was a lot about beauty and opulence visually within the show. So I think that the classical style, on a very basic level adopting the more elegant, less traditional TV style, I think it ultimately was a better fit with what one was seeing visually."[20] He also points out that the orchestral music forms another layer of extravagance within the world of the program.

Comedy and Music in Trump-Era Drama

Although *Succession* and *The Good Fight* are ostensibly regarded as drama, being suffused with dark comedy allows them to highlight the irrationality of contemporary times. Part of the comedy in *Succession* stems from the pedigree of the creative team. Armstrong, the showrunner for *Succession*, is the screenwriter behind blackly comedic sitcoms such as *Peep Show* (Channel 4, 2003–15) and the tragicomic series *Fresh Meat* (Channel 4, 2011–16). He was also a writer for the political comedies *Veep* (HBO, 2012–15) and *The Thick of It* (BBC, 2005–12). The team also features writers such as Will Tracy, the former editor of the satirical website and newspaper *The Onion*, who also currently writes for the late-night satirical talk show *Last Week Tonight with John Oliver* (HBO, 2014–). Further to this, the pilot episode for *Succession* was directed by the former comedy writer Adam McKay, the director of the biting feature films *Vice* (2018) and *The Big Short* (2015), and was executive produced by McKay and his longtime collaborator, the actor and comedian Will Ferrell. Part of the comedy stems from the sharpness and musicality of the dialogue, part from individual characters positioned as figures of fun, such as cousin Greg (Nicholas Braun), and part of it emanates from the manner in which it is shot. Appropriating aspects of the mock-documentary aesthetic from *Veep* and *The Thick of It*, the humor is often conveyed through the lingering reaction shots of the Roy clan and their entourage, the camera zooming into faces, ensuring that the joke lands.

Often the humor in both shows comes from the ridiculousness of modern life. In the second season, the Roys begin to liquidate Vaulter, the digital media company for which Kendall overpays in the first season to help inject some cool and credibility into the Waystar Royco brand. Television screens in the Vaulter offices display increasingly preposterous headlines in the background, such as "Soylent Green Could Become a Delicious Reality" and "This Tinder for Pedophiles App Sounds Like a Really Bad Idea," headlines that would not look out of place in *The Onion* and yet are plausible enough to appear on the digital news and entertainment platform Buzzfeed. *The Good Fight* is more of an explicitly comic proposition. Although considerable comedy stems from the eloquence of the dialogue and the often consciously ostentatious performances from supporting characters, much of the comedy emerges from the blurring of fact and fiction, the surrealness of the plots, and the preposterousness of social situations.

It is much more difficult to articulate what makes music funny, especially in shows that adopt an understated approach to humor. The musicologist Miguel Mera points out that cultural and personal context and understanding have much to do with how audiences perceive music as humorous. Further to this, he asserts that "humor is connected with expectation. Almost all humor is set up by creating a sense of anticipation that is then subverted or dislocated. For an audience to find something funny, they must be complicit into this anticipation; they must expect what you predict them to expect."[21] In classical music, humor can be understood through a subversion of audience expectations. Because established musical forms such as sonatas are governed by musical rules and structures, challenging them can unsettle audiences or interpellate those that understand the principles into the musical joke.

Mera makes a compelling case for why this formal context for the creation of music does not typically exist in film music. This is firstly due to the brevity of the average film-music cue, which typically does not allow adequate time for the establishment or development of complex musical forms such as the sonata. Secondly, the structure of the music is often subordinate to other aspects of the film, such as narrative, mise-en-scène, and editing. As Britell himself points out, the "picture is the ultimate arbiter of things."[22] However, Buckley considers classical idioms to permit him to negotiate the fine line between comedy and drama in a way that much contemporary television scoring does not allow for: "It's harder to turn to the comedic. One obvious thing is just being able to use a diminished harmony or a dominant harmony, which you tend not to hear too much in normal everyday television music. It's sort of seen as a slightly archaic chord structure, but just being able to put that in would suddenly be able to let you bend into a comedic thing without being absurd, without being on the nose, and then you could go back to whatever serious business was at hand."[23] Both Britell and Buckley, however, do draw on established musical forms. Buckley uses musical forms such as the fugue in his musical scores. Britell also draws on established eighteenth-century musical forms such as the minuet, a slow dance in a 3/4 time signature. "Tern Haven" (2.5) provides an example of this. A minuet based on a theme established earlier in the episode plays as Kendall exchanges looks with Naomi Pierce and the Roys prepare to leave the Pierces' ancestral home of Tern Haven to return to New York in their choppers. Minuets serve as a cipher for corporate machinations in the second season, often appearing when corporate strategy is being discussed.

Part of the humor from the music in *Succession*, and indeed *The Good Fight*, can also be found in the combinations of musical sounds and the balance of instruments within compositions. Some of the drums are proportionately overpowering in the opening theme when taken in concert with the other instruments. Some of the instrument tunings are off too. Buckley takes an understated approach to the more overtly funny moments in *The Good Fight* and the *Good Wife*, allowing the audience to "participate in the intellectual conceits."[24] He points out that fugues are not "inherently funny"; however, when deployed in an incongruous audiovisual context, they can prove amusing indeed. An example of this incongruence occurs in "Whack-a-Mole" (5.9) in *The Good Wife*, when the lawyer Damian (Jason O'Mara), a new hire at Lockhart Gardner, Alicia's former firm, seeks to undermine her new firm, Florrick Agos, by stealing its office furniture. The comedy of the scene is subtly underscored by a fugue as Damian and his merry band of Lockhart Gardner lawyers execute their prank. The punch line of the joke delicately lands through the music itself. There is a brief pause in the music, which returns as Alicia arrives back to her office and realizes that the furniture is gone. This natural break between musical phrases allows the audience to parse her reaction before the main theme from the piece is revisited and resolves.

Sometimes the music functions to elicit comedy by placing the audience in a position of superiority, where we can laugh at the super-rich. In *Succession*'s "Dundee" (2.8), we find Kendall dressed in a baseball shirt with bow tie and formal shirt, rapping a sycophantic ode to his father, Logan, as family and members of the business community gather in Scotland to celebrate Waystar Royco's fiftieth year in business. The moment is both absurd and toe-curling. Kendall's obsequious but polished rap is accompanied by a beat that is rooted in a hip-hop aesthetic, cooked up by "his boy Squiggle," and that is a reinterpretation of Johann Sebastian Bach's Prelude in C Minor (ca. 1717–23), a mangling of good taste and what Kendall supposes to be New York hipness. Lest the audience require tutelage on matters of musical palate, they are made aware of Kendall's cultural faux pas through the response and reactions of the extended Roy family ("It's burning my eyes, but I can't look away"), ranging from open-mouthed disbelief to witty quips to ironic dancing to laughing, while they film on smartphones for posterity.

Mera also suggests that music in film, and by extension television, is often required to act as "comic foil" to other comedic elements that occur in the narrative, remaining credible in order to counterbalance the other humorous features.[25] Britell's approach to scoring *Succession* was to create a juxtaposition between the absurdity onscreen and the relative seriousness of his music: "The thing I've found throughout the show is that serious stuff feels serious, musically, but the more absurd something gets onscreen, the more serious I play the music."[26] This is exemplified in "Tern Haven," in which the relatively new wealth of the Roys is juxtaposed with the old money of the blue-blooded New England Pierce family during a weekend summit at Tern Haven. The liberal, Shakespeare-quoting Pierce family preside over a venerable conglomerate of "quality" providers of "real news" that the Roys are attempting to buy. The constant contrasting of the Roys' taste and conspicuous trappings of wealth with the high cultural sensibility and noblesse oblige of the Brahmin brethren is subtly comedic. This is reflected in the musical score. Slow melancholic strings accompany Roman as he scuttles down the corridor of the Pierce mansion to the bedroom of Gerri (J. Smith-Cameron), the veteran Waystar Royco lawyer, for what transpires to become a nighttime assignation. Prior to this, he had been comically rejected by his beautiful paramour, Tabitha (Caitlin Fitzgerald), after encouraging her to pretend to be dead during sex. There is an incongruence between the gravitas of the music and the comedy of Roman's psychosexual situation. A similar musical cue had earlier served to underscore the ominous mood that marked the end of the Roy-Pierce dinner. Changing the context of the piece again harks back to the tension between the comedic and the broader societal concerns under consideration in *Succession*.

To conclude, this chapter has interrogated how the musical scores of Trump-era dramas *Succession* and *The Good Fight* embody for liberal audiences the absurdity and unease of contemporary life under the Trump presidency. Unusually for television, both scores overtly draw on established European art-music traditions. These traditions, typically associated with refinement, taste, and quality, demarcate a sonic world of money and power to be read and understood by the intended audiences of these shows. Yet the scores also subvert the melodic and harmonic structures associated with this long classical history through their collisions of styles, orchestration, and excess. Their breaking of musical rules and incongruence suggest an unraveling of existing political and societal rules to a demographic that is no longer sure of its position within this new era of global conservative populist politics, while their skirting of the line between comedy and solemnity accents the asininity, anxiety, and legacy of the Trump era, acting as an affective and intellectual code for the liberal resistance.

Notes

1   CBS All Access was rebranded as Paramount + in March 2021.
2   Katie Baker, "How Nicholas Britell Became the Sound of Money in Holly-wood," *Ringer*, July 13, 2018. https://www.theringer.com/features/2018/7/13/17567674/composer-nicholas-britell-succession-the-big-short-moonlight.
3   Michelle Goldberg, "The Only TV Show That Gets Life under Trump," *New York Times*, May 3, 2019.
4   Kate Storey, "All of the Similarities between the Murdochs and the Roy Family in HBO's *Succession*," *Esquire*, April 3, 2019, https://www.esquire.com/entertainment/a27033483/hbo-succession-true-story-murdoch/.
5   Jane Feuer, "HBO and the Concept of Quality TV," in *Quality TV: Contemporary American Television and Beyond*, ed. Janet McCabe and Kim Akass (London: I. B. Tauris, 2007), 147.
6   Dean DeFino, *The HBO Effect* (London: Bloomsbury Academic, 2001), 5.
7   DeFino, 5.
8   David Buckley (composer) in discussion with the author, November 2019.
9   Ron Rodman, *Tuning In: American Narrative Television Music* (Oxford: Oxford University Press, 2010), 105.
10   Kathryn Kalinak, *Settling the Score: Music and the Classic Hollywood Film* (Madison: University of Wisconsin Press, 1992); Justin London, "Leitmotifs and Musical Reference in the Classical Film Score," in *Music and Cinema*, ed. James Buhler, Caryl Flinn, and David Neumeyer (Hanover, NH: Wesleyan University Press, 2000), 85–98.
11   Rodman, *Tuning In*, 116
12   Buckley in discussion with the author.
13   Buckley.
14   Katey Rich, "The *Succession* Theme Song, Explained by Nicholas Britell," *Vanity Fair*, December 12, 2019, https://www.vanityfair.com/hollywood/2019/12/succession-theme-song-nicholas-britell.
15   Rich.
16   Rich.
17   Donald J. Grout and Claude V. Palisca, *A History of Western Music*, 4th ed. (London: Norton, 1988), 351.

18 Buckley in discussion with the author.

19 Michel Chion, *Audio-Vision: Sound on Screen*, ed. and trans. Claudia Gorb-man (New York: Columbia University Press, 1994), 36.

20 Buckley in discussion with the author.

21 Miguel Mera, "Is Funny Music Funny? Contexts and Case Studies of Film Music Humor," *Journal of Popular Music Studies* 14 (2002): 92.

22 Charles Bright, "Nicholas Britell ('Succession') on Differences Composing for Film and TV," *Gold Derby*, May 21, 2019, https://www.goldderby.com/article/2019/nicholas-britell-succession-composer-beale-street-moonlight-video-interview/.

23 Buckley in discussion with the author.

24 Buckley.

25 Mera, "Is Funny Music Funny?," 99.

26 Christopher Rosen, "*Succession* Composer Nicholas Britell Explains the Origins of Kendall's Cringeworthy Rap," *TV Guide*, October 8, 2019, https://www.tvguide.com/news/succession-composer-nicholas-britell-season-2/.

PART V

Renegotiating the Past

REMEMBER THE TIME WHEN

ANNOTATIONS ON BLACK HISTORIES
IN KENYA BARRIS'S *BLACK-ISH*

Kwakiutl L. Dreher

This chapter forages for annotations on Black histories in ABC's prime-time sitcom *Black-ish* (2017–). Its creator, the Black television writer and producer Kenya Barris, utilizes the symbolic power of the Black family to keep alive Black histories from the Obama era to the political climate of the presidency of Donald J. Trump. Megan Garber's assertion rings true: "Every once in a while, a primetime network sitcom will double as an urgent argument about the way we live."[1]

Barris's "double . . . argument" compels him to capitalize on Black history's ability to confront national amnesia and purposeful forgetfulness. Some semblance of utopia may have been realized by its featured upper-middle-class Black family, the Johnsons. Jean Baudrillard would estimate their achievements to have actualized utopia, or "everything that others have dreamt of—justice, plenty, rule of law, wealth, freedom."[2] *Black-ish*, however, disrupts the comfortable insularity of the sitcom to complicate the utopian ideal. Practically every episode explores the current anxieties of race relations and the history of them in the United States. Racial unease and racism thrive *still*, even though Americans elected their first Black president, Barack Hussein Obama Jr., in 2008 and 2012.

The nation's plantation regime installed ideologies on race/racism centuries ago, and the 2016 election of Trump and his "Make America Great Again" campaign slogan stoked a host of anxieties around them. Barris entrusts the sitcom's narrator and patriarch, Andre "Dre" Johnson, to unabashedly invoke historical and contemporary memories of the Black experience. His critique is important, given that the election of President Obama and his "Yes We Can" mantra lulled the United States of America into a sense that the nation had morphed into a postracial society. As Ta-Nehisi Coates contends, the term "postracial" is problematic: "The Obama-era qualifier . . . assumes that the long struggle that commenced when the first enslaved African arrived on American soil centuries ago could somehow be resolved in an instant, by the mere presence of a man who is not a king."[3]

Black-ish annotates Black histories every week on prime-time television to caution viewers of racism's robust operation in the United States. That *Black-ish* is on prime-time television signifies its lineage as "a space of opposition, a vehicle for challenging and resisting the representations perpetuated throughout the American cultural landscape."[4] Donald Bogle maintains as well that "the weekly primetime series had a greater effect on viewer perceptions of African-American experiences than almost any other form of television."[5]

Most significantly, *Black-ish* joins the continuum of popular Black families featured on prime-time television with the presence of Black fathers. To mark out the whole of the continuum would overwhelm this chapter; however, most notable is *Good Times* (1974–79), created by Norman Lear of *All in the Family* (1971–79) fame. Programmed by CBS, *Good Times* was the first Black two-parent family sitcom to debut on network television. The sitcom starred Esther Rolle as Florida Evans and John Amos as James Evans, a couple living in Cabrini-Green, an inner-city housing project in Chicago, with their three children, James "J.J." Evans Jr. (Jimmy Walker), Thelma (Bern Nadette Stanis), and Michael (Ralph Carter). CBS preferred a single-parent household because, as the *Good Times* creator Eric Monte reveals, the producers believed that "a strong Black man is not funny in a sitcom." Rolle, however, agreed to star only if the Black father remained in the script. She states, "I introduced the Black father [on prime-time television] to this country. There never had been one in the whole of the country, and I risked my job saying, 'I won't do it unless you give me a husband for my children.'"[6] The studio relented. In addition to the Black two-parent family in *Black-ish*, Barris affords viewers the Black extended family, the "multigenerational, interdependent kinship system which is welded together [and] generally organized around a 'family base' household."[7] Anthony Anderson stars as Andre "Dre" Johnson, a resilient Black father with a strong work ethic, who not only supports the nuclear family but also assumes responsibility for his parents.

Arthur Schomburg's belief in the power of history, sketched in his essay "The Negro Digs Up His Past," directs this chapter. His teacher's dismissive statement that "blacks had no history" motivated him to "devote most of his life both to recovering as much of the history of the black peoples of the world as he could and to disseminating information that would discourage or even prevent such gross misstatements."[8] To dig up the Black past, supposed Schomburg, restored "what slavery took away, for it is the social damage of slavery that the present generations must repair and offset."[9] Remembering Black history, then, is the balm for restoration, and remembering requires consistent attention. Just as Schomburg set out to disprove his teacher's assertion, every Tuesday night Barris, Schomburg's "present generation," *remembers the time* in Black history for approximately twenty-two minutes. In essence, Barris opens "certain chapters of American history" and, in the process, expands Schomburg's mission.[10] *Black-ish* addresses the angst/anxieties that Barris infers are curried still in the psyche, regardless of Black achievement. Barris exploits particular film forms to facilitate his expansion and nuances in the series. The manipulation of time-space relationships via flash projection allows glimpses into a character's mind in the present. Flashback works "to explain the connection between past and present."[11]

The term "blackish" suggests, says Aisha Harris, that "there is no hard and fast 'definition' of what it means to be black"; there is a gray area, and "*Black-ish* is all about exploring that grey area and expanding upon the idea of blackness in the 21st century."[12] Dre, however, judges a person *intensely* as black*ish* who identifies as Black but cavalierly dismisses Black culture and history. In Dre's mind, they fail miserably to, in the urban vernacular, keep it real. It is Rainbow "Bow" (Tracee Ellis Ross), his wife, who advises Dre from within the vortex of the blackish gray area.

The posters for the sitcom advertise a jubilant Black family pointing to the audience. They resemble the "All the Colors in the World" ad campaign launched in 1984 by Benetton, dressed in vibrant colors of pink, green, yellow, orange, purple, and blue/turquoise. The art director Oliviero Toscani's marketing strategy for Benetton "became a common way of referring to a group of ethnically mixed people."[13] In the ads, "young children and teenagers from different countries and ethnic groups were laughing and smiling together . . . using the language of racial harmony to transcend the cultural barriers."[14] The *Black-ish* cast and characters correspond to Benetton's construction of racial harmony. Its multiracial cast represents a host of ethnicities: African American and Jewish (Tracee Ellis Ross and Daveed Diggs); African American, Choctaw, and Iranian (Yara Shahidi); African American and Mexican (Miles Brown); African American and white (Marcus Scribner and Rashida Jones); white (Beau Bridges); and African American (Anthony Anderson, Laurence Fishburne, Marsai Martin, and Jenifer Lewis).

Black-ish, the Pilot

Two years into the second term of President Obama and two years before the election of Donald Trump as the forty-fifth president of the United States, the pilot episode of *Black-ish* aired on ABC on September 24, 2014. At the heart of each episode, the patriarch of the family, Dre, narrates the sociocultural, historical, and political subjects concerning Black Americans and Blackness to be covered in that episode.

A cornucopia of sociocultural, historical, and political themes sets out pertinent discussions about Blackness held within and between communities across nationalities and ethnicities. Specific to the pilot are conversations on relationships and histories: Blacks and the Jewish community; Blacks and Africa; and Blacks and the white community, to include the workplace. Several issues such as the appropriation of Black culture, or the "Black man's go tos," by other races and nationalities, such as dance (Asian), rhythm and blues (R&B; white), and bootylicious (white women), as well as generational conflict, abound throughout.

The characters, also introduced by Dre, the show's narrator, reflect the multiracial makeup of the series. Dre is a "standard old, incredibly handsome, unbelievably charismatic" Black senior vice president marketing executive from Compton, California. Rainbow "Bow" Johnson is a "pigment-challenged, mixed-race" doctor. Rainbow's parents, Alicia (Anna Deavere Smith) and Paul (Beau Bridges), were hippies who raised Rainbow in a commune. Animal waste powers the RV within which they live; the license plate reads "BLKWYF" to express Paul's pride as a white husband married to a woman of African descent. Bow's sister is Santamonica, a reality-TV star (Rashida Jones); her brother, Johan, is a free-spirited poet (Daveed Diggs). Dre and Bow have four children: twins Jack (Miles Brown)

and Diane (Marsai Martin), son Andre Jr. (Marcus Scribner), and daughter Zoey (Yara Shahidi). Special to *Black-ish* is the extended Black family,
whereby Dre's parents are highly integrated into the Johnson nuclear family
unit. Dre's mother, Ruby (Jenifer Lewis), and Dre's father, Earl "Pops" Johnson (Laurence Fishburne), live under the same roof, though Pops sometimes
resides elsewhere. In all, the Johnson household is a "hip, cool, and colorful"
family.

That the Johnsons live in a four-bedroom, four-bath, two-story home in
the predominantly white suburb of Sherman Oaks signifies their realization
of the American Dream. The American Dream bends to a seductive ideology
that *anyone* and *everyone* in the United States can achieve the dream of life
and liberty in their pursuit of happiness. An ethos of integrity, industry, and
virtue is part of the ideology to which a US citizen has to aspire. According
to Jennifer Horschild, "the *idea* of the American dream has been attached to
everything from religious freedom to a home in the suburbs. . . . The American dream consists of tenets about achieving success . . . the attainment
of a high income, a prestigious job, economic security."[15] Significant to the
story of the Johnsons is the proverbial joy of having "mov[ed] on up, finally
got a piece of the pie" after a "whole lot of tryin' just to get up that hill,"
to paraphrase the opening of the theme song to the popular Black television sitcom *The Jeffersons*, which debuted in 1975 on CBS. Dre's move up
from the all-Black neighborhood of Compton, California, to Sherman Oaks
earned him access to the "big leagues, getting his turn at bat" (*Jeffersons*
lyrics). In his comparison of Compton to Sherman Oaks, via flashback, a
young Dre is pictured in front of a graffitied wall in Compton. The camera
cuts to the manicured lawns of the Sherman Oaks suburb. He remarks, "I
promised my parents I would get an education, graduate, and get myself
out of there [Compton]. I guess for a kid from the 'hood, I am living the
American Dream."

The attainment of the American Dream, however, causes Dre some
anxiety. In the pilot, he remarks, "The only problem is whatever American had this dream probably wasn't where I'm from, and if he was, he
should have mentioned the part about how, when brothers start getting a
little money, stuff starts getting a little weird." Dre thinks to himself as he
retrieves his mail, "In my neighborhood [of Sherman Oaks], sometimes I
feel like a bit of an oddity." Flash projection creates an alternate time in the
space of Dre's mind. An "Ultimate Hollywood Tours" van passes through

the neighborhood. The tour guide announces to the group of excited white tourists, "And if you look to your left, you will see the mythical and the majestic Black family out of their natural habitat and still thriving. Go ahead and wave; they'll wave right back. They're just . . . just amazing." All the tourists gawk and smile at the Johnsons, who have arranged themselves at the curbside of the front lawn to wave back at them; an intercut labels them "The Mythical Majestic Black Family White Neighborhood (circa 2014)." The Johnsons are the *happy* Black family.

Flash projection of the "Mythical Majestic Black Family" invokes the infamous history of the display of the sensational, if not *exotic*, other out of their "natural habitat" of the stereotypical crime-riddled ghetto. Specifically, the "Ultimate Hollywood Tours" moment brings to relief the history of the human zoo or the ethnological exposition, whereby European human traffickers and rarities agents brought Africans from disparate parts of the African continent and transported them to Europe to be exhibited at world's fairs and circuses. According to Shoshi Parks, "Like the inclusion of rare beasts from foreign lands, human zoos and other displays of indigenous peoples offered audiences a hierarchical narrative of race where the West triumphed over 'uncivilized' cultures."[16] As do the white tourists in the van, white tourists visited reconstructed African villages replete with peoples paraded for their viewing pleasure. Leopold Lodewijk Filips Maria Victor, or King Leopold of Belgium, built one of the most notorious of human zoos. In 1897, 297 Congolese lived in a mock African village on his estate and were displayed to visitors.[17] In the United States of America, the 1904 St. Louis World's Fair hosted twenty million visitors, who came to "see electricity for the first time, to hear the first telephone, and to witness around 3,000 'savages' from Africa, Asia, and the Americas living in 'displays' that resembled their native villages."[18] Fast-forward to the 1958 Brussels World's Fair, where a group of Congolese traveled to Belgium and found themselves behind a bamboo fence being taunted by white patrons who made monkey noises and threw at them bananas and peanuts.[19]

No matter Black achievement, no matter the incantations of "I am my ancestors' wildest dreams" in Dre's mind,[20] the specter of historical horror and trauma lurks in the psyche of the Black achiever. The Johnsons have quashed the stereotype of the Black family as headed only by single Black mothers. Dre, in particular, has canceled the stereotype of the Black man as athlete, drug dealer/user, criminal, pimp, and absentee father. A cohesive and vibrant Black family exists in Barris's world. No matter. The Elder Nana Peazant declares in Julie Dash's film *Daughters of the Dust* (1991), "We carry these memories inside of we," even in the simple task of retrieving the mail.

The upper-middle-class status of the Johnsons illustrates utopia attained by them in the United States. *Black-ish*, however, is deeply reflexive. The sitcom answers Schomburg's call to "open up the Negro past" because "the bigotry of civilization . . . begins far back and must be corrected at its source."[21] In the pilot, Andre Jr. requests a bar mitzvah for his birthday party in anticipation of his father's disagreement. "I know we're not Jewish," he interrupts, "but Zach [his Jewish friend] knows a rabbi who is great at pushing through conversions." Dre reprimands him and explains, "When you turn thirteen, you're becoming a . . . a *Black* man because I'm throwing you an African Right of Passage ceremony. . . . It is important for you to hold onto your culture and realize how special *it* is." Barris acknowledges the taproot of Black lineage: the African diaspora or the "migrations . . . and the dynamics of dispersed communities," *not* the Jewish faith.[22]

The sitcom creator's acknowledgment of this Black lineage, in addition, invokes one of the ideals of the Black Arts Movement, wherein artists embraced the continent of Africa as its source for artistic expression. "The Black Arts Movement (BAM) of the 1960s and the 1970s . . . clearly accepted Africa," writes Haki Madhubuti. "Black . . . spoke to one's *culture, consciousness*."[23] Andre Jr.'s euphoria over the possibility of converting to Judaism makes known, interestingly, that Dre and Rainbow, in their move on up, have yet to lay bare at least a modicum of Black history; or, if they have, Andre Jr. demonstrates no Black cultural awareness, nor any understanding of its significance to *him*. Dre's refusal to allow Jr. to *pass* for Jewish at the expense of denying his African history and Black culture is significant to the African Right of Passage ceremony. As it was in the Black Arts Movement, Dre's starting point is the source, Africa.

The ceremony takes place in the backyard, decorated with African drums, baskets, and statues. Father and son are dressed in garments made of African print. Pops, puzzled, admonishes Dre, "This ain't *our* culture; we Black, not African. Africans don't even like us." Undeterred, Dre throws some bones at Jr. and blows something that looks like rice onto his face. Bow is livid, and out of the vortex of the black*ish* gray area, she says, "This 'keeping it real' BS has got to stop! I'm not going to have you going around torturing my son. What *are* you wearing? Whatever issues you are working through, you need to get over them . . . now!" Pops's and Bow's black*ish* admonishment responds to Madhubuti's caution to those Blacks who embrace African culture. He writes, "We must be careful not to buy into the feel good history of Black superiority."[24] Dre ends up organizing a multicultural birthday celebration: a "Hip-Hop Bro-Mitzvah," blending Jr.'s desire for a bar mitzvah and an homage to hip hop, Dre's coming-of-age culture in Compton, California. This blend is an indirect nod to Pop's statement, "We're not African."

"Who's Afraid of the Big Black Man?": Season 3, Episode 4

"Who's Afraid of the Big Black Man?" premiered on October 4, 2016, during Trump's campaign for the presidency. One of the most notable details of the campaign was Trump's stance as the "defender of white maidenhood against Mexican rapists."[25] The long-held stereotype of the man of color who lusts after white female flesh runs parallel to Trump's accusation. Specifically, national memory serves well of the racial fear that George H. W. Bush stirred up during his 1988 presidential campaign. Bush circulated a "Bush & Dukakis On Crime" ad, in which Bush accused Michael Dukakis of being soft on crime and a candidate who "allowed murderers to have weekend passes";[26] Willie Horton's mug shot looms large in the ad. Horton, on furlough under Dukakis's watch, raped a white Maryland woman and stabbed her partner. Michael Nelson (author of *41: Inside the Presidency of George H. W. Bush*) says, "In some ways, the Willie Horton ad is the 1.0 version of Trump's relentless tweets and comments about African-Americans."[27]

"Who's Afraid of the Big Black Man?" opens with Dre walking with a confident stride on his way to the elevator, but when the doors open to reveal a blond white toddler, Dre panics. The passenger elevator in the advertising firm Stevens & Lido functions as a perfect space to *remember the time when . . .* This enclosed, *contained* space, seven feet wide and six feet deep, is "an actor in its own right."[28] Not only does the elevator move cargo and people to chosen floors in buildings, but for a few seconds, it fosters a visceral faux-intimacy and privacy between strangers with whom that space is shared. At the elevator's threshold, Dre surveys the area for others, then cautiously walks away as the doors close. Mr. Stevens (his boss) and Josh (his white coworker) view a recording of the incident in the conference room and repeat derisively, "The horror! The horror!"—a phrase from

Joseph Conrad's novel *Heart of Darkness*. Dre defends himself: "That was a little white girl and as a Black man . . ." Josh slams the table and retorts, "No! No! You do not get to play the race card today [*whimpering*], not with that. . . . You monster! [*points to the screen*]." In the meantime, Charlie, a Black coworker, arrives out of breath: "There was a little snowflake on the elevator, so I had to take the stairs." Curtis, another Black coworker, enters: "Sorry I'm late boss, but there was a little white girl on the elevator. . . . I saw my freedom flash right before my eyes."

Dre relates the incident to Pops and Rainbow at home. Pops gives his account of a similar encounter he had in the 1940s. He says, "To be fair, as a Black man, we can never be too careful. I remember my first little-white-girl-in-an-elevator experience." In flashback, Pops, dressed in the regalia of a 1940s elevator attendant/operator, immediately leaves his post when a white girl enters. "You did the right thing, son. I'm proud of you." This episode conjures a historical truth: death and life have resided in the tongue of a white female, regardless of age, regardless of the truth. *This* is Dre's horror. The blond, blue-eyed, white toddler is unnamed, but that is just the point. In Dre's world, as well as in Charlie's and Curtis's, she does not have to be named.

One has only to rewind in history to arrive at the horror of Emmett Till, a fourteen-year-old Black male whom Roy Bryant and his half brother J. W. Milam (two adult white males) lynched in Money, Mississippi, in 1955. Carolyn Bryant Donham, a twenty-one-year-old white woman, accused Till of speaking in "crude, sexual language," whistling at her, and grabbing her around the waist while she cashiered in Bryant's Grocery and Meat Market.[29] On her word, Bryan and Milam kidnapped Till from his home, tortured him, tied a seventy-pound cotton-gin fan around his neck, and threw him into the Tallahootchie River. In 2008, Carolyn Bryant Donham admitted, "That part's not true. . . . Nothing that boy did could ever justify what happened to him."[30] On *her word*, however, Bryant and Milam justified their lynching of Emmett Till.

It is worth noting Barris's casting of a nameless three-year-old white *toddler* to tell this story rather than an *adult* white woman. The age does not matter, either. The history of lynching *and* the history of "reckless eye-balling" reveal that close proximity to a white female could result in grave consequences, even death, no matter her age. For example, in 1951, Willa Jean Bosewell, a seventeen-year-old white girl, accused Matt Ingram, a Black tenant farmer and father of nine children in Yanceyville, North Carolina, of stopping "at some plum bushes watching her, [and] she . . . was scared."[31] The prosecutor argued for a conviction for "assault with intent to rape . . . declaring that 'young womanhood must be protected from niggers.'"[32] According to the nineteenth-century antilynching activist Ida B. Wells-Barnett, "Opportunity is not given the Negro to defend himself against the unsupported accusations of white men and women," not even a toddler.[33]

"I married a monster!" replies Rainbow to Dre and Pops, and her reaction mirrors those of white employees at Stevens & Lido—contemporary responses to a historical moment. In the twenty-first century, Dre *can* see the girl in the elevator as only a toddler in need of help. Rainbow, incredulous, asks, "What do you think would have happened if you'd helped the little white girl?" Dre imagines kneeling to the toddler in the elevator, reassuring her, "I'm going to help you find your mom, okay?" The elevator opens. A gaggle of white news reporters lean in: "So, Andre," asks one reporter, "what were your *plans* here today?" The "rape myth" that "black men were driven biologically to desire white women and to fulfill those desires by force" haunts Dre, as well as Charlie, Curtis, and Pops.[34]

Rainbow's brother Johan, after an unsuccessful citizen's arrest attempt on a white police officer for roughing him up, admits, "We are very, very far away from things being completely different." Andre Jr.'s slam poetry affirms Johan's admission: "It's still a crime to be Black." This tying up of loose ends, however, feels shallow. Of note is Rainbow's and Josh's labeling of Dre as a *monster*. He is not *inconsiderate*, not even a *scaredy-cat*, but a *monster*. Barris's and the writers' decision to exploit the loaded term *monster* to advance this particular interracial dynamic is questionable. They conjure racist tropes historically mapped onto the body of the Black male. Since Barris assumes a responsibility to facilitate memories of historical residue, audiences trust him to get it right. In "Who's Afraid of the Big Black Man?," Barris fails. On close read, *monster*, as Dre is called, not only by his white coworkers but by his *wife* and in his own *home*, is an *apology* to the audience for remembering this horrific time in the history of the United States.

"Juneteenth": Season 4, Episode 1

To lay bare African American histories, "Juneteenth" uses the potency of storytelling across genres: hip hop and rap, animation, musical theater, folklore, and flash projection. A year after the debut of "Who's Afraid of the Big

Black Man?" and ten months into Trump's presidency, "Juneteenth" aired on October 3, 2017. Ta-Nehisi Coates observed the foundation of the Trump presidency the same month, writing, "[Trump's] political career began in advocacy of birtherism, that modern recasting of the old American precept that black people are not fit to be citizens of the country they built."[35]

"Juneteenth" begins with Dre's lamentation on "fake history," dramatized in Jack and Diane's history skit on the "1492 Columbus Sailed the Ocean Blue" theme. He chastises their teacher: "Ms. Davis, *you* should be ashamed of yourself. Where you really failed is this isn't how it went down." In flash projection, Jack and Diane break out into a rap song that revises the history of Christopher Columbus:

> *Everything you know about Columbus is a joke.*
> *He didn't discover America*
> . . . .
> *And it's cool how your men killed three thousand people in one day . . .*
> *Celebrating Columbus is celebrating a slavery pioneer . . .*

Pops observes of the play, "Everybody's represented here: St. Patrick's Day, Columbus Day, Cinco de Mayo. What about . . . Juneteenth?" An angry Dre leaves, but not before he upbraids the audience and the teacher: "I hope you enjoy the rest of your racist pageant! Johnsons! We're out!"

In this episode, animation and musical theater forge points on enslavement and emancipation in the United States. Motivated by Pops's suggestion to celebrate Juneteenth, Dre presents his ideas to Stevens & Lido. In deliberations with his colleagues, Dre senses from the comments by Mr. Stevens, his white boss—"Your people, well, they have been free for a long time"—that they fail to register the magnitude of this historical moment. A brief history of Juneteenth makes known that the celebration originated in Galveston, Texas. The Emancipation Proclamation was signed in 1863, but the emancipation of enslaved people did not occur until June 19—Juneteenth—1865, when Justice Livingston Lindsay decreed, "The liberation in Texas took effect from the date of the surrender of the insurgent forces, and the proclamation of that fact by the commanding general, dated 19th June, 1865. . . . That was the day of jubilee of the freedom of the slaves in Texas."[36] New freedmen and women celebrated in Galveston, Texas, the town where Juneteenth originated.

The Grammy Award–winning singer-songwriter Aloe Blacc asks Dre, "What do you want?" as he brainstorms with Stevens & Lido. They agree to dramatize the history of Juneteenth through song and dance. The theme song to its animated song-story, "I'm Just a Slave" (sung by The Roots-Questlove), is a musical variation on the acclaimed song "I'm Just a Bill" (1975) from *Schoolhouse Rock!* (ABC, 1973–2009). It is set in 1865 in a Texas plantation shack. Of the project, Barris remarks, "Slavery is America's recessive gene and it's time we all dealt with it."[37]

Central to Barris's "historically significant think-piece" is Dre's attempt to "put an end to Columbus Day" in order for Juneteenth to live.[38] Aloe Blacc flash-projects the viewers through time and space, landing on June 19, 1865, and he deploys musical theater to tell the story. The choice to embed the genre into the narrative is apropos, since musical theater "questions and explores the dynamics of our lives—and it does this in song and dance."[39] Barris and Peter Satji collaborated on the libretto; the Grammy Award winner Pharrell Williams and his partner, Mimi Valdés, composed the music.

In the musical's mise-en-scène, the newly freed Johnson family dance in jubilee in their one-room plantation shack. The dance number is shot in deep focus: the gospel choir is down stage right and left, and the family is center stage. Deep focus entices the audience to feel the gravity of the historical moment. The musical, overall, impresses on the spectator to *remember the time when*. A gospel choir bolsters the performances as the song "Juneteenth" passes through time, from slavery on through to the 1960s civil rights movement; the freed people sing of reparations, voting, equality, and moving to the suburbs.

Black-ish's answer to Aloe Blacc's question to Dre, "What do you want?" is to *remember the time when*. Black progress and achievement require remembering Black history to stave off historical amnesia. It requires digging it up, as Arthur Schomburg urged present and new generations, *especially* in this post-Obama era and during and following the Trump era of politics. Obama recognized the Johnsons in his own experience. Trump tweeted "that the title alone is 'racism at highest level'"; Barris "simply wanted to open a dialogue" on the strains of race relations in the United States.[40] His embrace of Black history and its power accords audiences wide berth for a dialogue to occur every week on prime-time television. Isn't that part of the American Dream?

Notes

1 Megan Garber, "*Black-ish* Embraces the Urgency of History," *Atlantic*, October 2017, https://www.theatlantic.com/entertainment/archive/2017/10/black-ish-juneteenth-musical/541953/.

2 Jacques Baudrillard, *America* (London: Verso, 1999), 77.

3 Ta-Nehisi Coates, "There Is No Post-Racial America," *Atlantic*, July–August 2015, https://www.theatlantic.com/magazine/archive/2015/07/post-racial-society-distant-dream/395255/.

4 David Leonard and Lisa Guerrero, *African Americans on Television: Racing for Ratings* (Santa Barbara, CA: Praeger, 2013), 13.

5 Donald Bogle, *Primetime Blues* (New York: Farrar, Straus and Giroux, 2001), 5, 6.

6 reelblack, "Good Times—The True Hollywood Story (2000)," YouTube, November 24, 2018, https://www.youtube.com/watch?v=fA4fCXSPr4I.

7 Elmer P. Martin and Joanne Mitchell Martin, *The Black Extended Family* (Chicago: University of Chicago Press, 1978), 1.

8 "Arthur Schomburg," in *The Norton Anthology of African American Literature*, ed. Henry Louis Gates Jr. and Valerie A. Smith (New York: Norton, 2014), 945–50.

9 Arthur Schomburg, "The Negro Digs Up His Past," *Survey Graphic*, March 1925, 670–72.

10 Schomburg, 672.

11 Bernard F. Dick, *Anatomy of Film* (Boston: Bedford / St. Martin's, 2010), 270.

12 Aisha Harris, "How *Black-ish* Earned the Right to Call Itself *Black-ish*," *Slate*, April 2015, https://slate.com/culture/2015/04/black-ish-on-abc-the-shows-title-may-be-provocative-but-its-not-offensive-video.html.

13 Yomi Adegoke, "United Colors of Benetton Blazed a Trail for Diversity in Fashion," *Medium*, June 7, 2019, https://medium.com/@yomiadegoke/united-colors-of-benetton-blazed-a-trail-for-diversity-in-fashion-a61746de0517.

14 Jonathan Mantle, *Benetton: The Family, the Business, and the Brand* (London: Werner Brooks, 1999), 130–31.

15 Jennifer Horschild, *Facing Up to the American Dream* (Princeton, NJ: Princeton University Press, 1995), 15 (emphasis added).

16 Shoshi Parks, "These Horrifying 'Human Zoos' Delighted American Audiences at the Turn of the 20th Century. 'Specimens' Were Acquired

from Africa, Asia, and the Americas by Deceptive Human Traffickers,"
Timeline.com, March 19, 2018, https://timeline.com/human-zoo-worlds
-fair-7ef0d0951035.

17 Joanna Kakissis, "Where 'Human Zoos' Once Stood, a Belgian Museum
Now Faces Its Colonial Past," NPR.org, September 26, 2018, https://
www.npr.org/2018/09/26/649600217/where-human-zoos-once-stood-a
-belgian-museum-now-faces-its-colonial-past.

18 Parks, "These Horrifying 'Human Zoos.'"

19 Parks.

20 Brianna James, "'I Am My Ancestors' Wildest Dreams': This Black History
Month I'm Celebrating Myself," *Teen Vogue*, February 7, 2018, https://www
.teenvogue.com/story/i-am-my-ancestors-wildest-dreams.

21 Schomburg, "Negro Digs Up His Past," 672.

22 Patrick Manning, *The African Diaspora: A History through Culture* (New
York: Columbia University Press, 2010), 2.

23 Haki Madhubudi, *Tough Notes: A Healing Call for Creating Exceptional
Black Men* (Chicago: Third World, 2002), 8 (emphasis added).

24 Madhubudi, 9.

25 Ta-Nehisi Coates, "The First White President: The Foundation of Donald
Trump's Presidency Is the Negation of Barack Obama's Legacy," *Atlantic*,
October 2017, https://www.theatlantic.com/magazine/archive/2017/10/
the-first-white-president-ta-nehisi-coates/537909/.

26 Peter Baker, "Bush Made Willie Horton an Issue in 1988, and the Racial
Scars Are Still Fresh," *New York Times*, December 3, 2018, https://www
.nytimes.com/2018/12/03/us/politics/bush-willie-horton.html.

27 Baker.

28 James A. Tyner, *Space, Place, and Violence* (New York: Routledge, 2012), 15.

29 Alan Blinder, "U.S. Reopens Emmett Till Investigation, Almost 63 Years
after His Murder," *New York Times*, July 12, 2018, https://www.nytimes
.com/2018/07/12/us/emmett-till-death-investigation.html; Tyner, *Space,
Place, and Violence*, 15.

30 Timothy Tyson, *The Blood of Emmett Till* (New York: Simon and Schuster,
2017), 6–7.

31 Mary Francis Berry, "'Reckless Eyeballing': The Matt Ingram Case and the
Denial of African American Sexual Freedom," *Journal of African American
History* 93, no. 2 (2008): 225.

32 Berry, 227.

33 Ida B. Wells-Barnett, *A Red Record: Tabulated Statistics and Alleged Causes of Lynching in the United States* (1895), Project Gutenberg, http://www .gutenberg.org/files/14977/14977-h/14977-h.htm.

34 Lisa Lindquist Dorr, *White Women, Rape, and the Power of Race in Virginia, 1900–1960* (Chapel Hill: University of North Carolina Press, 2004), 6.

35 Coates, "First White President."

36 Texas Supreme Court, *Reports of Cases Argued and Decided in the Supreme Court of the State of Texas* (Austin, TX: News Office, 1870), 773, https://play .google.com/books/reader?id=RucaAAAAYAAJ&hl=en&pg=GBS.PA773.

37 Greg Evans, "Kenya Barris & Pharrell Williams Team for 'Juneteenth' Stage Musical," *Deadline*, June 8, 2018, https://deadline.com/2018/06/ kenya-barris-pharrell-williams-juneteenth-stage-musical-black-ish -1202413429/.

38 Megan Garber, "*Black-ish* Embraces the Urgency of History," *Atlantic*, October 2017, https://www.theatlantic.com/entertainment/archive/2017/ 10/black-ish-juneteenth-musical/541953/.

39 Millie Taylor and Dominic Symonds, *Studying Musical Theatre: Theory and Practice* (London: Red Globe, 2014), 2.

40 Homa Khaleeli, "Obama Loves It, Trump Called It Racist: Why Black-ish Is TV's Most Divisive Show," *Guardian*, February 25, 2017, https://www .theguardian.com/tv-and-radio/2017/feb/25/series-creator-kenya-barris -on-abc-sitcom-black-ish.

You Can't Go Home Again

The Recuperative Reboot and
the Trump-Era Sitcom

Jessica Ford and Martin Zeller-Jacques

For many people, the 2016 election of President Donald Trump triggered a reexamination of some fundamental assumptions that structure US life and culture in the twenty-first century. This rethinking of American values and culture manifests itself on television in various ways, including in a cycle of reboots that reexamine and recuperate the politics of their original versions. Since 2016, US television has seen a wave of these reboots, including *Fuller House* (Netflix, 2016–20), *One Day at a Time* (Netflix, 2017–19; Pop, 2020), *Roseanne* (ABC, 2018), *Will & Grace* (NBC, 2018–20), *Murphy Brown* (CBS, 2018), *Charmed* (The CW 2018–), *Roswell: New Mexico* (The CW, 2019–), and *The L Word: Generation Q* (Showtime, 2019–).

Reboots are not a new phenomenon in cinema or television. CBS attempted to replicate the success of *I Love Lucy* (CBS, 1950–55) with reboots for decades. However, reboots seem to be having a cultural moment in the "Peak TV" era. In 2018, the *Vulture* television critic Josef Adalian wrote, "Forget Peak TV: The era of Peak Reboot has arrived."[1] The proliferation of new platforms in the Peak TV era means that there is an enormous amount of television content in circulation but also that there are more distribution avenues than ever before and thus a larger demand for content. Owing to streaming services' existence outside traditional television flow, they are particularly well suited to use reboots to capitalize on the nostalgia of niche audiences by investing in active fan cultures and leveraging media buzz and hype cycles. Likewise, traditional broadcast networks have used reboots of previously popular properties to leverage nostalgic capital invested in their own status as legacy media.

Our focus in this chapter is on what we are calling the "recuperative reboot," which refers to a recent kind of television reboot working to update, recuperate, or resituate the politics and situations of its originals for the contemporary moment. In doing so, these recuperative reboots often comment on the politics of the past and present. As Jessica Ford has argued, "Reboots operate around two key pleasures. First, there is the pleasure of revisiting and/or re-imagining characters that are 'known' to audiences. Whether continuations or remakes, reboots are invested in the audience's desire to see familiar characters. Second, there is the desire to 'fix' and/or recuperate an earlier series."[2]

In proposing the idea of the recuperative reboot, we aim to move beyond what journalists have called the "woke reboot." This term typically refers to "progressive" remakes and revivals that employ diverse casts, are overtly political, and are drawing on and contributing to contemporary cultural conversations.[3] We contend, however, that focusing on "wokeness" provides only a partial picture of this phenomenon and that decidedly "unwoke" reboots such as *Roseanne* and *Fuller House* attempt a form of recuperation similar to overtly progressive texts such as *One Day at a Time* (*ODAAT*) and *Roswell: New Mexico*. In reviving and/or redeveloping established series in response to life in Trump's America, each of these series attempts to recuperate its earlier version. Some perform their recuperation by updating the original's gender and racial politics, while others invoke the nostalgic appeal of the original text's values, which they construct as missing from or a solution to the contemporary moment.

This chapter focuses on two key series in the recuperative reboot cycle: *Roseanne* and *ODAAT*. While each revisits a sitcom premise and setting known for exploring the feminist politics of its time, they take very different approaches to the recuperation of the original series and the resituating and reimagining of its characters for a contemporary context. *ODAAT* retains a conventional studio sitcom format but adapts the premise of the original series, focusing on a Cuban American family and exploring the intersections of gender, sexuality, race, and age across its three-season run. In contrast, *Roseanne* is a continuation of the '90s series, which enacts its thesis about the tribulations of white working-class Americans by revisiting the Conner family twenty years after we last saw them. Of course, *Roseanne* also attempts to recuperate its controversial star, Roseanne Barr, whose aggressively pro-Trump Twitter presence eventually led to the revival's cancellation. Through an analysis of *ODAAT* and *Roseanne*, we argue that recuperative reboots share a nostalgic perspective on the past, which is positioned as a solution to the present and future.

Recuperative Reboots

In journalistic circles, the term "reboot" is often used as a catchall for different kinds of revivals, retellings, spin-offs, adaptations, and remakes.[4] Despite the many different iterations of the reboot, there are clear differences between remakes and revivals. Remakes are derivations or reimaginings of known properties with new characters, casts, and stories, while revivals bring back an existing property in the form of a continuation with the same cast and/or setting. Both remakes and revivals, however, seek to capitalize on nostalgia for a specific kind of past and access the (presumed) existing audience of earlier series.[5] We contend that despite the many differences between recent reboots, they are ultimately grappling with the same questions and are united by the kind of recuperative politics they perform.

This cycle of revivals and remakes repositions understandings of the original series. This often takes the form of revisiting a situation, characters, and/or setting in order to address a generally perceived flaw or shortcoming with the original series. These perceived flaws or shortcomings might include appearing retrograde by contemporary standards, as in the case of *The Bionic Woman* (NBC, 2007), or a perceived "error" or misgiving in the original, such as with *Gilmore Girls: A Year in the Life* (Netflix, 2018), or the need to update or fundamentally reimagine the politics of the original for a new audience, as seen in *One Day at a Time*, *Battlestar Galactica* (Sci-Fi, 2004–10), *Roseanne*, *Murphy Brown*, and *Roswell* (UPN, 1999–2000). While some remakes, like *Battlestar Galactica* or *ODAAT*, significantly reimagine or update the politics of their original, others, like *Will & Grace* and *Murphy Brown*, position the politics of the original as an answer, or even a rebuke, to the confusion of the current moment.

This recent recuperative reboot cycle is enabled by economic and industrial conditions specific to the Peak TV era and cultural and political conditions specific to Trump's United States. Due to the rapid expansion of the US television industry, there is an increased demand for content that will attract audiences. At the same time, the fragmentation of mass audiences has created niche audiences who are drawn to both nostalgic intellectual property from earlier eras and politically and ideologically driven reimaginings of them.[6] Many of these recuperative reboots position themselves in response to the election of President Trump. For instance, *ODAAT* and *Roswell: New Mexico* directly focus on the experiences of Latinx Americans who are grappling with the racist rhetoric and policies of the Trump White House, while *Murphy Brown* attempts to examine the reasons the US failed to elect a woman with the same kind of power-suited '90s feminist bona fides as the series's titular character.

Nostalgia is central to the appeal and address of recuperative reboots, but it operates textually and extratextually across various series. *Fuller House* and *ODAAT* are presented as traditional multicamera studio sitcoms popularized by broadcast networks, which is at odds with the Netflix distribution model. *Will & Grace* and *Roseanne* invest in the audiences' familiarity with the setting and characters. While it is reductive to frame nostalgia as necessarily conservative, reboots demand a looking back and reverence for another time. There are also nostalgic clusters around particular characters and/or types of character. In the case of the sitcom, much of the nostalgic function of these recuperative reboots involves recentering television on the family and the domestic space at a time of political, economic, technological, and social change.

The current slate of recuperative reboots have not been particularly successful at remaining on the air beyond their first seasons. Even those that garnered significant initial buzz, like *Roseanne* or *Murphy Brown*, have been canceled rather swiftly. These reboots have been pitched as urgent responses in the moment, which propose a political thesis about what went wrong or what needs to go right, but the closer they are to the intractability of the political moment, the less likely their answer is to be convincing. For instance, the *Roseanne* reboot is, at least partially, about the waning centrality of the white working class in US culture, which is one issue on which many observers argued the 2016 election hinged.

Both the original and reboots of *Roseanne* and *ODAAT* are "socially conscious" sitcoms, therefore they have a preexisting political function, which is only compounded by their recuperative tendencies. The questions that *ODAAT* and *Roseanne* are exploring are questions that US television has been asking throughout most of its history, such as, What does the American family look like? And what is the social value and function of various

American families? Whether a show is liberal or conservative leaning, there is often a flattening of social difference and class stratification in the name of creating characters and families that are considered "relatable." This chapter examines two very different attempts to recenter the American family in the sitcom.

One Day at a Time

While many of the television series in this recent reboot cycle are reexamining texts from the 1990s or early 2000s, the original version of *One Day at a Time* (CBS, 1975–84) emerges out of a much earlier era of American television and culture. The original *ODAAT* was produced as part of a wave of television series that sought to work through the ideas being raised by second-wave feminism. Made by Embassy Television, Norman Lear's consolidated production house, *ODAAT* worked within the same tradition of "relevance programming" as the rest of Lear's output in the 1970s.[7] Norman Lear television series like *All in the Family* (CBS, 1971–79), *Good Times* (CBS, 1974–79), and *Maude* (CBS, 1972–78), as well as *ODAAT*, worked to make television "more responsive to the social and political milieu of the 1970s."[8] By bringing Norman Lear out of retirement to produce the new *ODAAT*, Netflix explicitly invokes the legacy of his earlier "relevant" sitcoms, which are now valued as much for their challenging politics as for their central place in the history of American popular culture.

The 1970s incarnation of *ODAAT* depicted Ann Romano (Bonnie Franklin), the newly divorced mother of two teenagers, starting her single life in a new city. Bonnie J. Dow argues that *ODAAT* emerged in a cultural moment when the force of radical feminism had been spent and the movement's goals adopted or co-opted by liberal feminism.[9] This made feminist politics a less risky subject for US broadcast television, as "only when radical feminism was no longer a visible threat could some of its issues receive sustained treatment in prime-time."[10] For Dow, the original *ODAAT* frequently raises political issues highlighted by radical feminism, such as women's agency and self-determination and the precarious economic situation of divorced women, but subsumes these ideas within the rhetoric of a "therapeutic feminism," which "recasts material issues of power between the genders into therapeutic obstacles to be conquered through self-transformation."[11]

The Netflix reboot changes little about the original's attitude toward the systemic and social problems faced by women and leans even more heavily into the therapeutic feminism of the original. While the series's title has always recalled the slogans and advice of twelve-step recovery programs for alcohol and drug abuse, the revival renders that context literal by placing its protagonist, Penelope Alvarez (Justina Machado), in a veteran's support group and dealing explicitly with the struggles of addiction faced by both her ex-husband, Victor (James Martinez), and her building's superintendent and close friend, Schneider (Todd Grinnell).

It is tempting to dismiss the *ODAAT* revival as an essentially conservative and nostalgic text, and Netflix's early marketing of it encourages this reading. As noted by Kathleen Loock, Netflix's #TGIAnytime campaign for *Fuller House, Gilmore Girls: A Year in the Life,* and *ODAAT* worked to establish the platform as a place for nostalgic family viewing.[12] Loock argues that the packaging of these reboots "promise[s] to provide a fixed constant from the past and ideological reassurance," both through the revisiting of old familiar characters and the emphasis Netflix places on "the temporal experience [of these television series as] defined by a 'slowness' that is deeply enmeshed with a nostalgia for the already seen."[13] Yet the *ODAAT* reboot provides more than a comforting revival of familiar and declawed feminist politics. Uniquely among the reboot cycle that Loock examines, *ODAAT* echoes its original using new characters, rather than revisiting old ones. If *Gilmore Girls: A Year in the Life* asks whether we can ever go back home again and *Fuller House* asks if it is such a bad thing to want things to stay the same, *ODAAT* uses a conservative form to communicate its more nuanced (and sometimes radical) politics.

At the center of the *ODAAT* reboot is the rhetorical gesture of presenting a self-consciously traditional, laugh-tracked, multicamera sitcom populated almost entirely by Latinx characters. By placing people of color at the center of a family sitcom and presenting significant portions of the dialogue in unsubtitled Spanish, *ODAAT* refutes the idea that it is a simplistic exercise in nostalgic formalism and implicitly claims a place for its characters at the heart of the symbolic American family. While this gesture is far from intrinsically radical, in the context of a US politics in which Latinx people have been vilified and stigmatized by one of the two main political parties, it is hardly safe. Therefore, while the series's form is willfully old-fashioned, its form does not necessarily signal nostalgia, comfort, or a lack of challenge to contemporary audiences. In US television culture, the single-camera-style sitcom is now "a model for newly legitimated 'classy' TV comedy" and the default approach to sitcom production; as such, *ODAAT*'s choice to return to "the most loathed convention of the traditional multi-cam style: the audience's audible laughter" is radical.[14] This is especially apparent when the series performs its frequent and abrupt changes in tone, moving from a broad classical sitcom style for its jokes to soap-inflected pathos for moments of character drama. *ODAAT*'s unusually long running time (ranging from twenty-five to thirty-five minutes, compared to the twenty-two minutes typical of its network contemporaries) affords it the opportunity for moments of slow and deliberate explorations of its characters' emotions, during which the laughter of the audience is notable by its absence. In the first episode of the series, as Penelope tells her mother about her difficulties sleeping since leaving her husband and her need for greater support in parenting, the camera stays focused on Penelope for nearly a full minute as she speaks, with no laughter from the audience. Brett Mills has argued that the presence of a laugh track in sitcoms typically works to link the domestic audience with the live audience, helping to generate a sense of intimacy, while also cueing our emotional responses.[15] Yet in *ODAAT*, the shifts from broad humor accompanied by laughter to long periods of dramatic conflict, with no vocal cues from the studio audience, force the domestic audience to navigate their responses to the characters' emotional anguish in a very direct and intimate way.

The most conservative aspects of the series are embodied not in any specific invocation of its 1970s original but in the casting of Rita Moreno as Penelope's mother, Lydia, whose presence in the household adds a third generation into the original's familial dynamic. Lydia is the voice of traditional Cuban values, and the series's mise-en-scène positions her centrally. Her curtained-off bedroom is directly behind the family sofa, and her Cuban music is audible throughout their small apartment. Lydia is also the vessel for the beneficent face of patriarchy in the series. Her conversations with her deceased and much-beloved husband, Berto (Tony Plana), form a recurring motif, which culminates in him appearing to her as a vision on several occasions throughout the series. Berto is one of the series's structuring absences—a model of a kind of simultaneously "good" and "old-fashioned" masculinity, which remains unproblematic because it exists primarily in memory rather than in day-to-day reality.

In addition to providing us with *ODAAT*'s standard for romantic love and masculine virtue, Lydia is the ideal embodiment of traditional morality and Cubanness. Moreno's stardom is intimately associated with an earlier era of American film and television in which family viewing (and family values) was the normative paradigm of the sitcom. Her appearances on classic series like *The Love Boat* (ABC, 1976–90) and *The Cosby Show* (NBC, 1984–92) made her a common fixture on American television screens. The *ODAAT* reboot, however, is especially reliant on Moreno's status as one of the most visible Latinx actors thanks to her star turn as Anita in *West Side Story* (Robert Wise and Jerome Robbins, 1961). In the musical, Moreno leads the ensemble in the song "America," which juxtaposes an optimistic, feminine story of the Latinx immigrant experience with a pessimistic masculine version of the same story. In the role of Lydia, the "Abuelita" of the family, Moreno embodies and expresses a similarly optimistic view. Her often-expressed conservatism around issues of gender and economic inequality is grounded in a profound understanding that things could be and have been worse for people like those in her family and her determination to take advantage of the opportunities afforded by life in the United States.

This conservativism on Lydia's part is contrasted with the adoption by her granddaughter Elena (Isabella Gomez) of contemporary feminist and social justice causes. The series typically mocks Elena's approach to these issues as humorless, while admitting or even assuming that her ideas are valuable and accurate. In the series's second episode ("Bobos and Mamitas" 1.2), Elena immediately identifies "microaggressions and mansplaining" in her mother's descriptions of the behavior of an annoying male colleague. Penelope and Lydia initially dismiss Elena's concerns as overblown, with Penelope suggesting that the best way to handle sexism is by outperforming men and Lydia arguing that women should perform subservience while doing as they please. During a later encounter in which the same colleague steals Penelope's idea and she learns that he makes more money than she does, she storms out, vowing to quit her job rather than work under inequitable conditions. As the bearer of a cultural memory of immigrant precarity, Lydia calls her daughter crazy for quitting "because of principles." While Penelope says that she felt good about the decision in the moment, the series implicitly acknowledges the pragmatic concessions she must make because of her situation. When Penelope's employer, Dr. Berkowitz (Stephen

Tobolowsky), apologizes for the discrepancy in her pay and begs her to return, it is revealed that the male colleague asked for more money than she did. Penelope internalizes the blame, saying, "To be honest, I don't know if it's a woman thing or what. I didn't even think about negotiating. I was newly separated. I really needed a job. You said, 'Do you want one?' I said yes." Despite the structural inequality that shapes Penelope's life, the series positions it as a personal problem with a personal solution. The original *ODAAT*'s "therapeutic feminism" has morphed into "pragmatic feminism" in the reboot. This brand of pragmatic feminism highlights well-meaning individuals navigating the various intersections of class, ethnicity, nationality, and gender through highly personal lenses with economic necessity as the backdrop.

ODAAT is particularly notable for its integration of contemporary issues of gender and sexuality into its story in ways that create tension with its depiction of Cuban American culture and normative family structure. Much of the first season of *ODAAT* revolves around preparations for Elena's *quinces* celebration, a ritual she initially resists because of its sexist origins. The generational tensions around the *quinces* are initially centered on its importance in Cuban heritage, with Lydia articulating its cultural centrality and Penelope seeing it as a point of pride for a financially struggling single mother to maintain her family's traditions. As the season develops, however, Elena begins to explore her queer identity, and the *quinces* takes on an added dimension as a coming-out celebration. This provokes a direct conflict with Penelope's ex-husband, Victor, who refuses to acknowledge or accept Elena's queer identity. The series presents a multifaceted depiction of Cuban values by having Lydia make the grand gesture of understanding and acceptance when, despite not having been "told" about Elena's sexuality, she remakes the *quinces* dress into a chic suit. When Elena appears publicly in the suit, against her father's express wishes, he leaves the *quinces* celebration before the father-daughter dance ("Quinces" 1.13). In the final moments of the season, his absence is filled as the entire extended family group gathers around Elena, and Elena explicitly thanks her mother and grandmother for making her have a *quinces*.

Ultimately, *ODAAT* opposes Victor's retrograde, macho version of Cuban identity, which emphasizes pride, normativity, and convention, with a more open and accepting one that privileges community, mutual support, and nonexclusion. Despite the show's conservative form, *ODAAT* does not make the Alvarez family a proxy for any American family but shows it navigating the specificity of Cuban identity as it intersects with other identities and contexts and attempts to articulate a way through that accepts and respects them all.

Roseanne

Several years on from President Trump's entry into the White House, the *Roseanne* reboot remains one of the most explicit embraces of and responses to Trump seen on US television. While the series as a whole maintains a degree of ambivalence toward Trump, it both accepts and dramatizes the thesis that the disenfranchisement of the white working class in the United States led directly to Trump's rise to power and thus represents a very different response to the 2016 election than that of *ODAAT*. Notably, *Roseanne* reflects the overwhelming whiteness of US television at large, which is distinctly different from the intersectionality of contemporary online feminist movements or of more explicitly "woke" recuperative reboots. Yet it also retains much of the original's explicit focus on the experiences and lives of working-class people, providing a perspective that is rarely seen in US television comedy.

The original *Roseanne* is one of the most highly studied and canonized US sitcoms. The series follows the Conner family, a white working-class family in the fictional blue-collar town of Lanford, Illinois. Roseanne Barr's avatar, Roseanne Conner, is one of the more unusual matriarchs to have appeared on American television. Brash, loud, and overweight, she is the sort of character we are used to seeing marginalized and mocked on television, when we see them at all. Yet Roseanne Conner is also quick-witted, fearless, loving, and almost always the one mocking the world around her. In Kathleen Rowe's examination of Barr and *Roseanne*, she contends that Barr "uses a 'semiotics of unruliness' to expose the gap she sees between the ideals of the New Left and the Women's Movement . . . and the realities of working-class family life."[16] Roseanne's excesses, both as Barr and Conner, helped her to trouble hegemonic narratives about womanhood and motherhood and lent the series a powerful political resonance.

Even today, *Roseanne* remains one of only a few US television series centered on precariously employed families with low socioeconomic status. It follows the Conner family, which consists of Roseanne, father Dan

(John Goodman), aunt Jackie (Laurie Metcalf), and children Becky (Alicia Goranson), Darlene (Sara Gilbert), and D.J. (Michael Fishman). Although created by Matt Williams, *Roseanne* is based on the stand-up and life of comedian Roseanne Barr. Barr and her character Roseanne are icons of 1990s televisual feminism, and "for nearly a decade, Barr was one of the most powerful women in Hollywood."[17] Ford notes, "Roseanne/Barr's perspective (as fictional character and media personality) informs the narrative, sensibility, and tone."[18] Similarities between Roseanne Barr and her fictional alter ego Roseanne Conner go beyond name and biographical details. Over the course of nine seasons, audiences were trained to conflate Roseanne and Barr, and this is clear in the recent reboot, its reception, and its cancellation.

The season 10 reboot reunites the original cast for a short-lived but impactful nine-episode season, which erases many of the events of season 9, which saw the family winning the lottery and Roseanne's husband, Dan, dying. The reboot was a major televisual event because of Barr's controversial public persona in the Trump era. In a *New York Times* review of the reboot, Roxane Gay writes, "Whatever charm and intelligence she [Barr] brought to the first nine seasons of her show, a show I very much loved, are absolutely absent in her current persona, particularly as it manifests on Twitter."[19] Against the background of this current persona, ABC's decision to revive *Roseanne* was designed to court controversy and perhaps to combat public complaints that Hollywood fails to cater to, or adequately represent, conservative Middle America. Initially, the *Roseanne* reboot earned the highest ratings of any US sitcom in the past three years;[20] however, it was canceled in May 2018, after a racist tweet in which Barr compared a Black woman (the high-ranking Obama aide Valerie Jarrett) to an ape. Barr's tweet and the cancellation of *Roseanne* highlights the limits of the series's recuperative politics and capacity to operationalize Barr's contentious Twitter presence alongside her previously lovable, unruly character. Ultimately, Barr's contemporary politics are too at odds with those of both 1990s-era Barr and her television alter ego to be successfully accommodated by the reboot.

Before the cancellation of the *Roseanne* reboot, however, one of its stated objectives was to address the contentious US political landscape after the election of President Trump.[21] *Roseanne* explicitly addresses Trump (the person and the phenomenon) early in season 10, and Barr's character is signaled as being aligned with the series's own perspective. As a character, Roseanne seems less pro-Trump than she is anti-Hillary. Roseanne's determination to prove that her sister Jackie's performative liberalism is ridiculous provides much of the humor in the first episode ("Twenty Years to Life" 10.1). However, the series also finds Roseanne's performative MAGA-ism equally humorous. Principle, whichever side of the political aisle it hails from, is set up for mockery in this reboot, and the butt of Roseanne's jokes is no longer systems of power or the beneficiaries of those systems, as was often the case in the original series. Instead, Roseanne in the reboot skewers those who are different from her (like Jackie), whom she calls "snowflakes." Explicit discussion of election-centric politics is largely confined to the first few episodes, however, as the rest of the series focuses on the constrained economic and social circumstances of the Conners as they undergo a series of reversals and setbacks.

The *Roseanne* reboot is a sometimes bleak depiction of low-socioeconomic-status families in the contemporary moment. The characters rarely question the ruins of the social fabric that keeps failing them, just as they never question their fundamental, embittered commitment to one another. In the show's attempt to address a white Middle America, there is a flattening of what made the early seasons of *Roseanne* so notable and memorable. In season 10, Roseanne and Dan now have a Black granddaughter, D.J.'s daughter, Mary (Jayden Rey), but her race is never mentioned. In contrast, in season 7 ("White Men Can't Kiss" 7.19), race is explicitly addressed and reckoned with, as Roseanne is forced to confront her unconscious biases and that she may have passed them onto her son. In season 7, Roseanne is appalled at the idea that she may have raised a racist son, but in the reboot, race is ignored, unless it serves to locate Roseanne as the hero. As Ford writes in her analysis of the reboot, "Roseanne is proven wrong, she is not forced to reckon with her bigotry"; instead, "she is positioned as a 'hero.'"[22]

Television as a media form that shapes the cultural, social, and political lives of its audience is central to how *Roseanne*, in both its original and rebooted forms, articulates its shifting politics. In the opening episode of season 9 ("Call Waiting" 9.1), after having a fight with Dan, Roseanne is lying on Jackie's couch watching television. She imagines herself as "television's first feminist": Ann Marie (Marlo Thomas) from *That Girl* (ABC, 1966–71), sassy genie Jeannie (Barbara Eden) from *I Dream of Jeannie* (NBC, 1965–70), and single working woman Mary Richards (Mary Tyler Moore) from *The Mary Tyler Moore Show* (CBS, 1970–77). Barr as Roseanne

Conner literally sees herself in each of these seminal television women, taking on and performing the persona of each character, complete with iconic costumes and hair. Barr/Roseanne takes on each of these roles as a way to express her frustration with Dan, and in doing so, she inserts herself into the history of white women on television who have challenged the patriarchy in some form or another. Likewise, the season 7 episode "All About Rosey" (7.19) finishes with a scene during which Roseanne talks with some of US television's best-known (and most traditional) mothers. When Roseanne enters the Conners' kitchen set, June Cleaver (Barbara Billingsley) from *Leave It to Beaver* (ABC, 1957–63), Joan Nash (Pat Crowley) from *Please Don't Eat the Daisies* (NBC, 1965–67), Ruth Martin (June Lockhart) from *Lassie* (CBS, 1958–64), Norma Arnold (Alley Mills) from *The Wonder Years* (ABC, 1988–93), and Louise Jefferson (Isabel Sanford) from *The Jeffersons* (1975–85) are cleaning. While Roseanne is a distinctly different kind of mother from the others, she still feels part of the lineage.

In stark contrast, however, by the season 10 reboot, Dan and Roseanne have come to see themselves as sitting outside the dominant modes of storytelling on US television. In the third episode of the reboot ("Roseanne Gets the Chair" 10.3), Roseanne and Dan fall asleep in front of the television. Upon waking, Roseanne remarks, "It's 11:00 p.m. We slept from *Wheel* [*of Fortune*] to *Kimmel*. We missed all the shows about Black and Asian families." Dan replies, "They're just like us," and Roseanne responds, "There, now you're caught up." This short, seemingly benign exchange reveals Roseanne and Dan's discomfort with the changing demographics of the United States, both on and off television. Part of the joke is that Roseanne is literally sleeping through stories about people of color or people who are different from her.

At the end of the single-season *Roseanne* reboot, we find the Conner family nearly destitute. Roseanne and Dan are struggling to salvage their belongings in the aftermath of a storm. Roseanne's wit serves only as gallows humor in these final few episodes, providing some grim levity against a backdrop of unremitting bleakness. There is an irony in the fact that the family's potential salvation comes from the declaration of a state of emergency and the arrival of FEMA (the Federal Emergency Management Agency). *Roseanne* does not dwell on the political implications of this white working-class family being bailed out by a federal agency, which notably failed to support the (largely nonwhite) American families in Puerto Rico following the devastation caused by Hurricane Maria in 2017.

The 2018 revival and cancellation of *Roseanne* raise questions about the relationship between politics and stardom and ask us to consider to what extent the legacy of the original series is tied to its author-star, Roseanne Barr. The series's investment in whiteness and Barr's star persona makes it difficult to move beyond the limitations of the original. At the time of writing, the Conner family remains on the air in *The Conners* (ABC, 2018–), which has been renewed for a fourth season. The spin-off depicts Roseanne's family coping with the fallout from her off-screen death, but her ghost looms large.

Conclusion

Despite the clear narrative, branding, and political differences among recent reboots like *Roseanne* and *ODAAT*, they are often grappling with the same questions and performing a kind of recuperative politics. Both of these series reimagine their explicitly second-wave-feminist predecessors for the contemporary moment. While *ODAAT* infuses a new interpretation of its scenario with intersectional politics that span various ethnic, gender, sexual, and class identities, without really advancing beyond the therapeutic feminism of the original, *Roseanne* dramatizes the stagnation and stasis of its characters, rendering the suffering of its white working-class family eternal, as they are ever more failed by the systems that should support them and ever less able to articulate a critique of those systems. Despite the differences in their analyses of and answers to the cultural moment of Trump's America, each of these recuperative reboots looks to the past for ideas about how to understand and approach the present.

ODAAT and *Roseanne* highlight how the recuperative reboot employs a nostalgic perspective on the past, which is positioned as a solution to the present and future. In reviving and/or redeveloping established series in response to life in Trump's United States, these series are also attempting to recuperate their earlier versions. While *ODAAT* performs its recuperation by updating the original's gender and racial politics, *Roseanne* invests in the nostalgic appeal of the original text, constructed either as missing from or as a solution to our current moment. These reboots highlight the tendency to reconsider US values and culture through the sitcom form and the ideal of the American family.

Notes

1 Joseph Adalian, "Why Network TV's Obsession with Reboots Isn't a Bad Thing," *Vulture*, February 1, 2018, https://www.vulture.com/2018/02/network-tv-reboot-obsession-roseanne-murphy-brown.html.

2 Jessica Ford, "Rebooting *Roseanne*: Feminist Voice across Decades," *M/C Journal* 21, no. 5 (2018), http://journal.media-culture.org.au/index.php/mcjournal/article/view/1472.

3 Emma Grey Ellis, "TV Reboots Are Having a Great Awokening. It Sucks," *Wired*, December 12, 2018, https://www.wired.com/story/tv-reboots-are-having-a-great-awokening-it-sucks/; Jack Seale, "From Party of Five to The L Word: How TV Reboots Got Woke," *Guardian*, February 14, 2019, https://www.theguardian.com/tv-and-radio/2019/feb/14/from-party-of-five-to-the-l-word-how-tv-reboots-got-woke.

4 For a thorough unpacking of the taxonomy of terms associated with reboots in popular and journalistic discourse, see William Proctor, "Regeneration & Rebirth: Anatomy of a Franchise Reboot," *Scope* 22 (February 2012), https://www.nottingham.ac.uk/scope/documents/2012/february-2012/proctor.pdf.

5 See Jason Mittell, *Complex TV: The Poetics of Contemporary Television Storytelling* (New York: New York University Press, 2015); Derek Johnson, "Party like It's 1999: Another Wave of Network Nostalgia," *Flow Journal*, April 2015, https://www.flowjournal.org/2015/04/party-like-it%E2%80%99s-1999/.

6 Katharina Neimeyer and Daniela Wentz, "Nostalgia Is Not What It Used to Be: Serial Nostalgia and Nostalgic Television Series," in *Media and Nostalgia: Yearning for the Past, Present and Future*, ed. Katharina Niemeyer (Basingstoke, UK: Palgrave Macmillan, 2014), 130–31.

7 Kirsten Marthe Lentz, "Quality versus Relevance: Feminism, Race, and the Politics of the Sign in 1970s Television," *Camera Obscura: Feminism, Culture, and Media Studies* 15, no. 1 (2000): 46.

8 Lentz, 47.

9 Bonnie J. Dow, *Prime-Time Feminism: Television, Media Culture, and the Women's Movement since 1970* (Philadelphia: University of Pennsylvania Press, 1996).

10 Dow, 64.

11 Dow, 74.

12 Kathleen Loock, "American TV Series Revivals: Introduction," *Television and New Media* 19, no. 4 (2018): 299–309.

13 Loock, 367–68.

14 Michael Z. Newman and Elana Levine, *Legitimating Television: Media Convergence and Cultural Status* (New York: Routledge, 2012), 75.

15 Brett Mills, *Television Sitcom* (London: British Film Institute, 2005), 50–51.

16 Kathleen Rowe, "Roseanne: Unruly Woman as Domestic Goddess," *Screen* 31, no. 4 (1990): 409.

17 Melissa Williams, "'Excuse the Mess, but We Live Here': Roseanne Barr's Stardom and the Politics of Class," in *Film and Television Stardom*, ed. Kylo-Patrick R. Hart (Cambridge, UK: Cambridge Scholars, 2009), 180.

18 Ford, "Rebooting *Roseanne.*"

19 Roxane Gay, "The 'Roseanne' Reboot Is Funny. I'm Not Going to Keep Watching," *New York Times*, March 29, 2018, https://www.nytimes.com/2018/03/29/opinion/roseanne-reboot-trump.html.

20 Michael O'Connell, "TV Ratings: 'Roseanne' Revival Skyrockets with Stunning Premiere," *Hollywood Reporter*, March 28, 2018. https://www.hollywoodreporter.com/live-feed/tv-ratings-roseanne-revival-skyrockets-stunning-premiere-1097943.

21 Emily VanDerWerff, "The Roseanne Revival, and the Argument over How TV Depicts Trump Supporters, Explained," *Vox*, March 30, 2018, https://www.vox.com/culture/2018/3/30/17174720/roseanne-2018-reboot-controversy-trump-explained-review.

22 Ford, "Rebooting *Roseanne.*"

"THE COST OF LIES"

CHERNOBYL, POLITICS, AND COLLECTIVE MEMORY

Oliver Gruner

In a review for *Vanity Fair* magazine, the television critic Sonia Saraiya described HBO's miniseries *Chernobyl* (2019) as "paradigm-shifting historical television." Praising the series's attention to period detail and narrative force, Saraiya declared that "*Chernobyl* gets under your skin."[1] She was not the only critic to extoll this dramatic reconstruction of events surrounding the nuclear-reactor explosion of April 1986. *Chernobyl* enjoyed strong—if not unanimous—acclaim throughout its original broadcast in May and June 2019. Saraiya's creepy corporeal metaphor was not out of place in a media landscape where the series was being touted as "a gruesome disaster epic replete with oozing blisters" and "horrifying, masterly television that sears onto your brain."[2] One way or another, it seemed, *Chernobyl* had managed to get under the skin of so many commentators. It quickly generated a firestorm of political discussion in the United States, with spokespeople from diverse backgrounds interpreting its portrayal in line with current affairs. Some applauded what they perceived to be its anti-Trump agenda, noting the ways in which *Chernobyl* served as a "modern parable," an indictment of the post-truth, anti-intellectual climate fostered by their commander in chief.[3] Others suggested the series to be a critique of Soviet governance, a cautionary tale about the threat of socialism and an assertion of the United States' comparative stability.[4] Across the US and international media, heated conflicts over historical and political content raged.[5]

On one level, then, *Chernobyl* can be viewed as a television show that constructs what Gary Edgerton terms a "useable past," or a historical representation designed to "clarify the present and discover the future."[6] In interviews and in the much-publicized podcasts that accompanied each episode, the series creator, Craig Mazin, discussed how *Chernobyl* was developed in response to twenty-first-century debates on the environment, the role of experts, truth, lies, and governmental malfeasance.[7] But beyond the immediate political context, there were a number of other factors that contributed to *Chernobyl*'s impact. In an article published two months after the series finale, the film scholar Louis Bayman reflected on its relationship to a longer history of horror and science-fiction portrayals, suggesting that visual and narrative content engaged with themes such as "knowledge, authority, human happiness and its relationship to nature." Furthermore, *Chernobyl*'s power lay in "its vision of how reality is made up of hidden physical and political forces."[8] This chapter builds on Bayman's insights, situating *Chernobyl* within a wider cluster of discourses pertaining to genre, politics, and collective memory. In doing so, I argue that the series mobilized thematic tropes that had long resonated in public remembrance of the nuclear disaster and, more broadly, in visual culture of the 1990s and twenty-first century. The chapter begins with a discussion of Chernobyl in collective memory and the television series's participation in broader commemorative practices. This is followed by a detailed visual analysis. Here, I am concerned with *Chernobyl*'s political and historical representation, its attempts to visualize the ongoing (and "invisible") force of radiation, and its focus on the human body as, in Marita Sturken's words, a "receptacle of memory."[9]

"The Past or the Future": Remembering Chernobyl

Chernobyl can be seen as part of a broader trend in North American television to revisit 1980s politics and popular culture. Shows such as *The Americans* (FX, 2013–18), *GLOW* (Netflix, 2017–19), and *Stranger Things* (Netflix, 2016–) are set in the Reagan era and make liberal reference to its events, prominent public figures, films, television shows, toys, and other phenomena. In a volume on the streaming service Netflix, Kathryn Pallister highlights the importance of nostalgic content as a way of attracting new subscribers from the economically lucrative baby-boomer (born between 1946 and 1964) and Generation X (1965–80) audiences.[10] Many scholars have explored US popular culture of the 1970s, 1980s, 1990s, and 2000s and its obsession with "remembering" the 1950s and 1960s (often portrayed as the years in which older baby boomers came of age).[11] Given the rise to prominence—in politics and in the media—of younger boomers and Generation X, it is perhaps unsurprising that the twenty-first century has witnessed a surge in the revisiting of all things "'80s."[12] As is the case with 1950s and 1960s nostalgia, renderings of the 1980s return time and again to the era's youth-oriented styles and popular culture. Kevin J. Wetmore Jr. argues that reboots of 1980s franchise films (*The Karate Kid* [Harald Zwart, 2010], *Friday the 13th* [Marcus Nispel, 2009], and *Ghostbusters* [Paul Feig, 2016], to name but a few) became central to twenty-first-century Hollywood and paved the way for blockbuster television shows like *Stranger Things*.[13] Furthermore, the success of the latter "has been accompanied by a glut of critical think-pieces about collective American nostalgia for the 1980s."[14] And whether appearing on the big or small screen, onstage or on the catwalk, images of the era prevail across the US cultural landscape.[15]

Certainly, events at the V. I. Lenin (or, as it is popularly known, Chernobyl) Nuclear Power Plant are very much part of living memory for the same older audiences that apparently found appeal in the aforementioned television shows. Craig Mazin (b. 1971) is himself of the Generation X cohort. He has asserted that one of the reasons for creating this series is that he remembered hearing about Chernobyl as a fifteen-year-old but was not really aware of the full context or what caused the disaster.[16] One can also detect a certain "nostalgia" for older media texts in *Chernobyl* (especially in the way the series draws on formal and stylistic conventions associated with previous horror and science-fiction cinema). And yet it would be hard to place *Chernobyl*—at least with regard to setting and subject matter—squarely within the group of productions previously referenced. Firstly, the series is not a direct revisiting of the US past, though occasional references to Reagan and to American television do appear. Secondly, the series can hardly be considered nostalgic in the traditional sense in which the term is mobilized (i.e., as an affectionate, even if sometimes skeptical, return to a past time). Thirdly, the series participates less in a US-centric and more a decidedly global set of commemorative practices. In different ways, *Chernobyl* draws for visual inspiration and narrative content on this international context.

The early hours of April 26, 1986, are enshrined in collective memory for what was then (and by many criteria remains) the most devastating nuclear incident suffered during peacetime. A disastrous attempt to undertake a safety test culminated in an explosion that saw fifty million curies of radiation being released into the atmosphere: "the equivalent of 500

Hiroshima bombs."[17] Thirty-one deaths were officially recorded by Soviet authorities, but in the months and years to follow, various organizations have estimated the actual death toll to be in the thousands. Furthermore, the accident's impact was far-reaching, with an estimated 350,000 people evacuated from contaminated areas around the nuclear plant and the wildlife, landscape, and environment destroyed and/or altered in ways that continue to affect the region.[18] Nations across the world developed, and continue to develop, their own information programs, legislations, and governmental responses to the disaster. Chernobyl is, therefore, both a historical event and, as Karena Kalmbach notes, an "ongoing event," one that continues to impact the physical environment, just as it does the political and cultural imaginary.[19]

Kalmbach explores the ways in which the disaster has, since the 1980s, become central to politicized discourses on nuclear energy, international relations, and the legacy of the Soviet Union.[20] She covers mnemonic practices within a variety of national contexts, noting, for example, that, in Germany, Chernobyl is a touchstone in conflicts over the development of a nuclear energy program. In France, it is often referenced when people seek to challenge "lies" and "disinformation" propagated by the government.[21] Kalmbach also emphasizes the important role that visual culture has played in Chernobyl remembrance. For instance, the photography of Igor Kostin, who took the first widely circulated images of the disaster and continually returned to the region throughout the 1990s, captures Chernobyl's human cost—men dying from acute radiation poisoning, children suffering from radiation-related illnesses and ailments—the cleanup operation, and the empty urban and rural landscapes present within the exclusion zone. These photographs present "an accident that has brought unimaginable suffering upon humanity" and continues to pose a threat to future generations.[22]

The idea of Chernobyl wreaking an "invisible" and ongoing menace on the world, a disaster yet to run its course, has been at the center of much popular and academic writing. "What lingers most in my memory of Chernobyl," writes the Belarusian author Svetlana Alexievich, "is life afterwards: the possessions without owners, the landscapes without people. The roads going nowhere, the cables leading nowhere. You find yourself wondering just what this is: the past or the future."[23] These words appeared in *Chernobyl Prayer*, a high-profile collection of stories based on interviews with survivors of the nuclear disaster. The book provided much content and inspiration for Mazin when he began the *Chernobyl* screenplays (discussed in more detail shortly). *Chernobyl Prayer*'s evocation of apocalyptic landscapes and allusions to broken technology and disrupted temporal relationships raise a series of philosophical issues that would not feel out of place in science fiction, a genre long associated with "our relationship with technology and how it affects our daily life."[24] Alexievich draws parallels between the literal "malfunction" of the nuclear technology and a symbolic breakdown in human perception. She writes that "our eyes, ears and fingers were no longer any help . . . because radiation is invisible." Furthermore, "we'd acquired a new enemy. Now we could be killed by cut grass, a caught fish. . . . The world around us, once pliant and friendly, now instilled fear."[25]

Ideas contained in Alexievich's account are evoked time and again in images of the catastrophe. Considering photographic representations, Daniel Burkner argues that "the task of capturing the scale of the disaster on camera had to contend with the challenges posed by invisibility."[26] According to Burkner, it is the repetition of familiar iconography, such as the power plant itself, the empty landscapes, the "liquidators" (the name given to those involved in the cleanup operation), the Ferris wheel in the abandoned Ukrainian city of Pripyat, the radiation trefoil symbol, that has made its impact visible and meaningful. Numerous allusions to such iconography occur throughout *Chernobyl*. For example, in the screenplay for episode 2 (titled "Please Remain Calm"), Mazin includes scene directions for the camera to "silently drift" through Pripyat. We travel between empty school classrooms and an apartment where a "pair of old shoes [lie] next to an unmade bed." There is a restaurant "with food still on the tables," and our attention is drawn to the Ferris wheel, which in 1986 had just been constructed but was ultimately never used and which "creaks gently in the breeze."[27]

Images of Chernobyl "try to make the empire of standstill and void visible."[28] Photographers such as Rüdiger Lubricht and Robert Polidori have revisited the exclusion zone on various occasions to capture the stark juxtaposition of decrepit buildings, decaying technologies, and a natural world that is recolonizing an area now free, for the most part, from human interference. The images present nature as the one dynamic force in the region, symbolically taking revenge on the follies of human endeavor.[29] Indeed, though released some seven years before the disaster, Andrei Tarkovsky's *Stalker* (1979), which deals with very similar themes, is often cited as a key text in establishing the accident's visual and thematic motifs. A gloomy and opaque film that follows three men on a trip to an uninhabited "zone," the desolate landscapes dominated by a rampant nature, philosophical discourse, and physical and mental disintegration that constituted its narrative "started to be interpreted as prophesy after Chernobyl."[30]

These visual motifs have reached wider audiences through various media texts. In Western popular culture, video games such as *S. T.A.L.K.E.R.: Shadow of Chernobyl* (2007) and *Call of Duty 4: Modern Warfare* (2007) utilize Pripyat's eerie cityscape as a backdrop for action and adventure. The fashion for "extreme" or "dark" tourism has seen a dramatic rise in the number of people visiting and photographing the exclusion zone.[31] As well as a plethora of photographs and videos posted online by visitors, dark tourism was the inspiration for the horror film *Chernobyl Diaries* (Brad Parker, 2012). Taking radioactive effects to new levels of absurdity, the film focuses on six young people and a tour guide who pay an unsanctioned visit to Pripyat. Chased by a bear and attacked by dogs, mutant fish, and, ultimately, mutant humans, the visitors are picked off one by one in a vein familiar to aficionados of the teen slasher genre. While the film's producer, Oren Peli (of *Paranormal Activity* [2007] fame), claimed that the film was "raising awareness" of the disaster for a new generation, some critics found its over-the-top portrayals insensitive toward Chernobyl's victims.[32]

One can certainly say that *Chernobyl* eschews the exaggerated monsters and histrionics of *Chernobyl Diaries*. Much was made of Mazin and director Johan Renck's painstaking re-creation of life in the Soviet Union of the 1980s. Though the series was largely shot in Lithuania, the attention to detail when rendering the city of Pripyat, the power plant, and key events (the removing of debris from the reactor's roof, for example) was widely celebrated throughout its broadcast. Craig Mazin himself explained that the emphasis on accuracy was a "sign of respect" to those who had suffered during and in the wake of the disaster.[33] Nonetheless, if *Chernobyl* strives for a documentary-like fidelity with regard to its period setting, it also exploits several formal, stylistic, and narrative devices that are less concerned with realism than with investing the series with a dramatic and political resonance. Particularly difficult to miss is the series's liberal use of stylistic tropes associated with horror films. Mazin had, prior to *Chernobyl*, gained quite a pedigree in youth-oriented horrors and gross-out comedies, penning films such as *Scary Movie 3* (David Zucker, 2003) and *4* (David Zucker, 2006), as well as parts 2 and 3 of the *Hangover* franchise (Todd Phillips, 2011; Todd

Phillips, 2013). A familiarity with genre conventions is on display throughout *Chernobyl* in a veritable barrage of dark corridors, eerie sounds, high angles, shadowy figures, surveillance shots, and Steadicam. These visual and aural devices combine to present onscreen "an awful reality shorn of the comforting illusions that usually sustain us," a Chernobyl that vividly dissects the past and anticipates a stormy future.[34]

History as Horror: Visualizing Chernobyl

Toward the end of *Chernobyl*'s first episode (titled "1:23:45," a reference to the time at which the initial explosion occurred), we are presented with a sequence that is both striking in its visual richness and reminiscent of so many classic horror productions. A leisurely tilt drifts up over the wreckage of Reactor Four, ground zero of the disaster. Passing over building debris, machinery, and devastated architecture, the camera continues upward, settling on a plume of thick gray smoke. The extreme low angle invests the scene with horrific poignancy as a dark, apocalyptic accumulation engulfs the screen. Now we follow the smoke as it rises up above an expanse of luminous, unsullied woodland and begins its approach on Pripyat. From long shots of tower blocks, there is a sudden, disconcerting cut, which takes us into the city itself. Between the walls of an alleyway, we observe a woman walking through a residential estate. This visual jump, from an aerial shot to a ground-level "surveillance" point of view, implies that the smoke has become something akin to a stalker, eagerly watching its prey, preparing to attack (one might think here of similar techniques used in films such as *Halloween* [John Carpenter, 1978] and *Friday the 13th* [Sean S. Cunningham, 1980]). A series of cuts focus on other potential "victims"—women chatting beneath a tree, schoolchildren marching home. Hildur Guðnadóttir's eerie minimalist score provides accompaniment as the camera picks up speed, panning across a line of children's feet. The camera comes to a standstill as a bird drops from the sky, spasms, and dies on the concrete path. This entire sequence plays out as an exercise in atmospheric tension, the bird's death a grim augury of the invisible "monster" about to be unleashed on the people of Pripyat, the Soviet Union, and the world.

Shifts in point of view, surveillance shots, claustrophobic cinematography, the incessant clicking of Geiger counters, and various other formal and stylistic devices are used throughout the series to evoke the intangible threat that is nuclear radiation. Often, they disrupt perspective, forcing us to question *who* (or *what*) is watching *whom* and through *whose* eyes we are witnessing the disaster's unraveling. In doing so, these devices engage with two key themes in Chernobyl remembrance. Firstly, how might visual artists and filmmakers "represent" a catastrophe whose scale and ongoing impact were down to the invisible force of radiation? Secondly, who were the "villains" in this tragic historical episode? And, if form and style become one way in which *Chernobyl* invokes the generic legacy of horror, we might also consider the emphasis placed on bodies and bodily contamination. Ronald Allen Lopez suggests that "contemporary horror films play on the fear not of death but of one's own body and its potential destruction."[35] Many of *Chernobyl*'s thematic tensions are focused on bodies, whether those be visually decaying, decrepit, dying bodies of those who suffer acute radiation sickness or the promise/threat of bodily dysfunction enacted on those who suffer smaller doses of radiation. Certainly, we might say, following Linda Williams's work on "body genres," that the series often provides "the spectacle of the body caught in the grip of intense sensation or emotion."[36]

As has been well rehearsed, bodily contamination is something of a cliché when it comes to Soviet Union–themed Western popular culture. Peter Knight reminds us that "hysterical fears about bugs, germs, microbes, monsters, aliens and all manner of scapegoated Others dominated the political and popular culture of the McCarthy years."[37] Without suggesting strong parallels with these previous cultural manifestations, we can certainly explore the body in *Chernobyl* as a lens through which ideas on politics and society are brought into stark relief. The violence wrought on the bodies of Chernobyl's victims is used to highlight not only individual but also national and international trauma. Militarized iconography prevails throughout the series; men dressed in army uniform and carrying guns appear in scene after scene. Liquidators stroll around military-style camps with rifles in their hands and makeshift lead straps covering their testicles. In Sturken's discussion of cultural memory of the AIDS crisis, she discusses the ways in which military metaphors were frequently used in the mainstream media (the immune system is conceptualized as a high-tech bulwark against invasion from a foreign menace) and the emasculated male body became a symbol of the instability of personal and even national identity.[38] In a similar vein, *Chernobyl* represents and simultaneously critiques the futility of using a military approach/paradigm when faced with an invisible threat. The bellicose posturing of the Cold War stands impotent when faced with radioactivity; no guns can help the people dying in the hospital of radiation-related illnesses. As Alexievich asks in *Chernobyl Prayer*, "Who were they meant to fire at? . . . Physics? Unseen particles?"[39] Faith in military strength, power, dominance—so close to the hearts of governments past and present—is rendered useless. The enemy of this war cannot be destroyed by weaponry, no matter how sophisticated.

One of the series's central characters, Ulana Khomyuk (played by Emily Watson), is sent to a Moscow hospital where those who are suffering from the most acute forms of radiation sickness—the nuclear-plant operatives, the firefighters—lay dying. It is here that she begins to uncover the conspiracy and lies that led to the explosion. The abject bodies cocooned inside protective plastic curtains are both evidence of the devastation that Chernobyl has wrought and potential saviors, or figures who can help prevent further catastrophe. It is their testimony that enables Khomyuk's investigation and, ultimately, her discovery of a high-level cover-up. She also makes reference to the deaths of these men as a way of convincing her colleague and the central protagonist, Valery Legasov (Jared Harris), to "tell the truth" about the disaster during the series's courtroom denouement. Thus is the body in *Chernobyl* at once a site of horror, conflict, conspiracy, and revelation. Human bodies are under attack from the start, with burns, blisters, and blood the gruesome physical wages of disaster. But in many ways, bodily disintegration also serves a more symbolic role, becoming indicative of an entire society, its institutions, political beliefs, and values coming apart at the seams.

Chernobyl's narrative revolves around four key characters. The scientists Valery Legasov and Ulana Khomyuk, the high-ranked Communist Party apparatchik Boris Shcherbina (Stellan Skarsgård), and Lyudmilla Ignatenko (Jessie Buckley), a woman whose story is the first to appear in Alexievich's *Chernobyl Prayer* and whose marriage, pregnancy, and life are irrevocably impacted by the disaster and its fallout. Ostensibly set in the former Soviet Union, almost all the series's characters speak with British accents. Much like that other blockbuster series *Game of Thrones*, which reached its finale just before *Chernobyl* began, these different accents, ranging from "plummy" English for the scientists to Scottish for miners and a Lancashire accent for one of the firefighters, help to place the characters within "a densely layered social order."[40] Certainly, the series explores a range of lives and experiences throughout, jumping from scenes featuring the Soviet premier Mikhail Gorbachev (David Dencik) to the home life of firefighters and farmers. Paintings and plaques of Vladimir Lenin provide an expressionless backdrop, as the bustle of everyday activities unravels onscreen. The fates of Legasov, Shcherbina, and Khomyuk are intertwined throughout the series, as each plays a role in managing the disaster's aftermath and in investigating the culprits. Ignatenko, on the other hand, appears more as a representative of, or synecdoche for, the struggles of so many "ordinary people" in the wake of Chernobyl. It is explicitly stated in the series's finale that Khomyuk's character was not based on a single individual but rather on the wider scientific community within the Soviet Union, which struggled "for truth and humanity." However, in a broader sense, we can say that all four of these characters come to stand in for something larger than themselves. A range of political and social themes are—to adapt Robert Rosenstone's terminology—"condensed" into these characters, with their individual stories representing a collective experience.[41]

An atmosphere of paranoia and confusion is evoked from the series's opening. We meet Legasov two years to the day after the accident. "What is the cost of lies?" he asks. He is recording what will prove to be his final testimony, for, within a few moments, Legasov has committed suicide. A series of close-ups of a cat lounging on a sofa, a gas meter, a pile of documents, shoes, a cigarette burning in an ashtray, and a clock that reads 1:10 a.m. place the scene in an apartment. "It's not that we'll mistake them for the truth," he continues. "All we want to know is who is to blame. . . . In this story, it was [deputy chief engineer] Anatoly Dyatlov. He was the best choice—an arrogant, unpleasant man." But, Legasov admits, "there were far greater criminals than him at work." From the very beginning, then, *Chernobyl* appears to be self-conscious about the story it is about to tell. Has the right man been brought to justice? Or are the real culprits still at large? Can we *really* trust Legasov's account of events? He might have been a high-ranked, highly respected scientist, but, as the series reveals, he is also just another cog in a far greater machine, one that is as complex, illusive, and invisible as the horrors of nuclear radiation.

Such themes are simultaneously enhanced through visuals. As Legasov speaks these lines, a slow tracking shot makes its way down the apartment's dark corridor, heading toward the illuminated room in which he is recording them. It is as if the cinematography is suggesting that there is an intruder in the house, someone watching over Legasov. As with the scene discussed earlier, we could read this as a symbolic nod to the spread of radiation encroaching here on Legasov's apartment. Certainly, the man does not look well, rather pallid and pockmarked, with a stooped gait. Later on in this opening sequence, the camera lingers on Legasov's tissue, which contains specks of blood. Here, however, it could equally allude to the all-seeing eye of the Communist state and its intelligence operatives. Indeed, throughout the series, figurative connections are made between the invisible threat of radiation and the equally invisible threat of lies, authoritarianism, and corruption. A moment later, Legasov exits his apartment, as an unknown man, shrouded in shadows, watches him disappear down an alleyway. When, in episode 3 ("Open Wide, O Earth"), the scientist confronts the head of the KGB, First Deputy Chairman Charkov (Alan Williams), the latter ominously alludes to a "circle of accountability," where everyone is surveying (and, indeed, blaming) each other. This statement might be applied to *Chernobyl* as a whole. If Dyatlov and his colleagues shoulder the official blame, the series also indicts the Soviet government, which was symbolically "dissolving under the influence of the radiation in Chernobyl."[42]

In different ways, Legasov, Khomyuk, and Shcherbina play a part in bringing this idea into sharp relief. Legasov is called in by the Politburo to assist with the cleanup operation but ultimately turns whistleblower against his superiors, informing a court of the cover-up that prevented a decisive safety test coming to light. He is spurred on by Khomyuk, who is charged with investigating the disaster and ends up discovering a conspiracy that runs to the top of the Soviet government. Shcherbina begins the series as a hardened, committed Party man (he initially has little time for Legasov, threatening to throw the scientist out of a helicopter) but ends up expressing a far greater respect for scientific experts and cynicism toward the state. "For God's sakes, Boris," says Legasov in the final episode ("Vichnaya Pamyat"), "You were the one that mattered most." In recognition of his colleague's contribution to the cleanup operation, Legasov expresses his gratitude during an emotional climax to their relationship, moments before he makes his own final dramatic courtroom proclamation. It has been argued that filmic representations of Chernobyl and, indeed, films about nuclear anxieties more generally imbue their narratives with themes of individual and collective "rebirth" and self-discovery.[43] Certainly, *Chernobyl* follows in this tradition, presenting narrative trajectories for these three characters that emphasize positive transformation and hope that the good deeds of heroic individuals might prevent such events from occurring again.

Embodying the role of expert-turned-whistleblower, the character of Legasov resonates with a prominent theme in contemporary US and global politics. The activities of individuals such as Edward Snowden, Chelsea Manning, and Carmen Segarra have received ample commentary in popular and academic literature. "If the experience of Donald Trump's presidency inspired anything," writes Allison Stanger in a book on this subject, "it is the conviction that whistleblowers matter."[44] As Trump's tenuous relationship with the truth has become ever more apparent—and misinformation, cover-ups, and outright lies have threatened the very foundations of democracy—the need for people willing to stand up to corruption is all the more urgent. Legasov is, therefore, playing the very embodiment of contemporary heroism: a man willing to sacrifice his own career and even his life for a greater principle. Ulana Khomyuk's story is equally potent in its evocation of wider social and political ideas. As noted earlier, she both discovers the cover-up of vital safety information and is the spur for Legasov to take his stand against the powers that be.

Of the four main characters, only Lyudmilla Ignatenko is not directly involved in the cleanup operation or investigation. Rather, she becomes a channel through which the disaster's impact on ordinary people is made manifest. Episode 5, titled "Vichnaya Pamyat" (approximately translated as "memory eternal"), is instructive in this respect. The episode begins with a flashback to life in Pripyat before the explosion. We see characters who, by this stage in the series, have died or suffered intolerable losses because of the radiation. People are going about their ordinary lives, looking after children, chatting, and cooking. The sequence is presented in saturated colors, as if this kind of normality is a distant memory and a thing of the past. The camera lingers on two familiar characters: Lyudmilla, who can be seen talking and laughing with a friend, and her husband, Vasily (Adam Nagatis), who is outside bouncing a baby in his arms. Throughout the series, Lyudmilla's story serves as an emotional core. Pregnant with her first child, she also comes to represent Chernobyl's effect on future generations. At the end of episode 4, we see her lying prostrate in a hospital bed, having just lost her baby. It was her extended exposure to Vasily, as she spent many hours with him in the hospital, that, *Chernobyl* suggests, led to her miscarriage. The opening of episode 5 is, therefore, a poignant flashback to happier times.

Lyudmilla, like so many people of Pripyat and surrounding areas, has witnessed the end of life as she knew it.

With regard to Lyudmilla's place within *Chernobyl*, it is notable the ways in which her everyday experiences are frequently presented as uncanny. The aforementioned sequence would, in another context, be little more than quotidian filler, people going about their daily lives. Here, however, it appears strange, dreamlike, and eerie. In "Open Wide, O Earth," Lyudmilla goes to visit Vasily at a hospital in Moscow. "There's no hiding from you, is there?" he says as he approaches his wife. What begins as an unremarkable greeting between husband and wife is, however, knocked askew by the cinematography, music, and lighting. The everyday becomes threatening as they embrace. First, Vasily bristles at her hug. "Take it easy. It's okay," he says, as a grating, high-pitched whistle provides aural accompaniment. Guðnadòttir's soundtrack was composed entirely of field recordings she made at power plants.[45] It is, therefore, interesting that these sounds play not only over scenes at Chernobyl but also at hospitals, in apartments, hotels, farmland, and many other settings. The soundtrack becomes symbolic of the radiation's spread, suggesting that events at the Chernobyl plant have encroached on all aspects of day-to-day life. The image then begins to flicker, a visual equivalent to the clicking of the Geiger counter that appears so frequently on the soundtrack, at times becoming difficult to watch. Lyudmilla is absorbing radiation from her contaminated husband. Symbolically, perhaps, given the image's visceral, bordering on unwatchable flicker, we the viewers are also being "contaminated" by events.

After the opening flashback, episode 5 flashes forward to 1987 and the trial at which Legasov will break his silence against the state. The trial plays out as a combination of scientific exposition and dramatic revelation. For the first time, we see the catalogue of human errors that led up to the explosion and, in particular, the role played by Anatoly Dyatlov (Paul Ritter) in bringing about the catastrophe. Toward the end of Legasov's summation, he stumbles on his words. He wishes to speak further; but the "villain," Dyatlov, has been identified, and the court officials are now happy for him to conclude. It is left to Shcherbina to step in: "Let him finish," he declares as the judge and prosecutor look on, dumbfounded. Legasov continues with his damning indictment of the Soviet state. "Every lie we tell incurs a debt to the truth," he says. "Sooner or later, that debt is paid."

Legasov is certainly forced to pay for his debt. His fate is to be symbolically erased from Soviet society. As Charkov informs him, "You will remain so immaterial to the world around you that, when you finally do die, it will be exceedingly hard to know you ever lived at all." As he is driven away by KGB operatives, we cut to an aerial shot that is similar to that which followed the radioactive cloud on its advance toward Pripyat. If, in that earlier scene, radiation was constructed as the symbolic "stalker" and destroyer of lives, now it is the Soviet state—and the lies that shore up its power—that is presented as such. Like radiation, lies have no physical presence; they are invisible. And, also like radiation, argues *Chernobyl*, lies are the lethal portents of catastrophe. More than thirty years after the disaster, the threat of radiation sickness may be negligible, but the "cost of lies" continues to weigh heavy upon us.

Conclusion

On May 30, 2019, the author Stephen King posted what would turn out to be a much-discussed tweet. "It's impossible to watch HBO's *Chernobyl* without thinking of Donald Trump," reported King. "Like those in charge of the doomed Russian reactor, he's a man of mediocre intelligence in charge of great power—economic, global—that he does not understand." Receiving support from many people (including Craig Mazin himself) and criticism from a sizable few, King's tweet led to him being interviewed for various articles and think pieces. Of course, as noted earlier, he was hardly alone in reading *Chernobyl* as an anti-Trump invective. It was, however, apt that this master of horror became so prominently associated with debates on the series. Drawing on many tricks of the horror trade, *Chernobyl* constructed a historical representation of immense visual and narrative intensity. Past and present collide in this dramatic rendition of an event that continues to fascinate (or terrify) so many people. Assiduously devoted to period detail, the series also mobilized all manner of formal and stylistic pyrotechnics in order to engage with themes such as politics, surveillance, technology, and the environment. Drawing connections between the invisible force of radiation and the equally invisible (and no less devastating) forces of lies and corruption, it was only natural that many people would interpret the series as a metaphor for the contemporary era.

The series's closing credits provide documentary materials, which tie up some of the narrative's loose ends. We read that Legasov took his life in 1988 and that his recorded tapes were distributed among the Soviet scientific community, which ultimately pressed for change in the nuclear sector (their struggle embodied in the figure of Ulana Khomyuk). Shcherbina dies four years after the accident. Lyudmilla Ignatenko suffers a series of strokes: "Doctors told her she would never bear a child." And yet, providing a flicker of hope in a closing sequence otherwise packed with death and despair, the subtitles announce that "they [the doctors] were wrong." Lyudmilla has a son and continues to live with him in Kiev. A film of Premier Gorbachev appears. We are informed that in 2006 he wrote, "The nuclear meltdown at Chernobyl . . . was perhaps the true cause of the collapse of the Soviet Union." Contemporary footage of the new "Safe Confinement" at the nuclear plant appears onscreen with the statement that it is "designed to last 100 years." The very fact that this safety measure is not permanent—What will happen in a century's time?—is suggestive of a switch from past and present to the future. Images of an empty school room accompany a statement that cancer rates in children spiked after the explosion and that "we will never know the actual human cost of Chernobyl." A powerful rendering of history, a commemoration of "those who suffered and sacrificed," a call to arms for the next generation, *Chernobyl* ends, like so many portrayals of the explosion and its aftermath, caught between visions of the past, present, and future. Violently torn from the pages of history, the disaster becomes an ominous harbinger of struggles yet to be waged.

Notes

1 Sonia Saraiya, "The Unique, Addictive Dread of *Chernobyl*," *Vanity Fair*, June 3, 2019, https://www.vanityfair.com/hollywood/2019/06/chernobyl -hbo-catch-22-good-omens-nuclear-power-dread.

2 Sophie Gilbert, "*Chernobyl* Is a Gruesome, Riveting Fable," *Atlantic*, May 6, 2019, https://www.theatlantic.com/entertainment/archive/2019/ 05/chernobyl-gruesome-riveting-fable-hbo/588688/; Rebecca Nicholson, "*Chernobyl*: Horrifying, Masterly Television That Sears on to Your Brain," *Guardian*, May 29, 2019, https://www.theguardian.com/tv-and-radio/ 2019/may/29/chernobyl-horrifying-masterful-television-that-sears-on-to -your-brain.

3 See, for example, Clive Irving, "Our Own Chernobyl Is Coming. And We're Handling It Just like the Soviets," *Daily Beast*, June 14, 2019, https://www .thedailybeast.com/our-own-chernobyl-is-coming-and-were-handling

-it-just-like-the-soviets; Bret Stephens, "What *Chernobyl* Teaches about Trump," *New York Times*, June 20, 2019, https://www.nytimes.com/2019/06/20/opinion/chernobyl-hbo-lies-trump.html.

4 See, for example, Warren Henry, "HBO's *Chernobyl* Indicts Soviet Socialism: Establishment Reviews Downplay It," *Federalist*, May 30, 2019, https://thefederalist.com/2019/05/30/hbos-chernobyl-indicts-soviet-socialism-establishment-reviews-downplay/.

5 For just two examples of this, see Masha Gessen, "What HBO's *Chernobyl* Got Right, and What It Got Terribly Wrong," *New Yorker*, June 4, 2019, https://www.newyorker.com/news/our-columnists/what-hbos-chernobyl-got-right-and-what-it-got-terribly-wrong; Jim Smith, "Ten Times the Chernobyl Television Series Let Artistic Licence Get in the Way of Facts," *Conversation*, June 21, 2019, https://theconversation.com/ten-times-the-chernobyl-television-series-lets-artistic-licence-get-in-the-way-of-facts-119110.

6 Gary R. Edgerton, "Introduction: Television as Historian: A Different Kind of History Altogether," in *Television Histories: Shaping Collective Memory in the Media Age*, ed. Gary R. Edgerton and Peter C. Rollins (Lexington: University Press of Kentucky, 2001), 4.

7 See, for example, Jeffrey Fleishman, "Radioactive Power," *Los Angeles Times*, May 4, 2019, E1, E4; HBO, "The Chernobyl Podcast: Part 1," YouTube, May 6, 2019, https://www.youtube.com/watch?v=rUeHPCYtWYQ.

8 Louis Bayman, "Catastrophe and Meaning in HBO's *Chernobyl*," *Ecologist*, August 9, 2019, https://theecologist.org/2019/aug/09/catastrophe-and-meaning-hbos-chernobyl.

9 Marita Sturken, *Tangled Memories: The Vietnam War, the AIDS Epidemic, and the Politics of Remembering* (Berkeley: University of California Press, 1997), 12.

10 Kathryn Pallister, introduction to *Netflix Nostalgia: Streaming the Past on Demand*, ed. Kathryn Pallister (Lanham, MD: Lexington Books, 2019), 2.

11 See, for just a few examples, Daniel Marcus, *Happy Days and Wonder Years: The Fifties and the Sixties in Contemporary Cultural Politics* (New Brunswick, NJ: Rutgers University Press, 2004); Michael Dwyer, *Back to the Fifties: Nostalgia, Hollywood Film and Popular Film of the Seventies and Eighties* (New York: Oxford University Press, 2015); Oliver Gruner, *Screening the Sixties: Hollywood Cinema and the Politics of Memory* (London: Palgrave Macmillan, 2016).

12 Ann M. Ciasullo, "Afterword: In Love with the Past," in Pallister, *Netflix Nostalgia*, 236.

13 Kevin J. Wetmore Jr., "Introduction: Stranger (Things) in a Strange Land, or, I Love the '80s?," in *Uncovering "Stranger Things": Essays on Eighties Nostalgia, Cynicism and Innocence in the Series*, ed. Kevin J. Wetmore Jr. (Jefferson, NC: McFarland, 2018), 1–3.

14 Heather Freeman, "Shifting Nostalgia Boundaries: Archetypes and Queer Representation in *Stranger Things, GLOW* and *One Day at a Time*," in Pallister, *Netflix Nostalgia*, 91.

15 On theater and fashion, see, for example, Matthew Schneier, "Don't You Forget about Me! The Formerly Irredeemable '80s Return," *New York Times*, April 20, 2016, https://www.nytimes.com/2016/04/21/fashion/dont -you-forget-about-me-the-formerly-irredeemable-80s-return.html.

16 HBO, "Chernobyl Podcast."

17 Serhii Plokhy, *Chernobyl* (London: Penguin, 2019), xii.

18 Jim Smith and Nicholas A. Beresford, eds., *Chernobyl* (Berlin: Springer, 2005).

19 Karena Kalmbach, "Radiation and Borders: Chernobyl as a National and Transnational Site of Memory," *Global Environment* 6, no. 1 (2013): 137.

20 Kalmbach, 130–59.

21 Kalmbach, 145–52.

22 Kalmbach, 144.

23 Svetlana Alexievich, *Chernobyl Prayer: A Chronicle of the Future*, trans Anna Gunin, Kindle ed. (London: Penguin, 2016), 33.

24 Lincoln Geraghty, *American Science Fiction Film and Television* (Oxford, UK: Berg, 2009), 7.

25 Alexievich, *Chernobyl Prayer*, 28.

26 Daniel Burkner, "The Chernobyl Landscape and the Aesthetics of Invisibility," *Photography and Culture* 7, no. 1 (2014): 21.

27 Craig Mazin, *Chernobyl: Episode 2—"Please Remain Calm*," September 21, 2018, 57. All *Chernobyl* scripts are available for download at https://www .hbo.com/chernobyl/episode-scripts.

28 Melanie Arndt, "Memories, Commemorations, and Representations of Chernobyl: Introduction," *Anthropology of East Europe Review* 30, no. 1 (2012): 8.

29 Burkner, "Chernobyl Landscape," 30.

30   Olga Bryukovetska, "Chernobyl Films: Half-Life of the Soviet Imaginary,"
     KinoKultura, 2009, http://www.kinokultura.com/specials/9/bryukhovetska
     .shtml.

31   Paul Dobraszcyzk, "Petrified Ruin: Chernobyl, Pripyat and Death of the
     City," *City* 14, no. 4 (2010): 370–89.

32   Roth Cornet, "Interview: *Chernobyl Diaries* and *Paranormal Activity*
     Writer/Producer Oren Peli," *Screen Rant*, May 25, 2002, https://screenrant
     .com/chernobyl-diaries-interview-oren-peli/.

33   HBO, "Chernobyl Podcast." Comments made eighteen minutes into the
     podcast.

34   Bayman, "Catastrophe and Meaning."

35   Ronald Allen Lopez Cruz, "Mutations and Metamorphoses: Body Hor-
     ror Is Biological Horror," *Journal of Popular Film and Television* 40, no. 4
     (2012): 161.

36   Linda Williams, "Film Bodies: Gender, Genre, and Excess," *Film Quarterly*
     44, no. 4 (1991): 4.

37   Peter Knight, *Conspiracy Culture: From the Kennedy Assassination to the
     "X-Files"* (London: Routledge, 2000), 169.

38   Sturken, *Tangled Memories*, 221–31.

39   Alexievich, *Chernobyl Prayer*, 28–29.

40   Sam Wetherell, "Stalinism in a British Accent," *Verso Blog*, June 6, 2019,
     https://www.versobooks.com/blogs/4347-stalinism-in-a-british-accent.

41   Robert A. Rosenstone, *History on Film / Film on History* (Harlow, UK:
     Longman, 2006), 182.

42   Plokhy, *Chernobyl*, 201.

43   See, for example, Johanna Lindbladh, "Representations of the Chernobyl
     Catastrophe in Soviet and Post-Soviet Cinema: The Narratives of Apoc-
     alypse," *Studies in Eastern European Cinema* 10, no. 3 (2019): 240–56;
     Jerome F. Shapiro, *Atomic Bomb Cinema: The Apocalyptic Imagination on
     Film* (London: Routledge, 2002), 12; Toni A. Perrine, *Film and the Nuclear
     Age: Representing Cultural Anxiety* (London: Routledge, 1998), 3–4.

44   Allison Stanger, *Whistleblowers: Honesty in America from Washington to
     Trump*, Kindle ed. (New Haven, CT: Yale University Press, 2019), loc. 3306.

45   Maddy Shaw Roberts, "Chernobyl Soundtrack: Who Composed the Haunt-
     ing Music for the HBO Miniseries?," ClassicFM.com, July 22, 2019, https://
     www.classicfm.com/discover-music/chernobyl-soundtrack-composer
     -hildur-gunadottir/.

CONTRIBUTORS

Editor

KAREN MCNALLY is a reader in American film, television and cultural history at London Metropolitan University. Her work takes an interdisciplinary approach to ideas of stardom, gender, and race in relation to US history and culture and has been published widely in peer-reviewed journals and edited volumes. McNally is the author of *The Stardom Film: Creating the Hollywood Fairy Tale* (2020) and *When Frankie Went to Hollywood: Frank Sinatra and American Male Identity* (2008), the editor of *Billy Wilder, Movie-Maker: Critical Essays on the Films* (2011), and coeditor of *The Legacy of Mad Men: Cultural History, Intermediality and American Television* (2019).

Contributors

MICHAEL MARIO ALBRECHT is a visiting instructor of English at the University of South Florida with a PhD from the University of Iowa in communication studies with a focus in media studies. He has held teaching positions at Eckerd College, the University of New Hampshire, and the University of Wisconsin–Milwaukee. His research interests include television studies, masculinity, critical theory, popular culture, and contemporary politics. He is the author of *Masculinity in Contemporary Quality Television* (2014).

HANNAH ANDREWS is a senior lecturer in media, film, and television at Edge Hill University. She teaches and researches film and television fiction. Her book *Television and British Cinema* (2014) analyzes intermedial and industrial relations between film and television in the United Kingdom. Her second monograph, *Broadcasting Biography*, explores biographical drama as a television genre and will be published in 2021. Her work has been published in *Screen, Journal of Popular Television*, and *Critical Studies in Television*, among other publications. She is currently working on a project on cross-media caricature, which examines a range of moving-image texts, from children's comedy sketch shows to *RuPaul's Drag Race.*

KATHRYN CASTLE is a historian (Cornell University, University College London) with a long-standing interest in the mediation of information and knowledge. She has worked on nationalist images in history, the disinformation of the FBI, and the performative ideas of race in minstrelsy, all arenas that are more or less than they seem to the public eye. The Trump era echoes many of the same themes and concerns in its interaction with its audience. She is the recipient of the History of Education Book Prize for *Britannia's Children* (1996) and is an independent scholar.

STEVEN COHAN is Dean's Distinguished Professor Emeritus at Syracuse University. His books include *Masked Men: Masculinity and the Movies in the Fifties* (1997), *Incongruous Entertainment: Camp, Cultural Value, and the MGM Musical* (2005), *CSI: Crime Scene Investigation* (2008), *Hollywood: The Backstudio Picture and the Mystique of Making Movies* (2018), *Routledge Film Guide: Hollywood Musicals* (2019), and *Sunset Boulevard* (forthcoming). He has also edited or coedited *Screening the Male: Exploring Masculinities in Hollywood Cinema* (1993), *The Road Movie Book* (1997), *Hollywood Musicals: The Film Reader* (2002), and *The Sound of Musicals* (2010).

K. SCOTT CULPEPPER is a professor of history at Dordt University in Sioux Center, Iowa. He specializes in the fields of early-modern Europe and the Americas, with a particular emphasis on the interaction of politics, religion, and popular culture in the Atlantic world from 1400 to the present. The student body and faculty at Louisiana College honored him twice with the Professor of the Year Teaching Award. Culpepper is the author of *Francis Johnson and the English Separatist Influence: The Bishop of Brownism's Life, Ministry, and Controversies* (2011). He is currently working on a historical study of occult panics in American history and popular cultures.

KWAKIUTL L. DREHER is an associate professor of English and ethnic studies at the University of Nebraska–Lincoln. She conducts research in African American literature, including autobiography, film, visual and popular culture, and mass-marketed popular literature. She published *Dancing on the*

White Page: Black Women Entertainers Writing Autobiography in 2008. She is a director, playwright, screenwriter, and actor, and her film short *Anna* won Best Animation at the New Media Film Festival in Los Angeles. She is currently the director on a digital feature-length film titled *The Bell Affair*, funded by the National Endowment for the Humanities.

JESSICA FORD is a lecturer in screen and cultural studies and an early-career researcher in the Gender Research Network at the University of Newcastle, Australia. Her research examines women and feminism on TV, and she has published on *Orange Is the New Black*, *Girls*, *Crazy Ex-Girlfriend*, and *Better Things* in peer-reviewed journals, academic anthologies, and journalistic outlets.

TERESA FORDE is a senior lecturer in media at the University of Derby. She is coeditor of *The Legacy of "Mad Men": Cultural History, Intermediality and American Television* (2019). Forde has written on *True Blood* and *The L Word* in *Television Finales: From Howdy Doody to Girls* (2018) and the representation of Olivia Dunham and tropes of the American West in *Fringe* in the volume *Women's Space: Essays on Female Characters in the 21st Century Science Fiction Western* (2019). She has also published work on science fiction, including *Doctor Who*, *Solaris*, and *Strange Days*.

GREGORY FRAME is a lecturer in film studies at Bangor University. His research focuses on issues of politics and representation in American audiovisual culture. He has published on these topics in *Journal of American Studies*, *Journal of Popular Film and Television*, *Film & History*, and *New Review of Film and Television Studies*. He is the author of *The American President in Film and Television: Myth, Politics and Representation*, which analyzes portrayals of fictional US politicians in broader social and political contexts. He is currently working on research that explores how American film and television represent the nation after the 2008 financial crisis.

OLIVER GRUNER is a senior lecturer in visual culture at the University of Portsmouth. His research examines historical representations across a range of media. He is the author of *Screening the Sixties: Hollywood Cinema and the Politics of Memory* (2016) and coeditor (with Peter Krämer) of *Grease Is the Word: Exploring a Cultural Phenomenon* (2020). His essays have been published in the *Historical Journal of Film, Radio and Television, Rethinking History*, and *The Poster*, as well as in several edited collections.

RAFAŁ KUŚ has worked as an assistant professor at the Institute of American Studies and Polish Diaspora of the Jagiellonian University since 2011 and at the Jagiellonian University School of Rhetoric since 2017. Having received a grant from the Joseph P. Furgal Fund, Kuś was a visiting professor at Utica College (New York) during the spring semester of 2019. He has also lectured at the universities of Catania (Italy), Ljubljana (Slovenia), Santiago de Compostela (Spain), Plovdiv (Bulgaria), and Iasi (Romania). He is the author of books on the Public Broadcasting Service and Richard Nixon's rhetoric.

AIMEE MOLLAGHAN is a lecturer in film and screen studies at Queen's University Belfast. She is the author of *The Visual Music Film* (2015) and is the reviews editor for *Animation: An Interdisciplinary Journal*. Her research is concerned with exploring music, sound, and soundscape across disciplinary boundaries. Her current academic interests focus on the relationship between music, sound, and the moving image and on landscape, psychogeography, and hauntology. She continues to publish in these areas.

MARTIN MURRAY is the head of creative technologies and digital media at London Metropolitan University. His research is in the areas of media, cultural studies, creative industries, literature, art, philosophy, critical theory, and psychoanalysis. As well having written for magazines and blogs, he has published peer-reviewed articles on subjects as diverse as television, surrealism, pop art, popular music, and politics and has done so with reference to dialectics, phenomenology, postmodernism, and deconstruction. He is the author of *Jacques Lacan: A Critical Introduction* (2016) and is currently writing a paper on the migration of punk music and culture between and beyond New York and London.

DONNA PEBERDY is an associate professor of performance, sex, and gender at Solent University, Southampton. Donna's research focuses on acting, performance, and the politics of identity. She is the author of *Masculinity and Film Performance: Male Angst in Contemporary American Cinema* (2011), coeditor of *Tainted Love: Screening Sexual Perversion* (2017), and series coeditor of the *Screening Sex* book series for Edinburgh University Press. Her research has been published in the journals *Transnational Cinemas, Celebrity Studies, New Review of Film and Television Studies,* and *Men and Masculinities* and in numerous edited collections.

DOLORES RESANO is a Marie Skłodowska-Curie Fellow at the Clinton Institute for American Studies, University College Dublin, and visiting scholar at the Department of English and Creative Writing at Dartmouth College. Her current research is focused on contemporary American and European literary fiction from a transatlantic perspective, with a special interest in the intersections of literature, politics, affect, and public discourse. An edited collection, *American Literature in the Era of Trump,* is forthcoming in 2021. She is also coeditor in chief of the journal *Lectora: Revista de dones i textualitat,* which is dedicated to gender studies.

SIMON STOW is the John Marshall Professor of Government and American Studies at the College of William and Mary in Williamsburg, Virginia. He works at the intersection of political theory, American politics, history, and literature, paying particular attention to issues of race. Most recently, he is the author of *American Mourning: Tragedy, Democracy, Resilience* (2017).

MARTIN ZELLER-JACQUES was a senior lecturer in film and media at Queen Margaret University in Scotland until January 2021 and published research related to television narrative, adaptation studies, and gender and sexuality in the media. He has since left academia and embarked on a new career as a chef.

INDEX